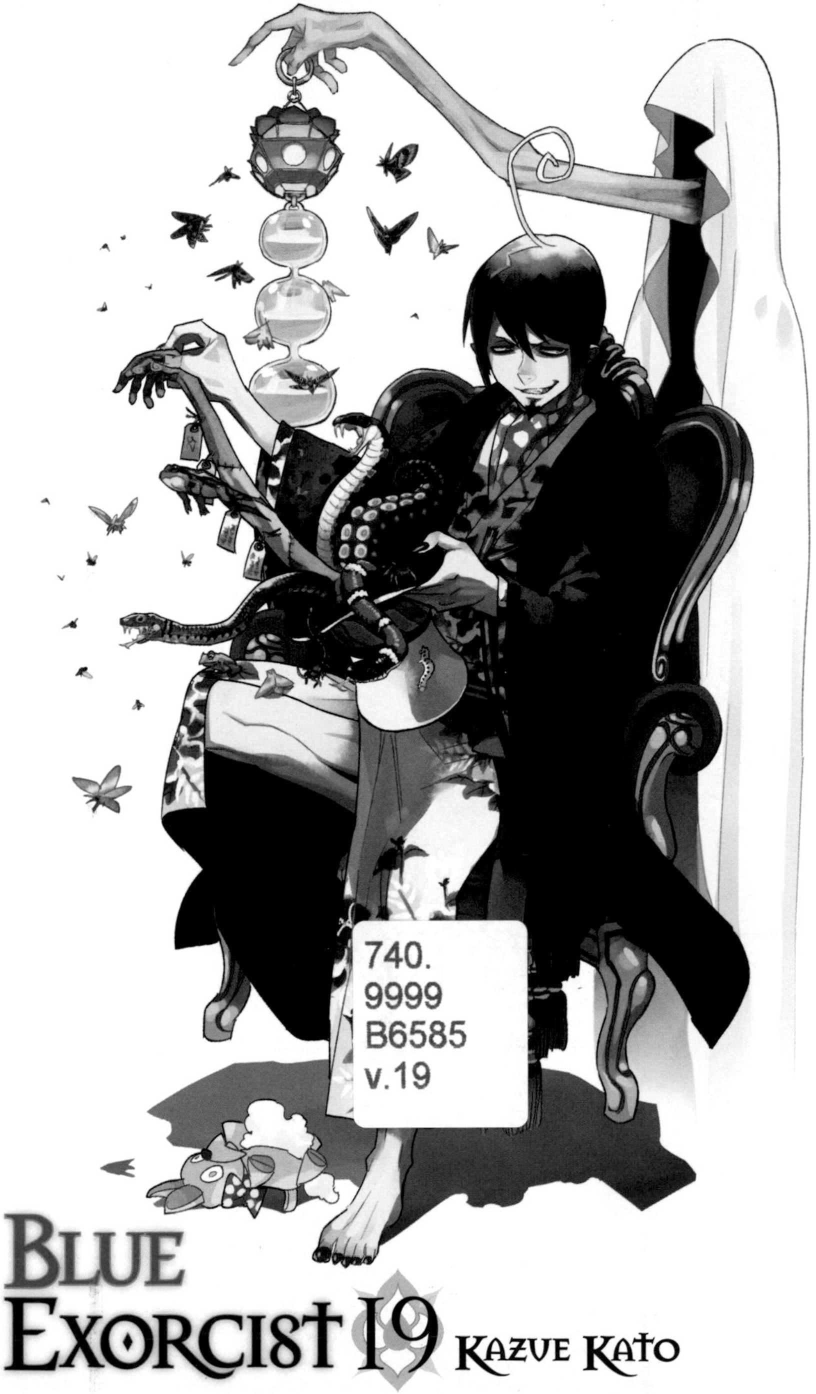

BLUE EXORCIST 19

KAZUE KATO

BLUE EXORCIST

Contents 19

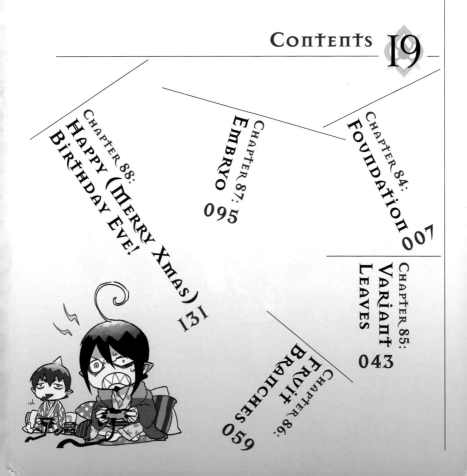

CAST OF CHARACTERS

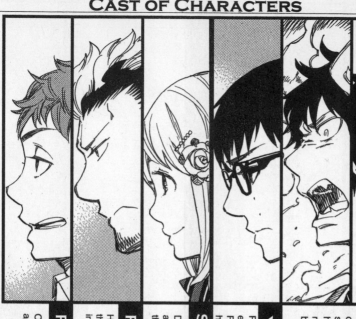

RIN OKUMURA

Born of a human mother and Satan, the God of Demons, Rin Okumura has powers he can barely control. After Satan kills Father Fujimoto, Rin's foster father, Rin decides to become an Exorcist so he can someday defeat Satan. Now a first-year student at True Cross Academy and an Exwire at the Exorcism Cram School, he hopes to someday become a Knight. When he draws the Koma Sword, he manifests his infernal power in the form of blue flames. He told Shiemi he likes her, but she turned him down.

YUKIO OKUMURA

Rin's brother. Hoping to become a doctor, he's a genius who is the youngest student ever to become an instructor at the Exorcism Cram School. An instructor in Demon Pharmaceuticals, he possesses the titles of Doctor and Dragoon. Todo told him that his true nature is that of a demon.

SHIEMI MORIYAMA

Daughter of the owner of Futsumaya, an Exorcist supply shop. She possesses the ability to become a Tamer and can summon a baby Greenman named Nee. She passed the high school entrance exam, so now she is a classmate of Rin and the others.

RYUJI SUGURO

Heir to the venerable Buddhist sect known as Myodha in Kyoto. He wants to achieve the titles of Dragoon and Aria. He is Lightning's apprentice and they are conducting an investigation together.

RENZO SHIMA

Once a pupil of Suguro's father and now Suguro's friend. Currently, he is a double agent providing information to both the Illuminati and the Knights of the True Cross.

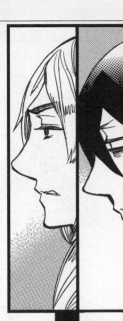
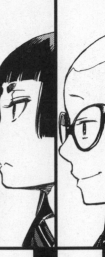
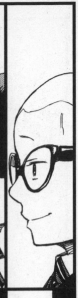

KONEKOMARU MIWA

He was once a pupil of Suguro's father and is now Suguro's friend. He's an Exwire who hopes to become an Exorcist someday. He is small in size and has a quiet and composed personality.

IZUMO KAMIKI

An Exwire with the blood of shrine maidens. She has the ability to become a Tamer and can summon two white foxes. The Illuminati had taken her captive, but with help from Rin and the others, she escaped and settled her grudge against the insane professor Gedoin.

NORIKO PAKU

An old friend of Izumo. The two girls joined the Exorcism Cram School together, but Paku dropped out when she couldn't keep up. Now she takes classes in the general curriculum at True Cross Academy Private High School.

SHURA KIRIGAKURE

A Senior Exorcist First Class who holds the titles of Knight, Tamer, Doctor and Aria. Rin and Yukio helped free her from a contract entered into by her ancestor.

MEPHISTO PHELES

President of True Cross Academy and head of the Exorcism Cram School. He was Father Fujimoto's friend, and now he is Rin and Yukio's guardian. The number two power in Gehenna and known as Samael, King of Time.

ARTHUR A. ANGEL

A Senior Exorcist First Class and the current Paladin. He wields the demon sword Caliban and is certain that Rin, as the bearer of Satan's blood, should be destroyed.

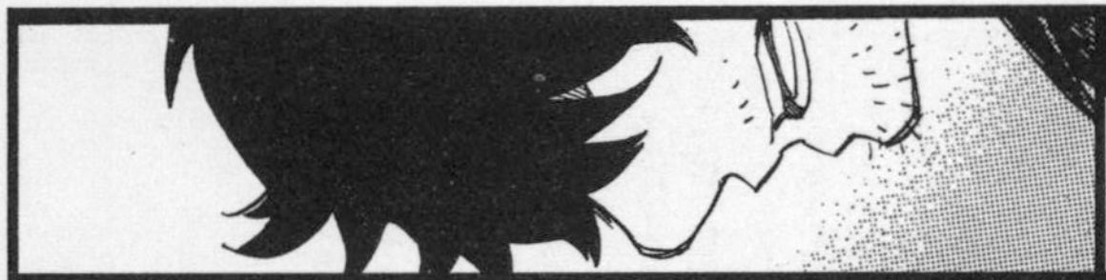

LEWIN LIGHT

As Arch Knight, he is Arthur's right-hand man as well as number two in the Order. An expert in Arias and summoning, he goes by the nickname "Lightning." He is currently stationed at the Japan Branch to investigate the Illuminati.

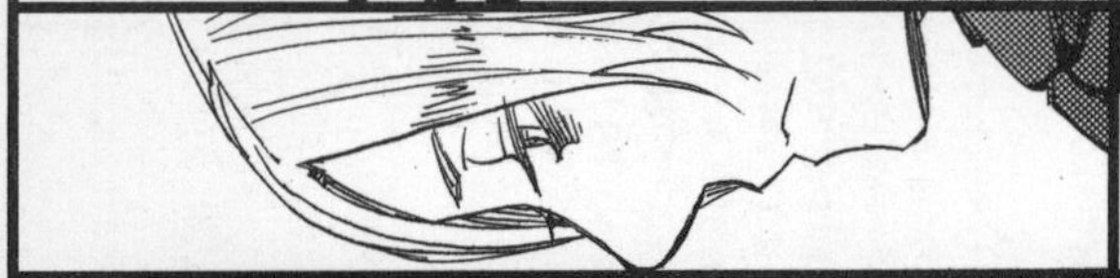

LUCIFER

Commander-in-chief of the Illuminati. Known as the King of Light, he is the highest power in Gehenna. He plans to resurrect Satan and merge Assiah and Gehenna into one.

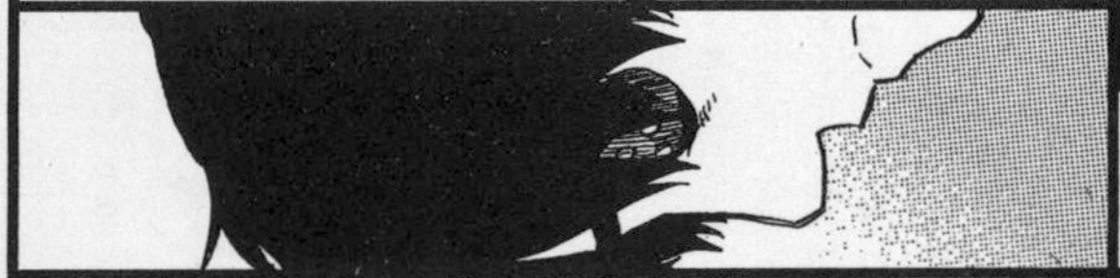

IGOR NEUHAUS

A Senior Exorcist First Class who holds the titles of Tamer, Doctor and Aria. After he tried to kill Rin, the Order suspended him.

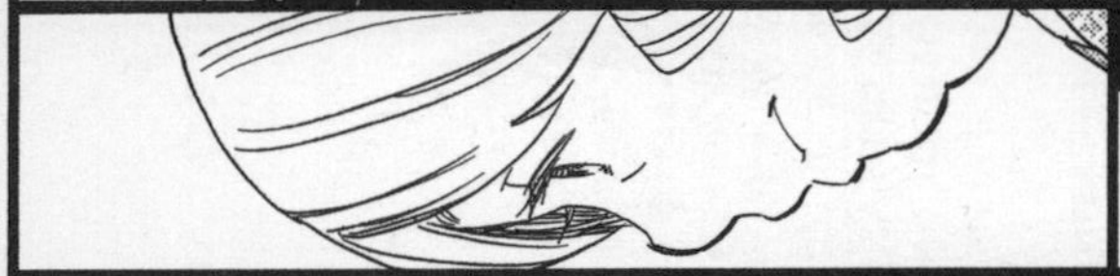

SHIEMI'S MOTHER

Owner of Futsumaya. She tends a garden left by her mother and watches over her daughter Shiemi, who has begun attending the Exorcism Cram School.

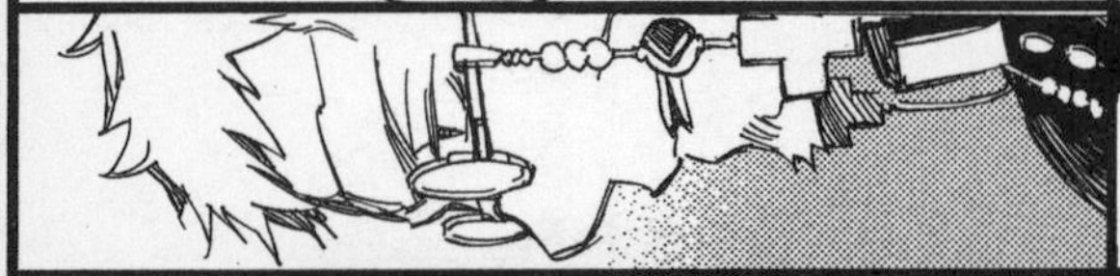

SHIRO FUJIMOTO

The man who raised Rin and Yukio. He was a priest at True Cross Cathedral. He held the rank of Paladin and once taught Demon Pharmaceuticals. Satan possessed him and he gave his life defending Rin.

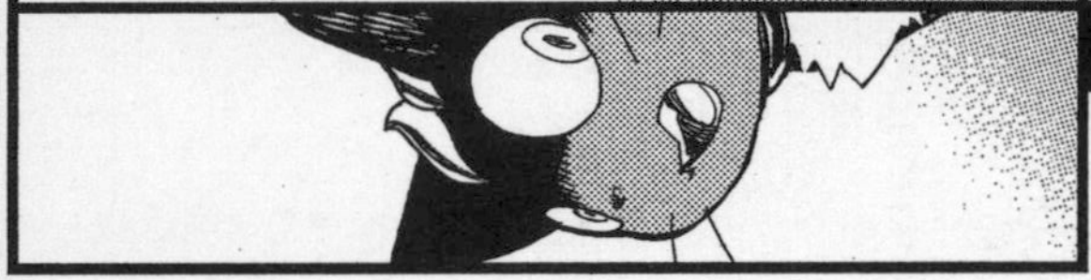

KURO

A Cat Sídhe who was once Shiro's familiar. After Shiro's death, he began turning back into a demon. Rin saved him, and now the two are practically inseparable. His favorite drink is the catnip wine Shiro used to make.

◉ THE STORY SO FAR ◉

UNKNOWN TO RIN OKUMURA, BOTH HUMAN AND DEMON BLOOD RUNS IN HIS VEINS. IN AN ARGUMENT WITH HIS FOSTER FATHER, FATHER FUJIMOTO, RIN LEARNS THAT SATAN IS HIS TRUE FATHER. SATAN SUDDENLY APPEARS AND TRIES TO DRAG RIN DOWN TO GEHENNA BECAUSE RIN HAS INHERITED HIS POWER. FATHER FUJIMOTO FIGHTS TO DEFEND RIN, BUT DIES IN THE PROCESS. RIN DECIDES TO BECOME AN EXORCIST SO HE CAN SOMEDAY DEFEAT SATAN AND BEGINS STUDYING AT THE EXORCISM CRAM SCHOOL UNDER THE INSTRUCTION OF HIS TWIN BROTHER YUKIO, WHO IS ALREADY AN EXORCIST.

RIN AND THE OTHERS SUCCEED IN DEFEATING THE IMPURE KING, AWAKENED BY THE FORMER EXORCIST, TODO. MEANWHILE, YUKIO FIGHTS TODO, AND AS THE BATTLE RAGES, HE SENSES THE SAME FLAME IN HIS OWN EYES AS HIS BROTHER. AFRAID, HE KEEPS IT A SECRET.

LATER, MYSTERIOUS EVENTS BEGIN OCCURRING AROUND THE GLOBE. A SECRET SOCIETY KNOWN AS THE ILLUMINATI IS BEHIND THESE INCIDENTS, AND SHIMA IS THEIR SPY. ON MEPHISTO'S ORDERS, HE HAD INFILTRATED THE ILLUMINATI TO WORK AS A DOUBLE AGENT AND WAS SUPPLYING INFORMATION TO BOTH SIDES.

MEPHISTO ORDERS RIN AND YUKIO TO FIND SHURA, WHO HAS DISAPPEARED. THEY FIND HER IN AOMORI PREFECTURE AND FREE HER FROM A DEADLY CONTRACT HER ANCESTOR ENTERED INTO WITH THE DEMON HACHIROTARO OKAMI. WHEN THEY RETURN TO SCHOOL, THEY DISCOVER AMAIMON IS NOW A CLASSMATE!

MEANWHILE, LIGHTNING AND SUGURO CONTINUE THEIR INVESTIGATION INTO THE ILLUMINATI. AT THE MONASTERY WHERE RIN AND YUKIO GREW UP, THEY OBTAIN INFORMATION REGARDING THE ENEMY ORGANIZATION!

Chapter 84: Foundation

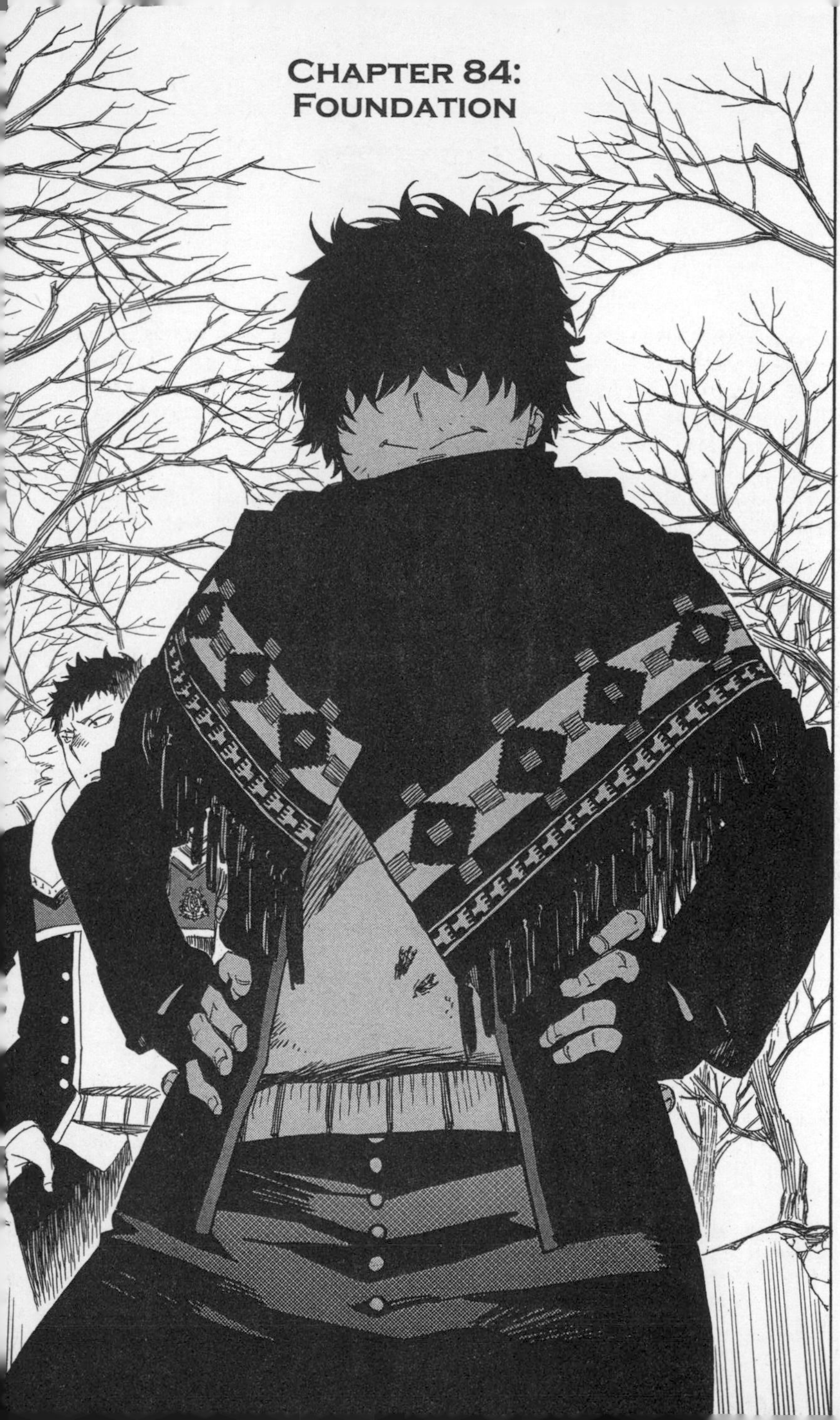

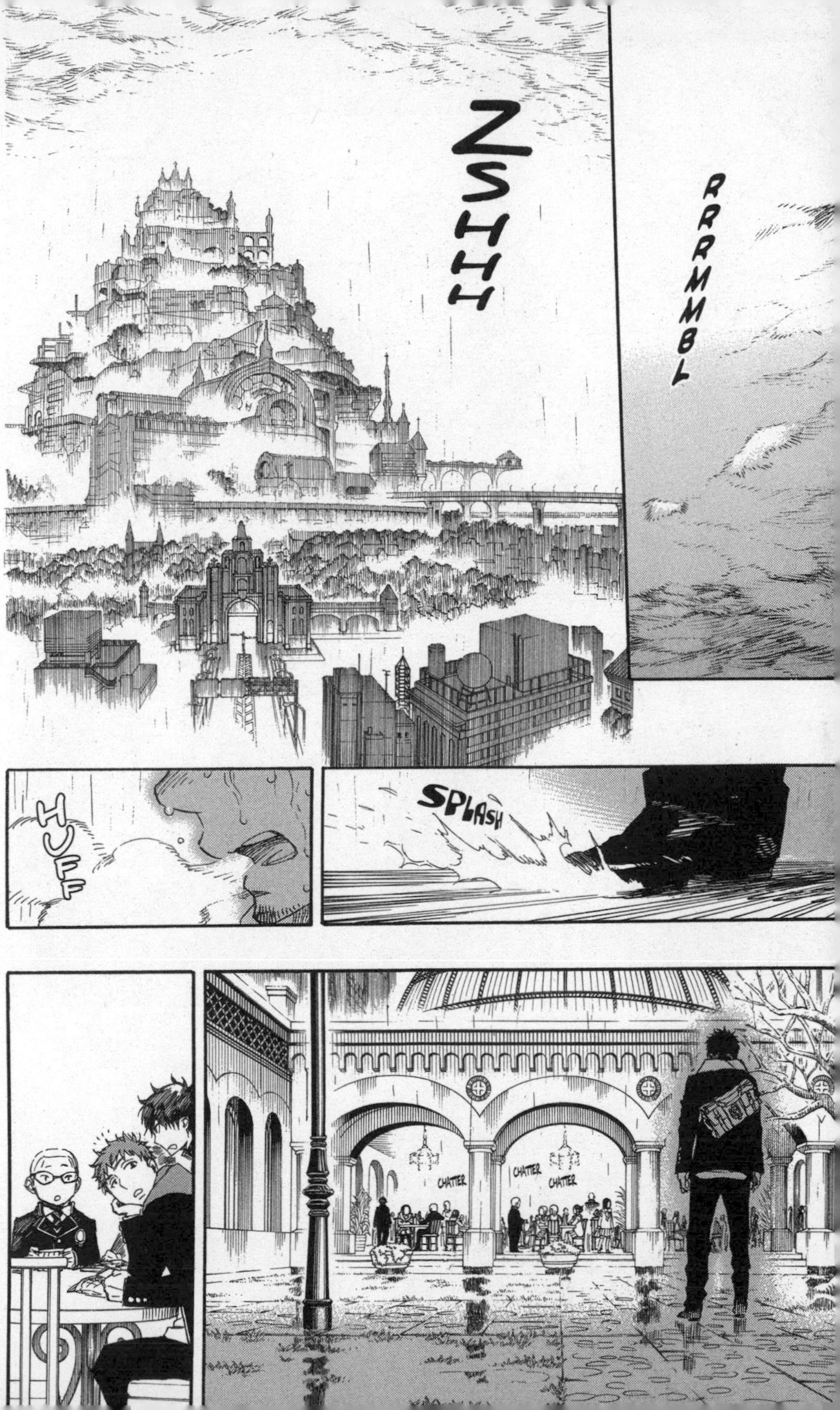
RRRMMBL
ZSHHH
SPLASH
HUFF
CHATTER
CHATTER
CHATTER

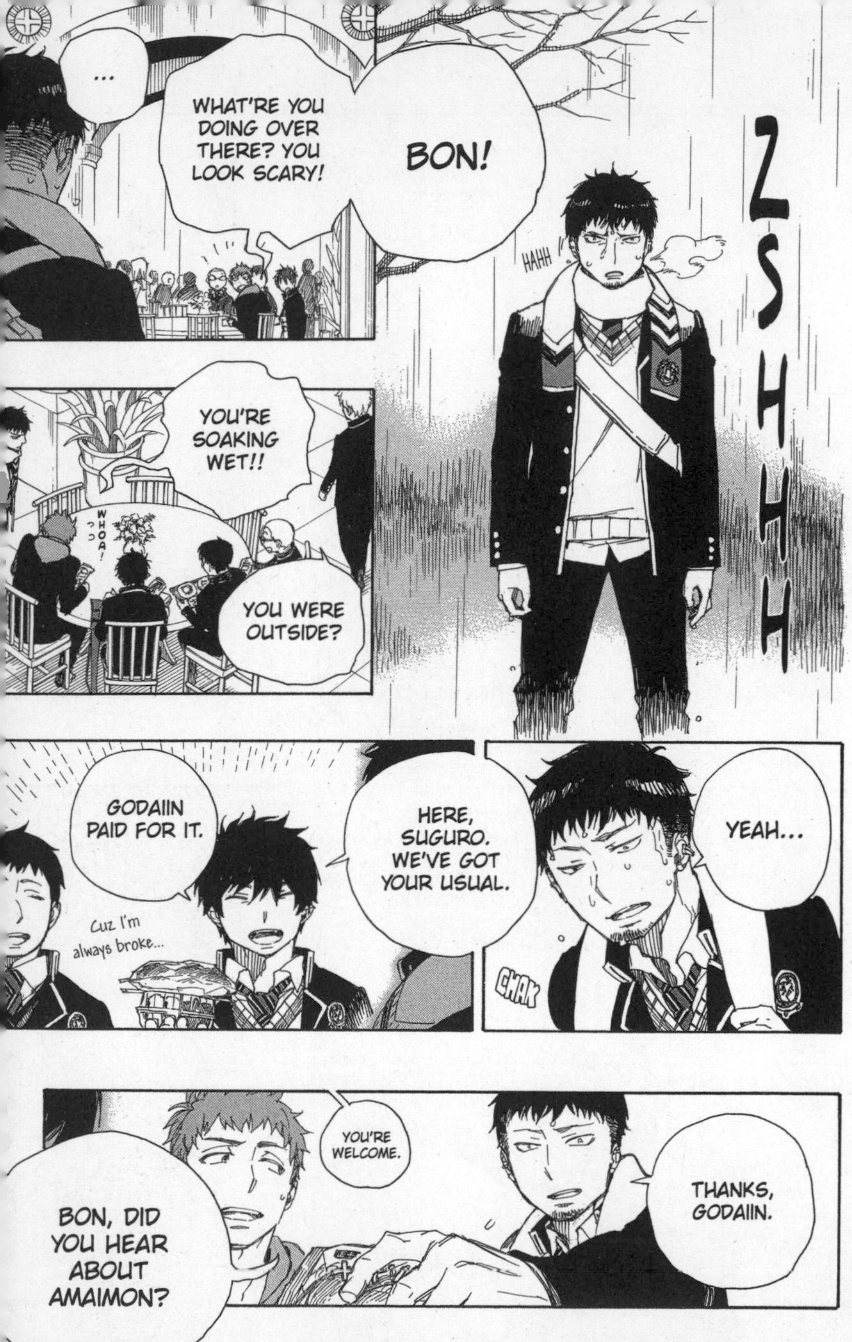
BON!
ZSHHH
HAHH
...
WHAT'RE YOU DOING OVER THERE? YOU LOOK SCARY!
YOU'RE SOAKING WET!!
WHOA!
YOU WERE OUTSIDE?
YEAH...
CHAK
HERE, SUGURO. WE'VE GOT YOUR USUAL.
GODAIIN PAID FOR IT.
Cuz I'm always broke...
THANKS, GODAIIN.
YOU'RE WELCOME.
BON, DID YOU HEAR ABOUT AMAIMON?

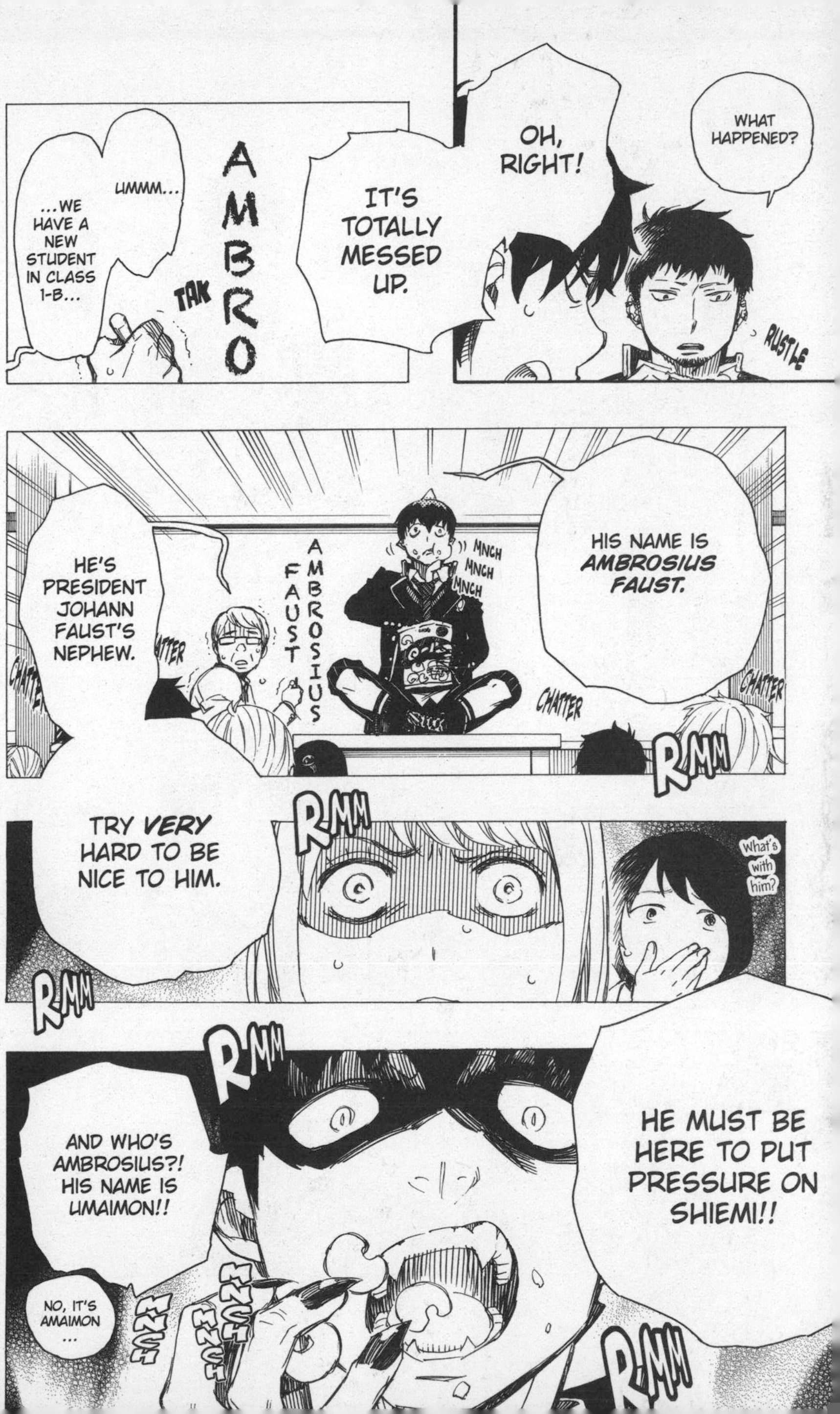
WHAT HAPPENED?
OH, RIGHT!
RUSTLE
IT'S TOTALLY MESSED UP.
AMBRO
UMMM...
...WE HAVE A NEW STUDENT IN CLASS 1-B...
TAK
HIS NAME IS *AMBROSIUS FAUST.*
CHATTER
MNCH MNCH MNCH
AMBROSIUS FAUST
HE'S PRESIDENT JOHANN FAUST'S NEPHEW.
CHATTER
RMM
What's with him?
RMM
TRY *VERY* HARD TO BE NICE TO HIM.
RMM
RMM
HE MUST BE HERE TO PUT PRESSURE ON SHIEMI!!
RMM
AND WHO'S AMBROSIUS?! HIS NAME IS UMAIMON!!
MNCH MNCH
NO, IT'S AMAIMON ...
MNCH

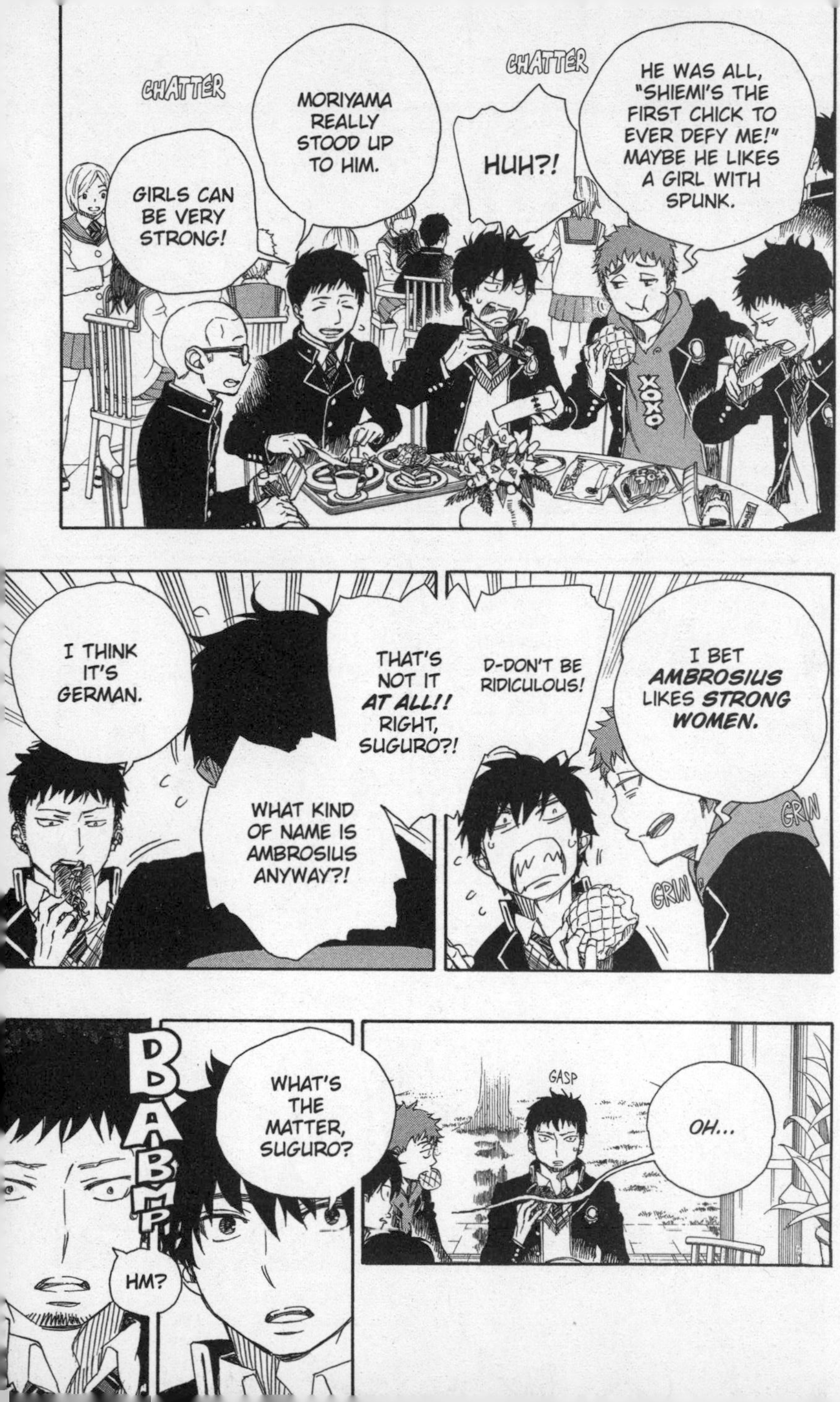
CHATTER
HE WAS ALL, "SHIEMI'S THE FIRST CHICK TO EVER DEFY ME!" MAYBE HE LIKES A GIRL WITH SPUNK.
HUH?!
MORIYAMA REALLY STOOD UP TO HIM.
CHATTER
GIRLS CAN BE VERY STRONG!
I BET **AMBROSIUS** LIKES **STRONG WOMEN.**
D-DON'T BE RIDICULOUS!
GRIN
GRIN
THAT'S NOT IT ***AT ALL!!*** RIGHT, SUGURO?!
I THINK IT'S GERMAN.
WHAT KIND OF NAME IS AMBROSIUS ANYWAY?!
GASP
OH...
WHAT'S THE MATTER, SUGURO?
BABMP
HM?

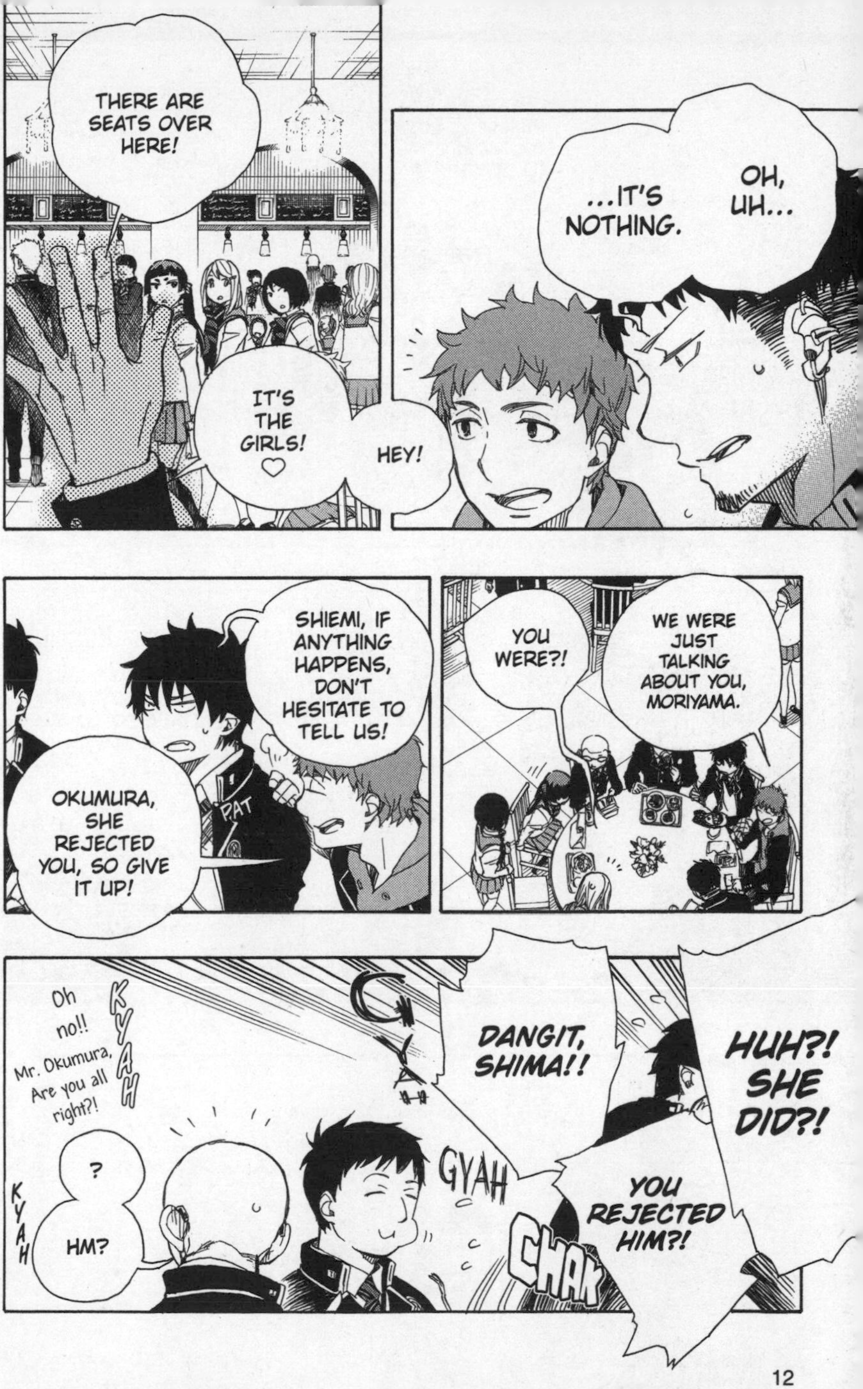
OH, UH...
...IT'S NOTHING.
HEY!
THERE ARE SEATS OVER HERE!
IT'S THE GIRLS! ♡
WE WERE JUST TALKING ABOUT YOU, MORIYAMA.
YOU WERE?!
SHIEMI, IF ANYTHING HAPPENS, DON'T HESITATE TO TELL US!
PAT
OKUMURA, SHE REJECTED YOU, SO GIVE IT UP!
HUH?! SHE DID?!
YOU REJECTED HIM?!
DANGIT, SHIMA!!
CHAK
GYAH
KYAH
Oh no!!
Mr. Okumura, Are you all right?!
?
HM?
KYAH

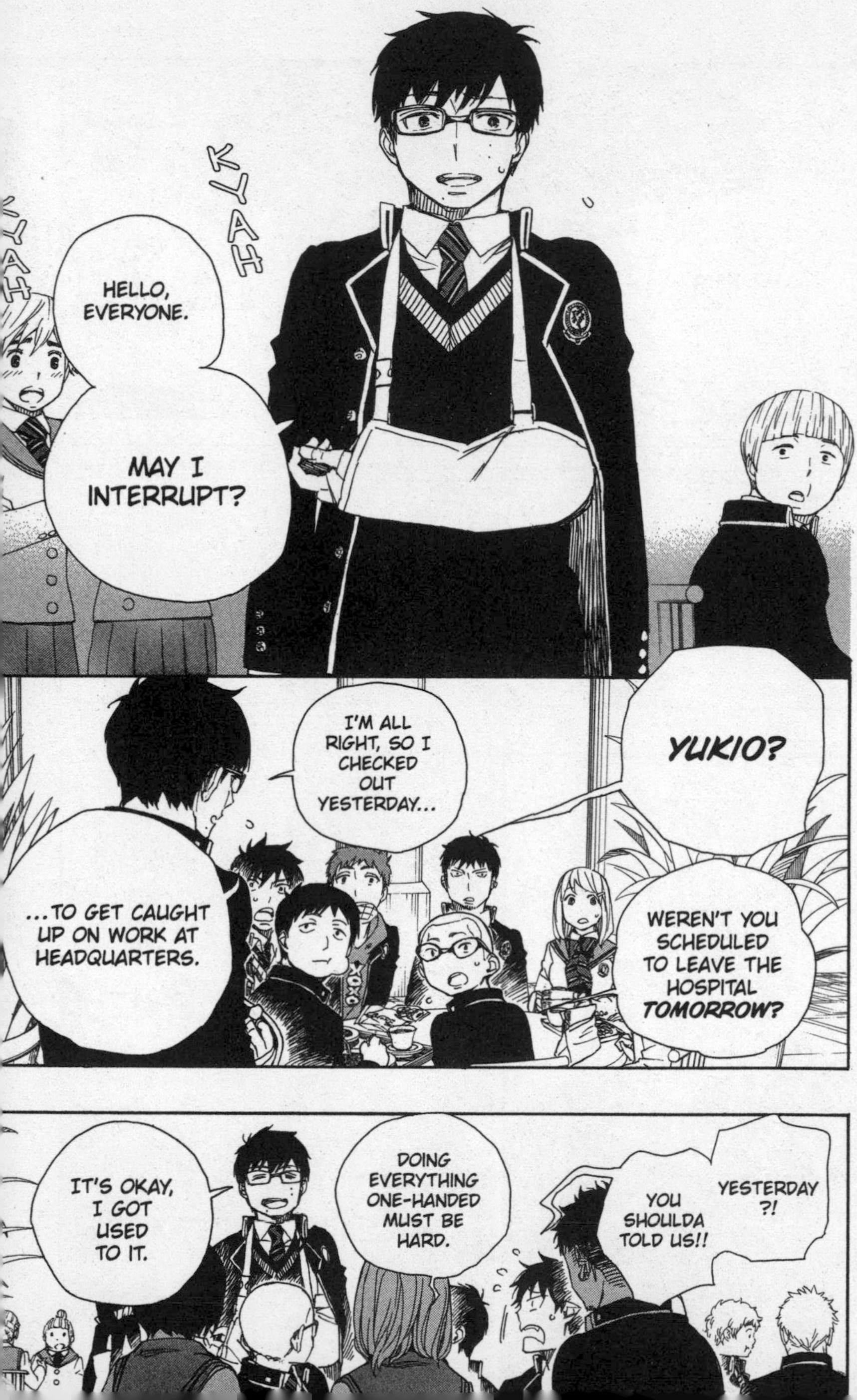
KYAH
HELLO, EVERYONE.
MAY I INTERRUPT?
YUKIO?
WEREN'T YOU SCHEDULED TO LEAVE THE HOSPITAL *TOMORROW?*
I'M ALL RIGHT, SO I CHECKED OUT YESTERDAY...
...TO GET CAUGHT UP ON WORK AT HEADQUARTERS.
YESTERDAY?!
YOU SHOULDA TOLD US!!
DOING EVERYTHING ONE-HANDED MUST BE HARD.
IT'S OKAY, I GOT USED TO IT.

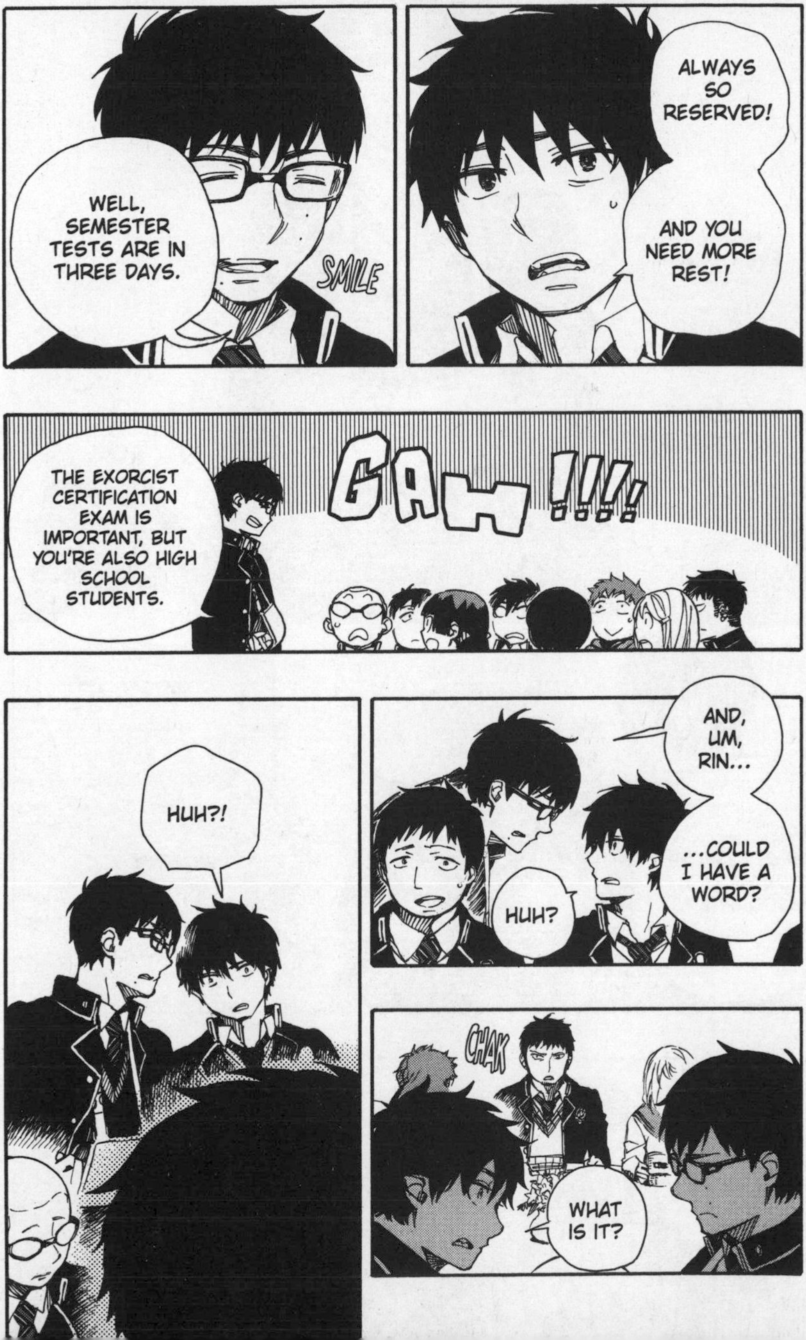
ALWAYS SO RESERVED!
AND YOU NEED MORE REST!
WELL, SEMESTER TESTS ARE IN THREE DAYS.
SMILE
GAH!!!!
THE EXORCIST CERTIFICATION EXAM IS IMPORTANT, BUT YOU'RE ALSO HIGH SCHOOL STUDENTS.
AND, UM, RIN...
...COULD I HAVE A WORD?
HUH?
CHAK
WHAT IS IT?
HUH?!

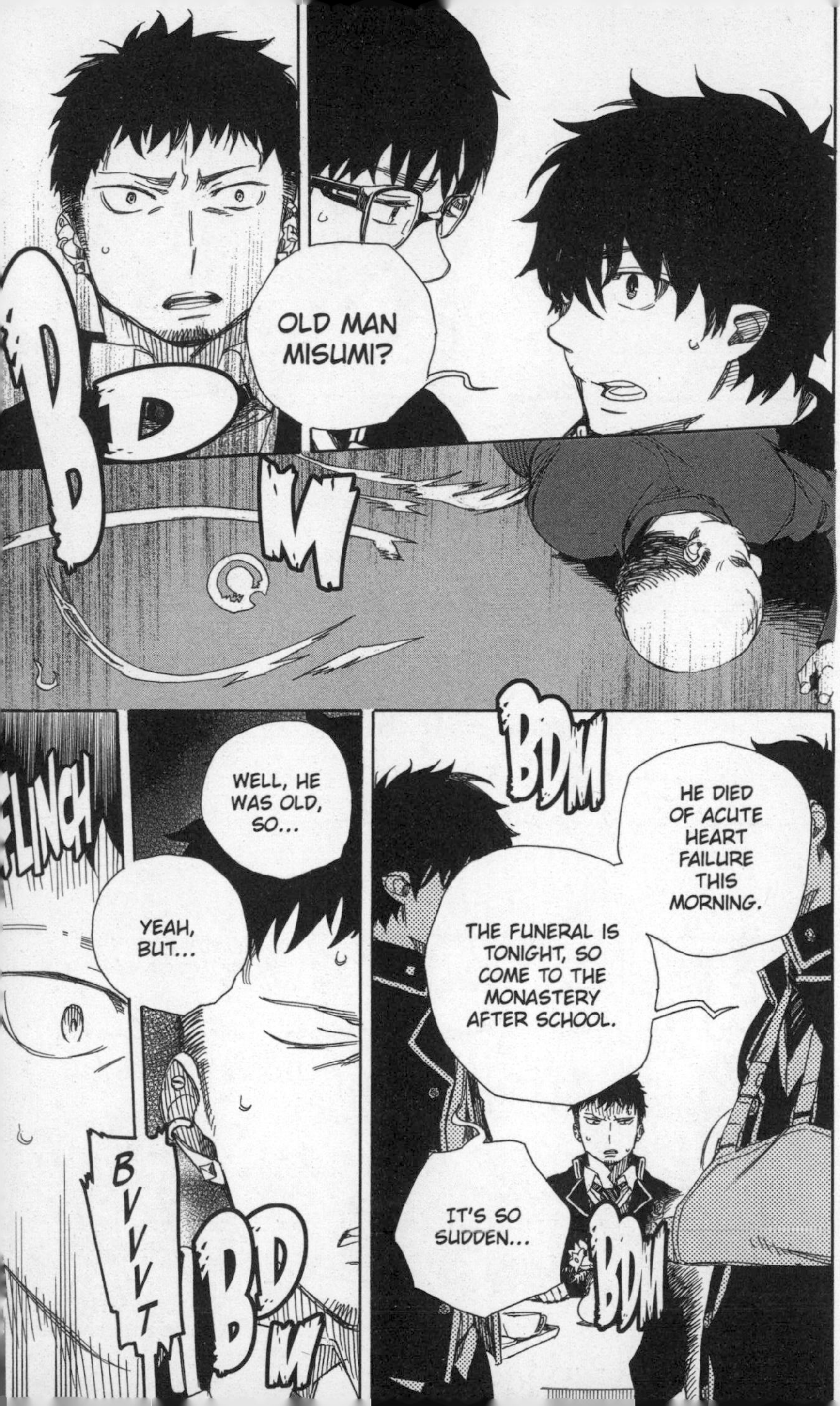
OLD MAN MISUMI?
BDM
BDM
HE DIED OF ACUTE HEART FAILURE THIS MORNING.
THE FUNERAL IS TONIGHT, SO COME TO THE MONASTERY AFTER SCHOOL.
IT'S SO SUDDEN...
BDM
FLINCH
WELL, HE WAS OLD, SO...
YEAH, BUT...
BVVVT
BDM

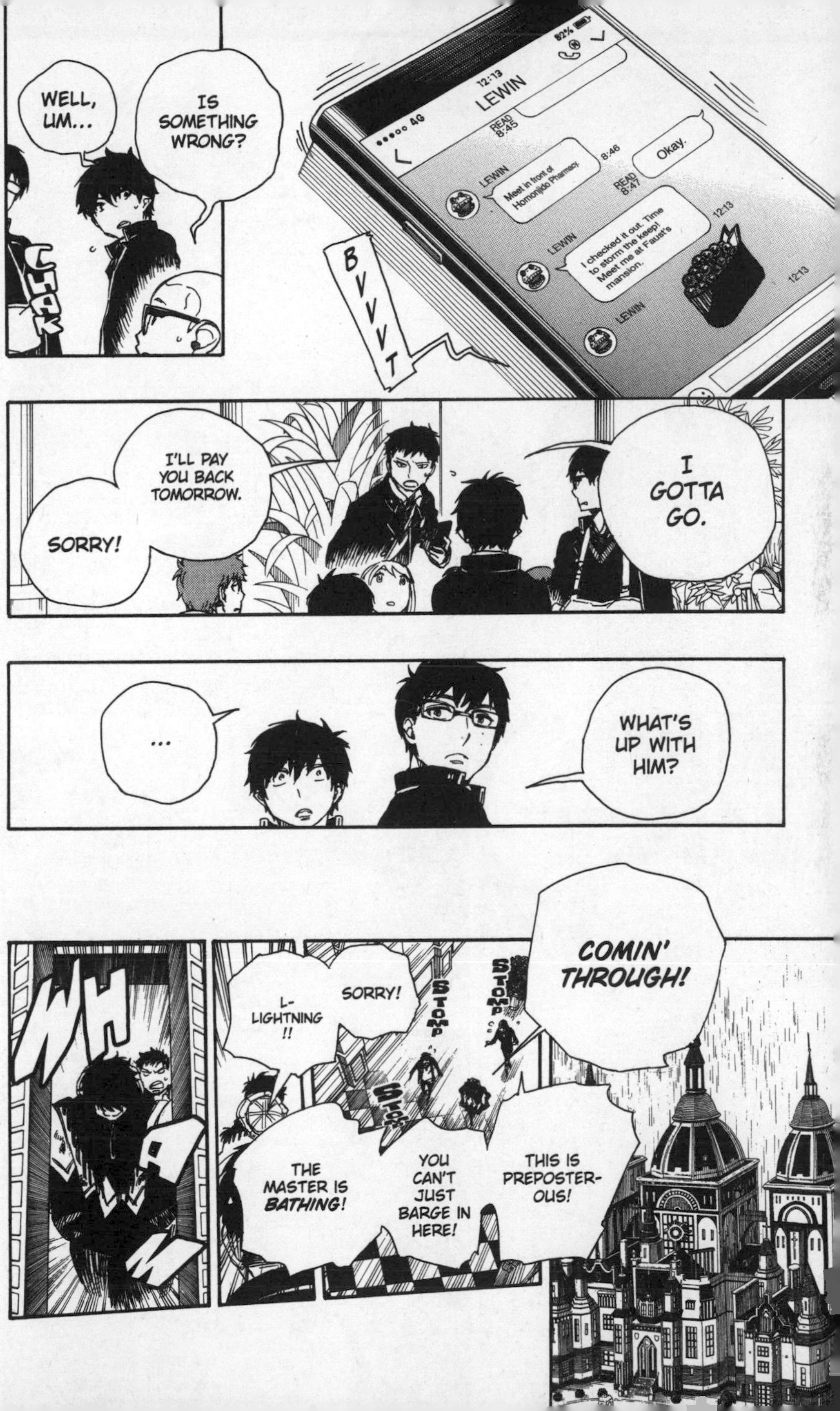
BVVVT
12:13
LEWIN
READ 8:45
LEWIN
Meet in front of Homonjido Pharmacy.
8:46
Okay.
READ 8:47
LEWIN
I checked it out. Time to storm the keep! Meet me at Faust's mansion.
12:13
LEWIN
12:13
LEWIN
IS SOMETHING WRONG?
WELL, UM...
CHAK
I GOTTA GO.
I'LL PAY YOU BACK TOMORROW.
SORRY!
WHAT'S UP WITH HIM?
...
COMIN' THROUGH!
THIS IS PREPOSTEROUS!
YOU CAN'T JUST BARGE IN HERE!
THE MASTER IS *BATHING*!
STOMP
STOMP
STOMP
SORRY!
L-LIGHTNING!!
WHAM

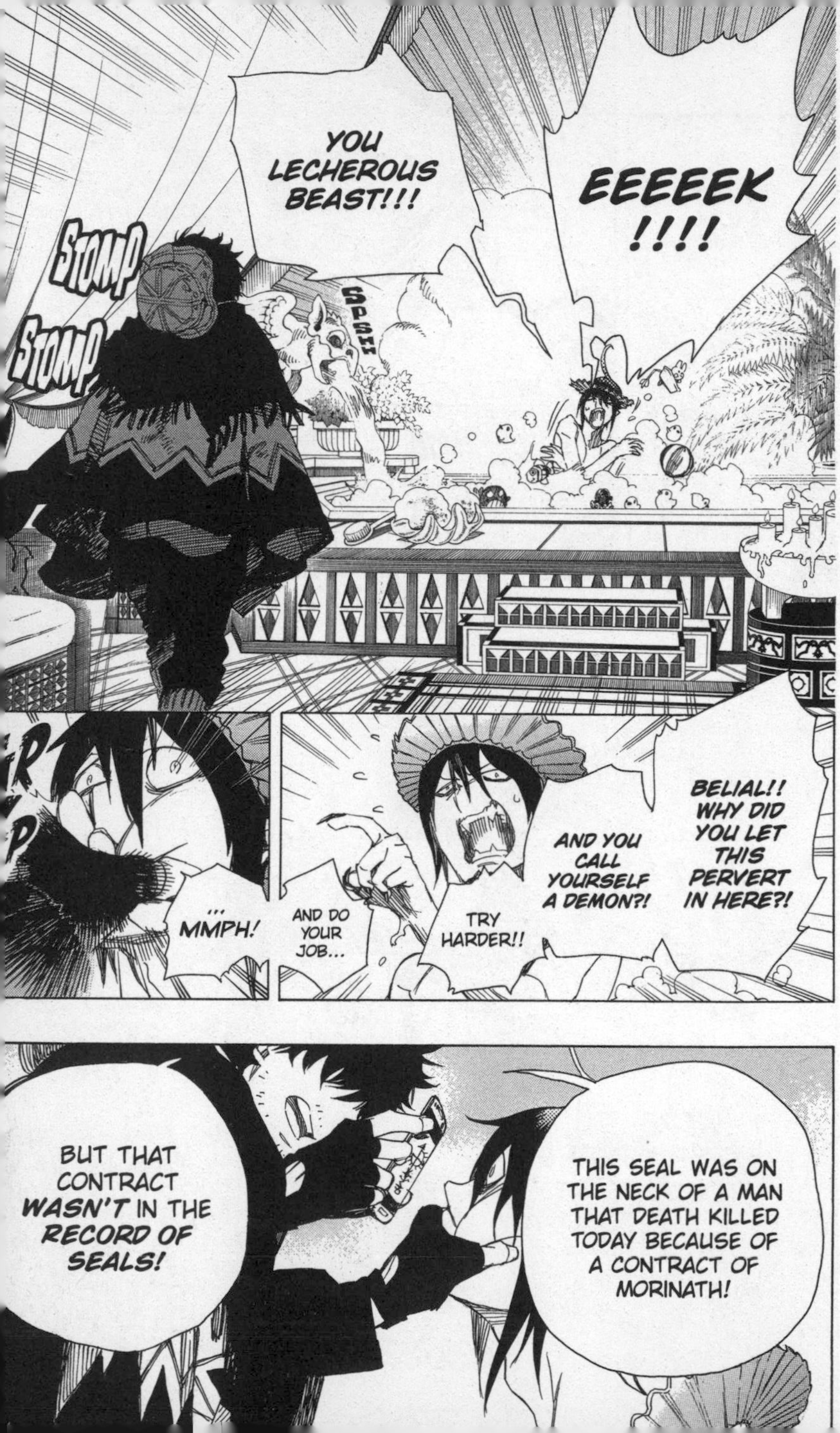
EEEEEK !!!!
YOU LECHEROUS BEAST!!!
SPSHH
STOMP
STOMP
BELIAL!! WHY DID YOU LET THIS PERVERT IN HERE?!
AND YOU CALL YOURSELF A DEMON?!
TRY HARDER!!
AND DO YOUR JOB...
... MMPH!
THIS SEAL WAS ON THE NECK OF A MAN THAT DEATH KILLED TODAY BECAUSE OF A CONTRACT OF MORINATH!
BUT THAT CONTRACT WASN'T IN THE RECORD OF SEALS!

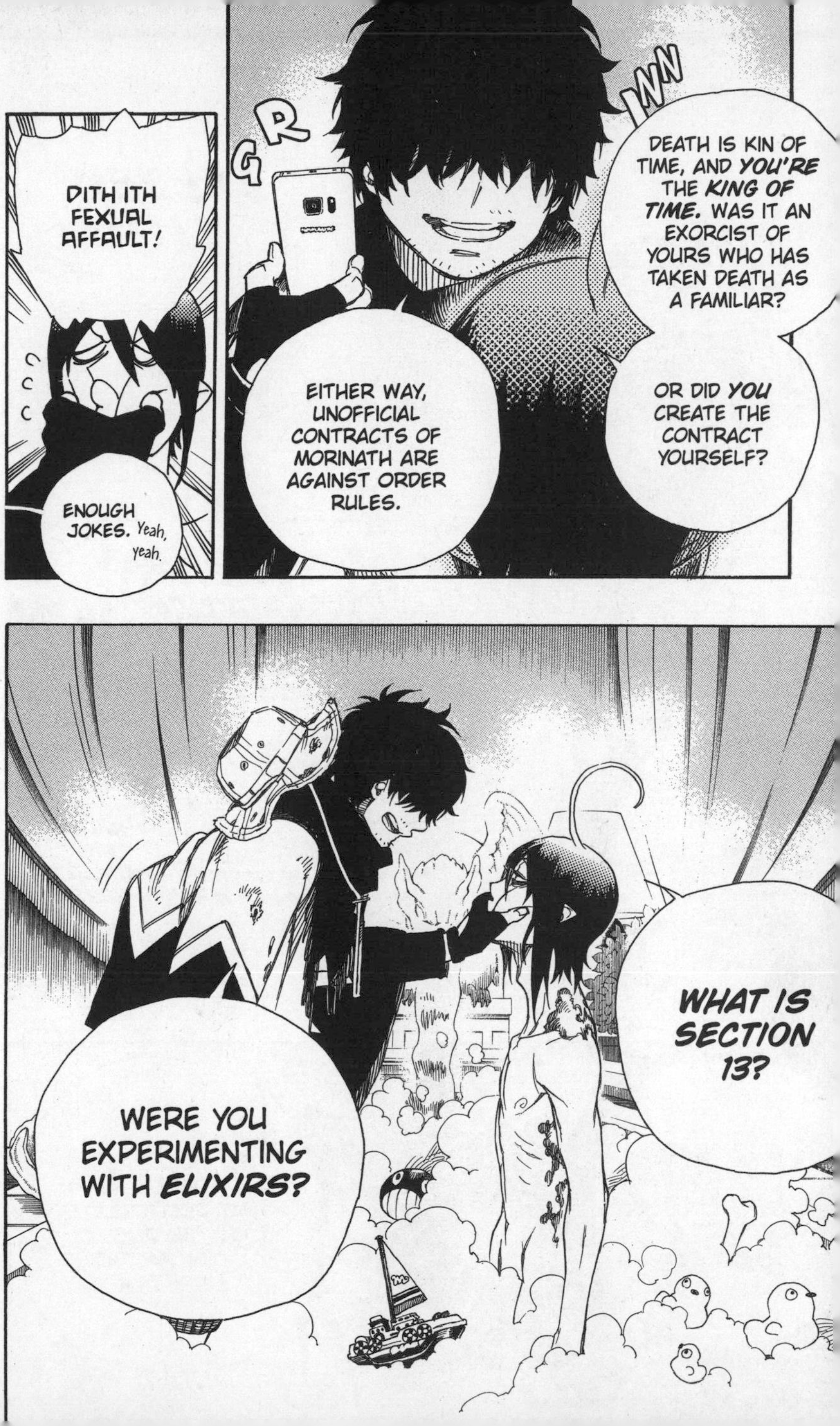
GR
INN
DEATH IS KIN OF TIME, AND *YOU'RE* THE *KING OF TIME.* WAS IT AN EXORCIST OF YOURS WHO HAS TAKEN DEATH AS A FAMILIAR?
OR DID *YOU* CREATE THE CONTRACT YOURSELF?
EITHER WAY, UNOFFICIAL CONTRACTS OF MORINATH ARE AGAINST ORDER RULES.
DITH ITH FEXUAL AFFAULT!
ENOUGH JOKES.
Yeah, yeah.
WHAT IS SECTION 13?
WERE YOU EXPERIMENTING WITH *ELIXIRS?*

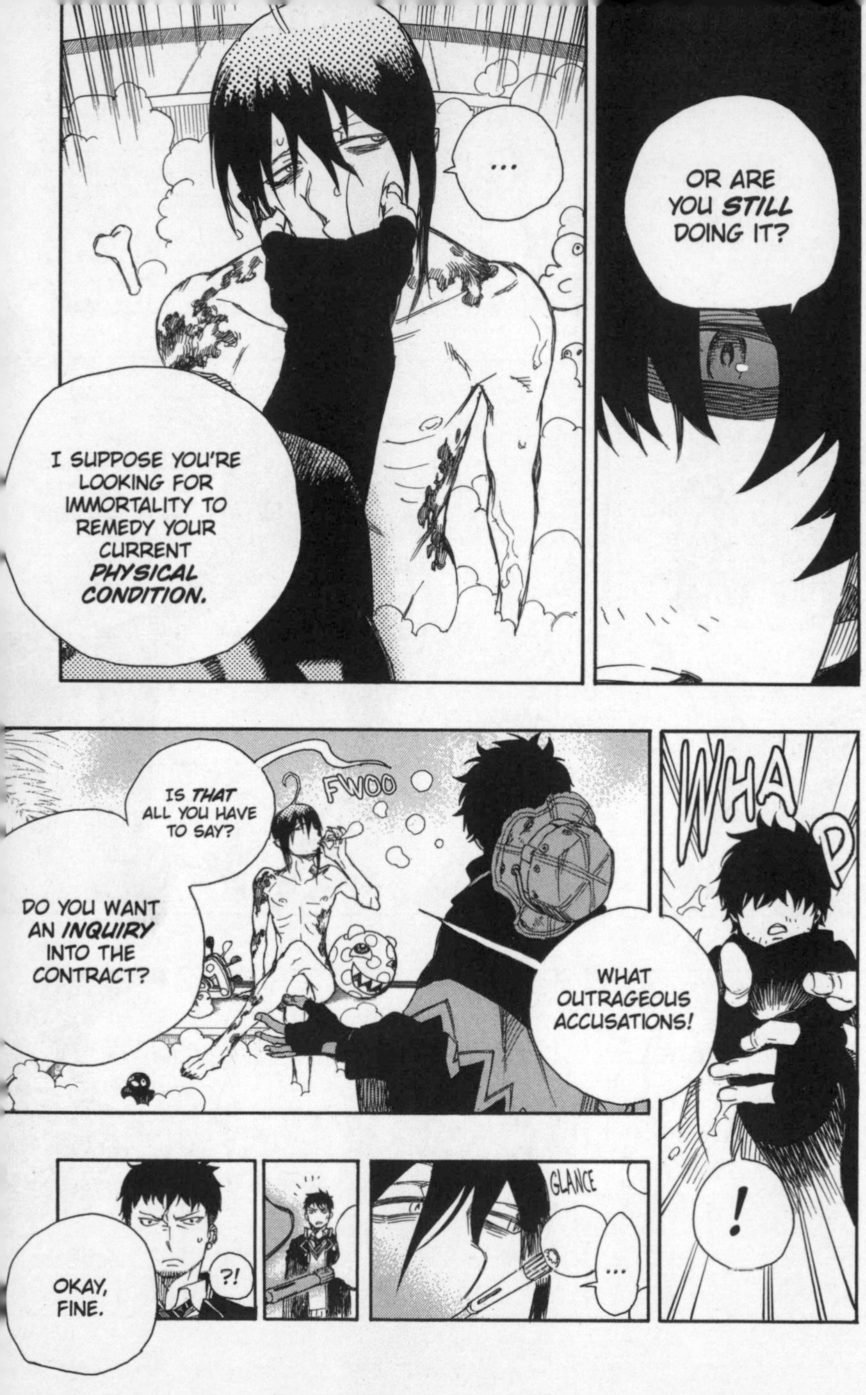
OR ARE YOU STILL DOING IT?
...
I SUPPOSE YOU'RE LOOKING FOR IMMORTALITY TO REMEDY YOUR CURRENT PHYSICAL CONDITION.
WHAP
!
FWOO
WHAT OUTRAGEOUS ACCUSATIONS!
IS THAT ALL YOU HAVE TO SAY?
DO YOU WANT AN INQUIRY INTO THE CONTRACT?
GLANCE
...
?!
OKAY, FINE.

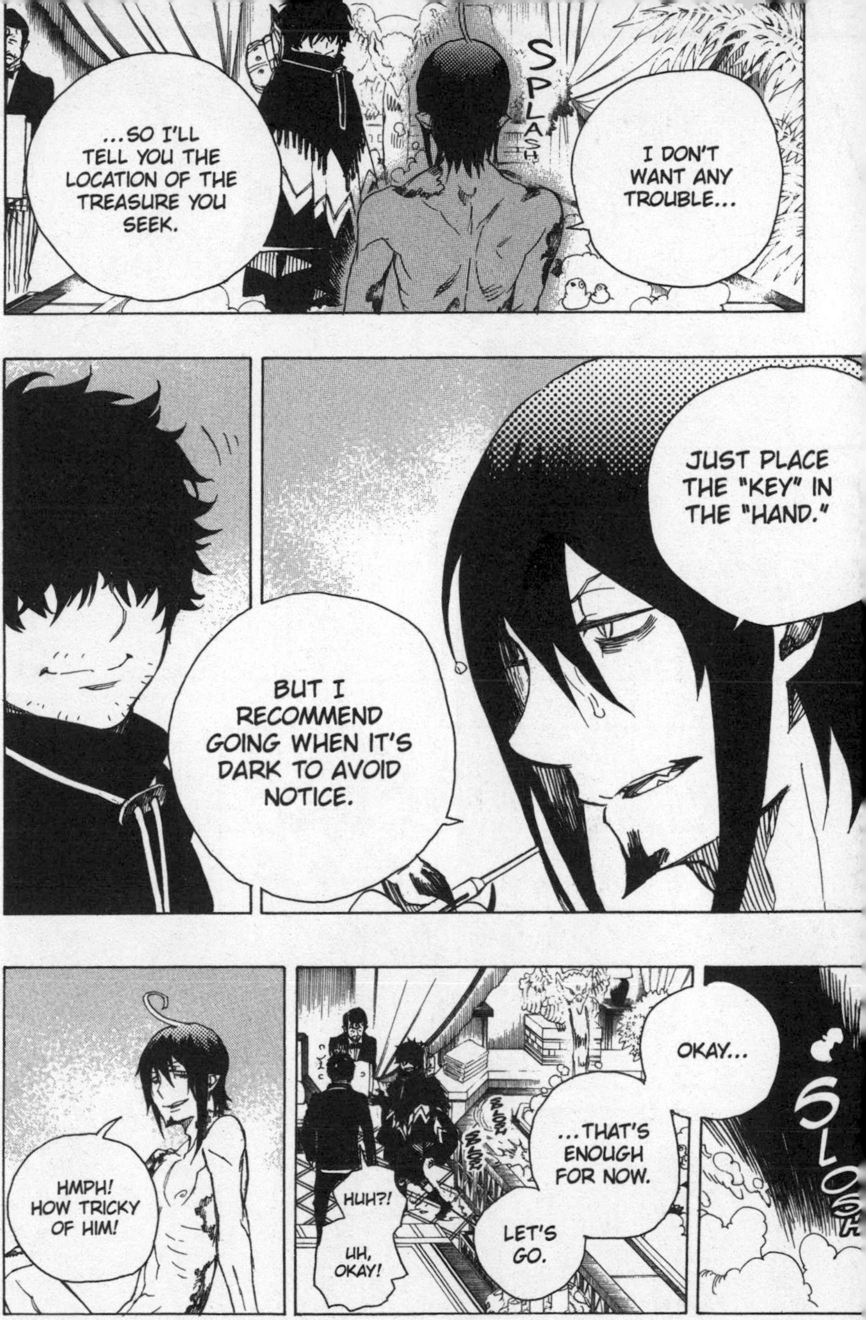
I DON'T WANT ANY TROUBLE...
SPLASH
...SO I'LL TELL YOU THE LOCATION OF THE TREASURE YOU SEEK.
JUST PLACE THE "KEY" IN THE "HAND."
BUT I RECOMMEND GOING WHEN IT'S DARK TO AVOID NOTICE.
SLOSH
OKAY...
...THAT'S ENOUGH FOR NOW.
LET'S GO.
HUH?!
UH, OKAY!
HMPH! HOW TRICKY OF HIM!

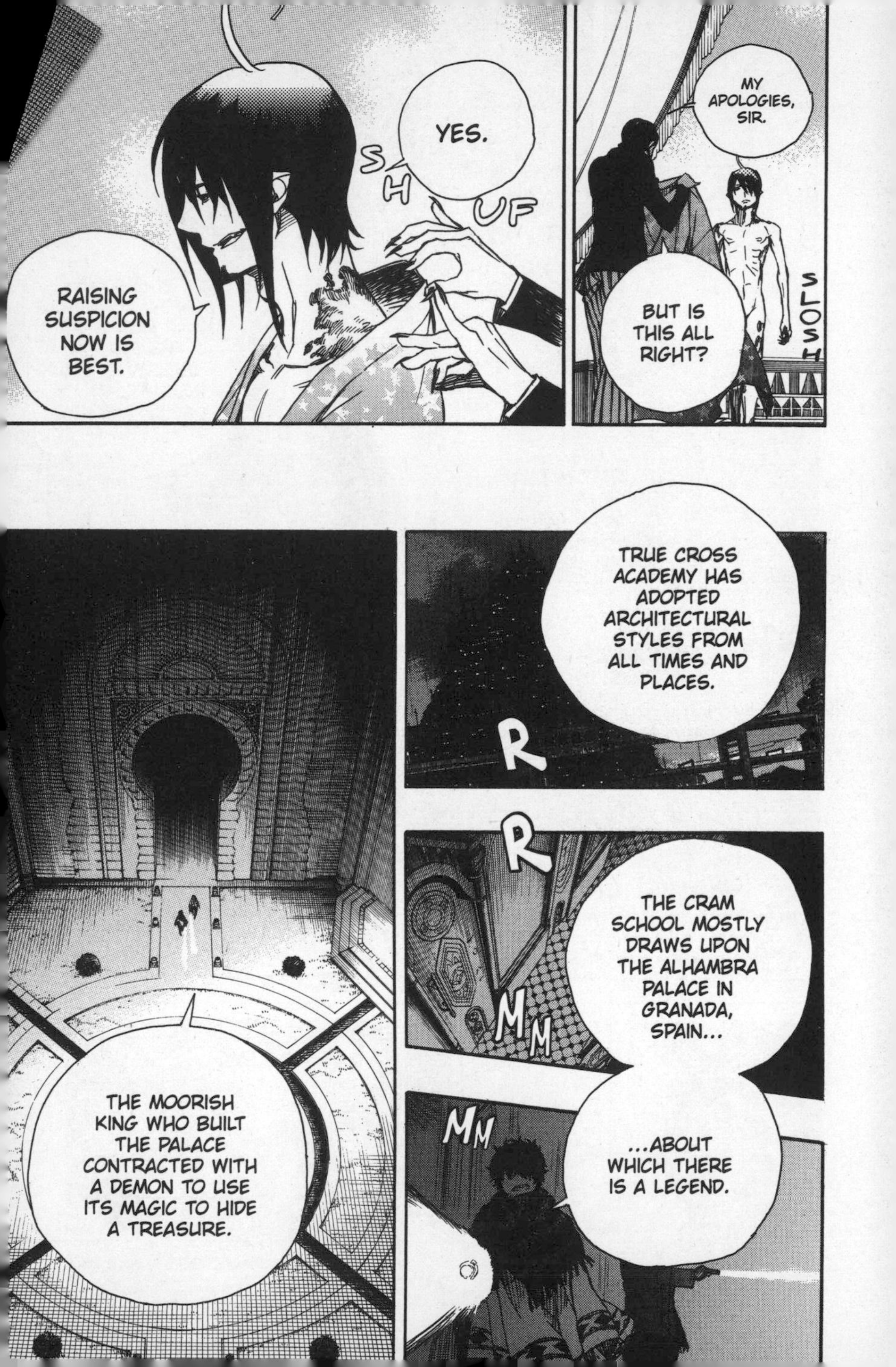
MY APOLOGIES, SIR.
BUT IS THIS ALL RIGHT?
SLOSH
YES.
SHUF
RAISING SUSPICION NOW IS BEST.
TRUE CROSS ACADEMY HAS ADOPTED ARCHITECTURAL STYLES FROM ALL TIMES AND PLACES.
R
R
THE CRAM SCHOOL MOSTLY DRAWS UPON THE ALHAMBRA PALACE IN GRANADA, SPAIN...
MM
MM
...ABOUT WHICH THERE IS A LEGEND.
THE MOORISH KING WHO BUILT THE PALACE CONTRACTED WITH A DEMON TO USE ITS MAGIC TO HIDE A TREASURE.

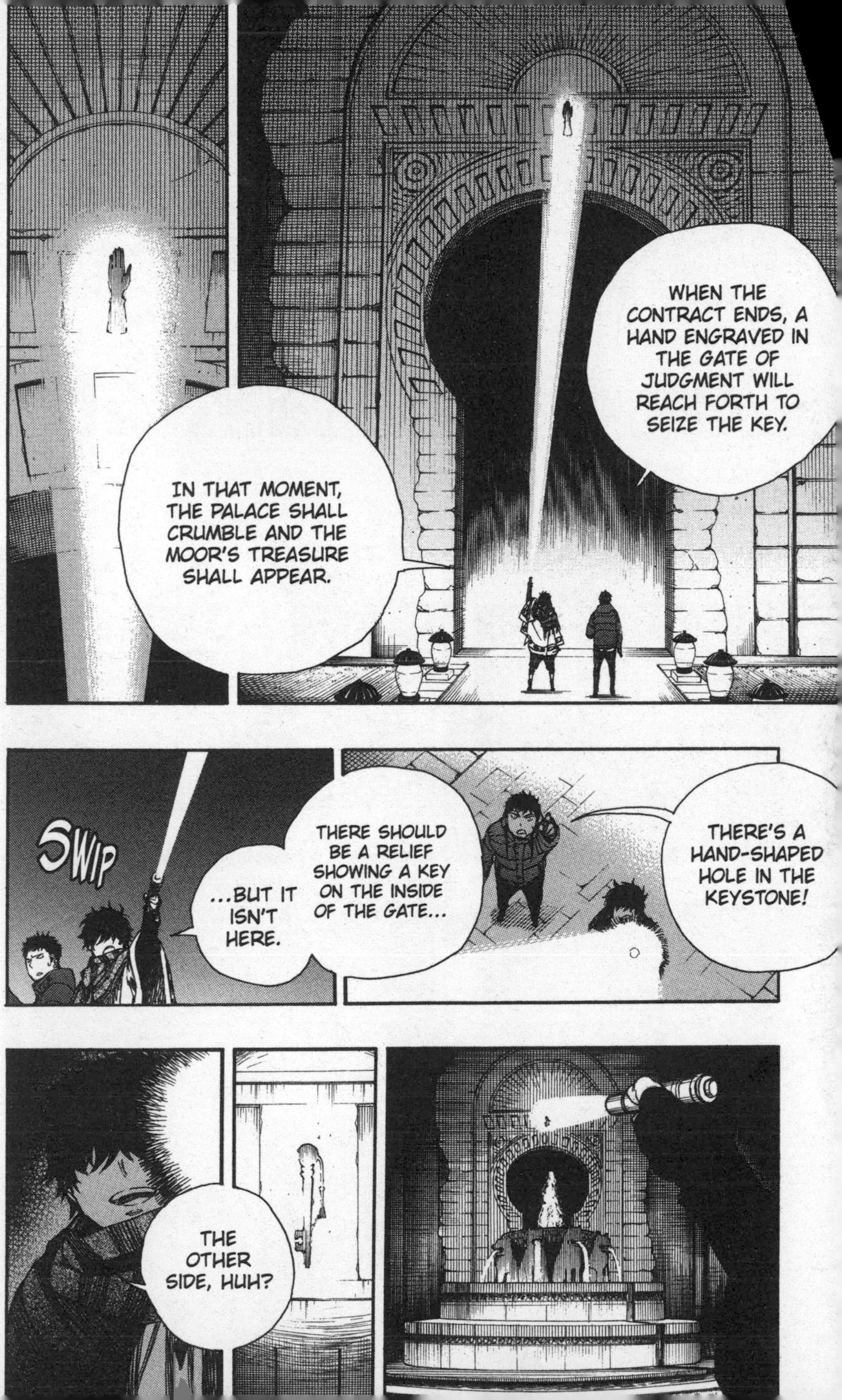
WHEN THE CONTRACT ENDS, A HAND ENGRAVED IN THE GATE OF JUDGMENT WILL REACH FORTH TO SEIZE THE KEY.
IN THAT MOMENT, THE PALACE SHALL CRUMBLE AND THE MOOR'S TREASURE SHALL APPEAR.
THERE'S A HAND-SHAPED HOLE IN THE KEYSTONE!
THERE SHOULD BE A RELIEF SHOWING A KEY ON THE INSIDE OF THE GATE...
...BUT IT ISN'T HERE.
SWIP
THE OTHER SIDE, HUH?

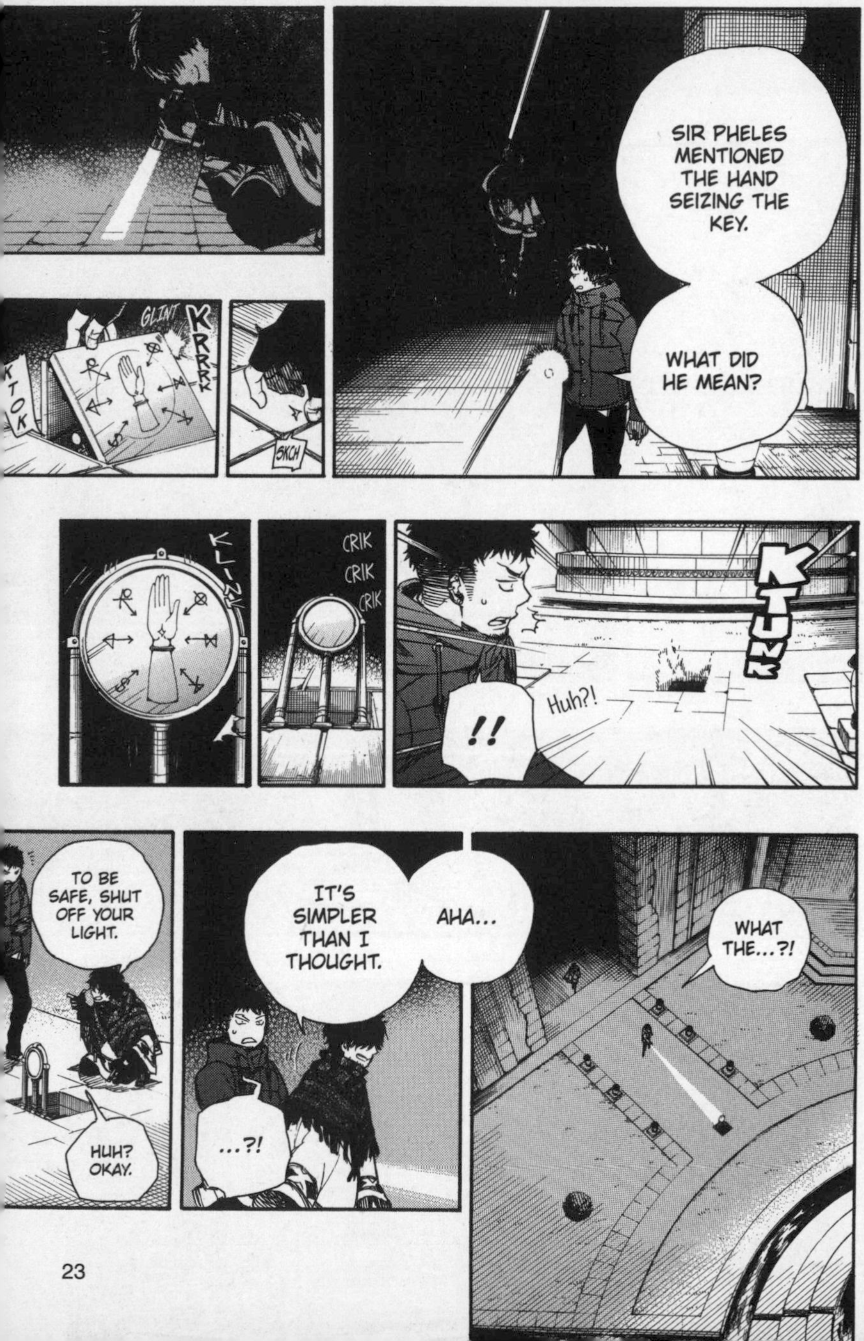
SIR PHELES MENTIONED THE HAND SEIZING THE KEY.
WHAT DID HE MEAN?
SKCH
GLINT
KRRRK
KTOK
KTUNK
Huh?!
!!
CRIK
CRIK
CRIK
KLINK
WHAT THE...?!
AHA...
IT'S SIMPLER THAN I THOUGHT.
...?!
TO BE SAFE, SHUT OFF YOUR LIGHT.
HUH? OKAY.

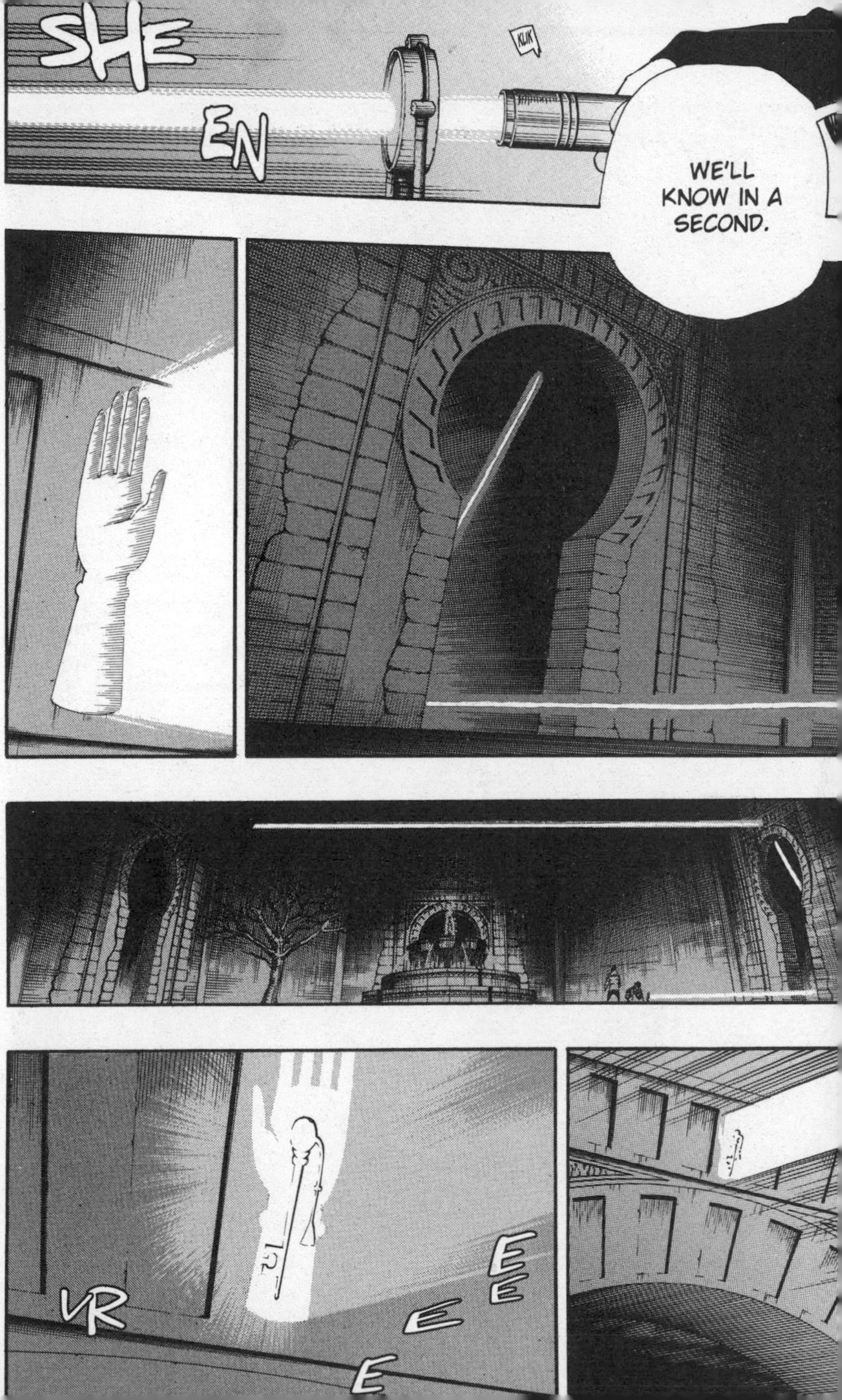
WE'LL KNOW IN A SECOND.
KLIK
SHE
EN
E
E
E
E
VR

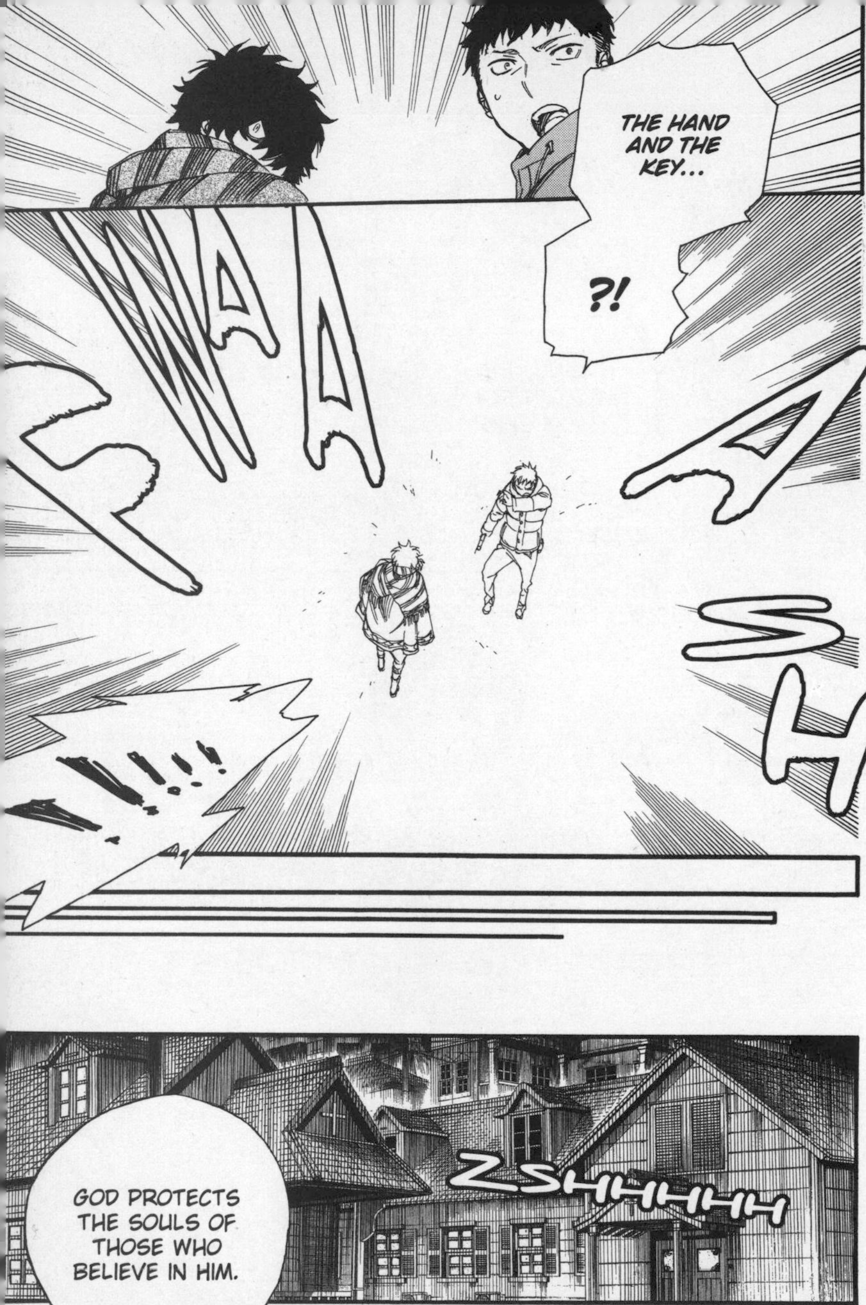
THE HAND AND THE KEY...
?!
WAAA
SH
!!!
ZSHHHHHH
GOD PROTECTS THE SOULS OF THOSE WHO BELIEVE IN HIM.

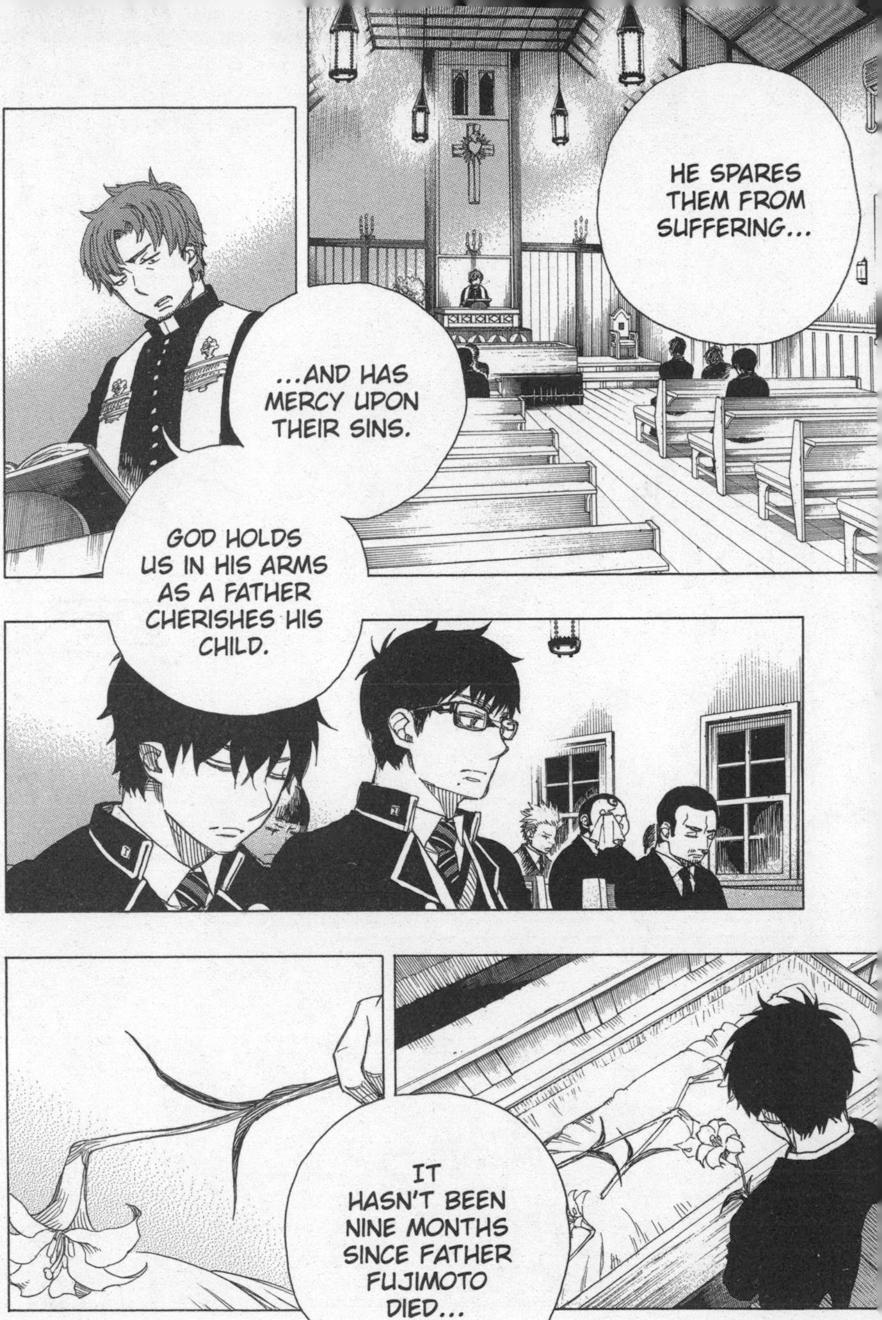
HE SPARES THEM FROM SUFFERING...
...AND HAS MERCY UPON THEIR SINS.
GOD HOLDS US IN HIS ARMS AS A FATHER CHERISHES HIS CHILD.
IT HASN'T BEEN NINE MONTHS SINCE FATHER FUJIMOTO DIED...

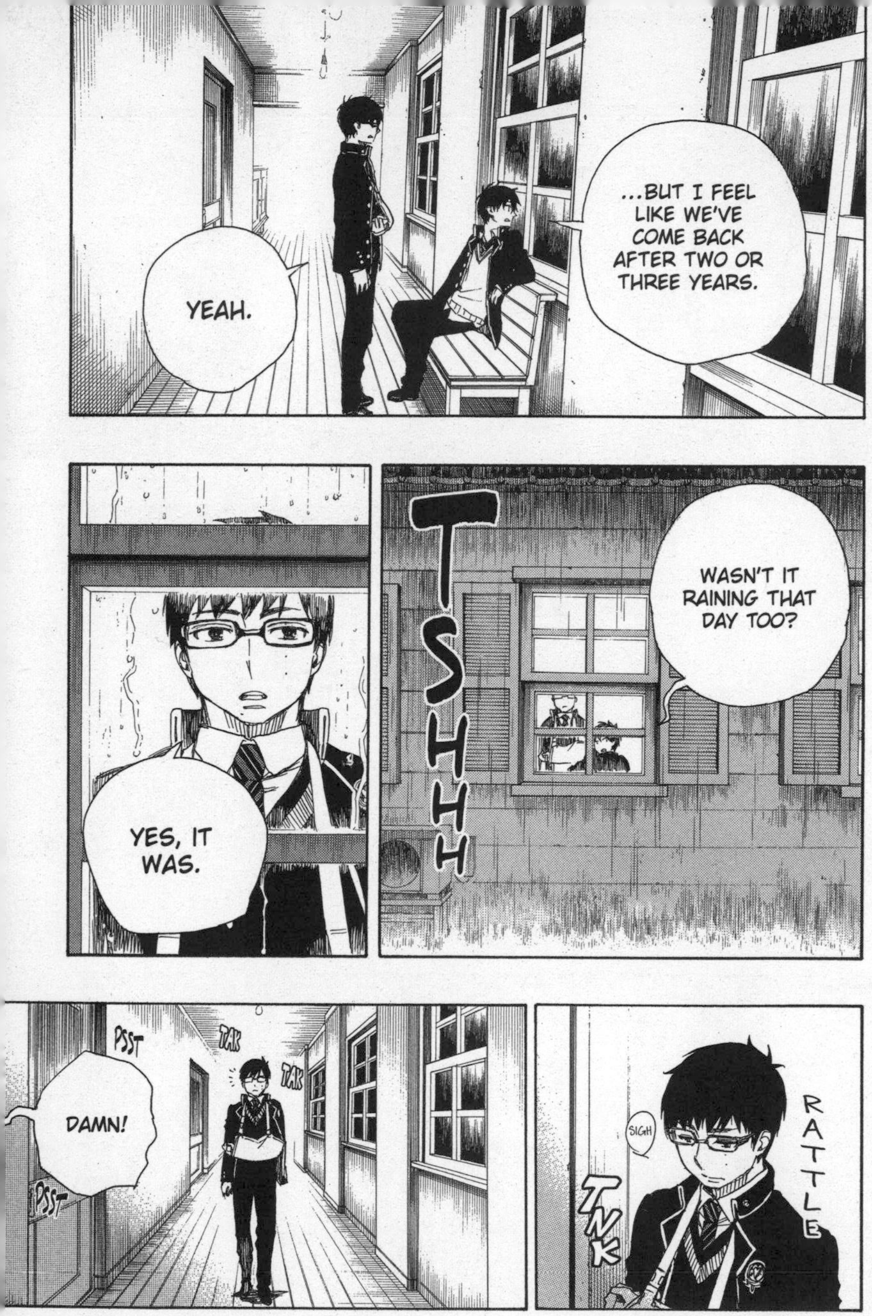

...BUT I FEEL LIKE WE'VE COME BACK AFTER TWO OR THREE YEARS.
YEAH.
TSHHH
WASN'T IT RAINING THAT DAY TOO?
YES, IT WAS.
RATTLE
SIGH
TNK
TAK
TAK
PSST
DAMN!
PSST

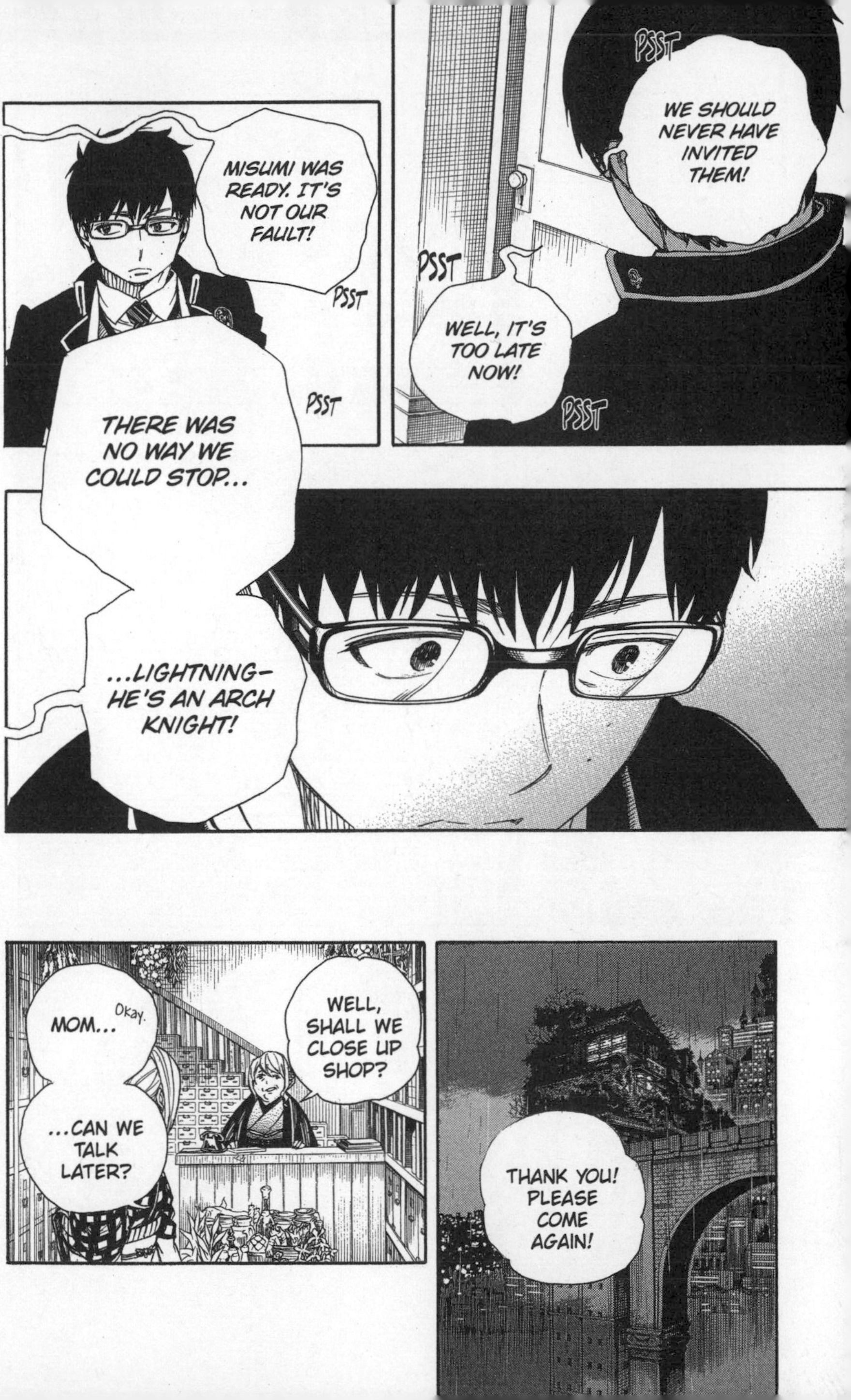
PSST
WE SHOULD NEVER HAVE INVITED THEM!
PSST
WELL, IT'S TOO LATE NOW!
PSST
MISUMI WAS READY. IT'S NOT OUR FAULT!
PSST
PSST
THERE WAS NO WAY WE COULD STOP...
...LIGHTNING—HE'S AN ARCH KNIGHT!
THANK YOU! PLEASE COME AGAIN!
WELL, SHALL WE CLOSE UP SHOP?
Okay.
MOM...
...CAN WE TALK LATER?

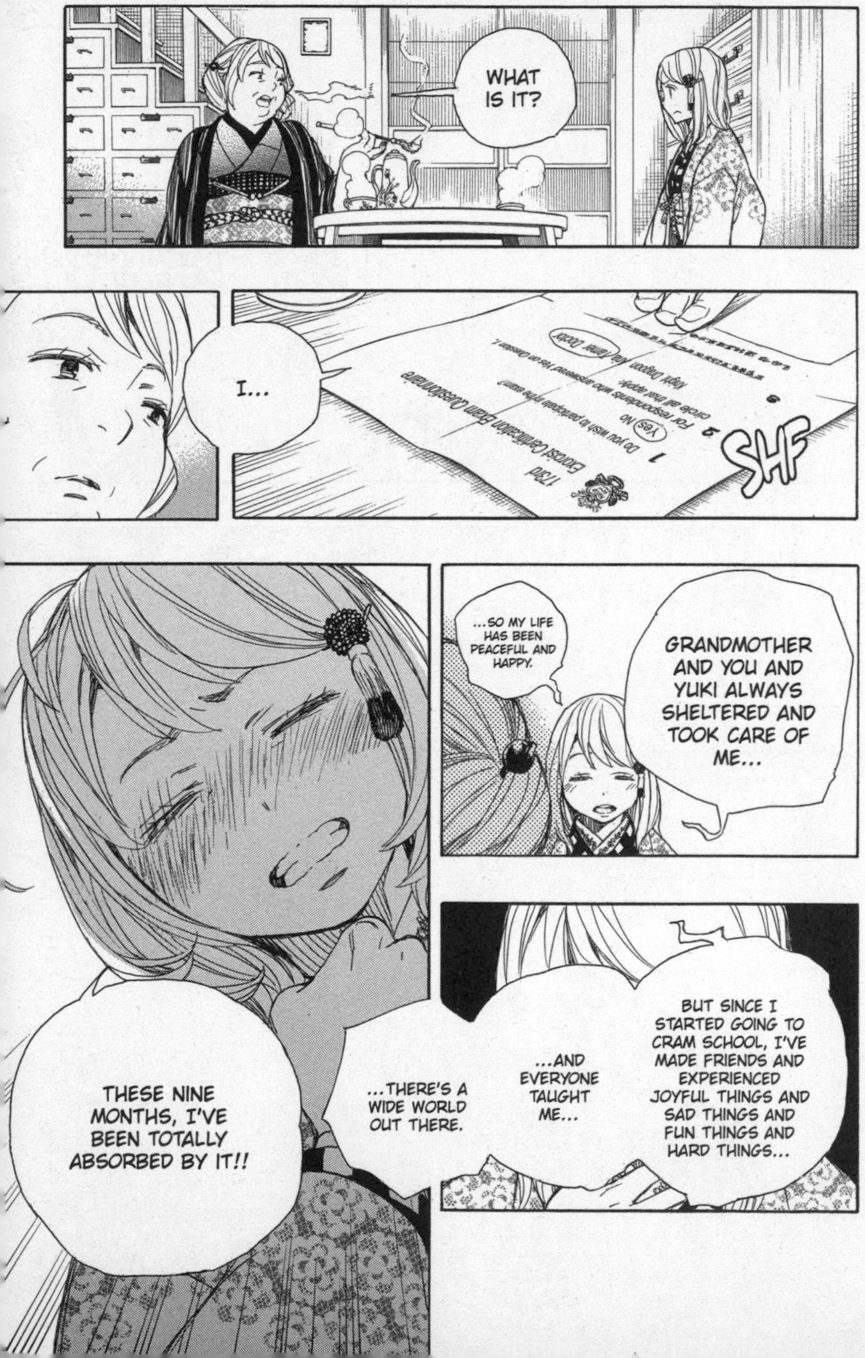
WHAT IS IT?
SHF
Exorcist Certification Exam Questionnaire
Do you wish to participate in the exam?
Yes No
For respondents who answered Yes on Question 1, circle all that apply.
Knight Dragoon Tamer Doctor
I...
GRANDMOTHER AND YOU AND YUKI ALWAYS SHELTERED AND TOOK CARE OF ME...
...SO MY LIFE HAS BEEN PEACEFUL AND HAPPY.
BUT SINCE I STARTED GOING TO CRAM SCHOOL, I'VE MADE FRIENDS AND EXPERIENCED JOYFUL THINGS AND SAD THINGS AND FUN THINGS AND HARD THINGS...
...AND EVERYONE TAUGHT ME...
...THERE'S A WIDE WORLD OUT THERE.
THESE NINE MONTHS, I'VE BEEN TOTALLY ABSORBED BY IT!!

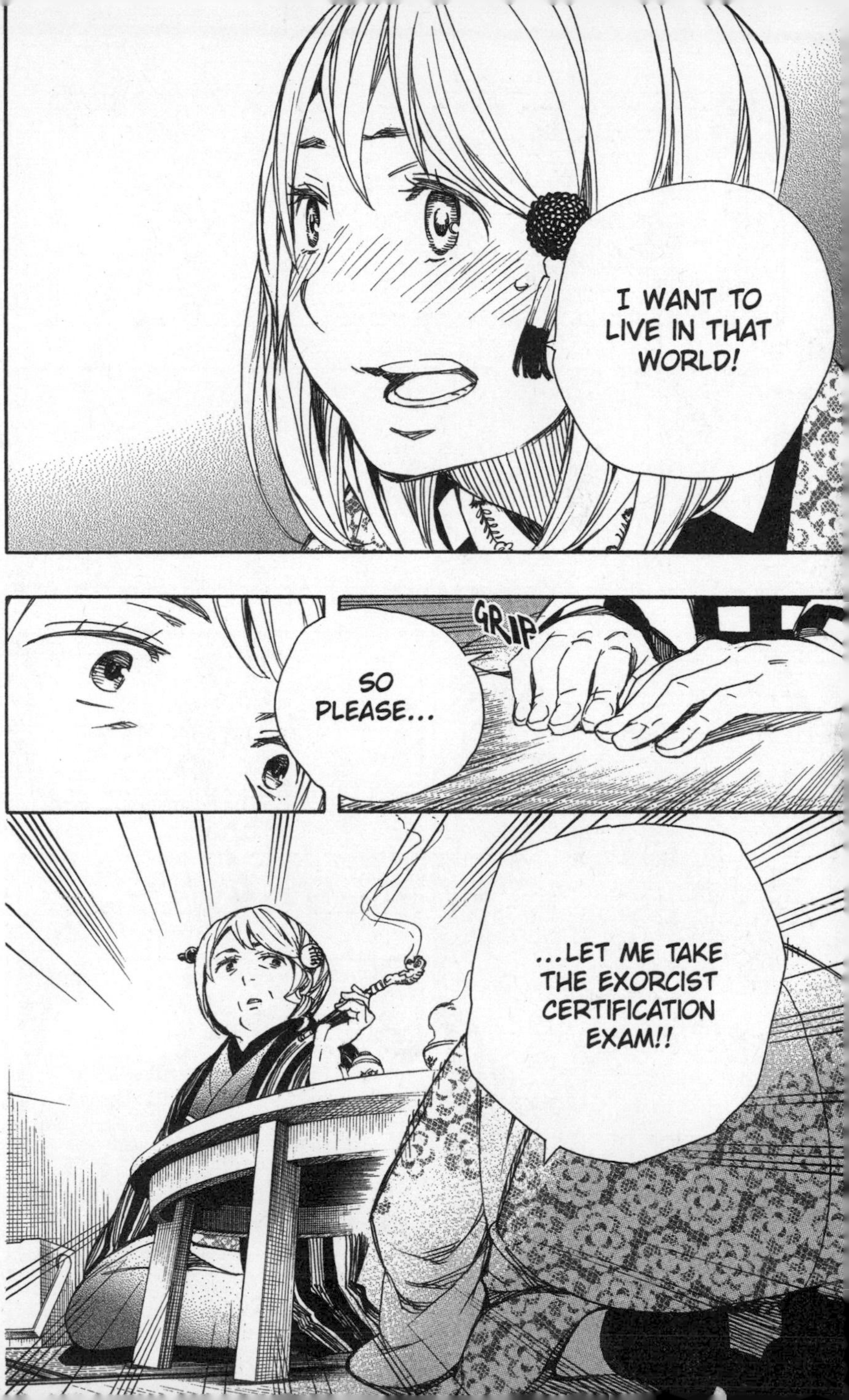
I WANT TO LIVE IN THAT WORLD!
GRIP
SO PLEASE...
...LET ME TAKE THE EXORCIST CERTIFICATION EXAM!!

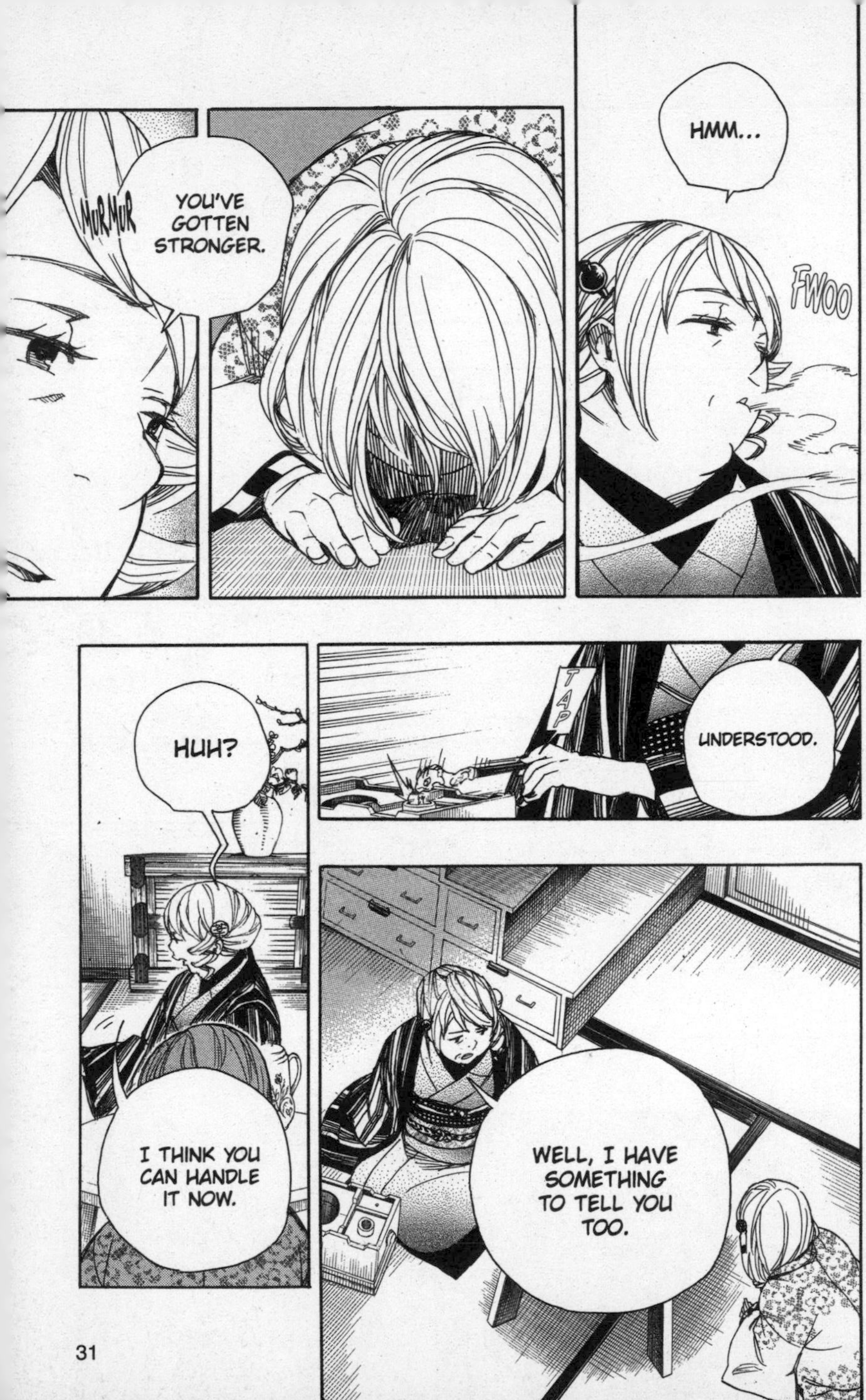
HMM...
FWOO
MURMUR
YOU'VE GOTTEN STRONGER.
TAP
UNDERSTOOD.
WELL, I HAVE SOMETHING TO TELL YOU TOO.
HUH?
I THINK YOU CAN HANDLE IT NOW.

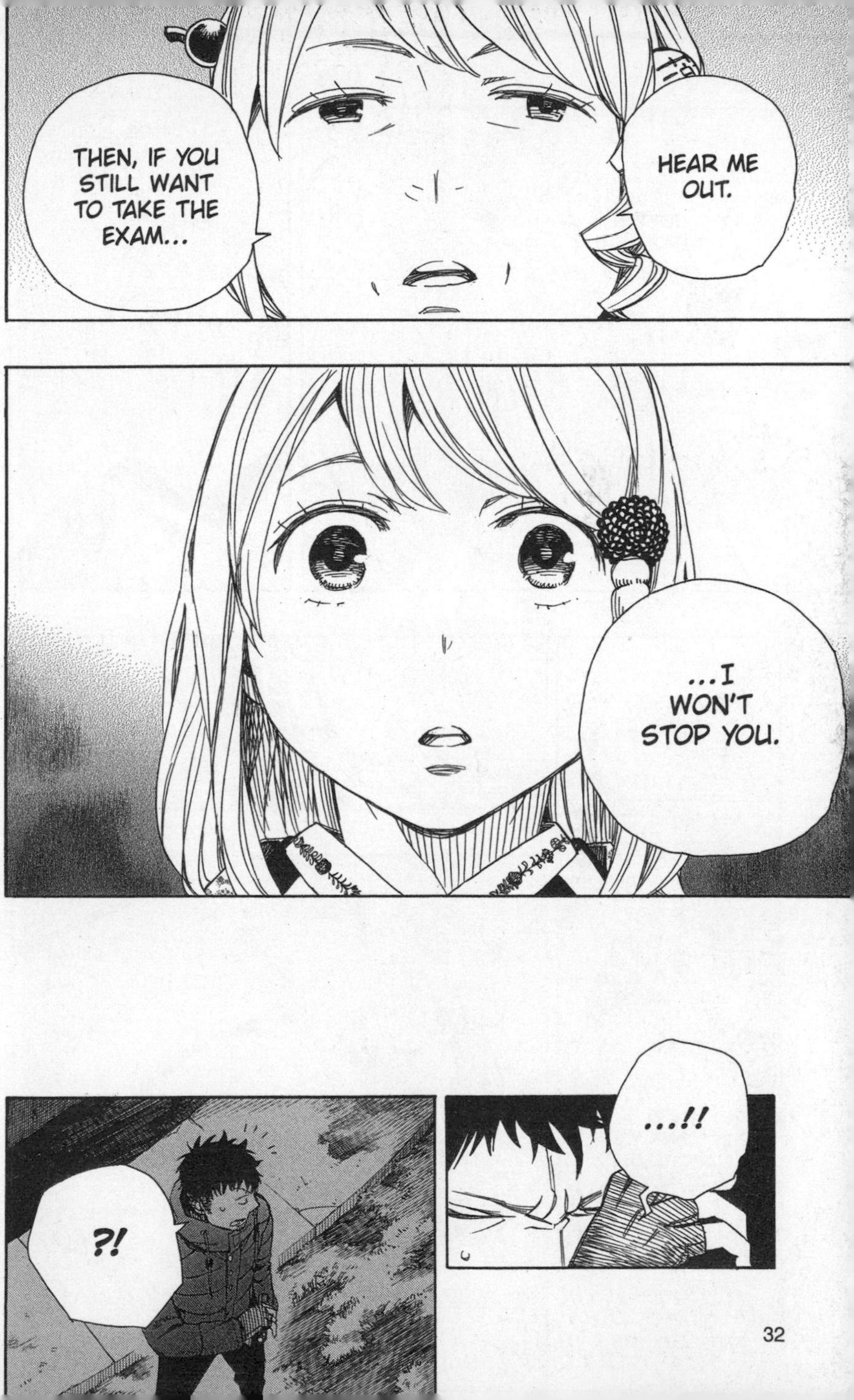
HEAR ME OUT.
THEN, IF YOU STILL WANT TO TAKE THE EXAM...
...I WON'T STOP YOU.
...!!
?!

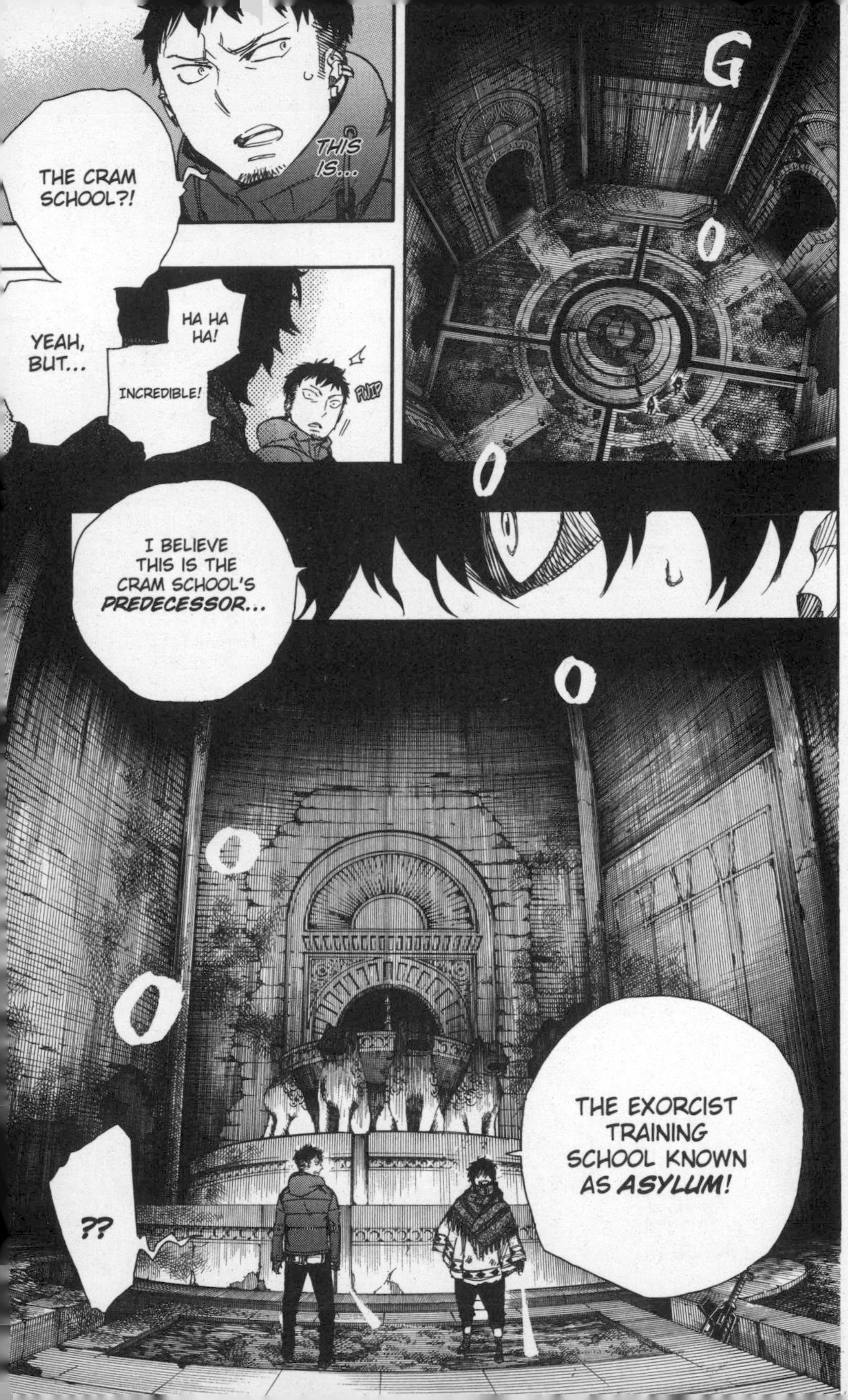
GWOOOOO
THIS IS...
THE CRAM SCHOOL?!
HA HA HA!
INCREDIBLE!
FWIP
YEAH, BUT...
I BELIEVE THIS IS THE CRAM SCHOOL'S ***PREDECESSOR***...
THE EXORCIST TRAINING SCHOOL KNOWN AS ***ASYLUM***!
??

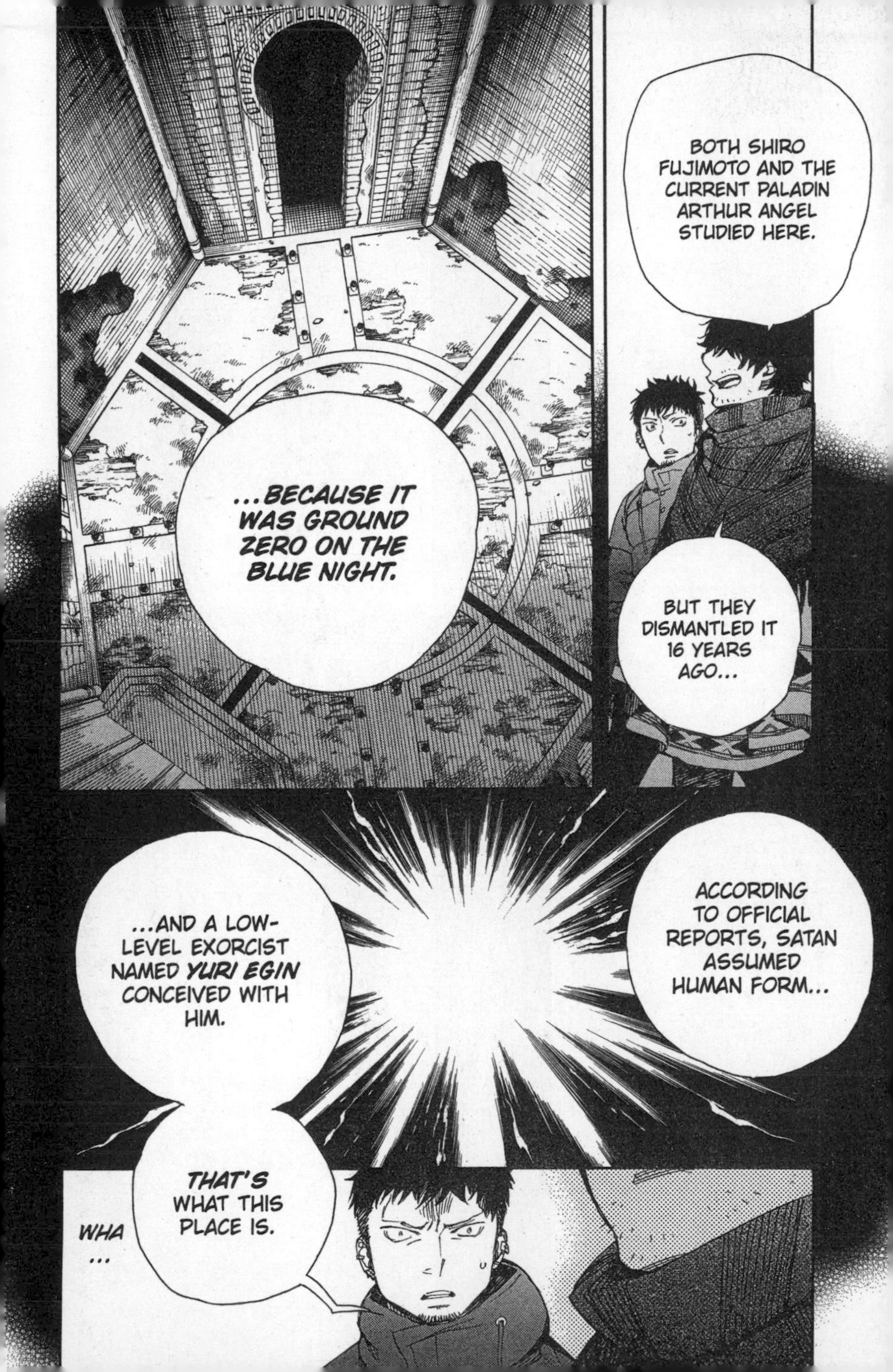
BOTH SHIRO FUJIMOTO AND THE CURRENT PALADIN ARTHUR ANGEL STUDIED HERE.
BUT THEY DISMANTLED IT 16 YEARS AGO...
...BECAUSE IT WAS GROUND ZERO ON THE BLUE NIGHT.
ACCORDING TO OFFICIAL REPORTS, SATAN ASSUMED HUMAN FORM...
...AND A LOW-LEVEL EXORCIST NAMED YURI EGIN CONCEIVED WITH HIM.
THAT'S WHAT THIS PLACE IS.
WHA...

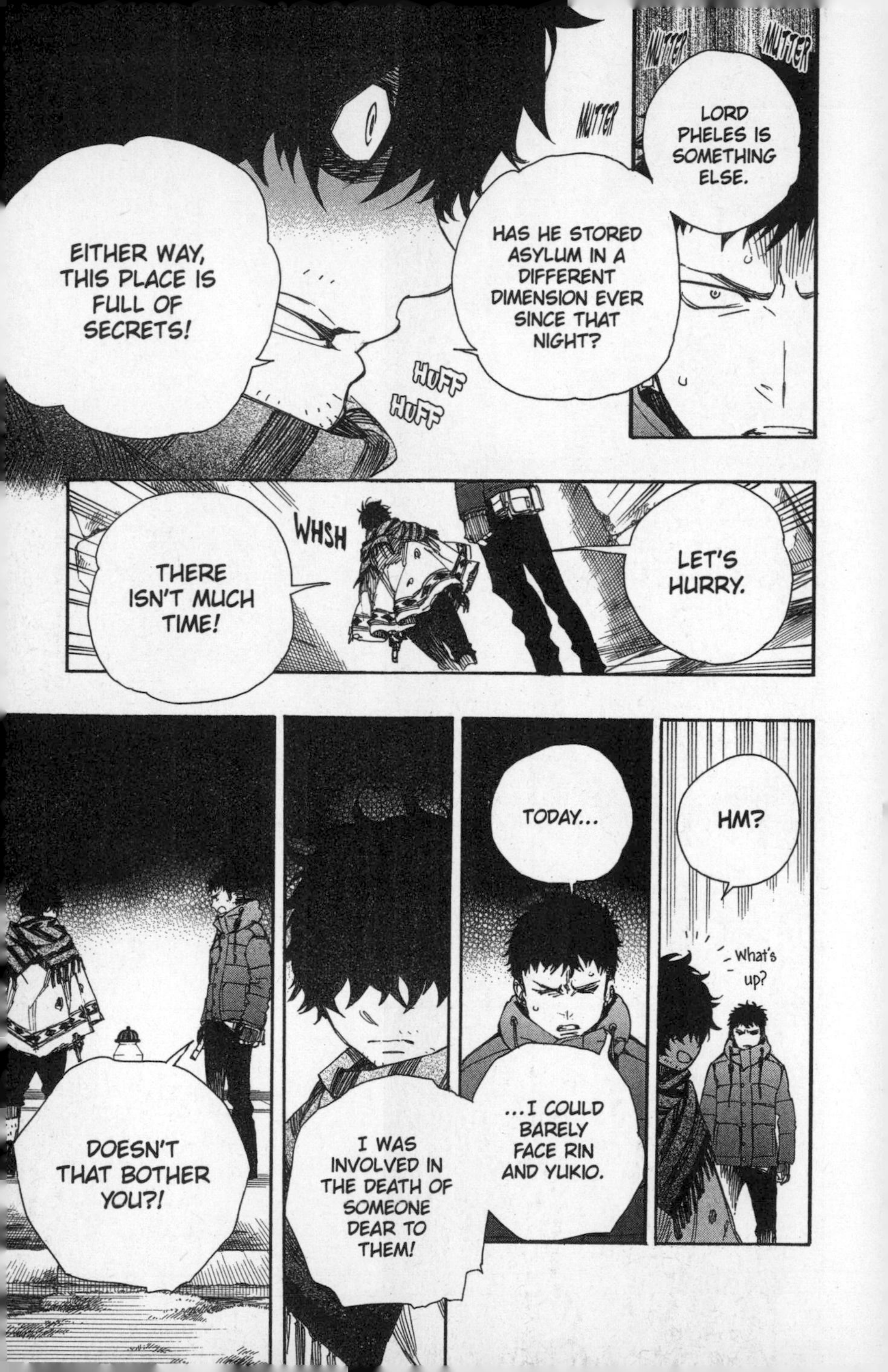
MUTTER
MUTTER
LORD PHELES IS SOMETHING ELSE.
MUTTER
HAS HE STORED ASYLUM IN A DIFFERENT DIMENSION EVER SINCE THAT NIGHT?
HUFF
HUFF
EITHER WAY, THIS PLACE IS FULL OF SECRETS!
LET'S HURRY.
WHSH
THERE ISN'T MUCH TIME!
HM?
What's up?
TODAY...
...I COULD BARELY FACE RIN AND YUKIO.
I WAS INVOLVED IN THE DEATH OF SOMEONE DEAR TO THEM!
DOESN'T THAT BOTHER YOU?!

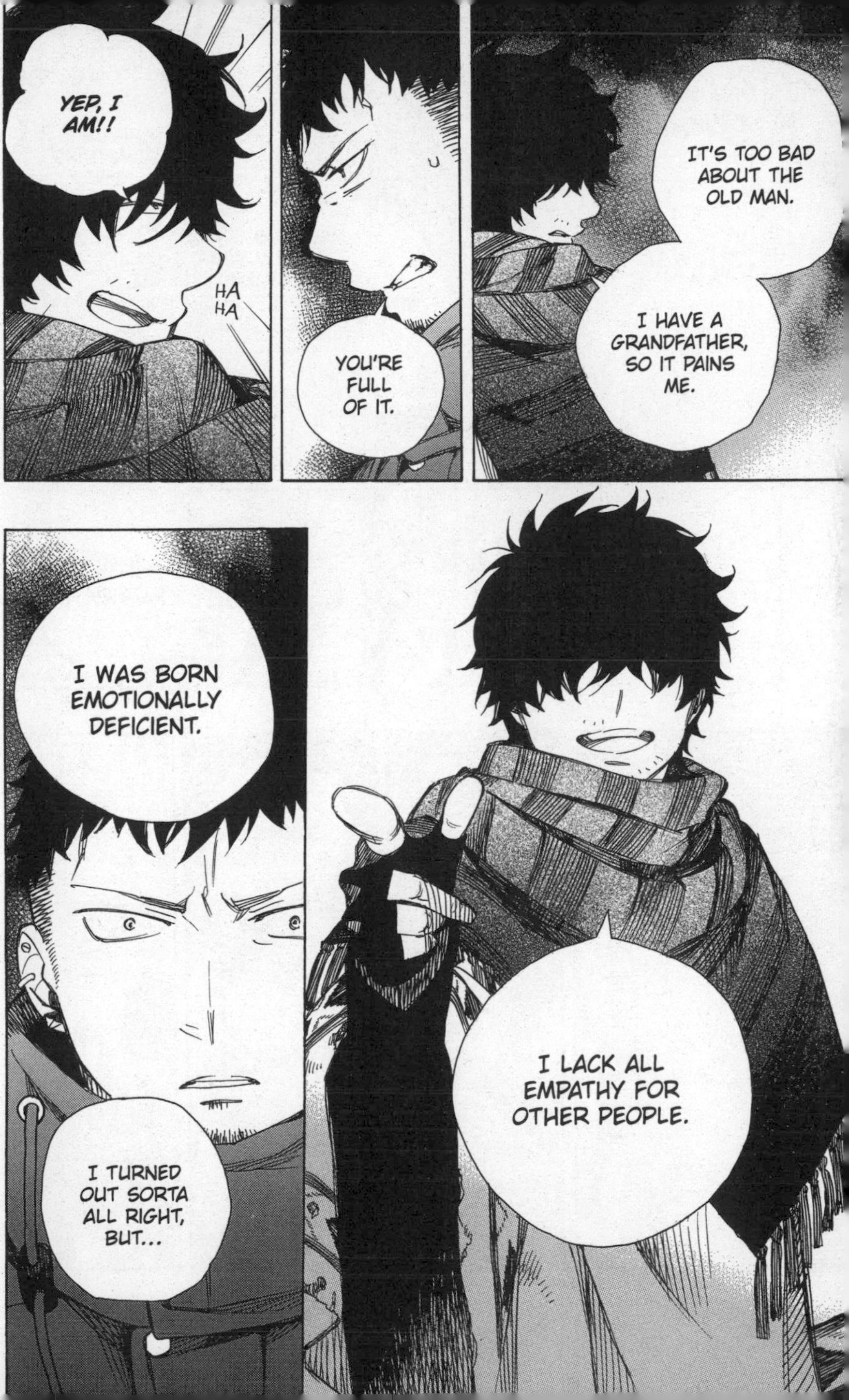
IT'S TOO BAD ABOUT THE OLD MAN.
I HAVE A GRANDFATHER, SO IT PAINS ME.
YOU'RE FULL OF IT.
YEP, I AM!!
HA HA
I LACK ALL EMPATHY FOR OTHER PEOPLE.
I WAS BORN EMOTIONALLY DEFICIENT.
I TURNED OUT SORTA ALL RIGHT, BUT...

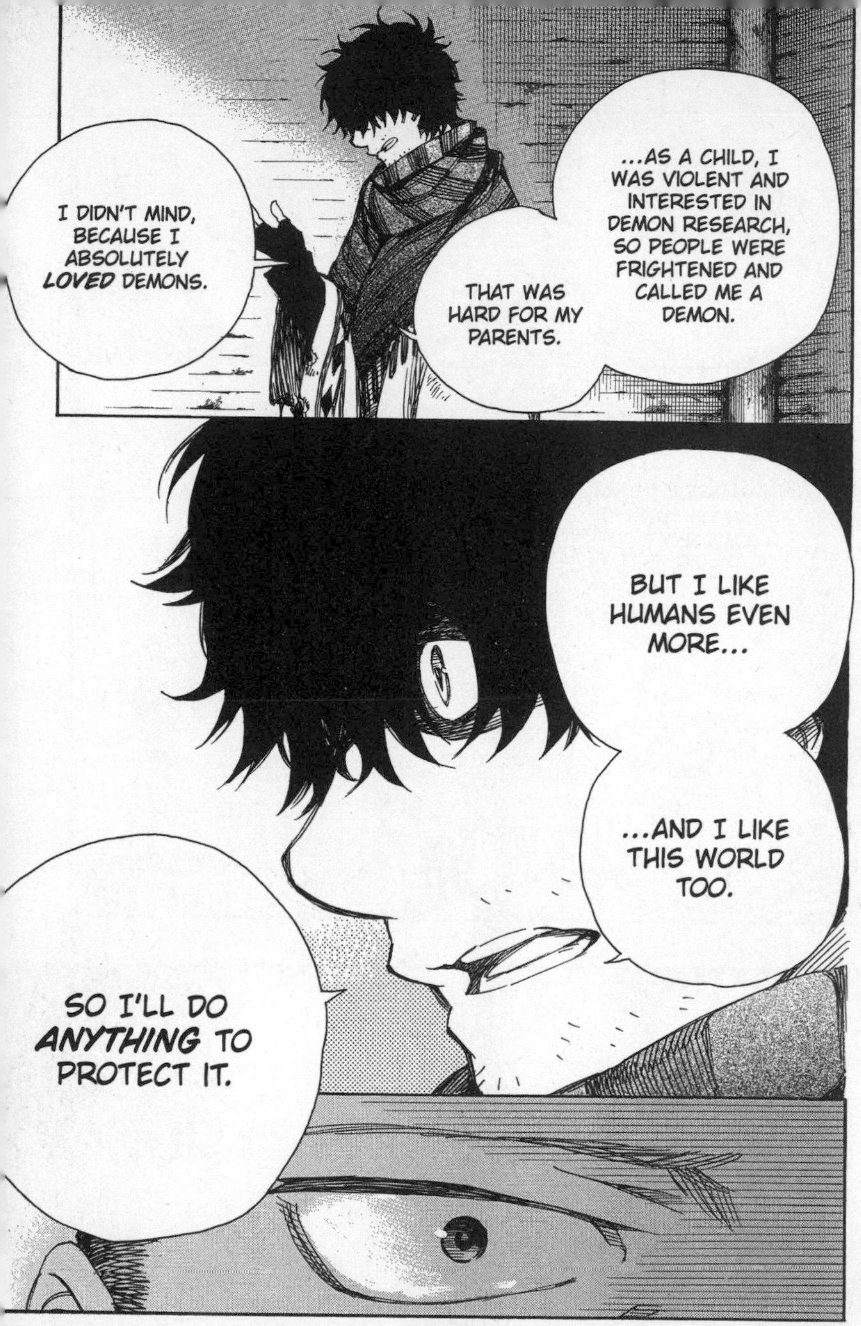
...AS A CHILD, I WAS VIOLENT AND INTERESTED IN DEMON RESEARCH, SO PEOPLE WERE FRIGHTENED AND CALLED ME A DEMON.
THAT WAS HARD FOR MY PARENTS.
I DIDN'T MIND, BECAUSE I ABSOLUTELY *LOVED* DEMONS.
BUT I LIKE HUMANS EVEN MORE...
...AND I LIKE THIS WORLD TOO.
SO I'LL DO *ANYTHING* TO PROTECT IT.

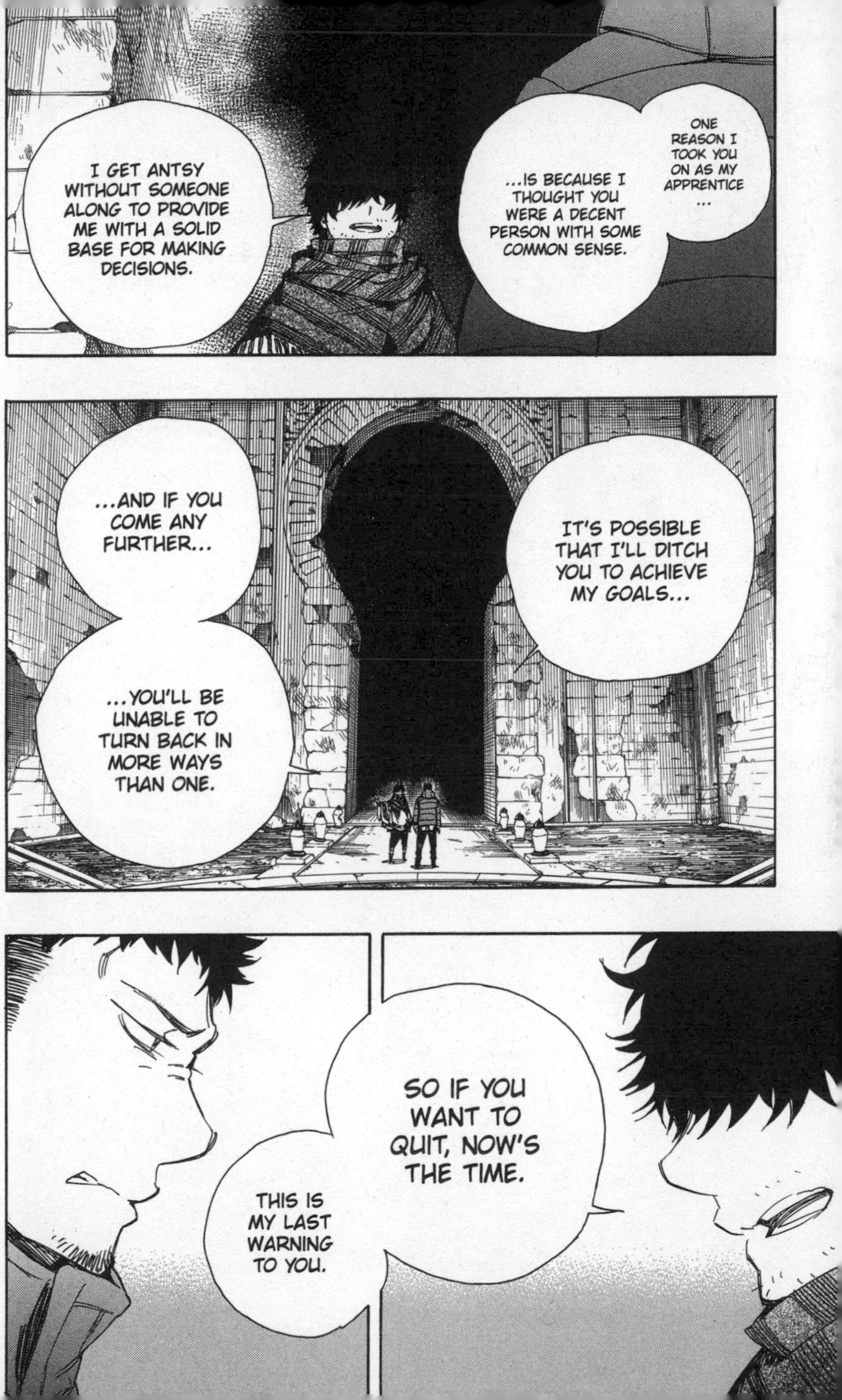
ONE REASON I TOOK YOU ON AS MY APPRENTICE ...
...IS BECAUSE I THOUGHT YOU WERE A DECENT PERSON WITH SOME COMMON SENSE.
I GET ANTSY WITHOUT SOMEONE ALONG TO PROVIDE ME WITH A SOLID BASE FOR MAKING DECISIONS.
IT'S POSSIBLE THAT I'LL DITCH YOU TO ACHIEVE MY GOALS...
...AND IF YOU COME ANY FURTHER...
...YOU'LL BE UNABLE TO TURN BACK IN MORE WAYS THAN ONE.
SO IF YOU WANT TO QUIT, NOW'S THE TIME.
THIS IS MY LAST WARNING TO YOU.

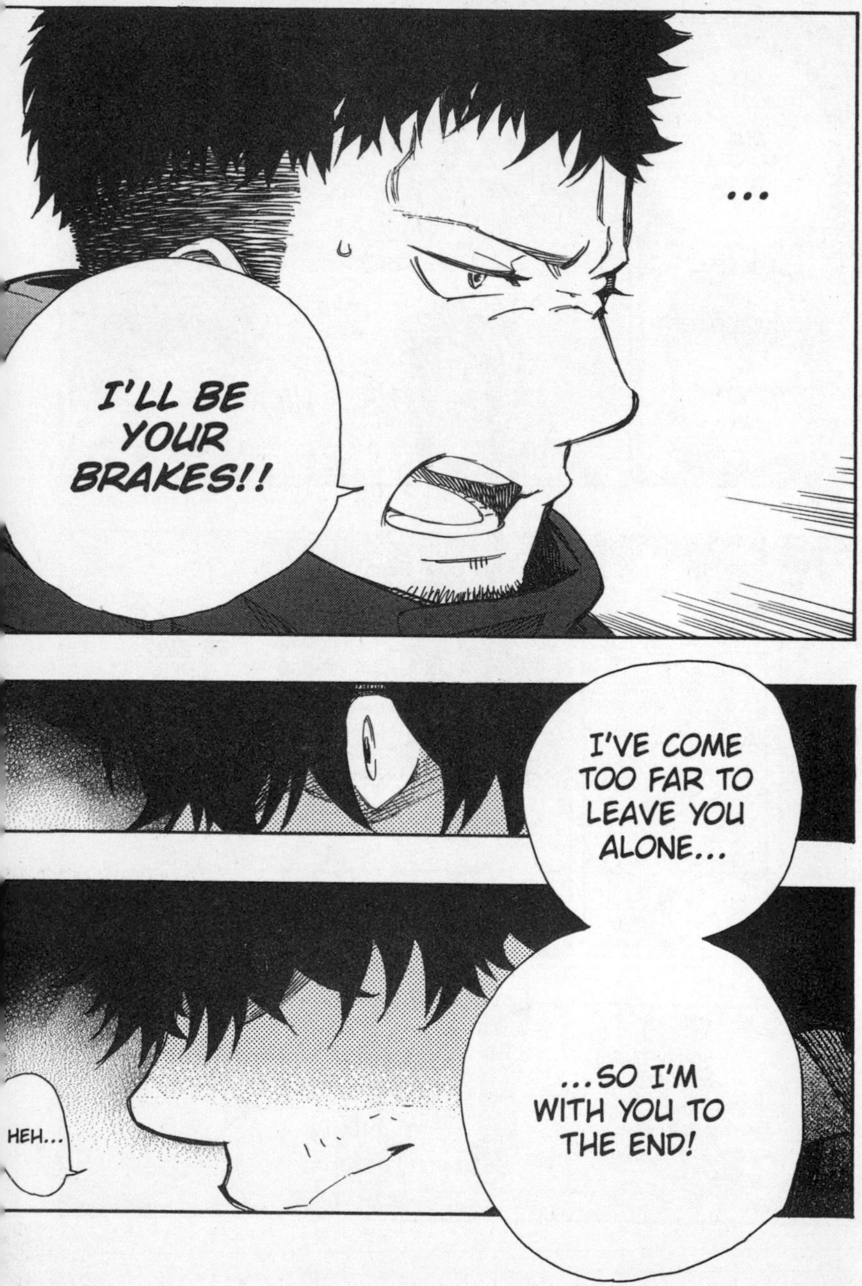
...
I'LL BE YOUR BRAKES!!
I'VE COME TOO FAR TO LEAVE YOU ALONE...
...SO I'M WITH YOU TO THE END!
HEH...

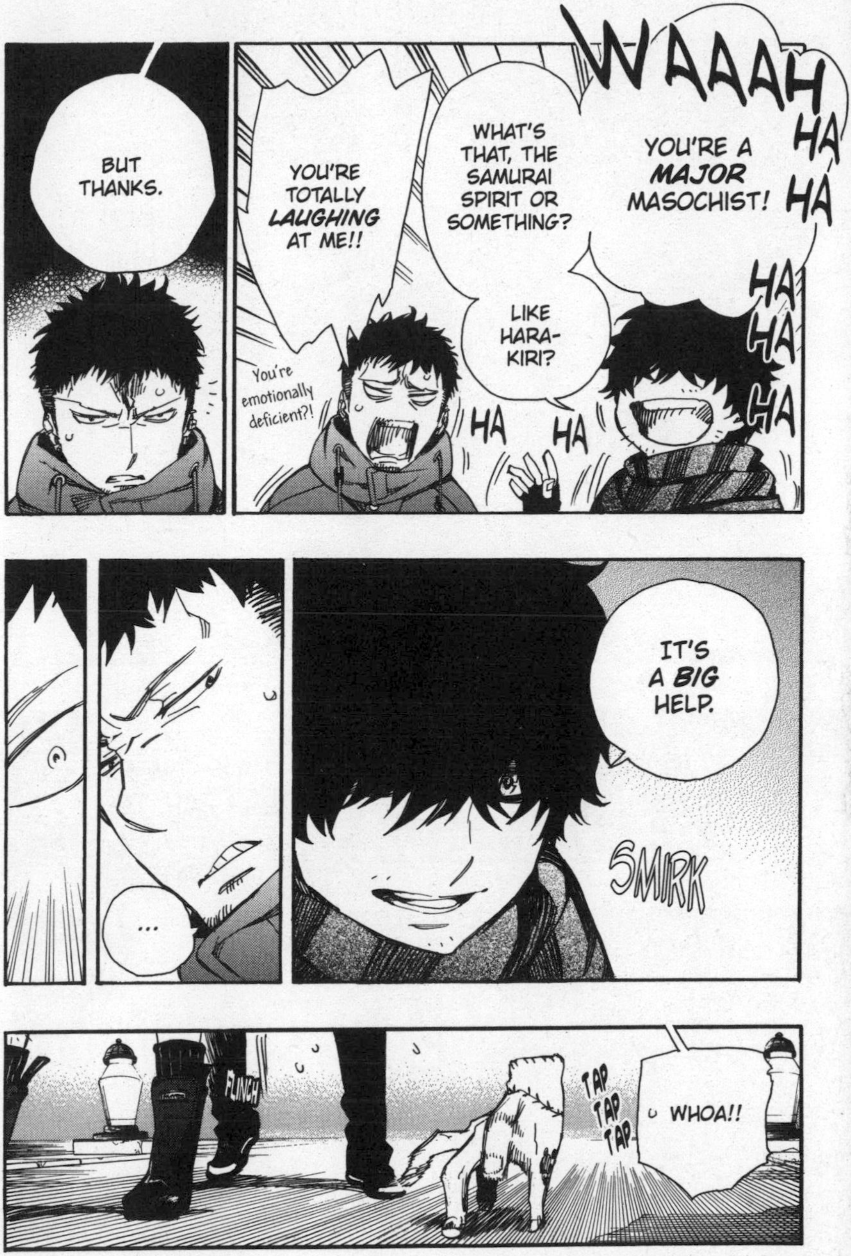
WAAAH
HA HA
YOU'RE A MAJOR MASOCHIST!
WHAT'S THAT, THE SAMURAI SPIRIT OR SOMETHING?
HA HA HA HA
LIKE HARA-KIRI?
HA
HA
YOU'RE TOTALLY LAUGHING AT ME!!
You're emotionally deficient?!
BUT THANKS.
IT'S A BIG HELP.
SMIRK
...
WHOA!!
TAP TAP TAP
FLINCH

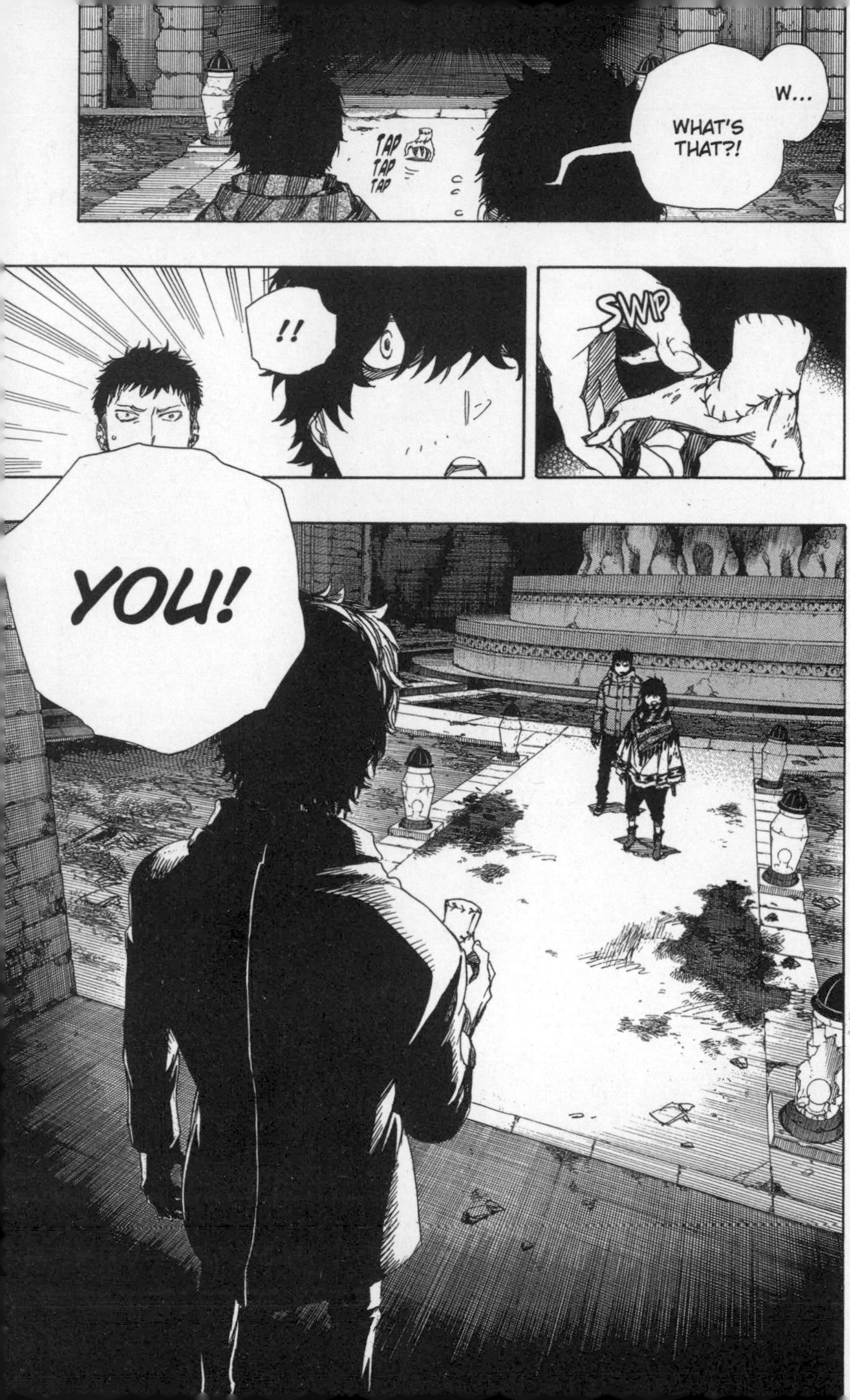
W...
WHAT'S THAT?!
TAP TAP TAP
SWIP
!!
YOU!

Blue Exorcist Chapter 84: Foundation

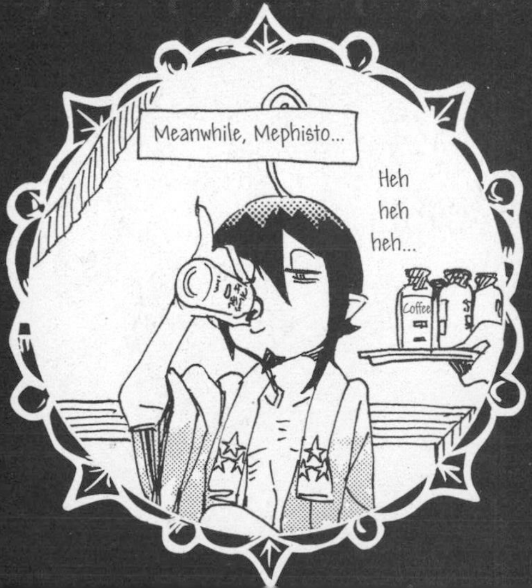
Meanwhile, Mephisto...
Heh heh heh...
Coffee

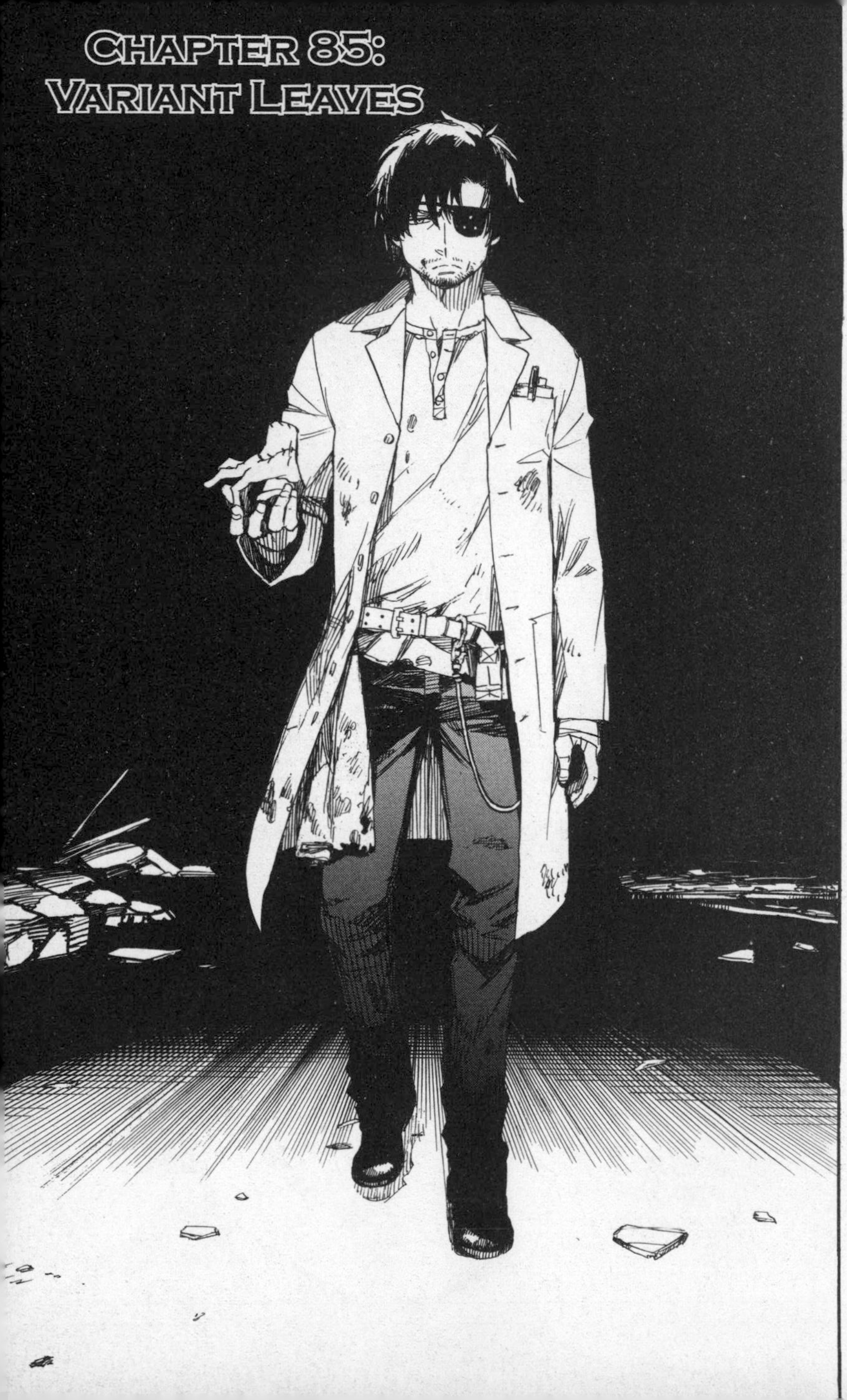
Chapter 85:
Variant Leaves

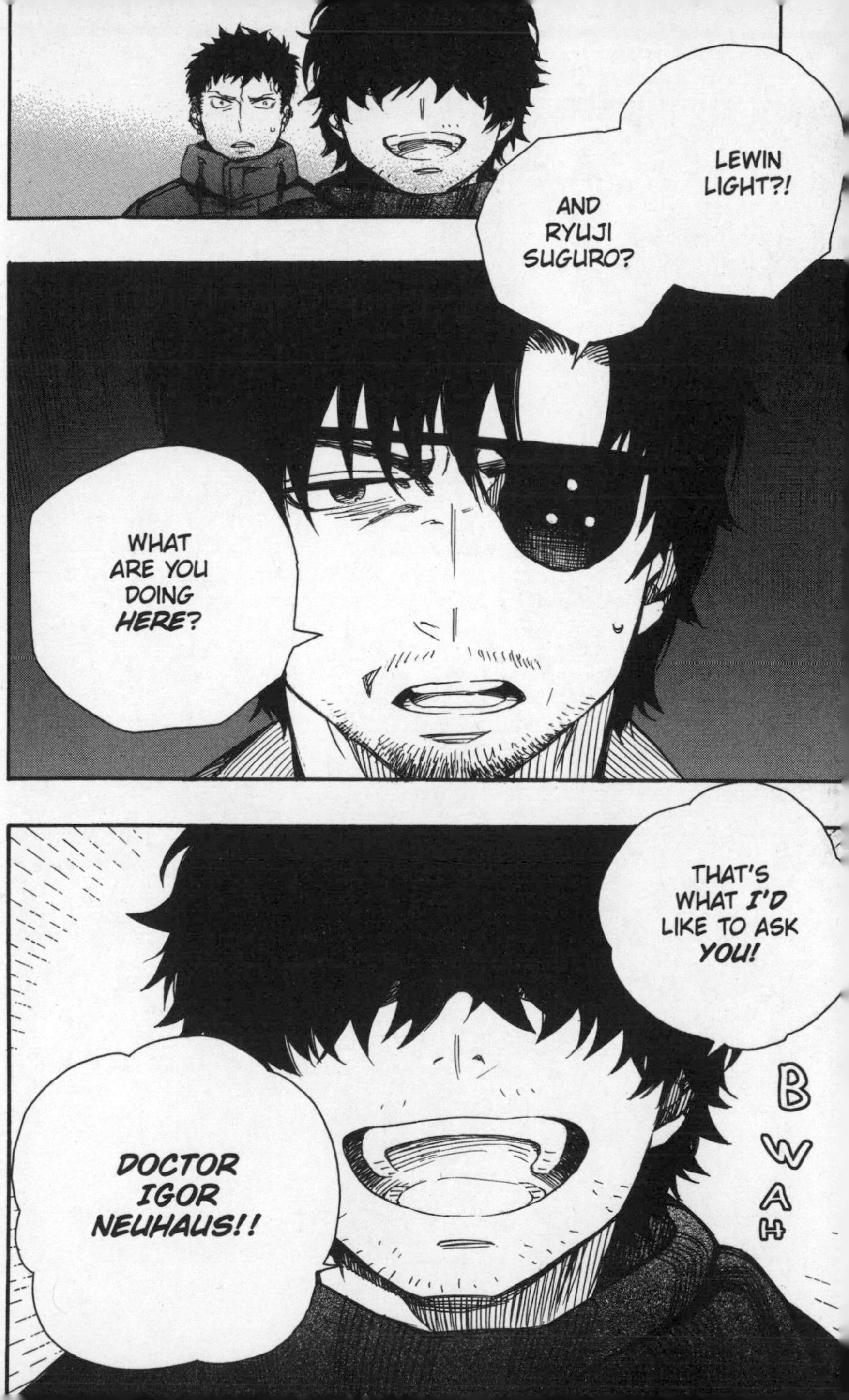
LEWIN LIGHT?!
AND RYUJI SUGURO?
WHAT ARE YOU DOING HERE?
THAT'S WHAT I'D LIKE TO ASK YOU!
DOCTOR IGOR NEUHAUS!!
BWAH

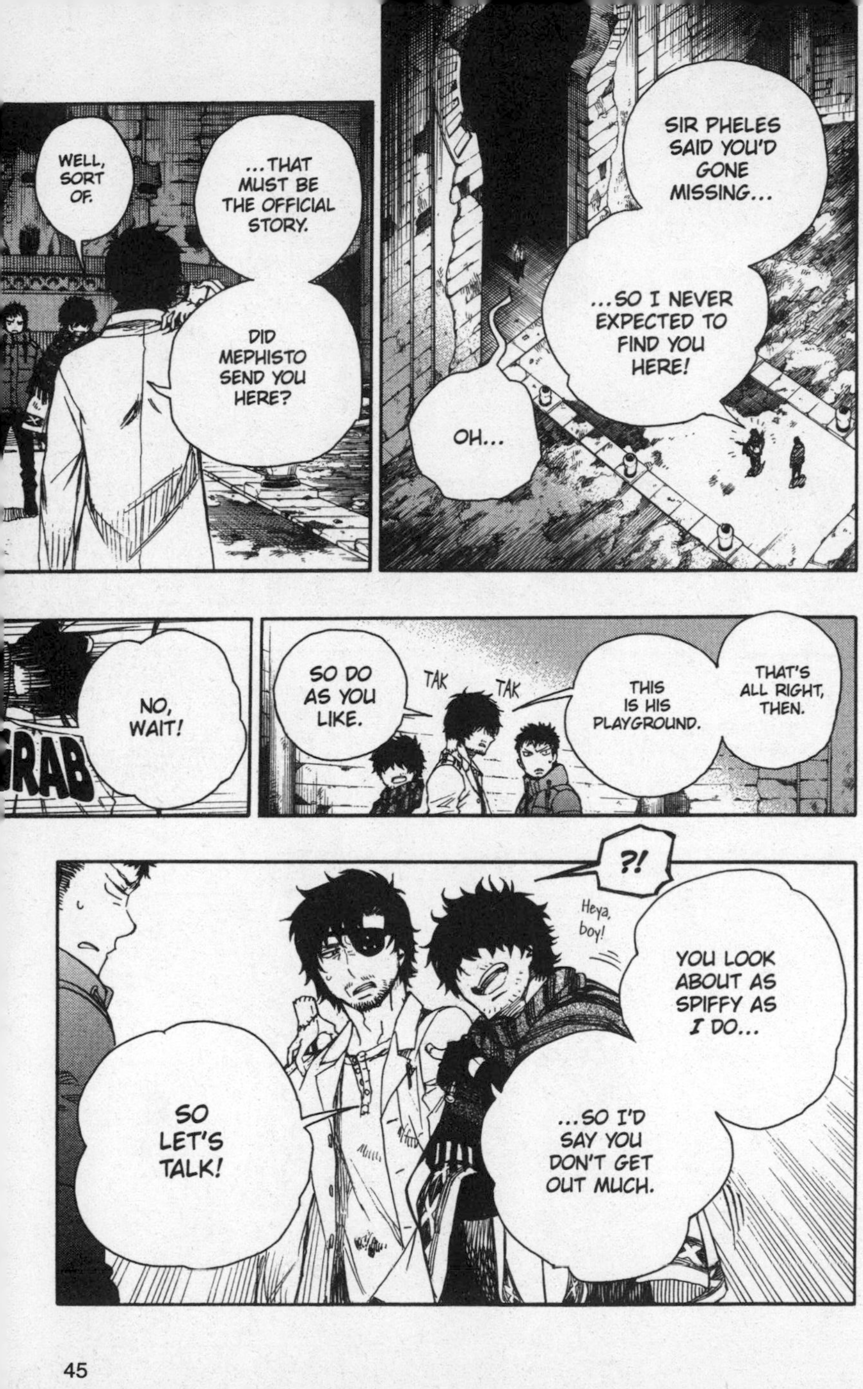
SIR PHELES SAID YOU'D GONE MISSING...
...SO I NEVER EXPECTED TO FIND YOU HERE!
OH...
...THAT MUST BE THE OFFICIAL STORY.
WELL, SORT OF.
DID MEPHISTO SEND YOU HERE?
THAT'S ALL RIGHT, THEN.
THIS IS HIS PLAYGROUND.
TAK
TAK
SO DO AS YOU LIKE.
NO, WAIT!
GRAB
?!
Heya, boy!
YOU LOOK ABOUT AS SPIFFY AS *I* DO...
...SO I'D SAY YOU DON'T GET OUT MUCH.
SO LET'S TALK!

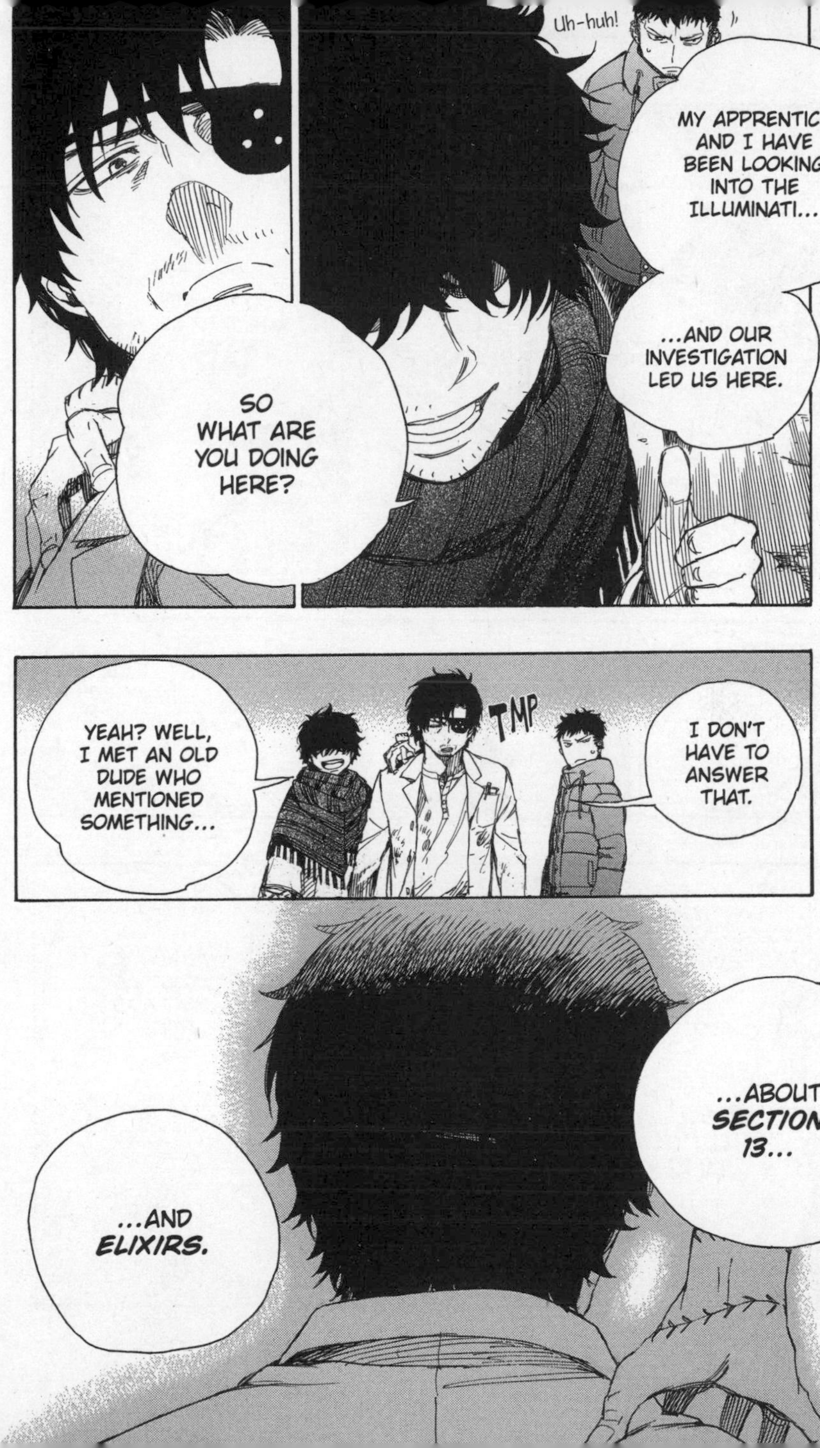

MY APPRENTICE AND I HAVE BEEN LOOKING INTO THE ILLUMINATI...
Uh-huh!
...AND OUR INVESTIGATION LED US HERE.
SO WHAT ARE YOU DOING HERE?
I DON'T HAVE TO ANSWER THAT.
TMP
YEAH? WELL, I MET AN OLD DUDE WHO MENTIONED SOMETHING...
...ABOUT **SECTION 13**...
...AND **ELIXIRS.**

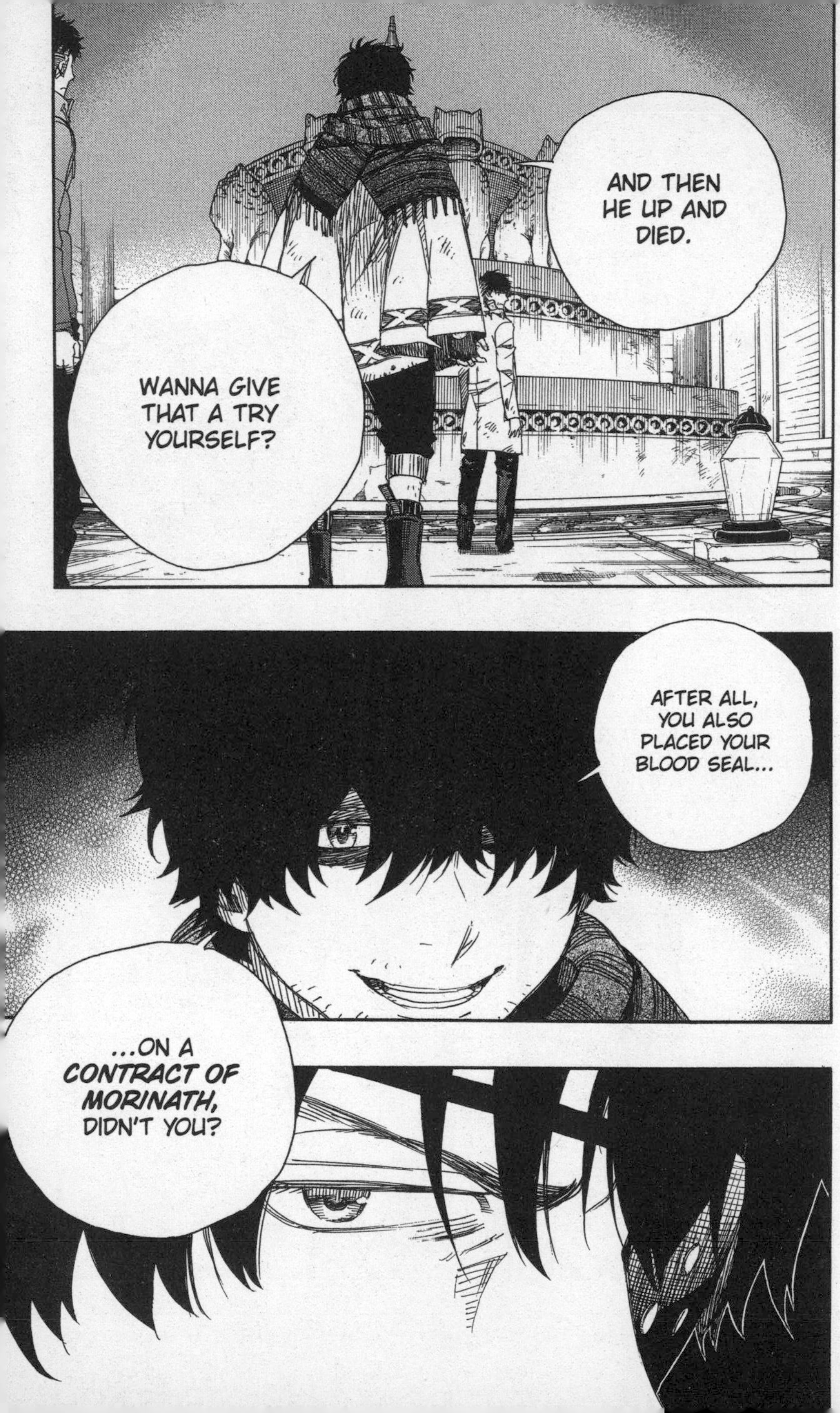
AND THEN HE UP AND DIED.
WANNA GIVE THAT A TRY YOURSELF?
AFTER ALL, YOU ALSO PLACED YOUR BLOOD SEAL...
...ON A *CONTRACT OF MORINATH,* DIDN'T YOU?

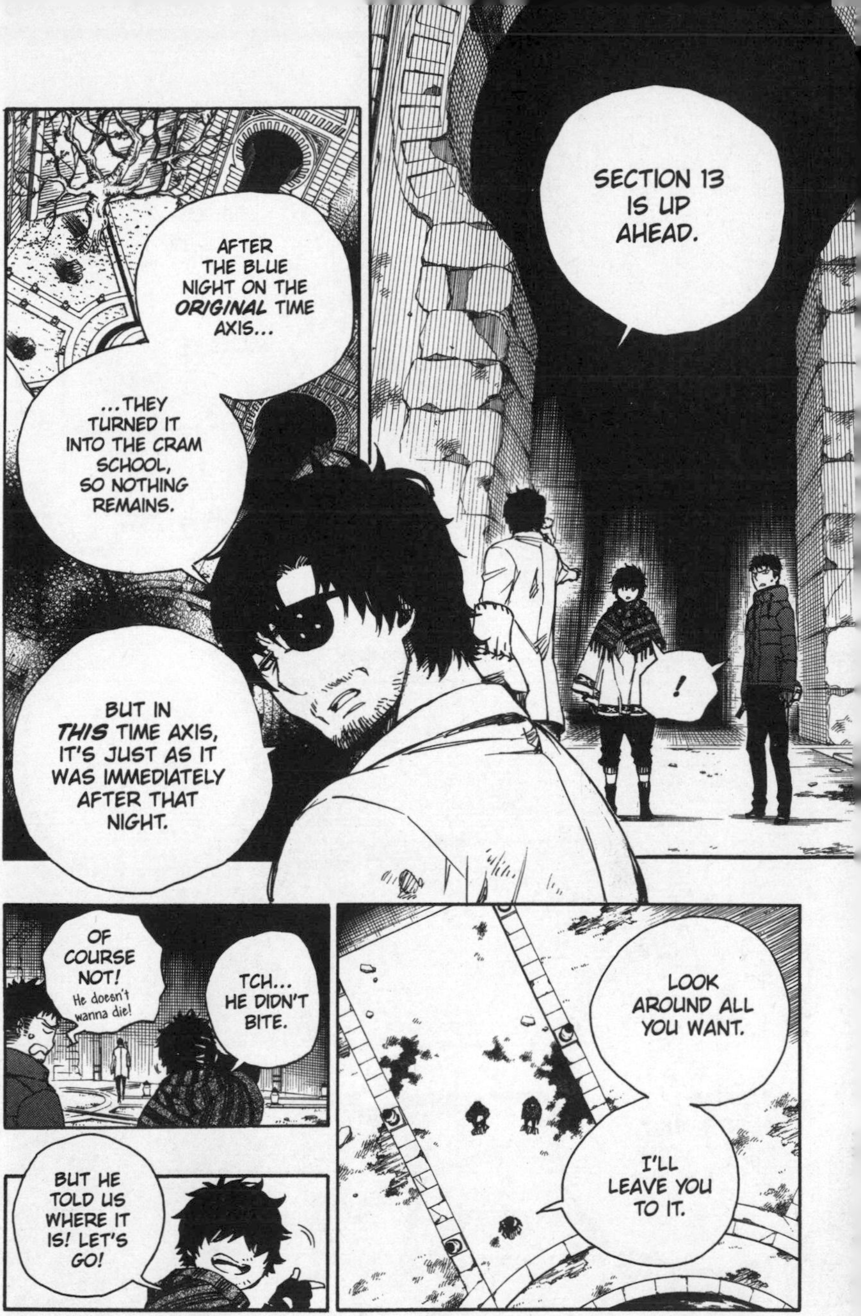
SECTION 13 IS UP AHEAD.
!
AFTER THE BLUE NIGHT ON THE *ORIGINAL* TIME AXIS...
...THEY TURNED IT INTO THE CRAM SCHOOL, SO NOTHING REMAINS.
BUT IN *THIS* TIME AXIS, IT'S JUST AS IT WAS IMMEDIATELY AFTER THAT NIGHT.
LOOK AROUND ALL YOU WANT.
I'LL LEAVE YOU TO IT.
TCH... HE DIDN'T BITE.
OF COURSE NOT!
He doesn't wanna die!
BUT HE TOLD US WHERE IT IS! LET'S GO!

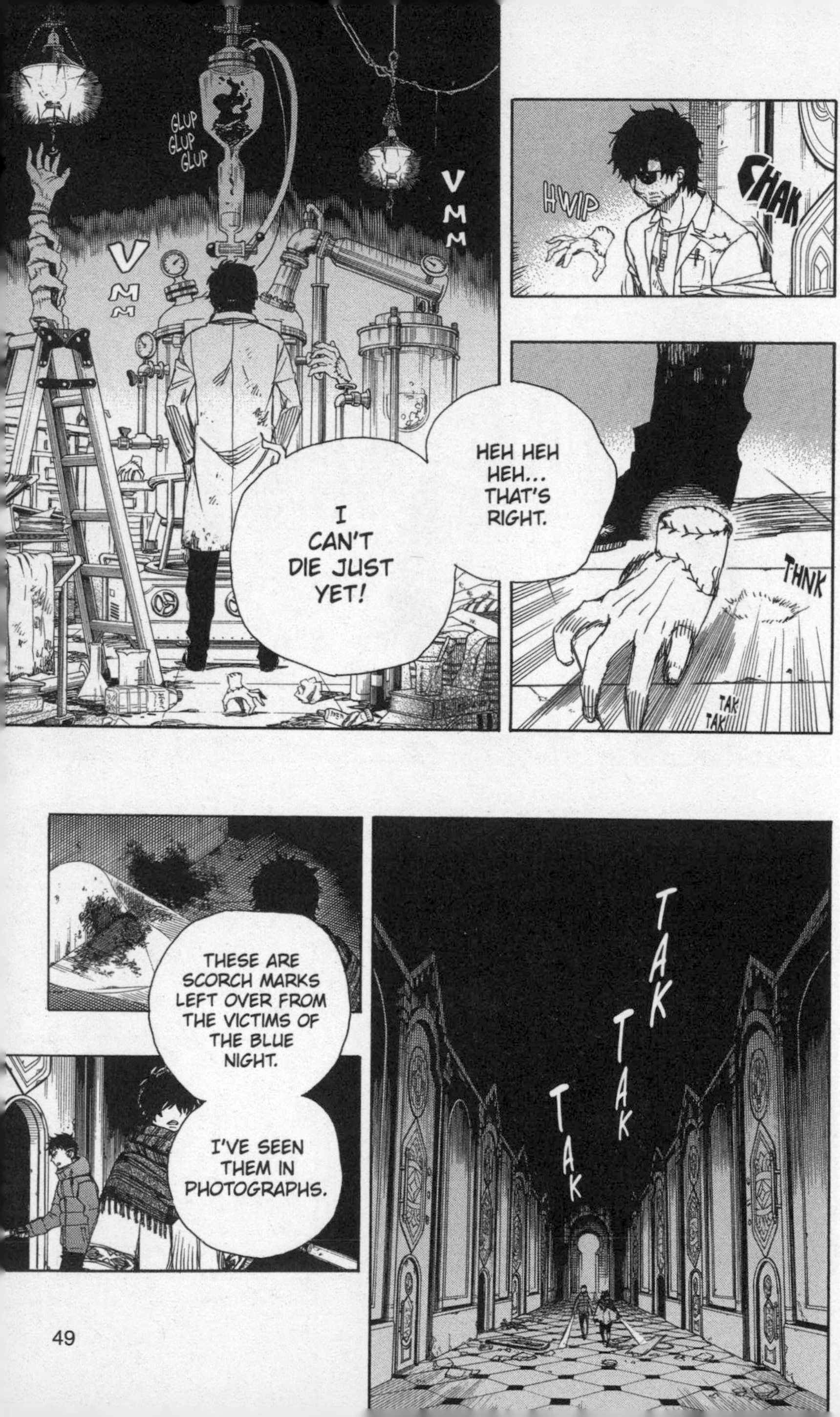
CHAK
HWIP
HEH HEH HEH... THAT'S RIGHT.
THNK
TAK TAK
I CAN'T DIE JUST YET!
VMM
GLUP GLUP GLUP
VMM
TAK TAK TAK
THESE ARE SCORCH MARKS LEFT OVER FROM THE VICTIMS OF THE BLUE NIGHT.
I'VE SEEN THEM IN PHOTOGRAPHS.

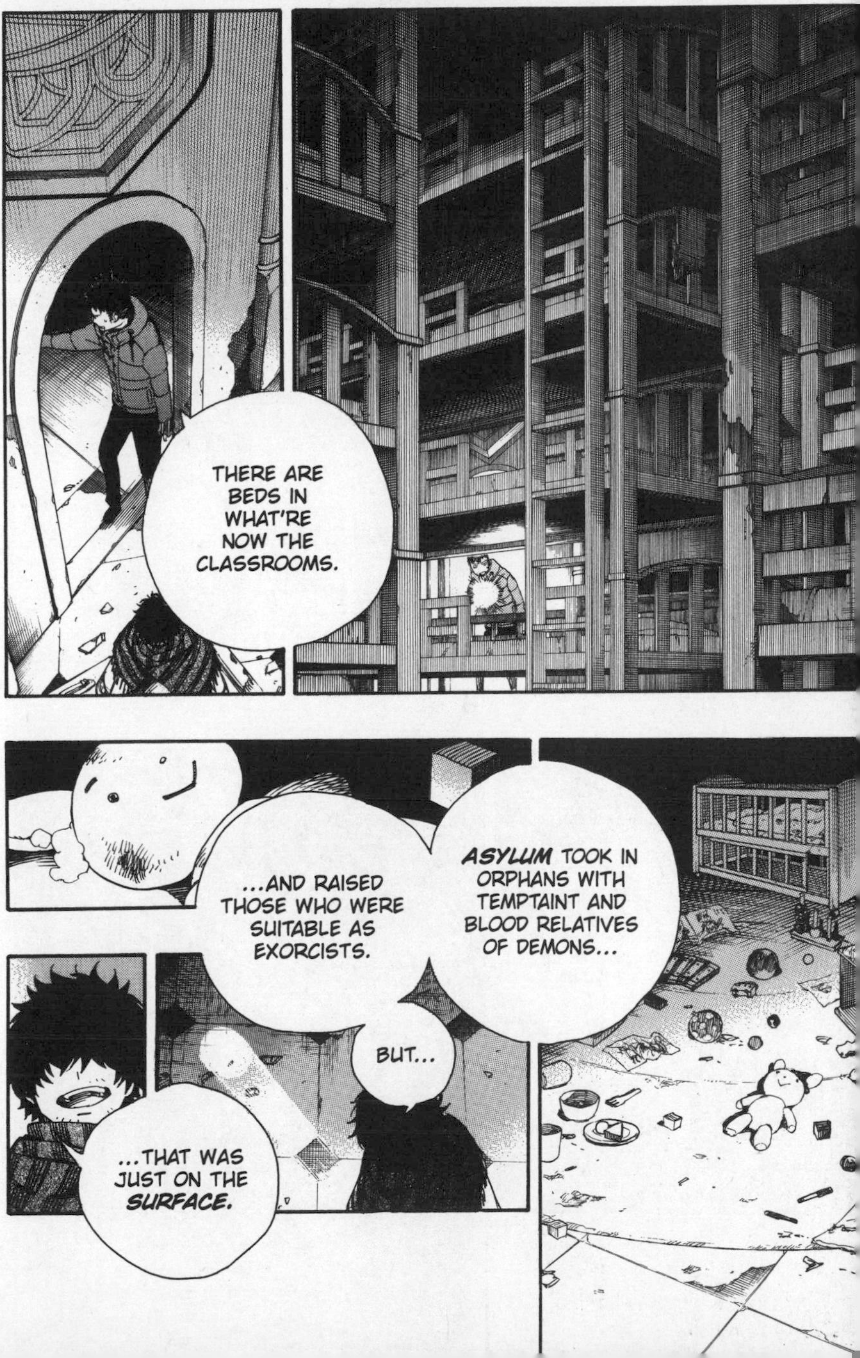
THERE ARE BEDS IN WHAT'RE NOW THE CLASSROOMS.
ASYLUM TOOK IN ORPHANS WITH TEMPTAINT AND BLOOD RELATIVES OF DEMONS...
...AND RAISED THOSE WHO WERE SUITABLE AS EXORCISTS.
BUT...
...THAT WAS JUST ON THE *SURFACE.*

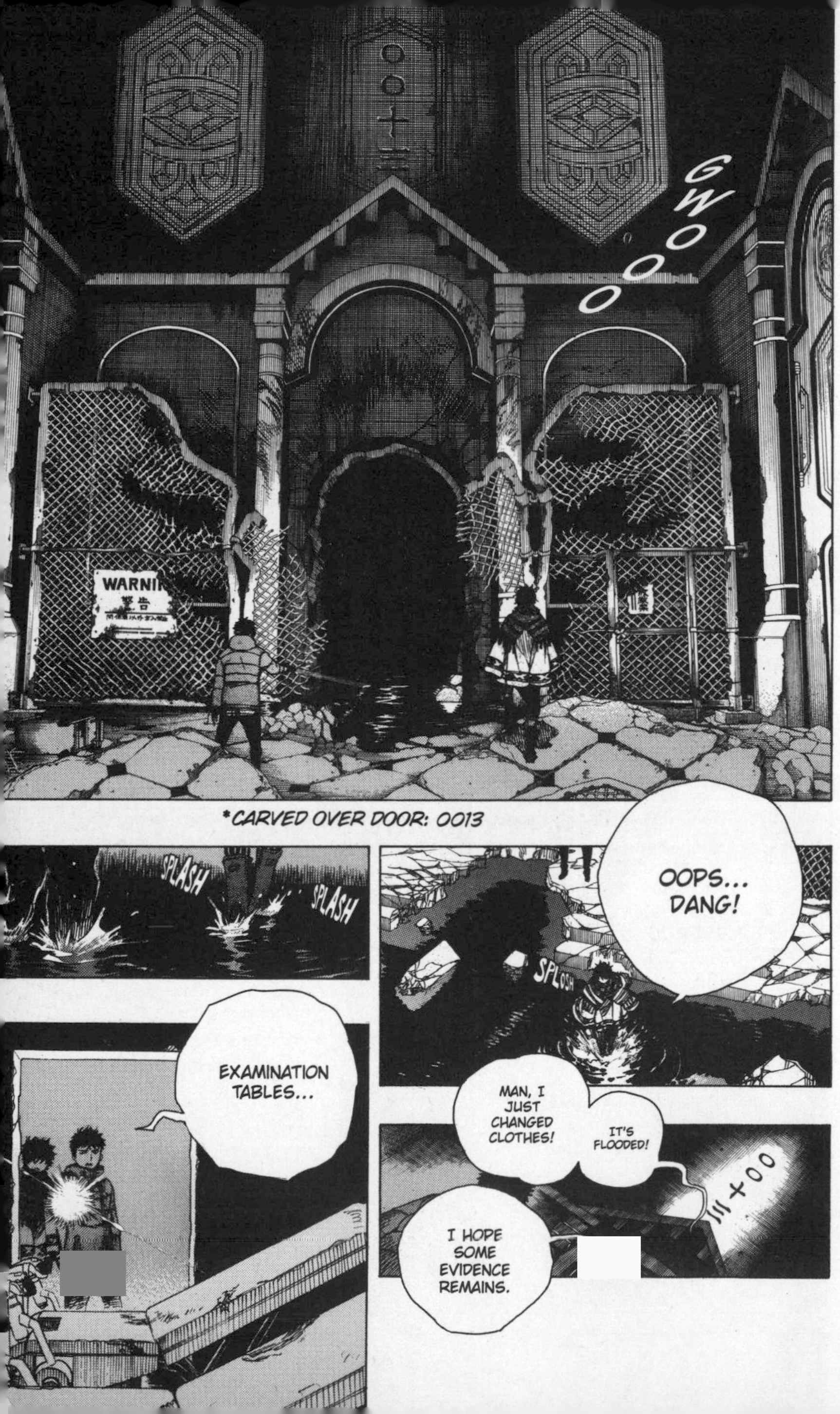
GWOOOO
WARNI
警告
*CARVED OVER DOOR: 0013
OOPS... DANG!
SPLOSH
SPLASH
SPLASH
IT'S FLOODED!
MAN, I JUST CHANGED CLOTHES!
I HOPE SOME EVIDENCE REMAINS.
EXAMINATION TABLES...

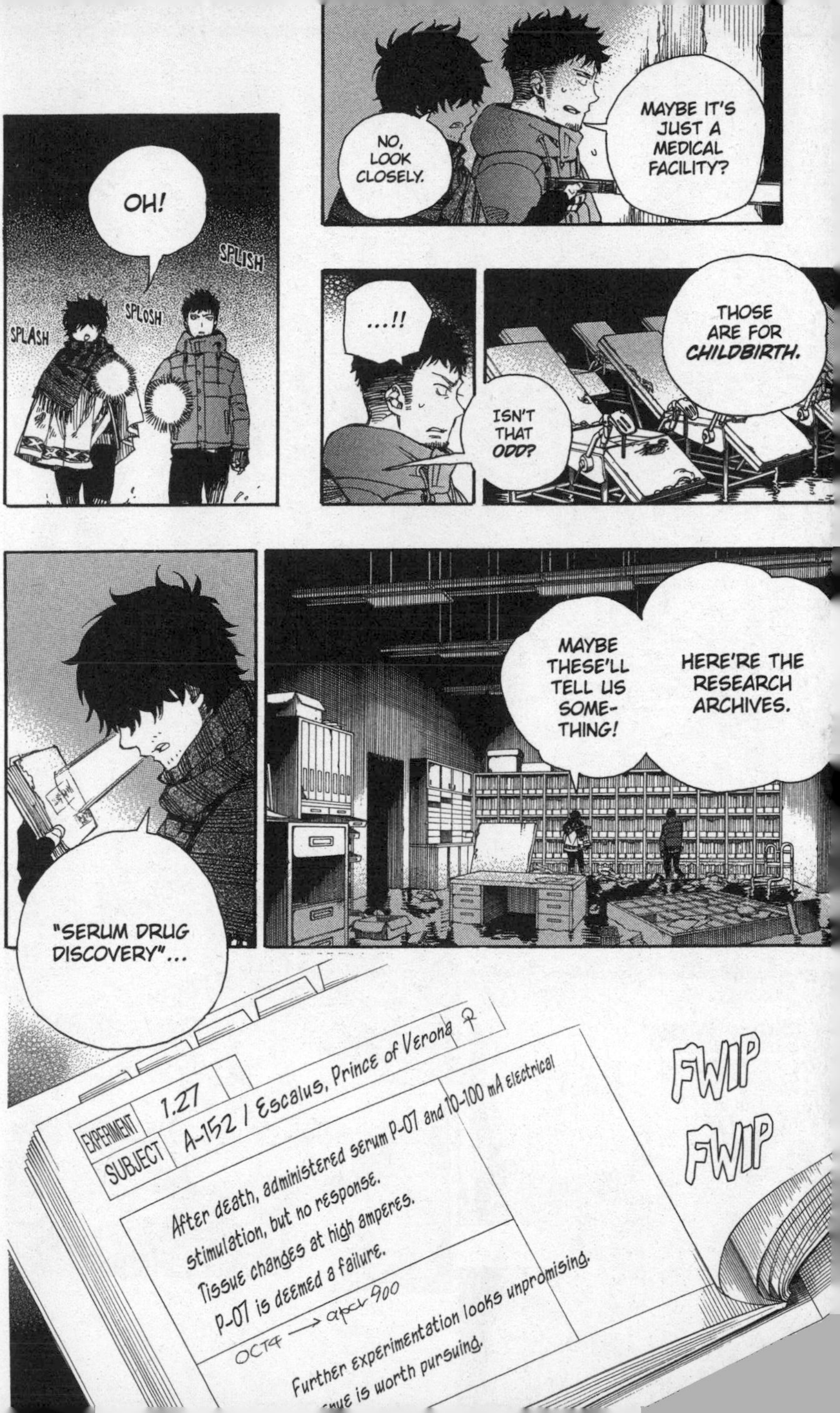
MAYBE IT'S JUST A MEDICAL FACILITY?
NO, LOOK CLOSELY.
THOSE ARE FOR CHILDBIRTH.
ISN'T THAT ODD?
...!!
OH!
SPLISH
SPLOSH
SPLASH
HERE'RE THE RESEARCH ARCHIVES.
MAYBE THESE'LL TELL US SOME-THING!
"SERUM DRUG DISCOVERY"...
EXPERIMENT 1.27
SUBJECT A-152 / Escalus, Prince of Verona ♀
After death, administered serum P-07 and 10-100 mA electrical stimulation, but no response.
Tissue changes at high amperes.
P-07 is deemed a failure.
Further experimentation looks unpromising.
FWIP
FWIP

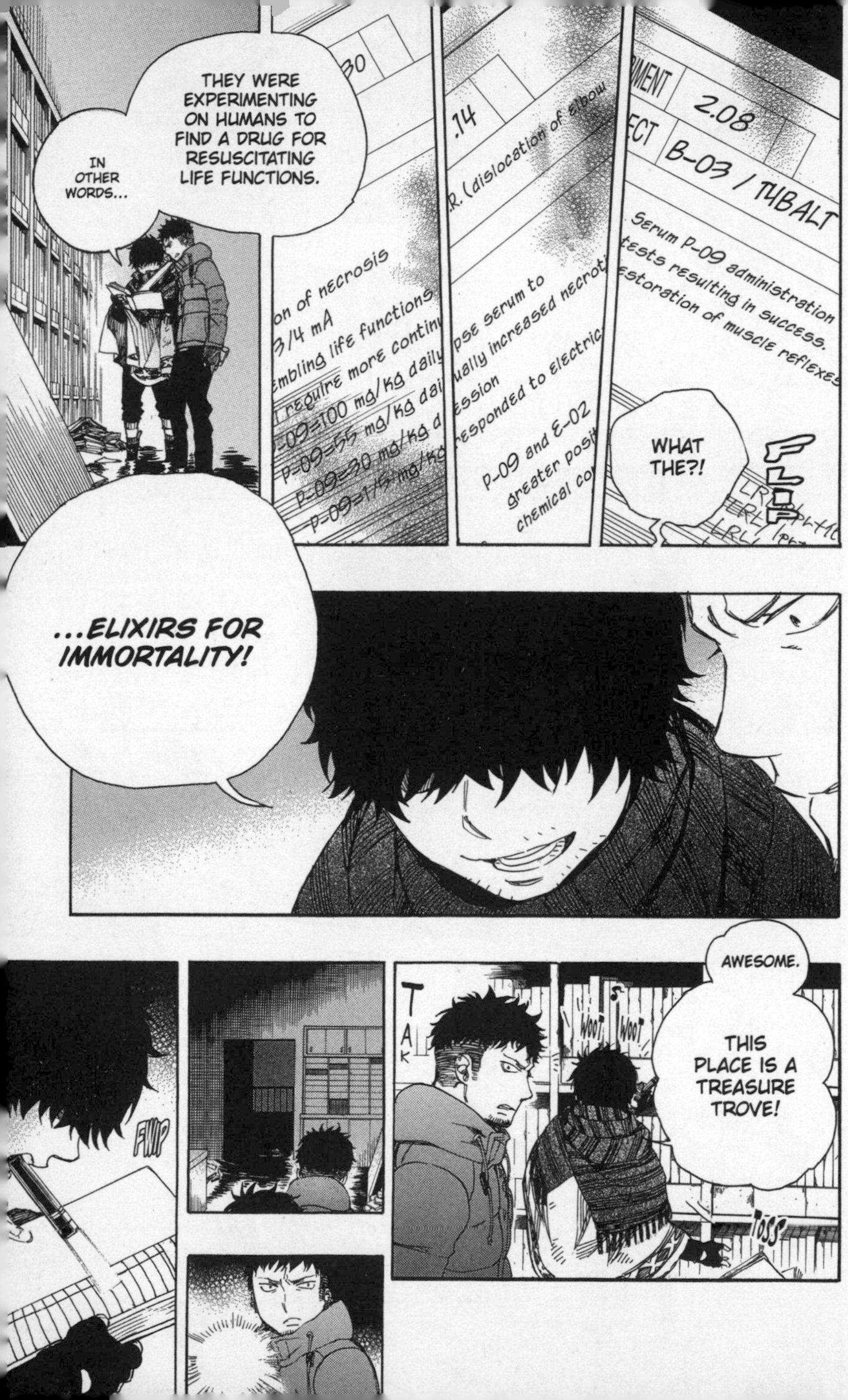
2.08
B-03 / TYBALT
Serum P-09 administration
tests resulting in success.
WHAT THE?!
FLIP
IN OTHER WORDS...
THEY WERE EXPERIMENTING ON HUMANS TO FIND A DRUG FOR RESUSCITATING LIFE FUNCTIONS.
...ELIXIRS FOR IMMORTALITY!
AWESOME.
THIS PLACE IS A TREASURE TROVE!
TAK
WOOT
WOOT
TOSS
FWIP

SECTION 13
RECORD OF HUMAN EXPERIMENTATION
IN CLONE STRENGTHENING
01
Reproductive cells with the donor's possession genes as
human donor possessed by a demon high in physical ch
regeneration and continuous recombination of gene se
resulting in an imperfect copy that is biologically a sibli
and observe the course of biological healing.
Donor Type – Lucifer
NO
NAME
01 ABEL
02 ADAM
03 ADOLPHUS
04 AL
05 ALASTAIR
06 ALFONSE
07 ALGERNON
08 ALLEN
09 AMOS
10 ANTHONY
11 ARSTUR
Lu-Ch001
Lu-Ch002
Lu-La003
Lu-La004
SECTION 13
RECORD OF HUMAN EXPERIMENTA
IN CLONE STRENGTHENING
01
Reproductive cells with the donor's possession genes a
human donor possessed by a demon high in physical
regeneration and continuous recombination of gene
resulting in an imperfect copy that is biologically a s
and observe the course of biological healing.
FWAP
DECEASED
Lu-Ku
03
DECE
Lu-La
Lu-La
FWAP
FWAP

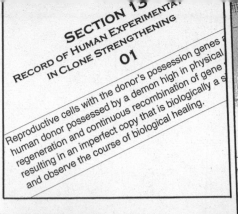

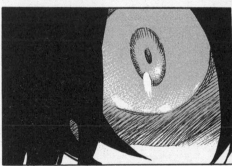

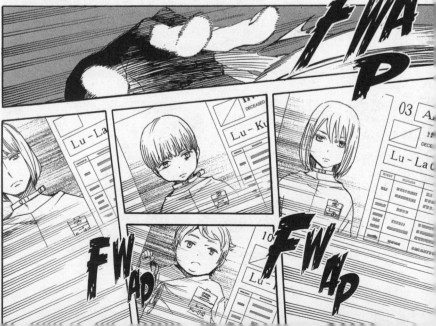

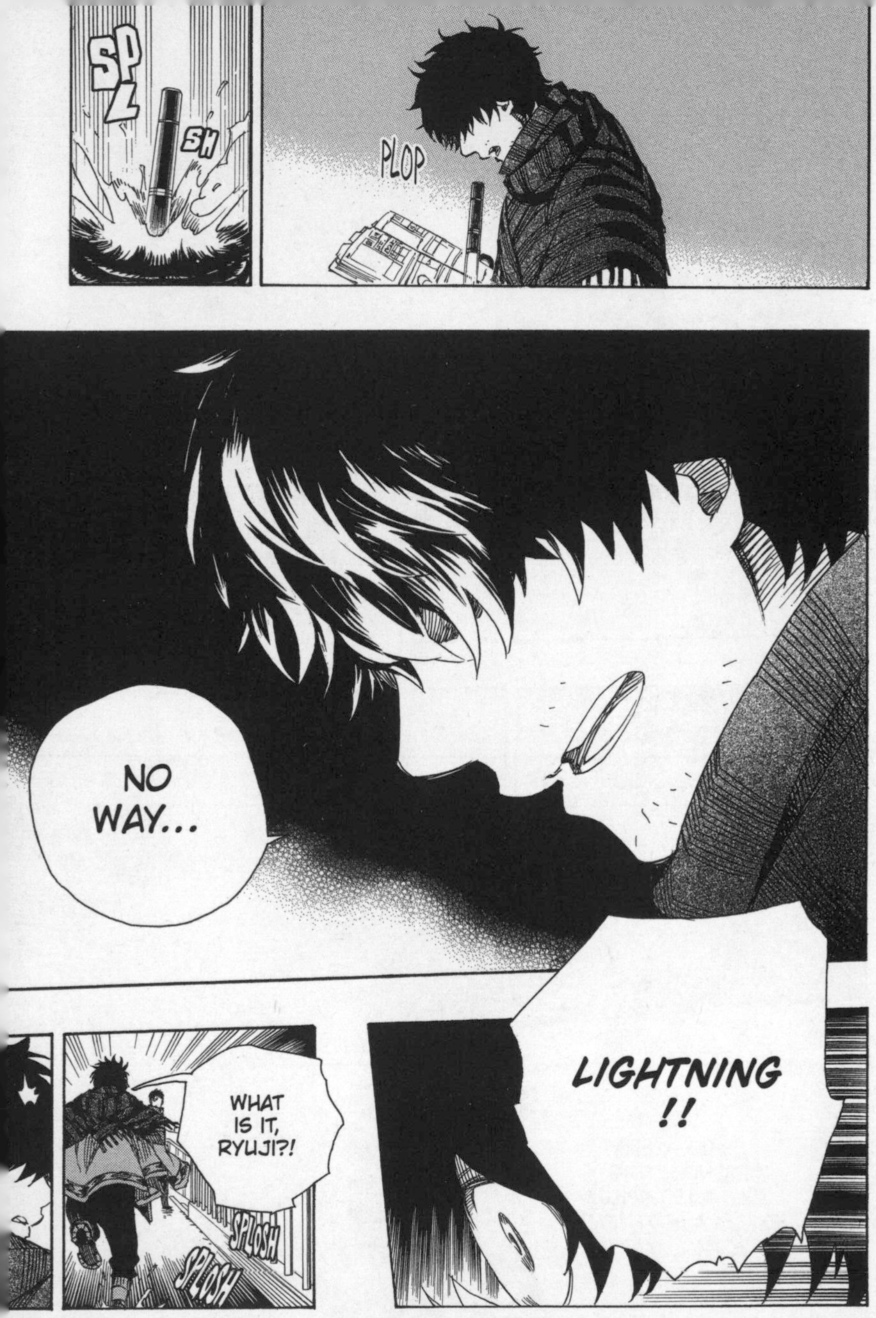
PLOP
SPLSH
NO WAY...
LIGHTNING !!
WHAT IS IT, RYUJI?!
SPLOSH
SPLOSH

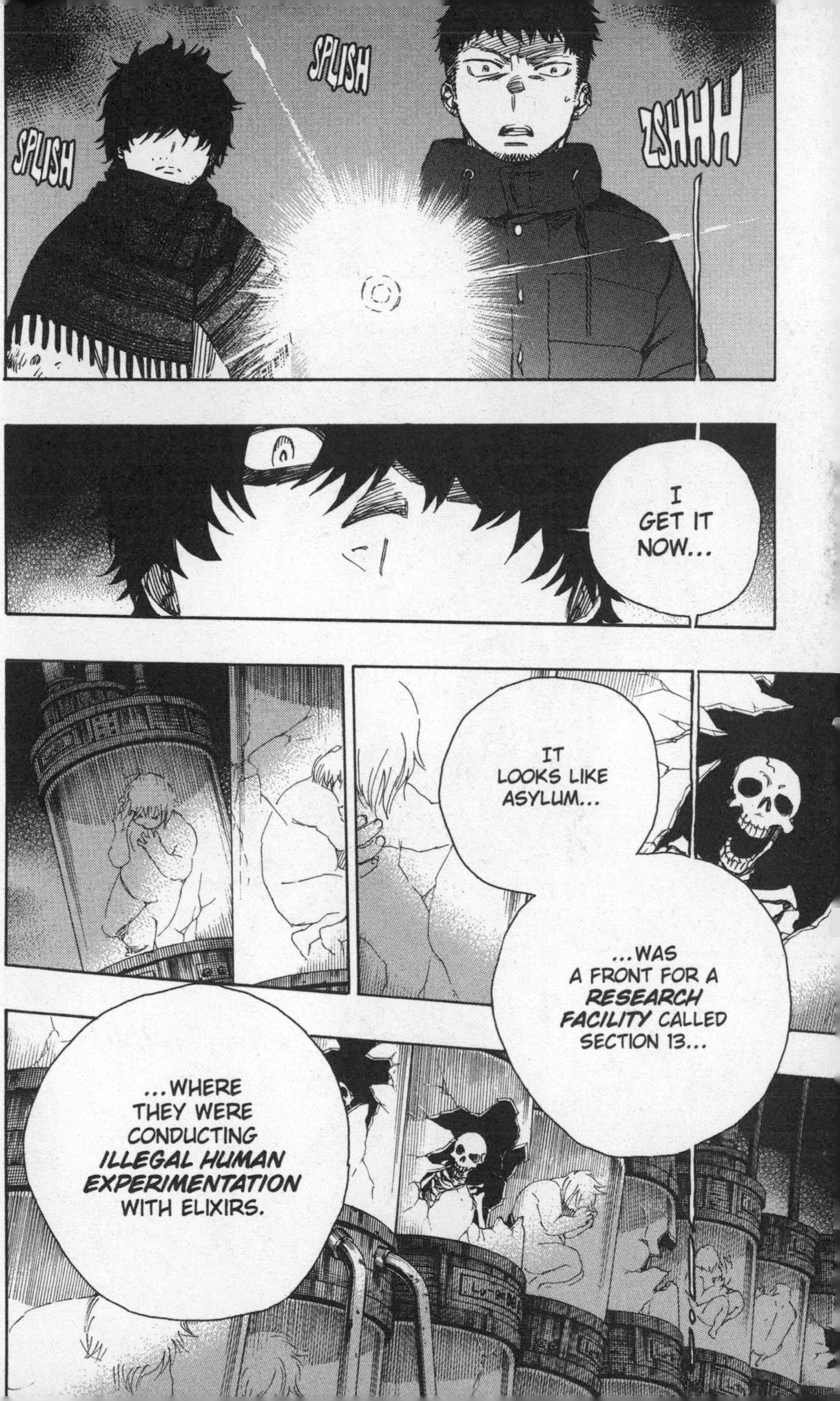
ZSHHH
SPLISH
SPLISH
I GET IT NOW...
IT LOOKS LIKE ASYLUM...
...WAS A FRONT FOR A RESEARCH FACILITY CALLED SECTION 13...
...WHERE THEY WERE CONDUCTING ILLEGAL HUMAN EXPERIMENTATION WITH ELIXIRS.

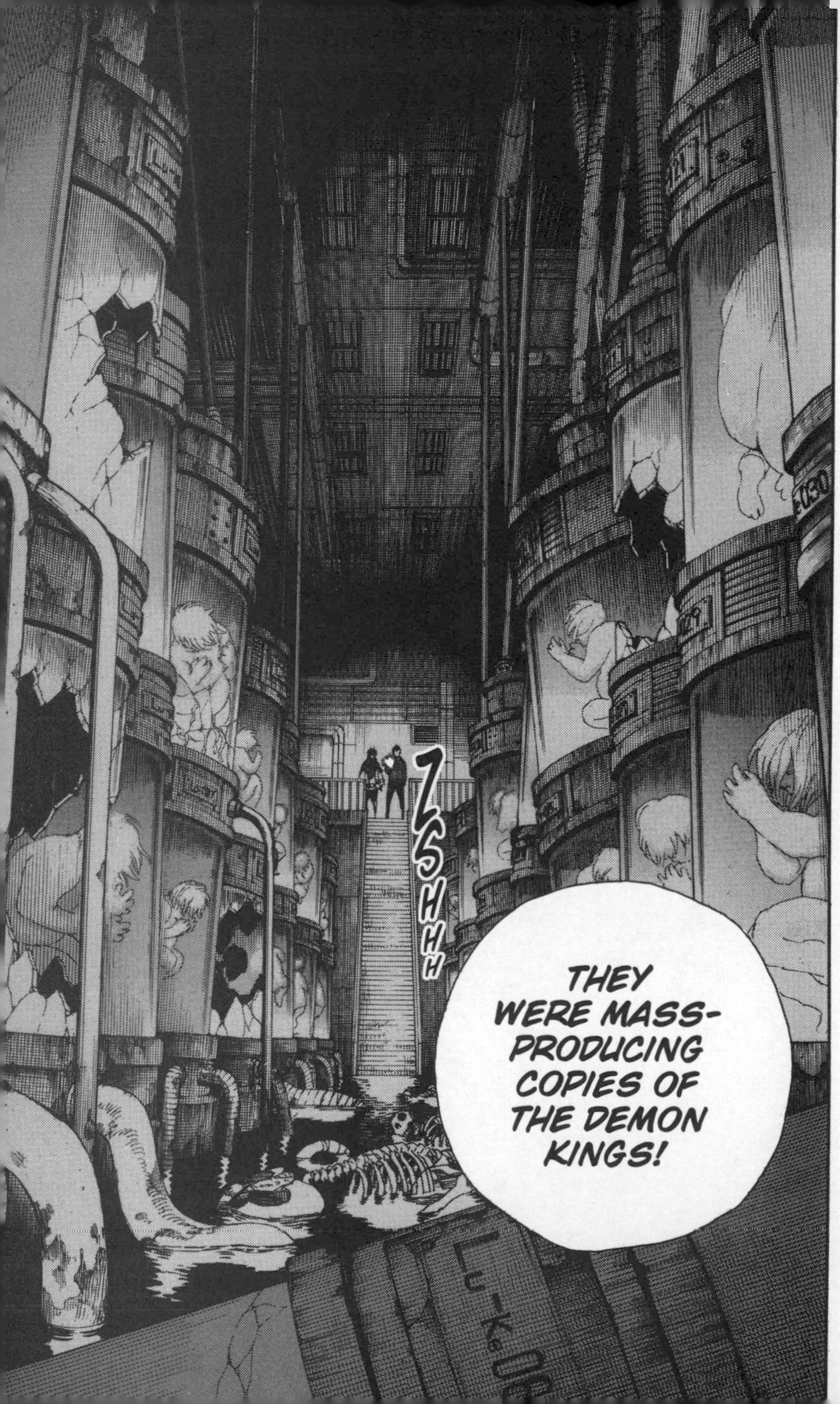
ZSHHH
THEY WERE MASS-PRODUCING COPIES OF THE DEMON KINGS!

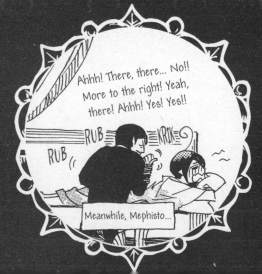

Blue Exorcist Chapter 85: Variant Leaves

Meanwhile, Mephisto...
Ahhh! There, there... No!! More to the right! Yeah, there! Ahhh! Yes! Yes!!
RUB
RUB
KRIK

Chapter 86: Fruit Branches

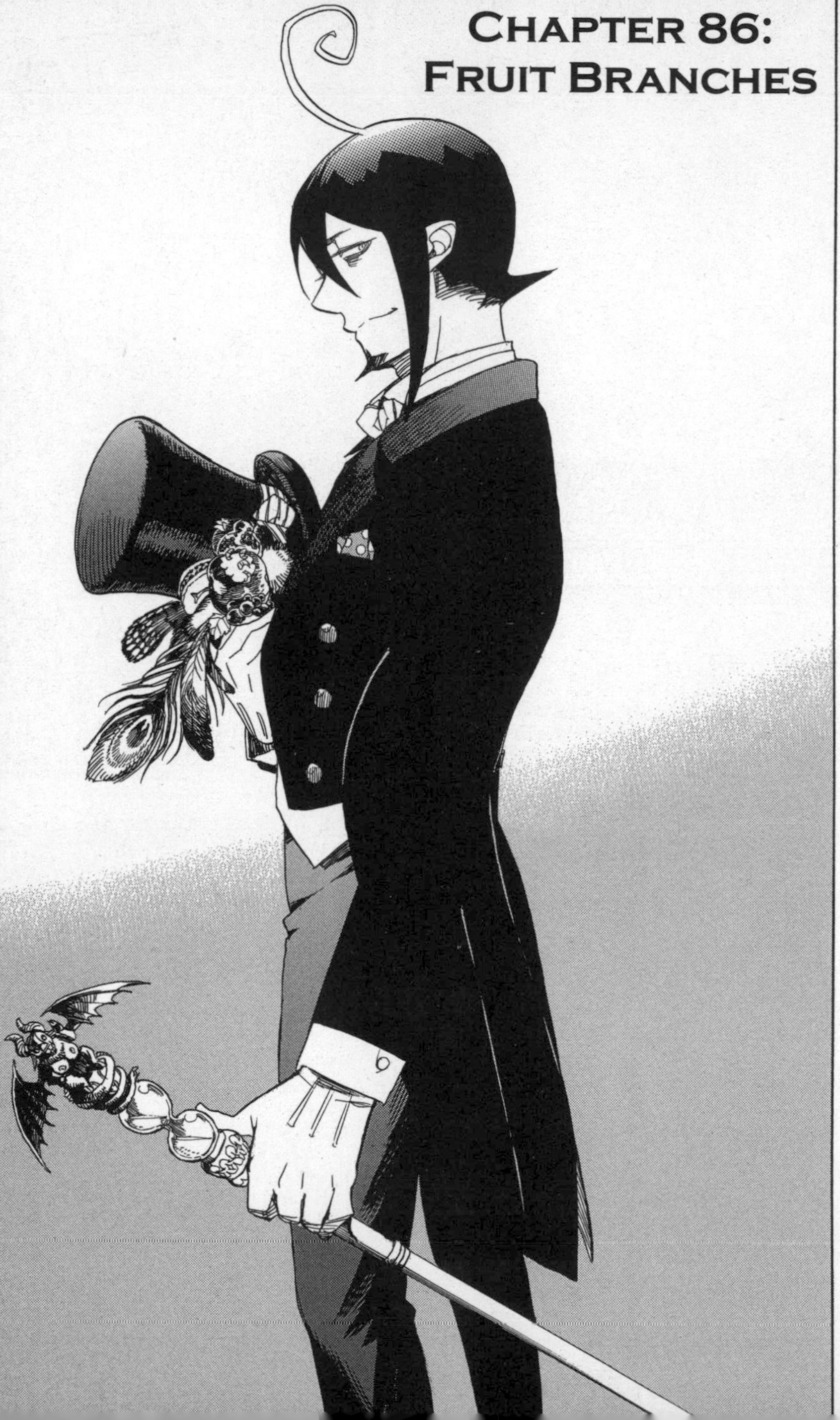

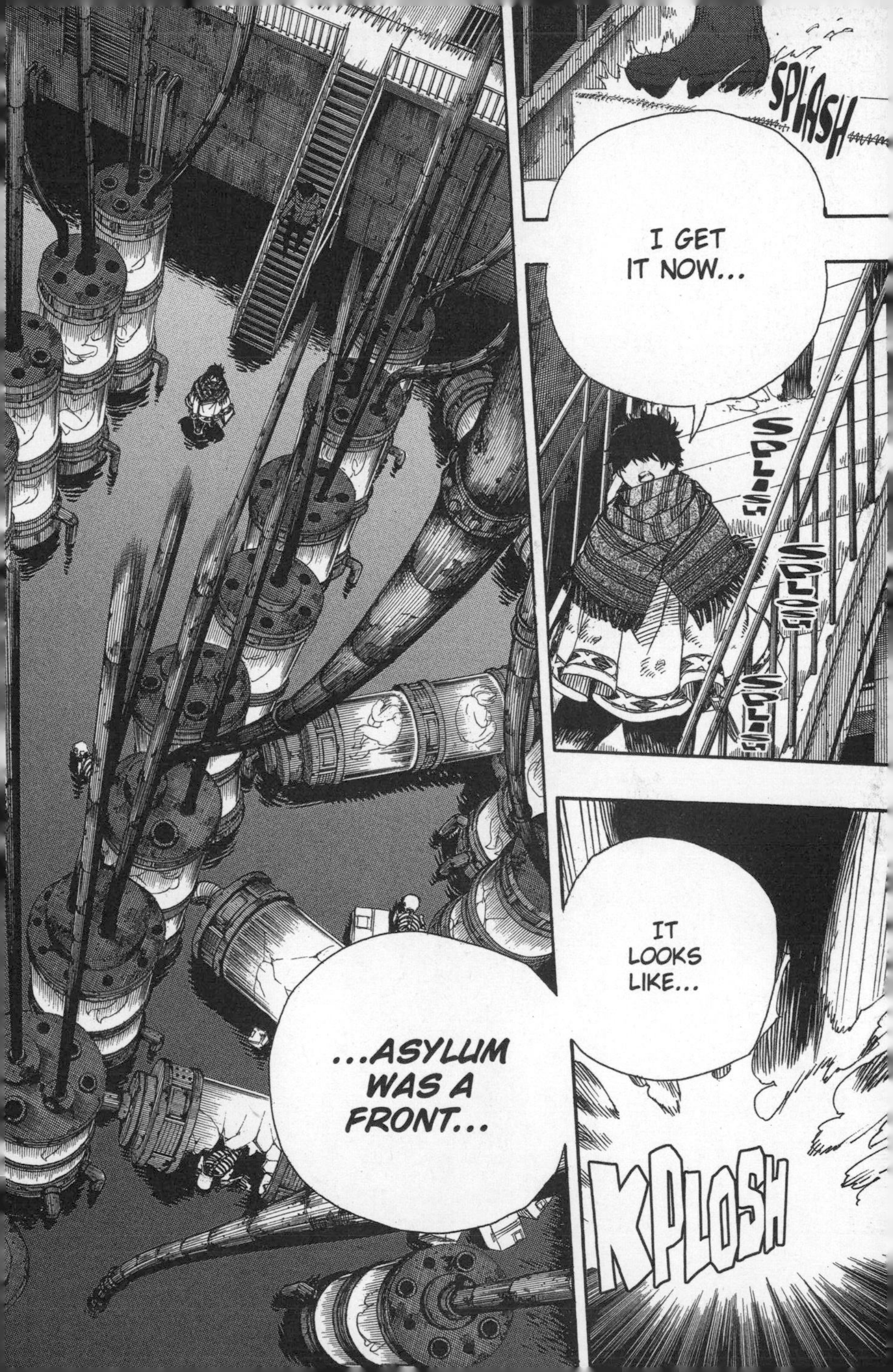
SPLASH
I GET IT NOW...
SPLISH
SPLISH
SPLISH
IT LOOKS LIKE...
KPLOSH
...ASYLUM WAS A FRONT...

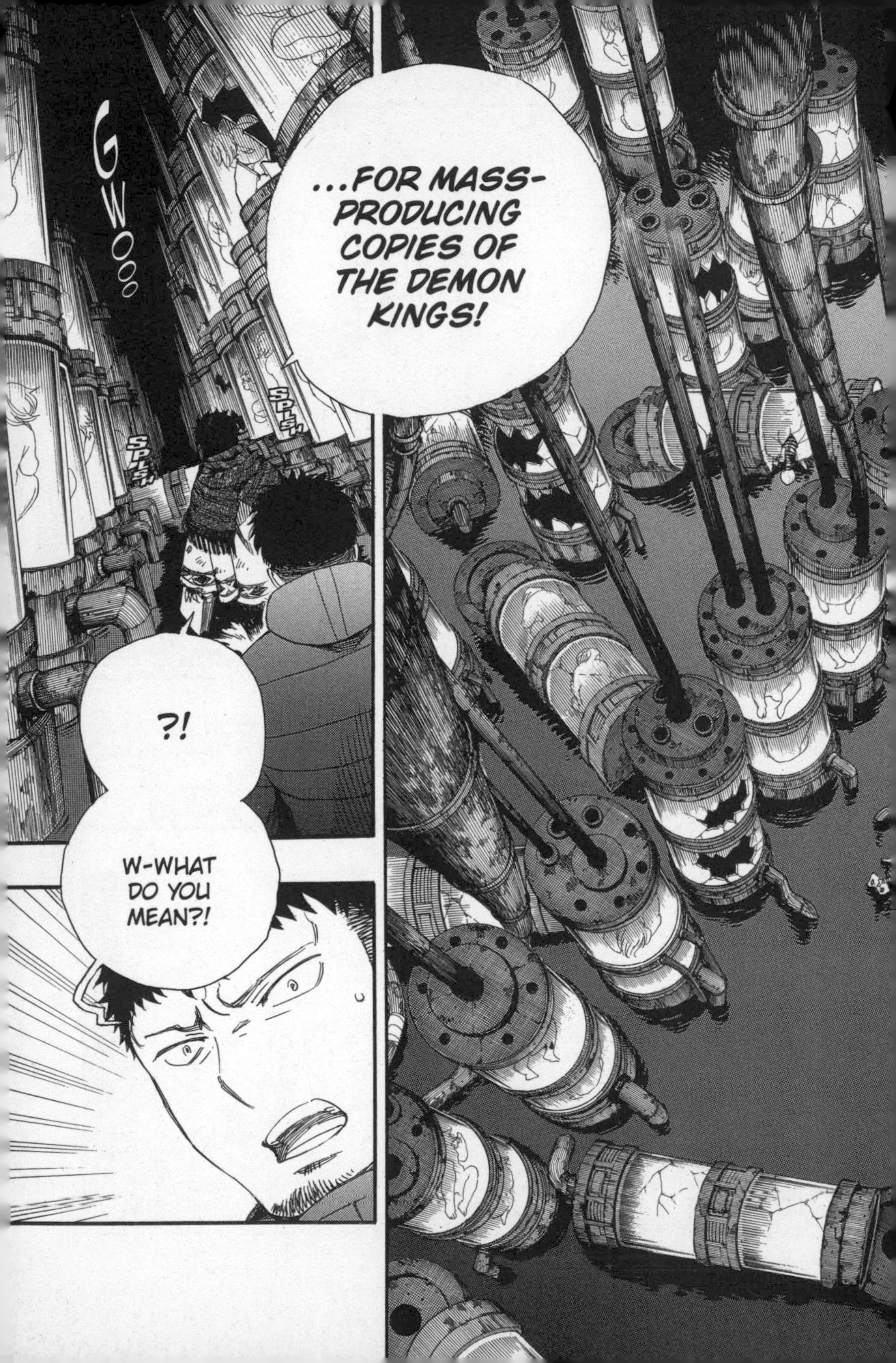
...FOR MASS-PRODUCING COPIES OF THE DEMON KINGS!
GWOOO
SPLSH
SPLSH
?!
W-WHAT DO YOU MEAN?!

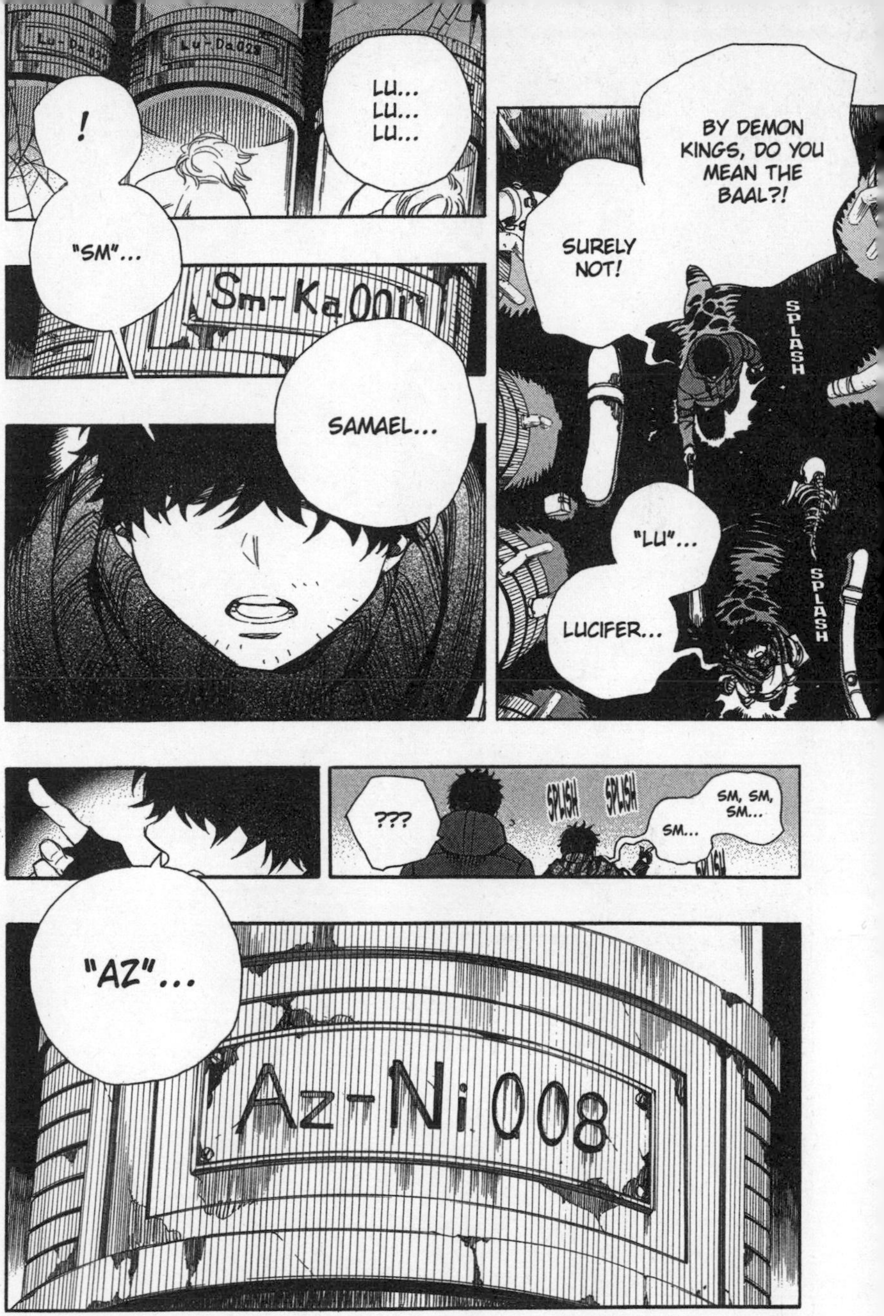
BY DEMON KINGS, DO YOU MEAN THE BAAL?!
SURELY NOT!
SPLASH
"LU"...
LUCIFER...
SPLASH
LU... LU... LU...
!
Lu-Da028
"SM"...
SAMAEL...
SM, SM, SM...
SM...
SPLISH
SPLISH
???
"AZ"...
Az-Ni 008

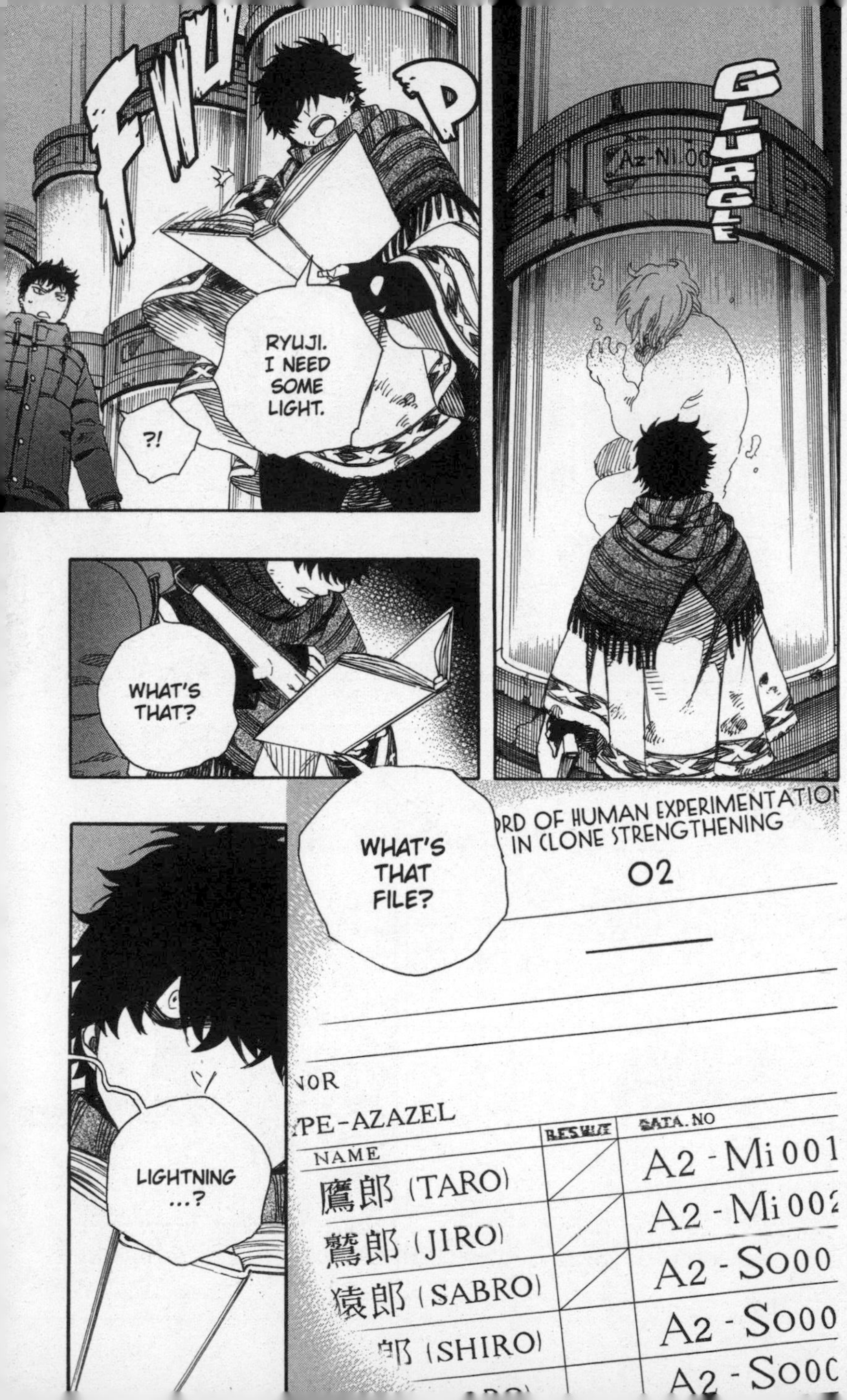
GLURGLE
Az-Ni.00
FWUP
RYUJI. I NEED SOME LIGHT.
?!
WHAT'S THAT?
WHAT'S THAT FILE?
ORD OF HUMAN EXPERIMENTATION
IN CLONE STRENGTHENING
02
NOR
PE-AZAZEL
NAME
鷹郎 (TARO)
A2-Mi001
鷲郎 (JIRO)
A2-Mi002
猿郎 (SABRO)
A2-So00
郎 (SHIRO)
A2-So00
A2-So00
LIGHTNING ...?

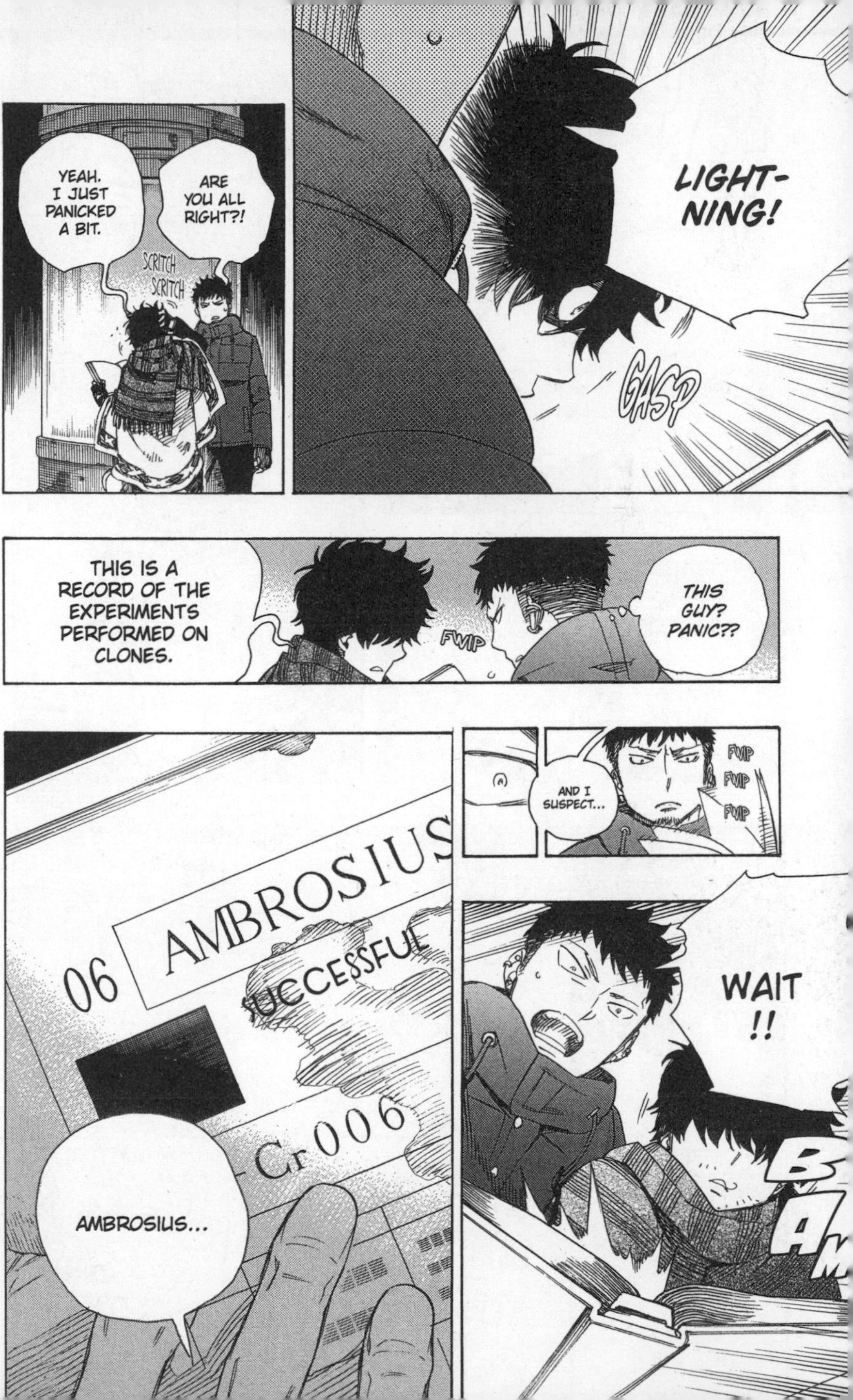
LIGHT-NING!
GASP
ARE YOU ALL RIGHT?!
YEAH. I JUST PANICKED A BIT.
SCRITCH SCRITCH
THIS GUY? PANIC??
FWIP
THIS IS A RECORD OF THE EXPERIMENTS PERFORMED ON CLONES.
AND I SUSPECT...
FWIP FWIP FWIP
WAIT!!
BAM
AMBROSIUS
06 AMBROSIUS
SUCCESSFUL
Cr006
AMBROSIUS...

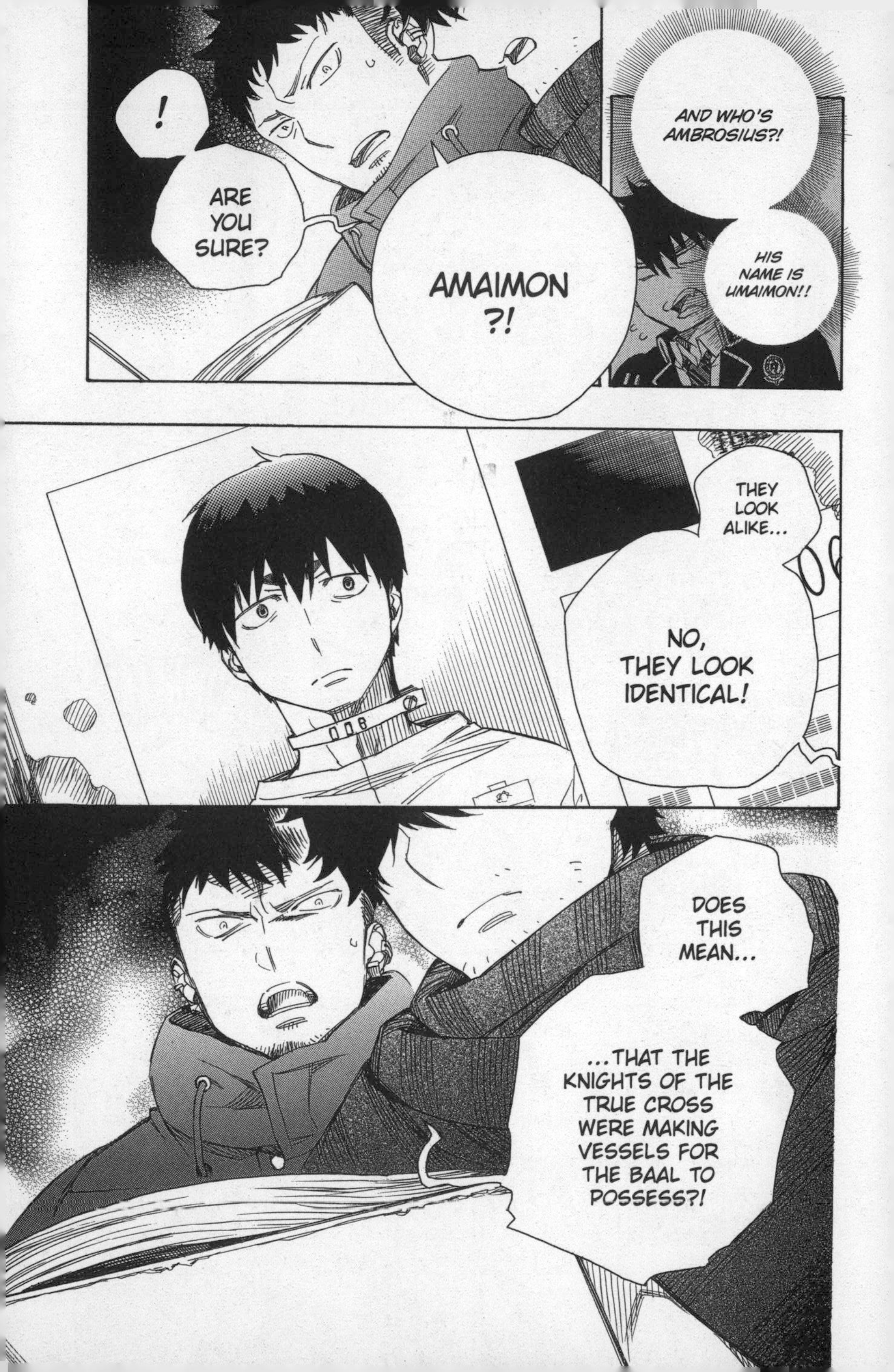
AND WHO'S AMBROSIUS?!
HIS NAME IS UMAIMON!!
AMAIMON ?!
!
ARE YOU SURE?
THEY LOOK ALIKE...
NO, THEY LOOK IDENTICAL!
DOES THIS MEAN...
...THAT THE KNIGHTS OF THE TRUE CROSS WERE MAKING VESSELS FOR THE BAAL TO POSSESS?!

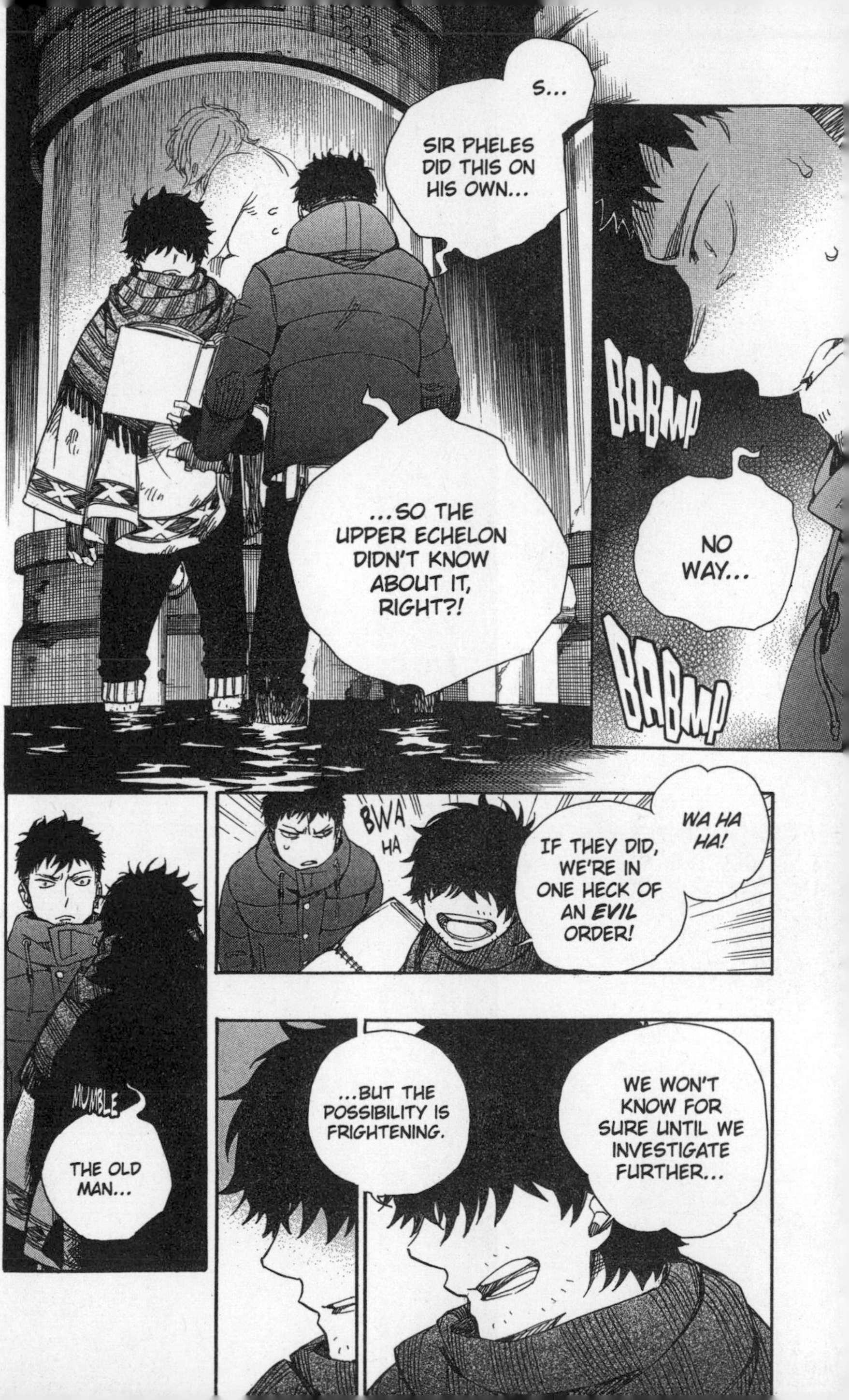
BABMP
NO WAY...
BABMP
S...
SIR PHELES DID THIS ON HIS OWN...
...SO THE UPPER ECHELON DIDN'T KNOW ABOUT IT, RIGHT?!
WA HA HA!
BWA HA
IF THEY DID, WE'RE IN ONE HECK OF AN EVIL ORDER!
WE WON'T KNOW FOR SURE UNTIL WE INVESTIGATE FURTHER...
...BUT THE POSSIBILITY IS FRIGHTENING.
MUMBLE
THE OLD MAN...

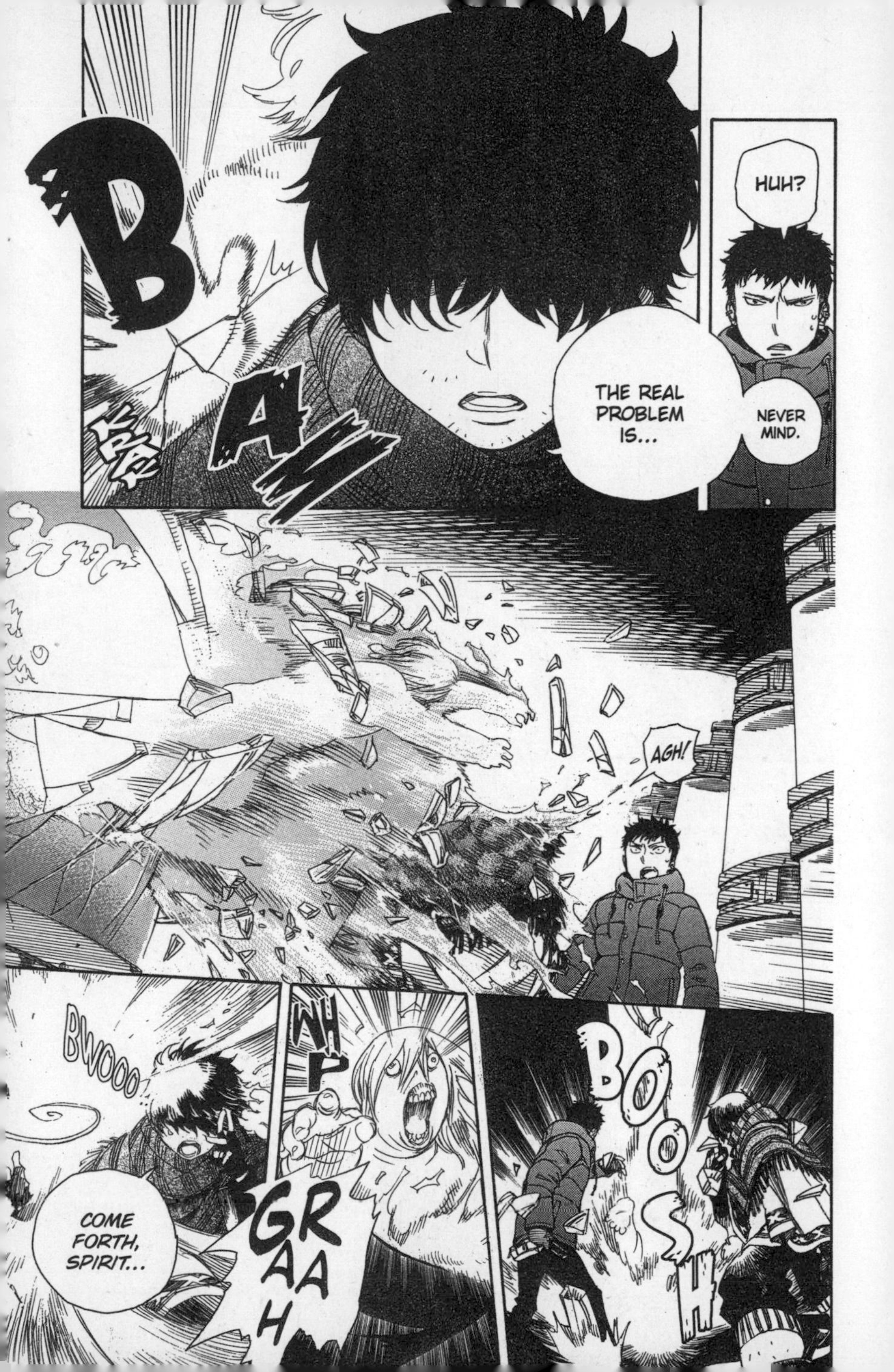

HUH?
NEVER MIND.
THE REAL PROBLEM IS...
BAM
AGH!
BOOOSH
WHP
GRAAAH
BWOOO
COME FORTH, SPIRIT...

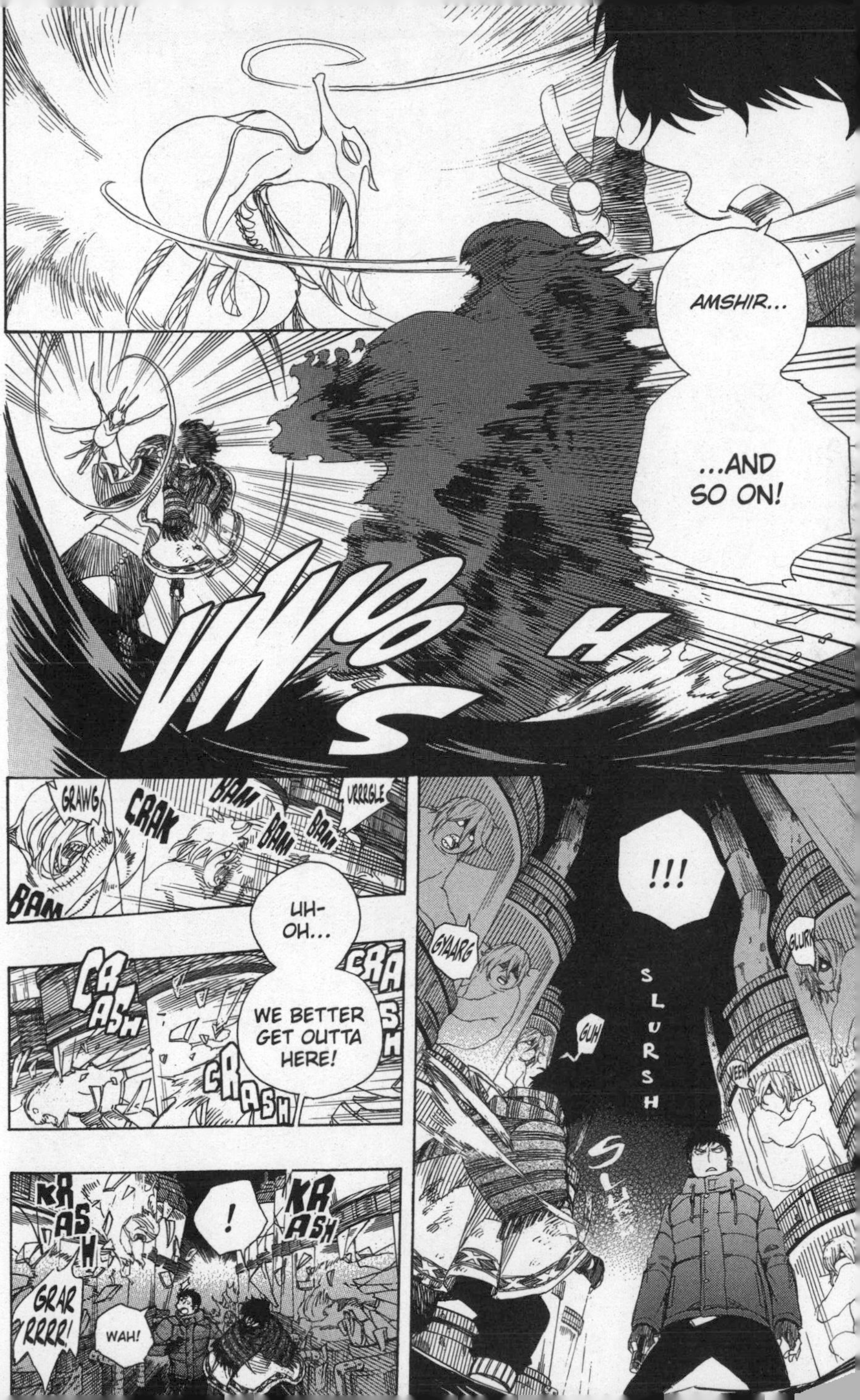
AMSHIR...
...AND SO ON!
VWOOSH
!!!
GYAARG
GUH
SLURSH
GLURK
GRAWG
CRAK
BAM BAM BAM BAM
URRRGLE
BAM
UH-OH...
WE BETTER GET OUTTA HERE!
CRASH
CRASH
CRASH
KRASH
!
KRASH
GRARRRRR!
WAH!

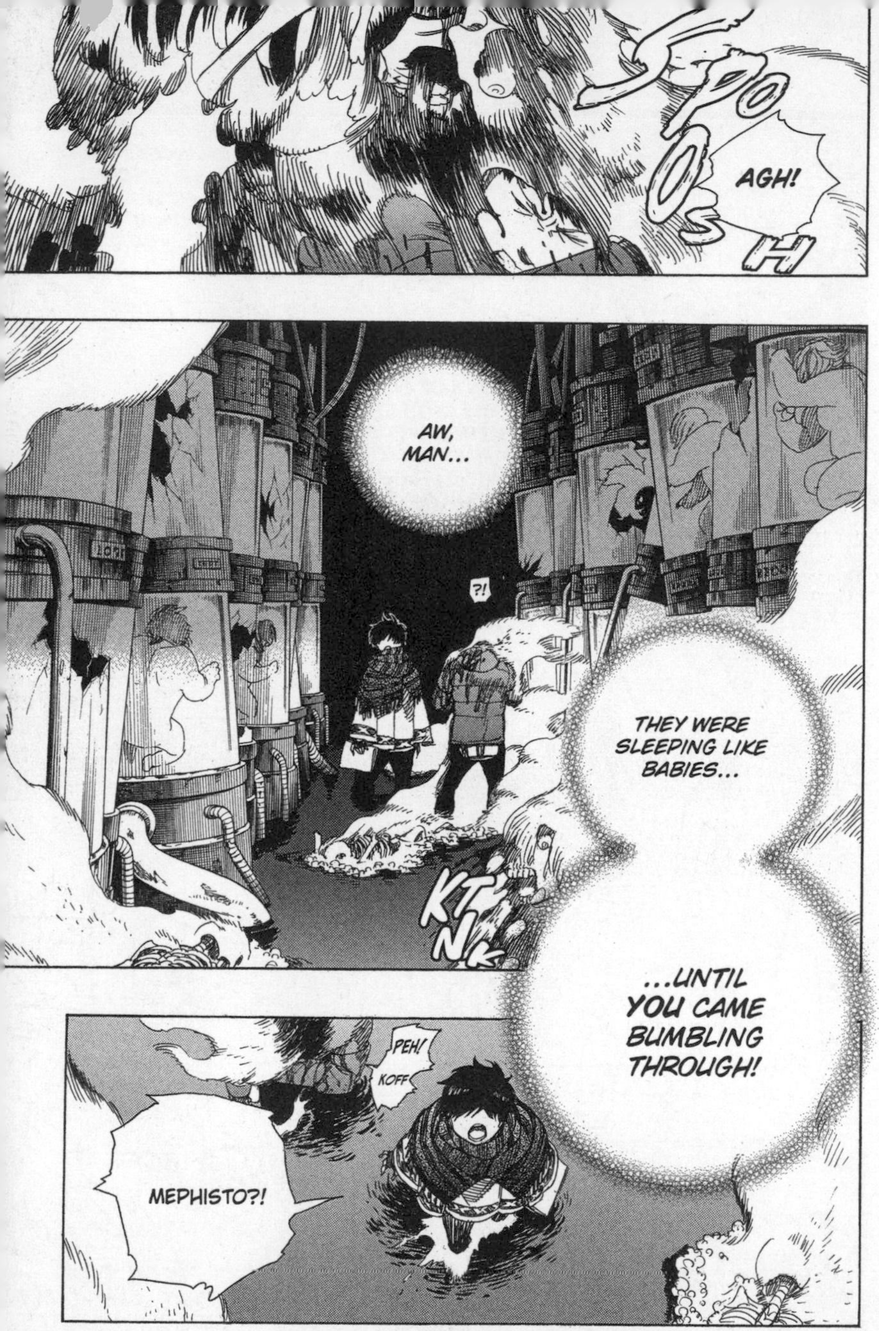
SPOOSH
AGH!
AW, MAN...
?!
THEY WERE SLEEPING LIKE BABIES...
KTINK
...UNTIL YOU CAME BUMBLING THROUGH!
PEH!
KOFF
MEPHISTO?!

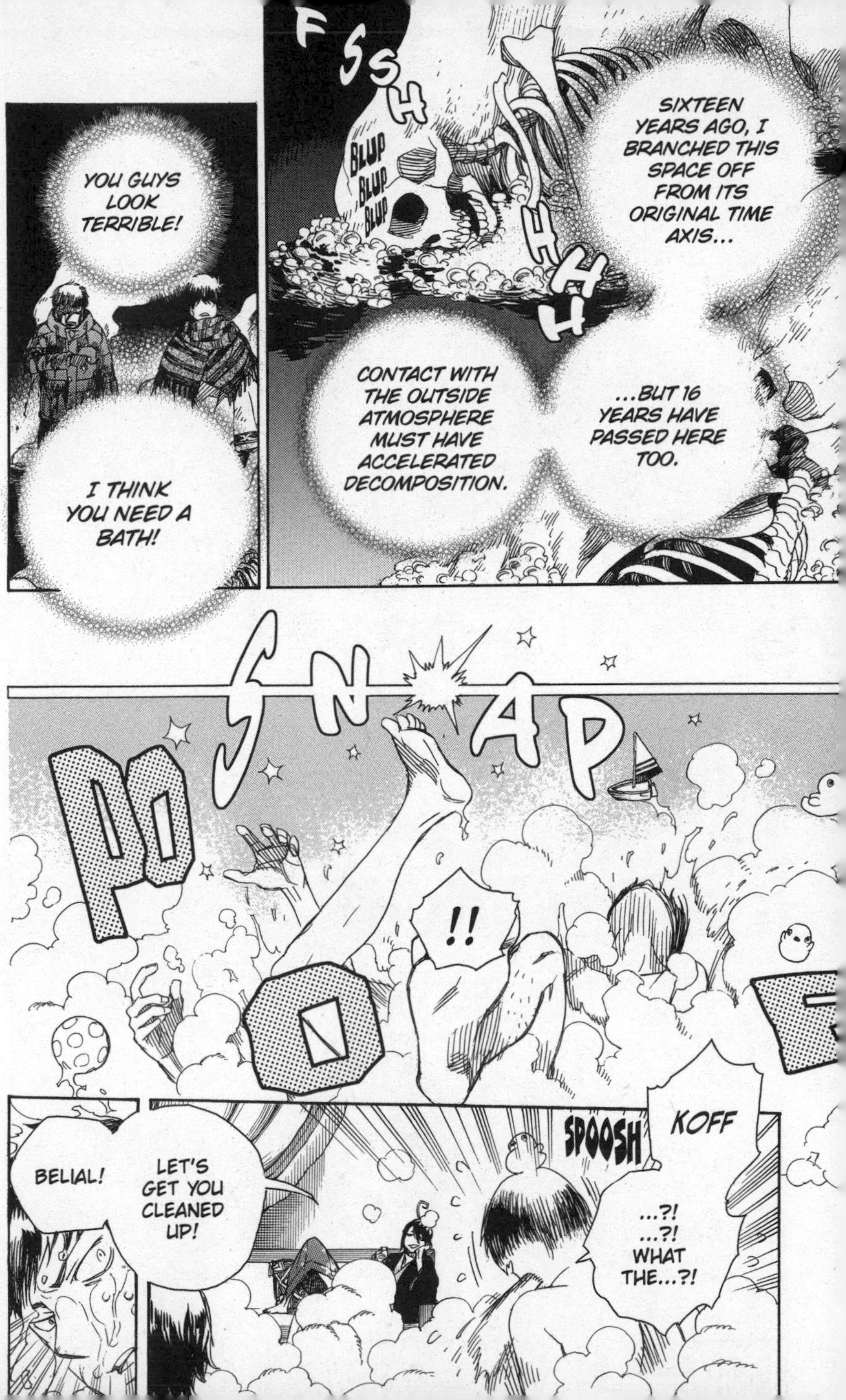
FSSHHHHH
BLUP BLUP BLUP
SIXTEEN YEARS AGO, I BRANCHED THIS SPACE OFF FROM ITS ORIGINAL TIME AXIS...
...BUT 16 YEARS HAVE PASSED HERE TOO.
CONTACT WITH THE OUTSIDE ATMOSPHERE MUST HAVE ACCELERATED DECOMPOSITION.
YOU GUYS LOOK TERRIBLE!
I THINK YOU NEED A BATH!
SNAP
POO
!!
KOFF
...?! ...?! WHAT THE...?!
SPOOSH
BELIAL!
LET'S GET YOU CLEANED UP!

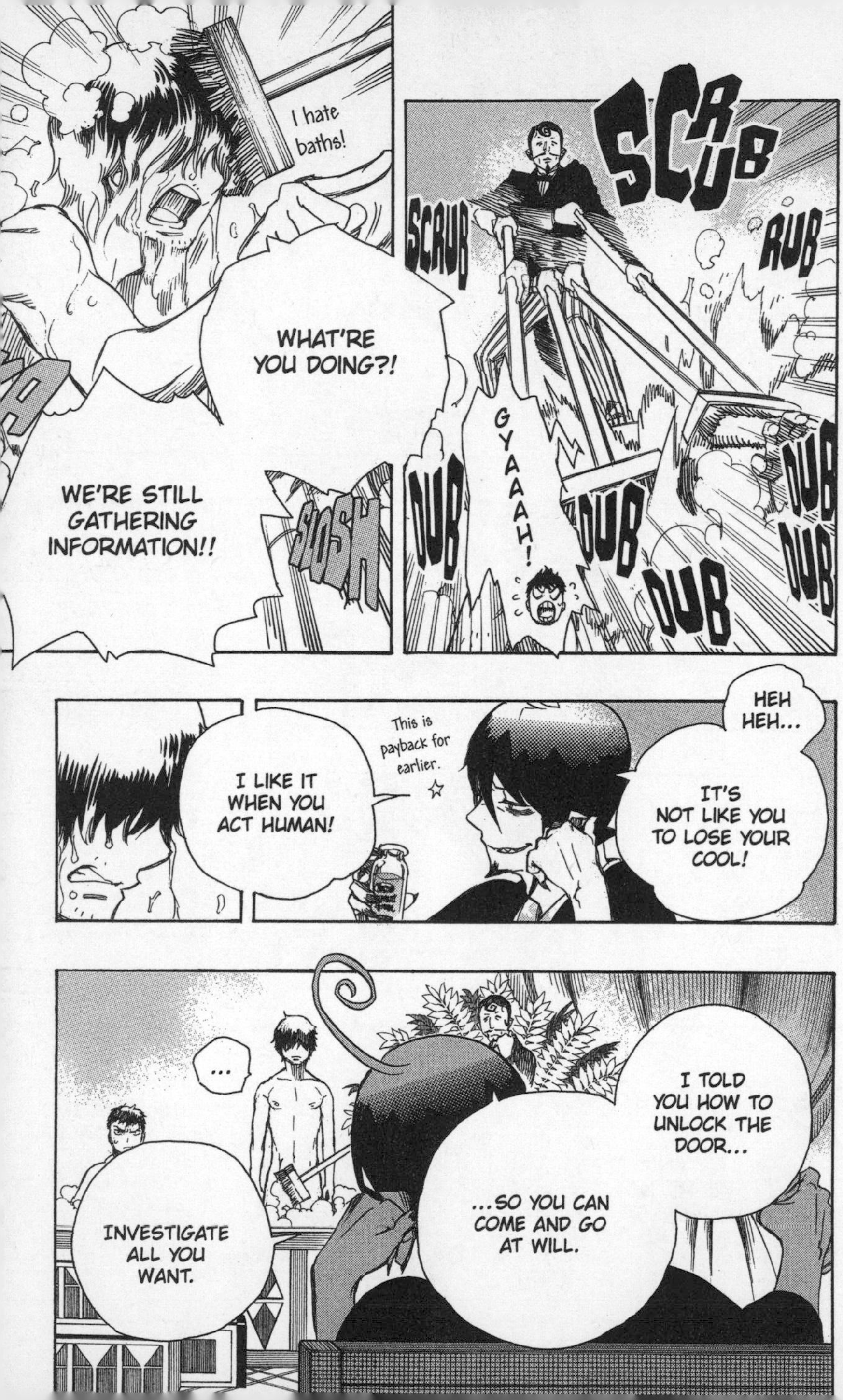
SCRUB
SCRUB
RUB
GYAAAH!
DUB
DUB
DUB
DUB
DUB
I hate baths!
WHAT'RE YOU DOING?!
SLOSH
WE'RE STILL GATHERING INFORMATION!!
HEH HEH...
IT'S NOT LIKE YOU TO LOSE YOUR COOL!
This is payback for earlier. ☆
I LIKE IT WHEN YOU ACT HUMAN!
I TOLD YOU HOW TO UNLOCK THE DOOR...
...SO YOU CAN COME AND GO AT WILL.
...
INVESTIGATE ALL YOU WANT.

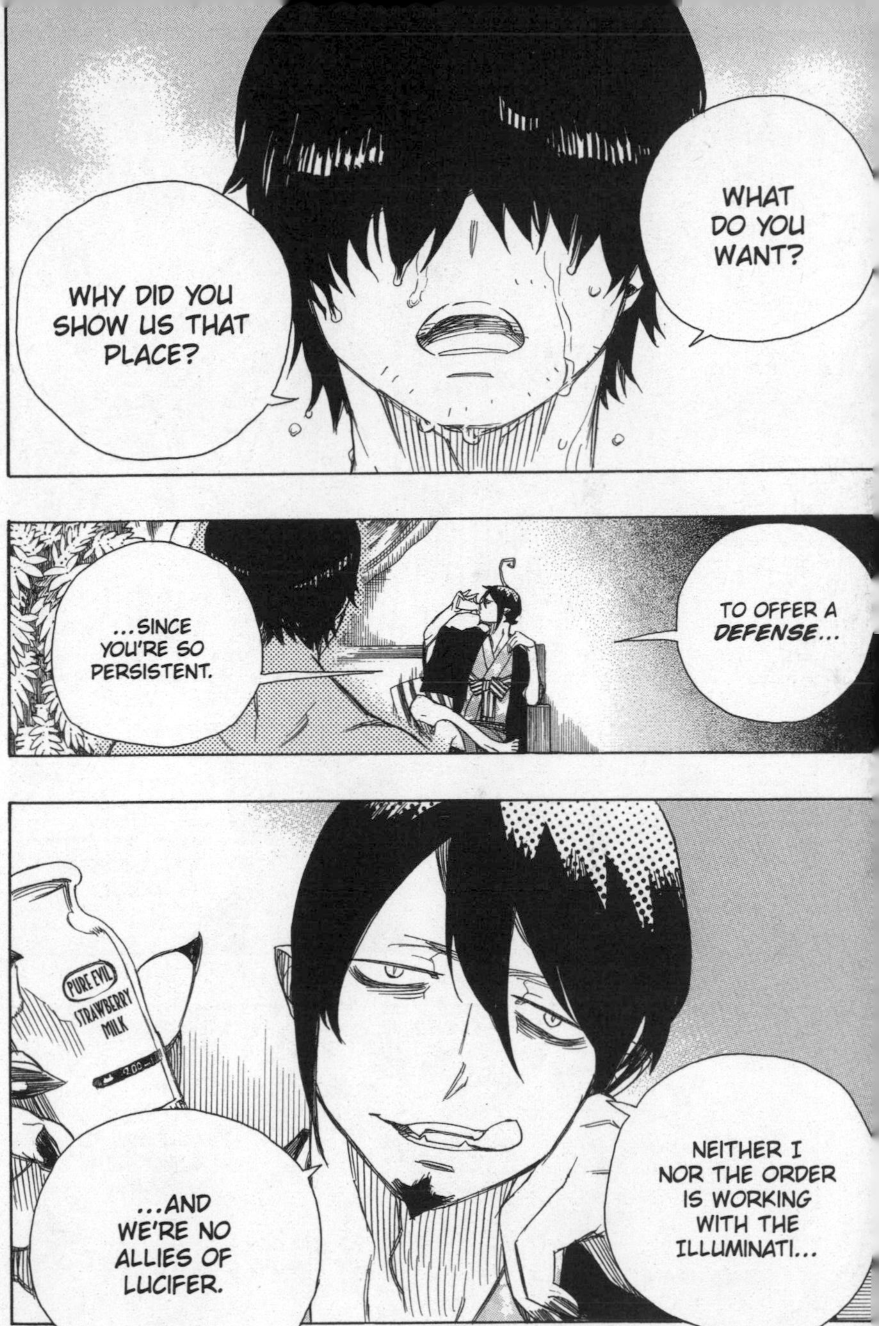
WHAT DO YOU WANT?
WHY DID YOU SHOW US THAT PLACE?
TO OFFER A *DEFENSE*...
...SINCE YOU'RE SO PERSISTENT.
PURE EVIL STRAWBERRY MILK
NEITHER I NOR THE ORDER IS WORKING WITH THE ILLUMINATI...
...AND WE'RE NO ALLIES OF LUCIFER.

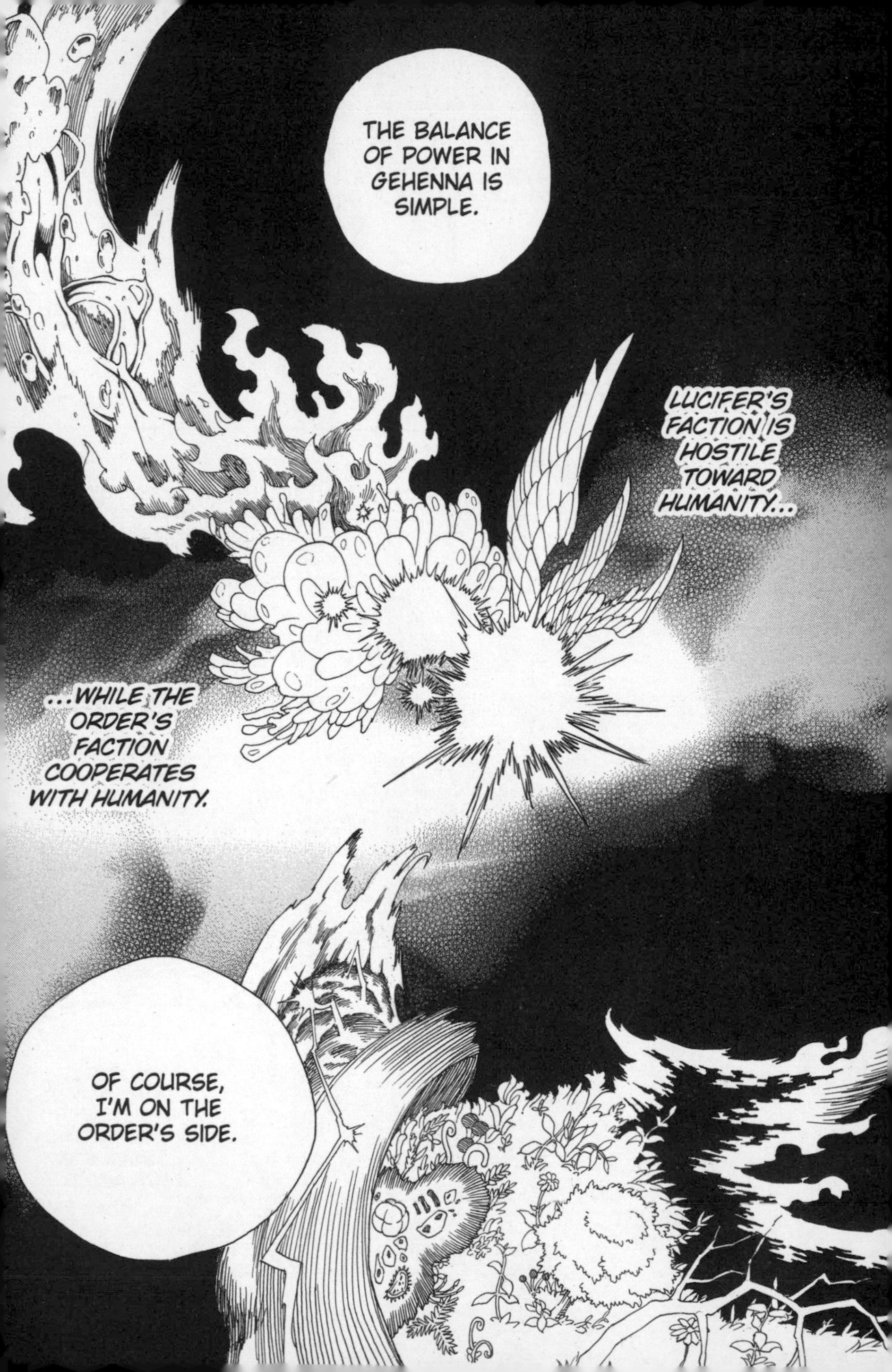
THE BALANCE OF POWER IN GEHENNA IS SIMPLE.
LUCIFER'S FACTION IS HOSTILE TOWARD HUMANITY...
...WHILE THE ORDER'S FACTION COOPERATES WITH HUMANITY.
OF COURSE, I'M ON THE ORDER'S SIDE.

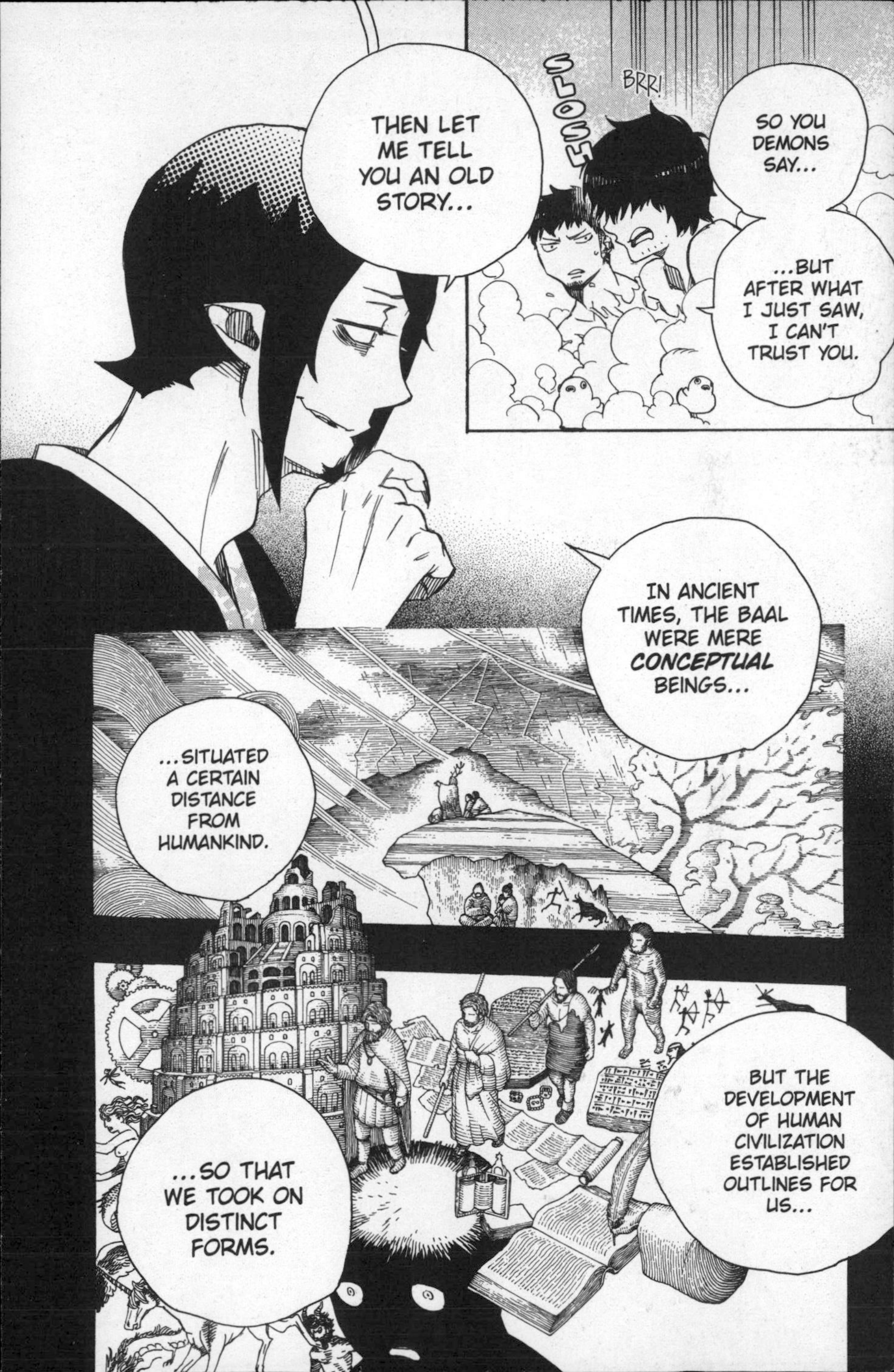
SLOSH
BRR!
SO YOU DEMONS SAY...
...BUT AFTER WHAT I JUST SAW, I CAN'T TRUST YOU.
THEN LET ME TELL YOU AN OLD STORY...
IN ANCIENT TIMES, THE BAAL WERE MERE CONCEPTUAL BEINGS...
...SITUATED A CERTAIN DISTANCE FROM HUMANKIND.
BUT THE DEVELOPMENT OF HUMAN CIVILIZATION ESTABLISHED OUTLINES FOR US...
...SO THAT WE TOOK ON DISTINCT FORMS.

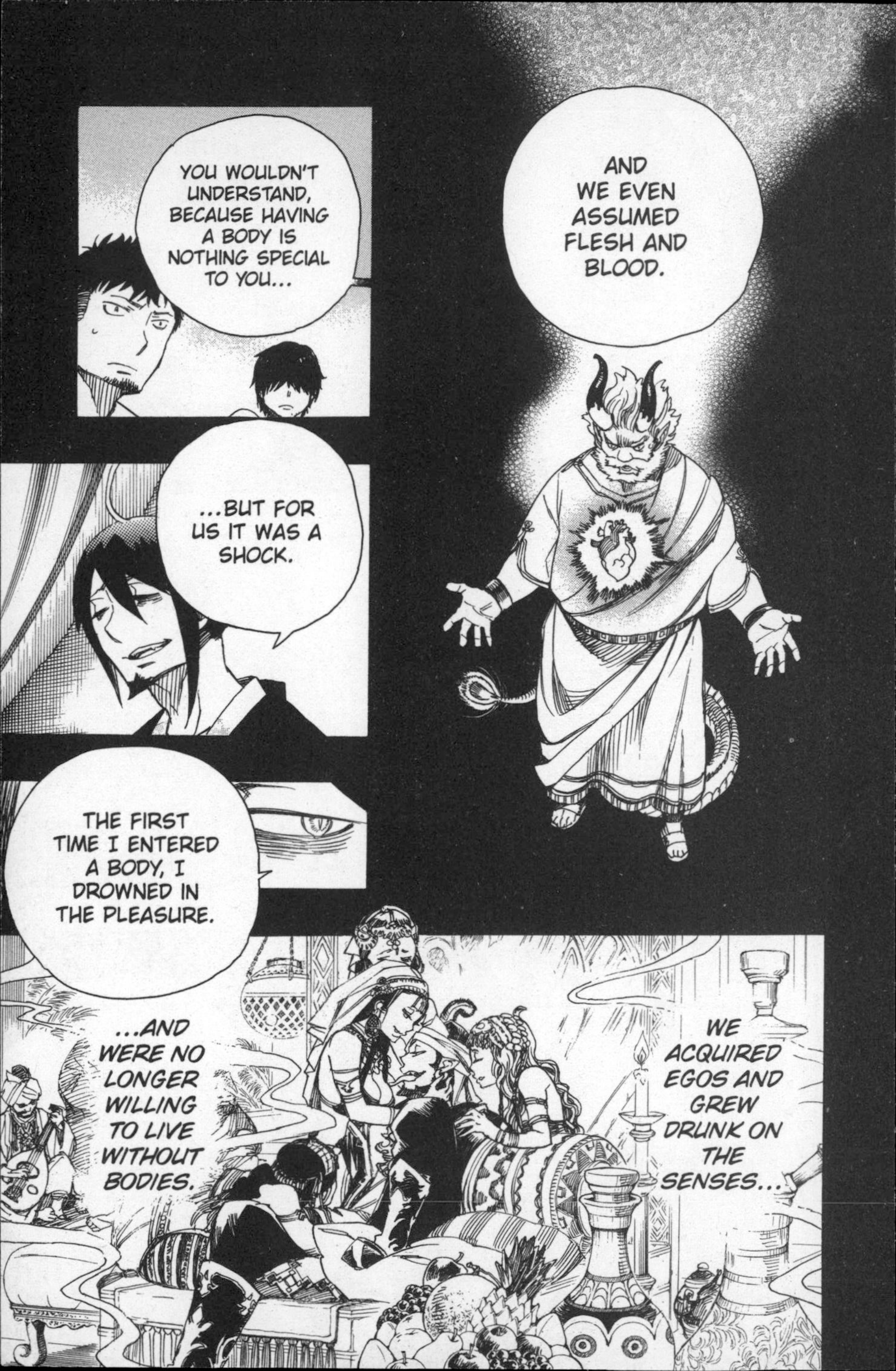
AND WE EVEN ASSUMED FLESH AND BLOOD.
YOU WOULDN'T UNDERSTAND, BECAUSE HAVING A BODY IS NOTHING SPECIAL TO YOU...
...BUT FOR US IT WAS A SHOCK.
THE FIRST TIME I ENTERED A BODY, I DROWNED IN THE PLEASURE.
WE ACQUIRED EGOS AND GREW DRUNK ON THE SENSES...
...AND WERE NO LONGER WILLING TO LIVE WITHOUT BODIES.

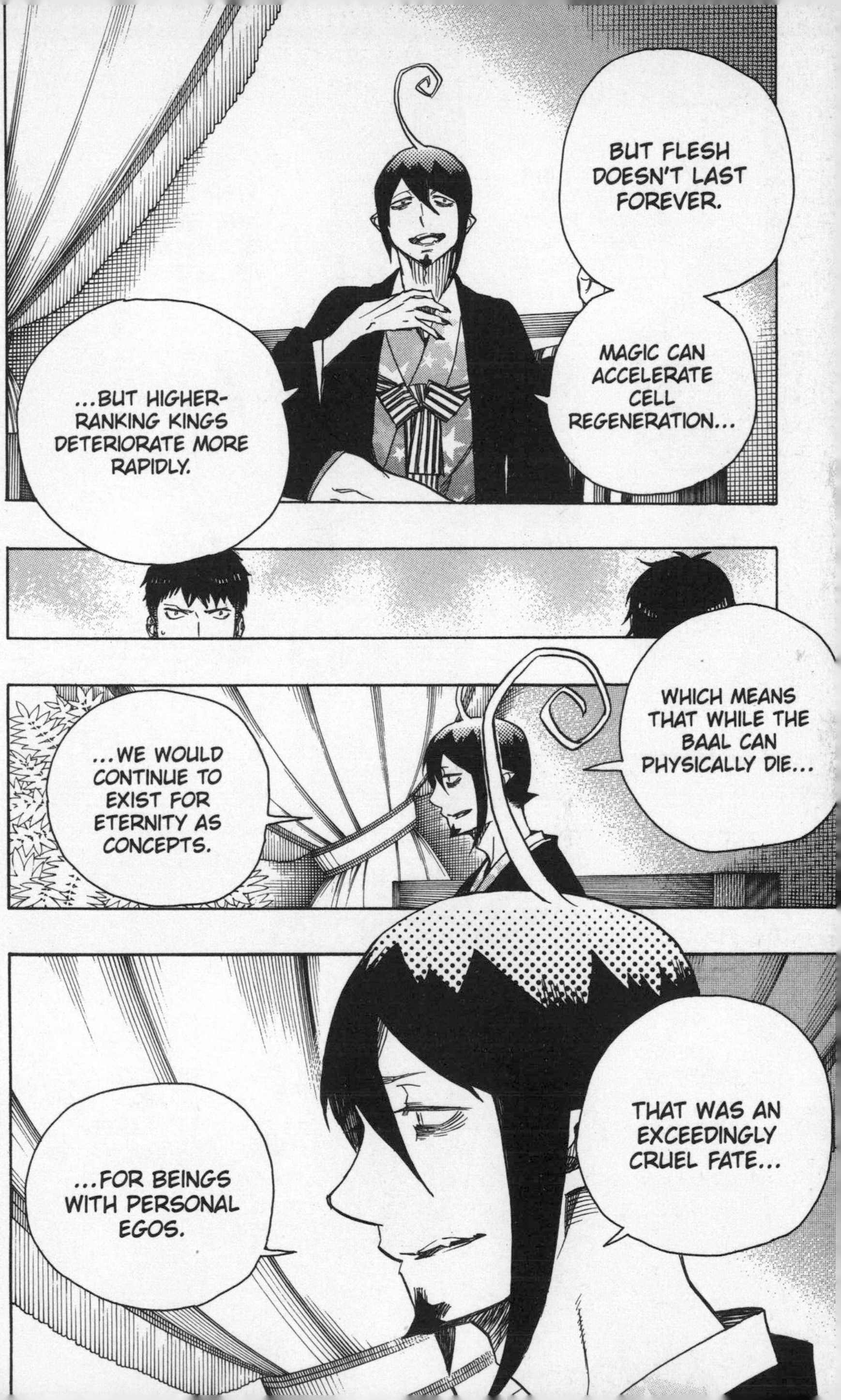
BUT FLESH DOESN'T LAST FOREVER.
MAGIC CAN ACCELERATE CELL REGENERATION...
...BUT HIGHER-RANKING KINGS DETERIORATE MORE RAPIDLY.
WHICH MEANS THAT WHILE THE BAAL CAN PHYSICALLY DIE...
...WE WOULD CONTINUE TO EXIST FOR ETERNITY AS CONCEPTS.
THAT WAS AN EXCEEDINGLY CRUEL FATE...
...FOR BEINGS WITH PERSONAL EGOS.

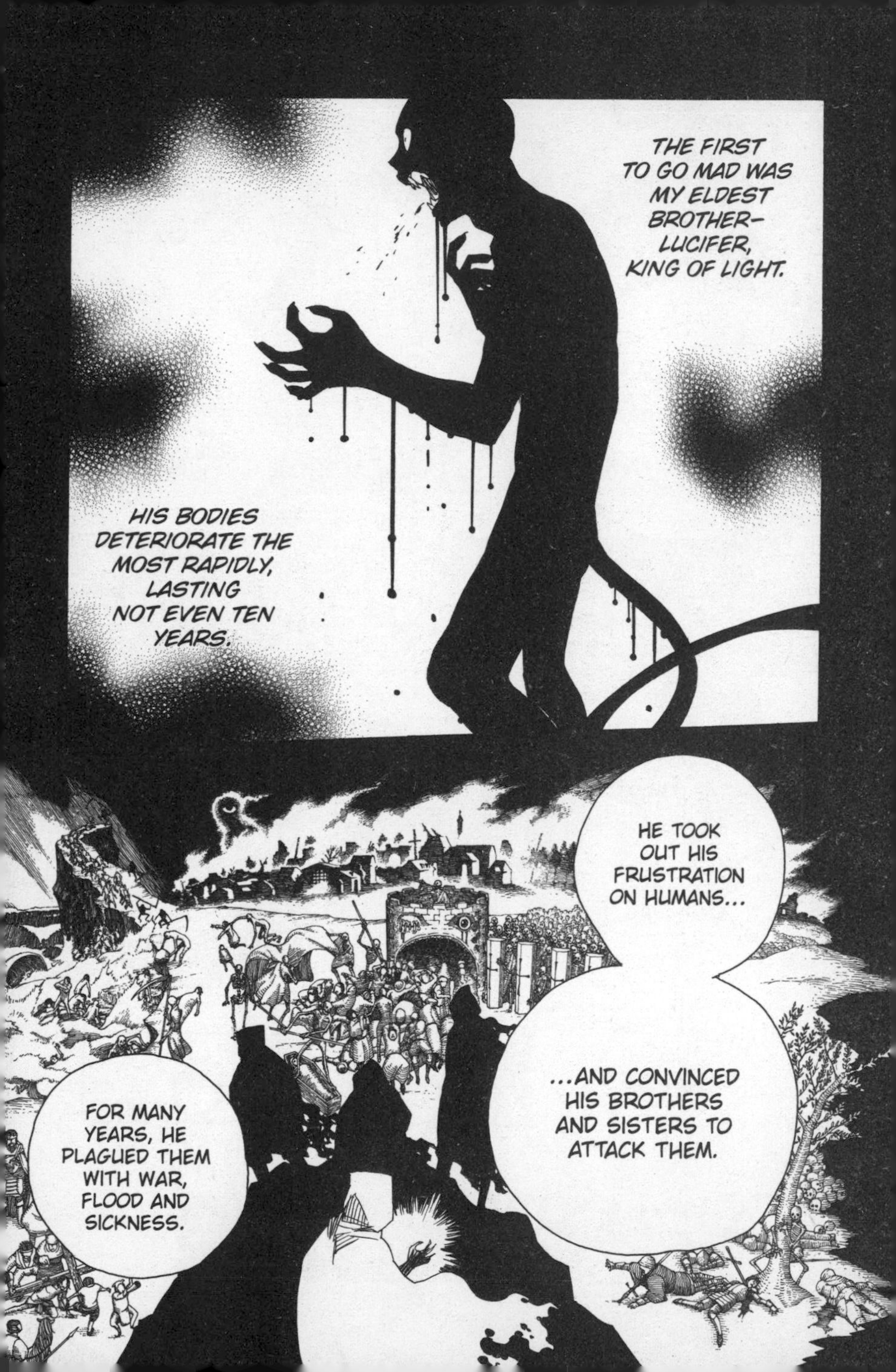
THE FIRST TO GO MAD WAS MY ELDEST BROTHER- LUCIFER, KING OF LIGHT.
HIS BODIES DETERIORATE THE MOST RAPIDLY, LASTING NOT EVEN TEN YEARS.
HE TOOK OUT HIS FRUSTRATION ON HUMANS...
...AND CONVINCED HIS BROTHERS AND SISTERS TO ATTACK THEM.
FOR MANY YEARS, HE PLAGUED THEM WITH WAR, FLOOD AND SICKNESS.

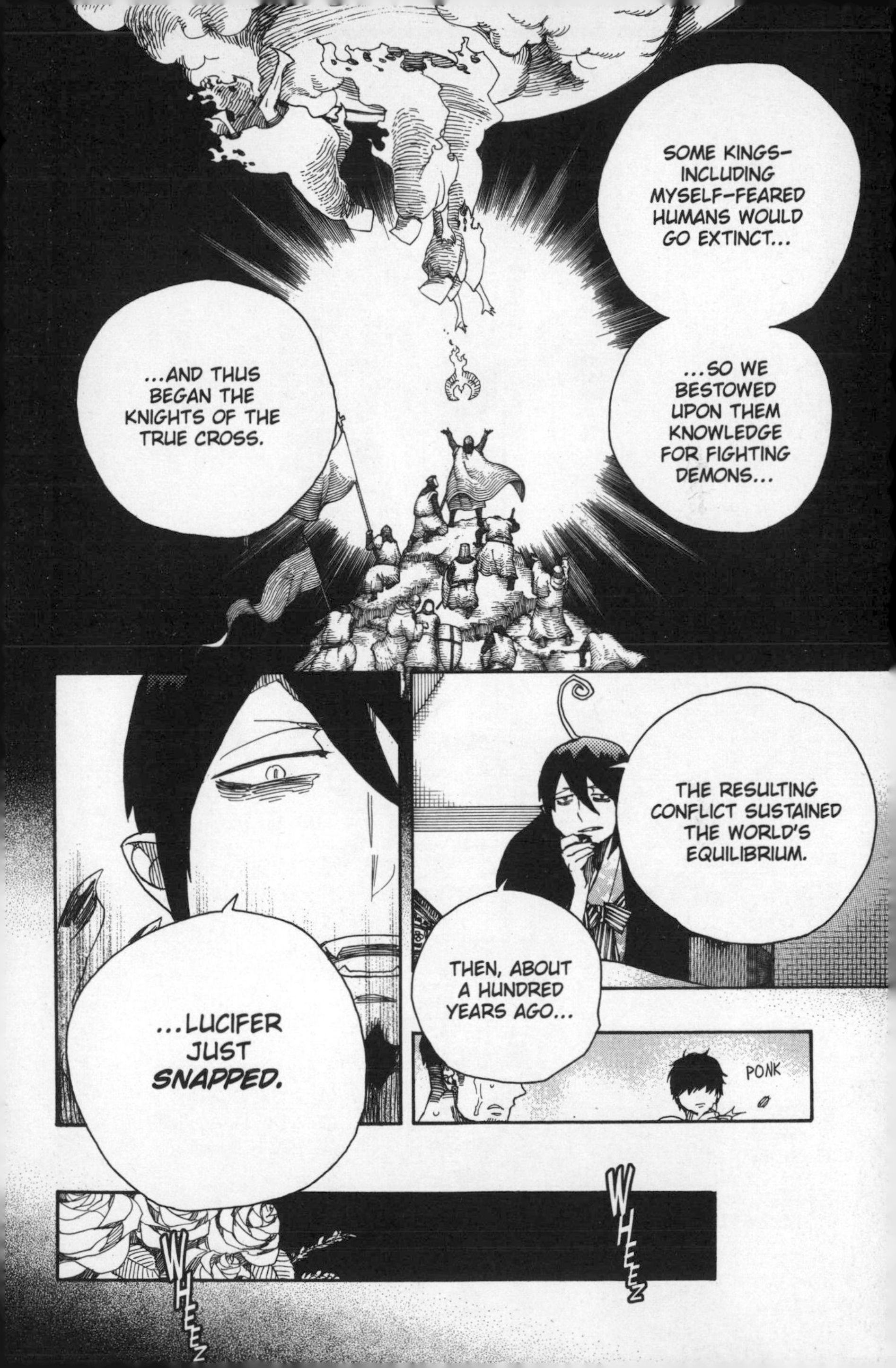
SOME KINGS—INCLUDING MYSELF—FEARED HUMANS WOULD GO EXTINCT...
...SO WE BESTOWED UPON THEM KNOWLEDGE FOR FIGHTING DEMONS...
...AND THUS BEGAN THE KNIGHTS OF THE TRUE CROSS.
THE RESULTING CONFLICT SUSTAINED THE WORLD'S EQUILIBRIUM.
THEN, ABOUT A HUNDRED YEARS AGO...
PONK
...LUCIFER JUST *SNAPPED.*
WHEEZ
WHEEZ

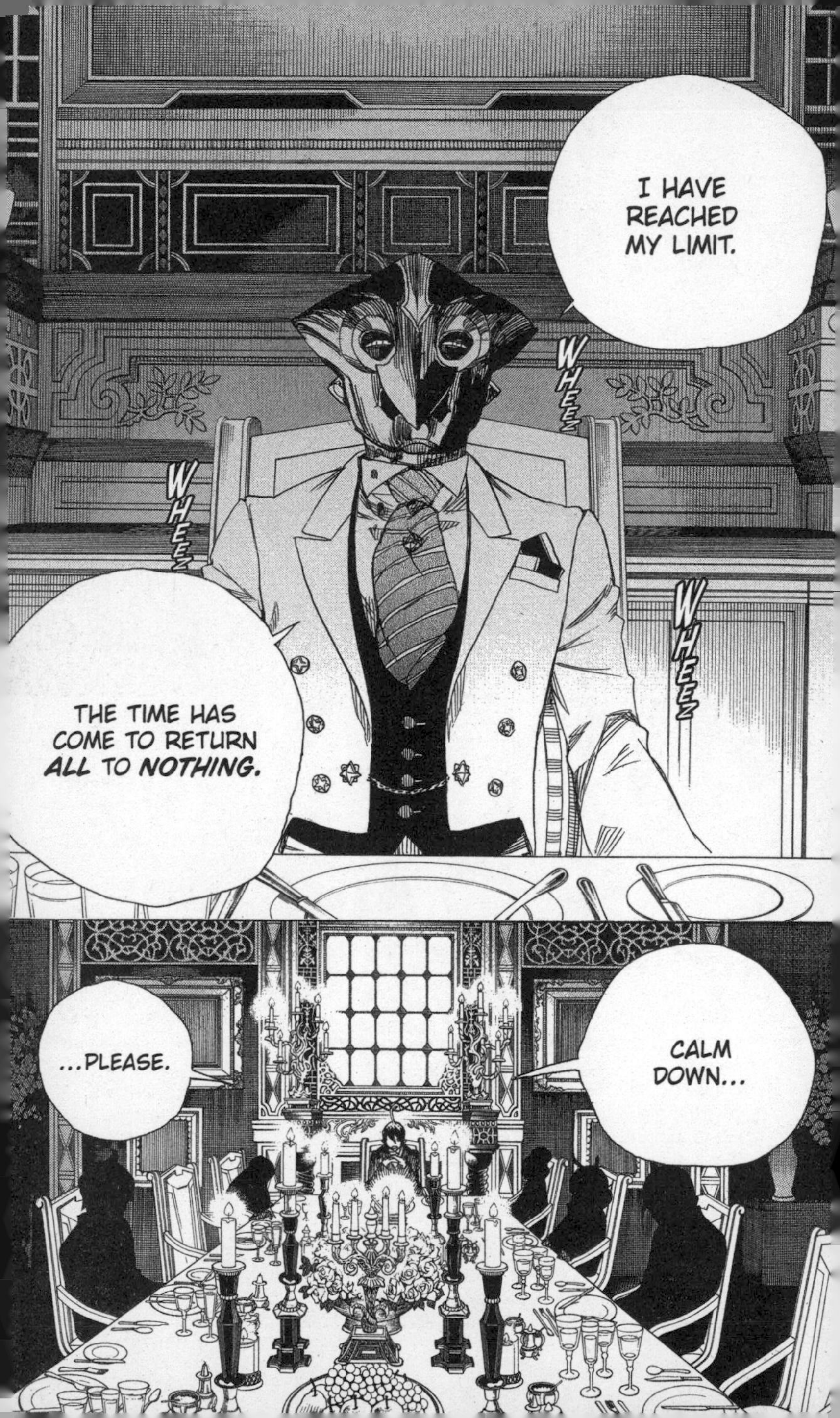

I HAVE REACHED MY LIMIT.
WHEEZ
WHEEZ
WHEEZ
THE TIME HAS COME TO RETURN ALL TO NOTHING.
CALM DOWN...
...PLEASE.

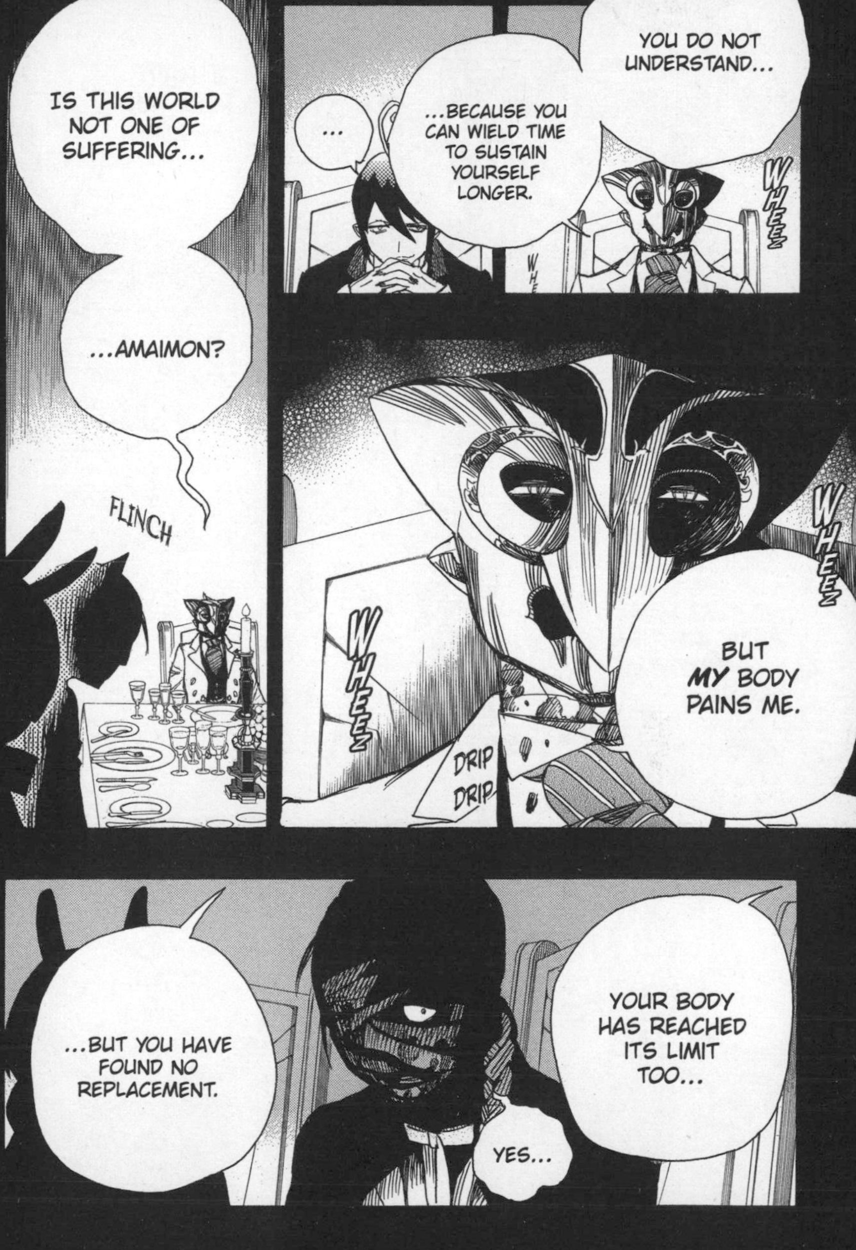
YOU DO NOT UNDERSTAND...
...BECAUSE YOU CAN WIELD TIME TO SUSTAIN YOURSELF LONGER.
WHEEZE
WHE
...
WHEEZE
WHEEZE
BUT MY BODY PAINS ME.
DRIP DRIP
IS THIS WORLD NOT ONE OF SUFFERING...
...AMAIMON?
FLINCH
YOUR BODY HAS REACHED ITS LIMIT TOO...
YES...
...BUT YOU HAVE FOUND NO REPLACEMENT.

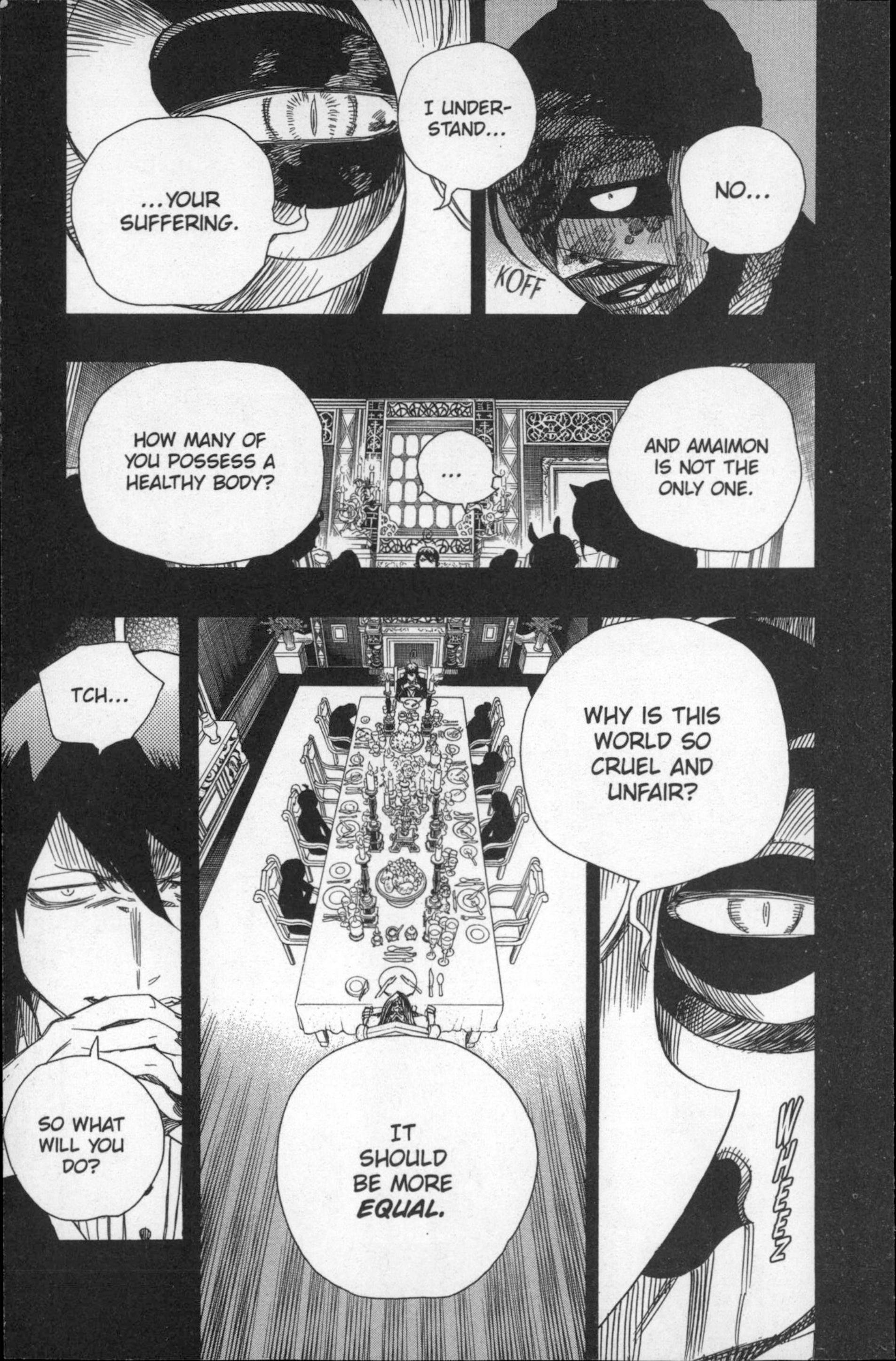
NO...
KOFF
I UNDER-STAND...
...YOUR SUFFERING.
AND AMAIMON IS NOT THE ONLY ONE.
...
HOW MANY OF YOU POSSESS A HEALTHY BODY?
WHY IS THIS WORLD SO CRUEL AND UNFAIR?
WHEEZ
IT SHOULD BE MORE **EQUAL.**
TCH...
SO WHAT WILL YOU DO?

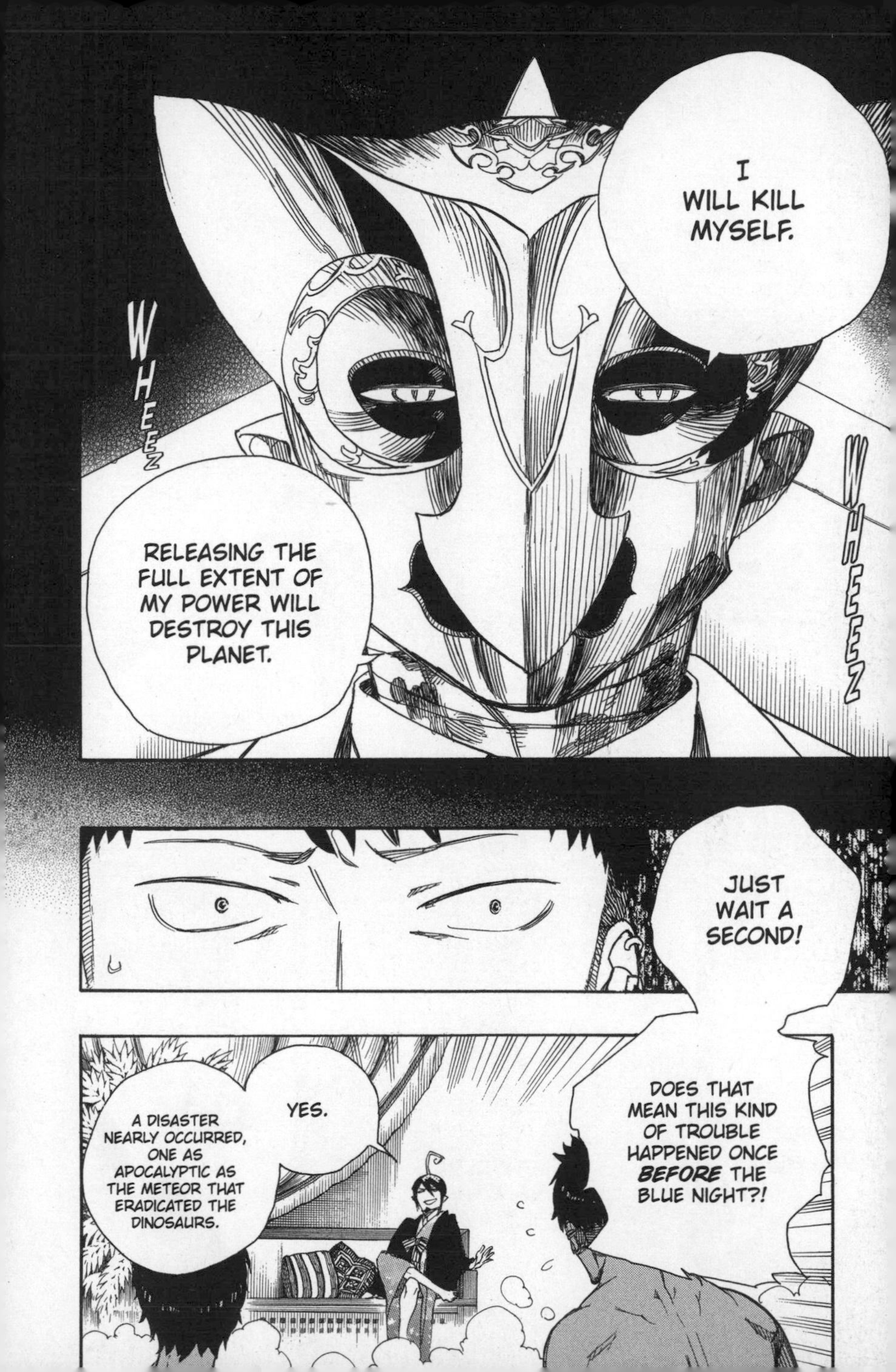
I WILL KILL MYSELF.
WHEEZ
RELEASING THE FULL EXTENT OF MY POWER WILL DESTROY THIS PLANET.
WHEEZ
JUST WAIT A SECOND!
DOES THAT MEAN THIS KIND OF TROUBLE HAPPENED ONCE *BEFORE* THE BLUE NIGHT?!
YES.
A DISASTER NEARLY OCCURRED, ONE AS APOCALYPTIC AS THE METEOR THAT ERADICATED THE DINOSAURS.

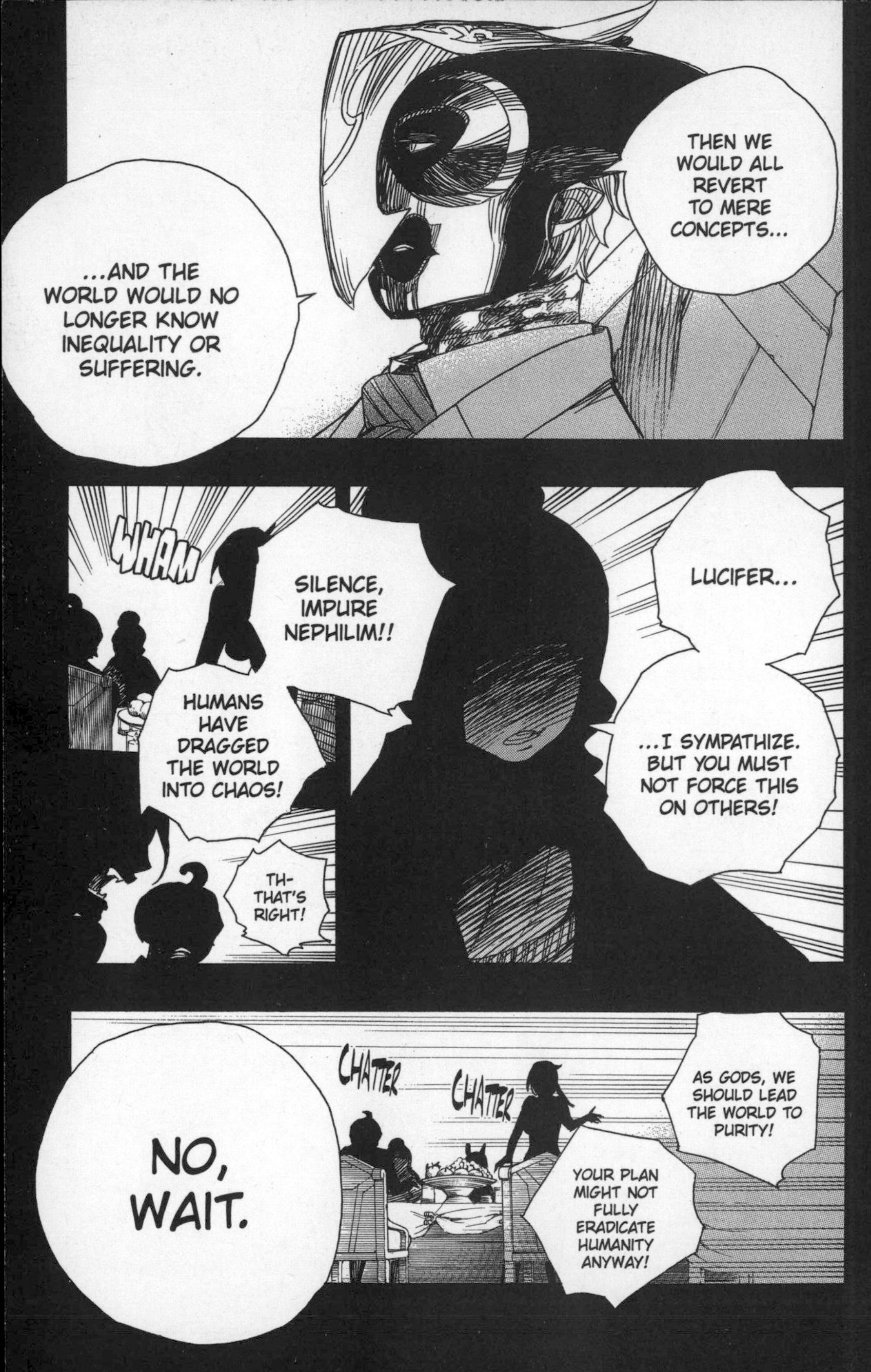
THEN WE WOULD ALL REVERT TO MERE CONCEPTS...
...AND THE WORLD WOULD NO LONGER KNOW INEQUALITY OR SUFFERING.
LUCIFER...
...I SYMPATHIZE. BUT YOU MUST NOT FORCE THIS ON OTHERS!
WHAM
SILENCE, IMPURE NEPHILIM!!
HUMANS HAVE DRAGGED THE WORLD INTO CHAOS!
TH- THAT'S RIGHT!
AS GODS, WE SHOULD LEAD THE WORLD TO PURITY!
YOUR PLAN MIGHT NOT FULLY ERADICATE HUMANITY ANYWAY!
CHATTER
CHATTER
NO, WAIT.

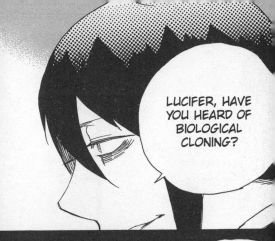

LUCIFER, HAVE YOU HEARD OF BIOLOGICAL CLONING?

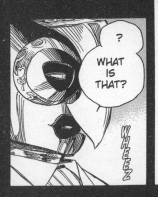

?

WHAT IS THAT?

WHEEZ

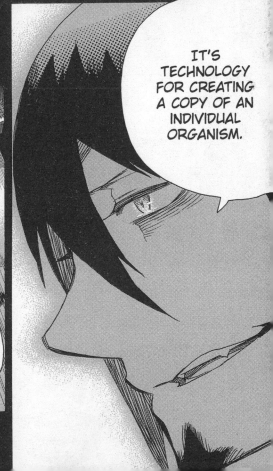

IT'S TECHNOLOGY FOR CREATING A COPY OF AN INDIVIDUAL ORGANISM.

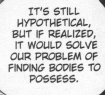

IT'S STILL HYPOTHETICAL, BUT IF REALIZED, IT WOULD SOLVE OUR PROBLEM OF FINDING BODIES TO POSSESS.

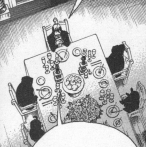

IF WE COULD EASILY ENTER A NEW BODY WHEN THE OLD ONE FAILED...

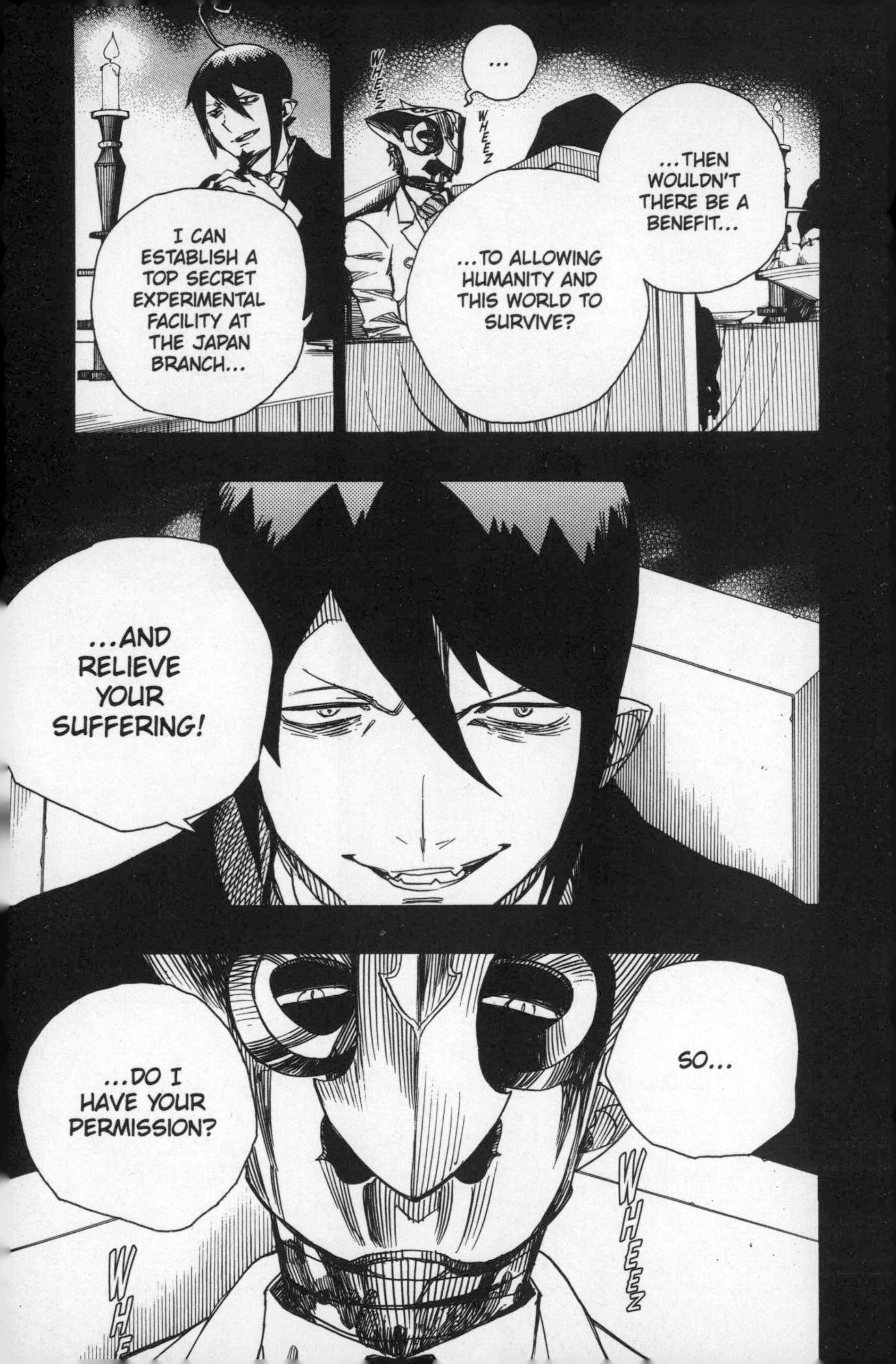
...
WHEEZ
WHEEZ
...THEN WOULDN'T THERE BE A BENEFIT...
...TO ALLOWING HUMANITY AND THIS WORLD TO SURVIVE?
I CAN ESTABLISH A TOP SECRET EXPERIMENTAL FACILITY AT THE JAPAN BRANCH...
...AND RELIEVE YOUR SUFFERING!
SO...
...DO I HAVE YOUR PERMISSION?
WHEEZ
WHE

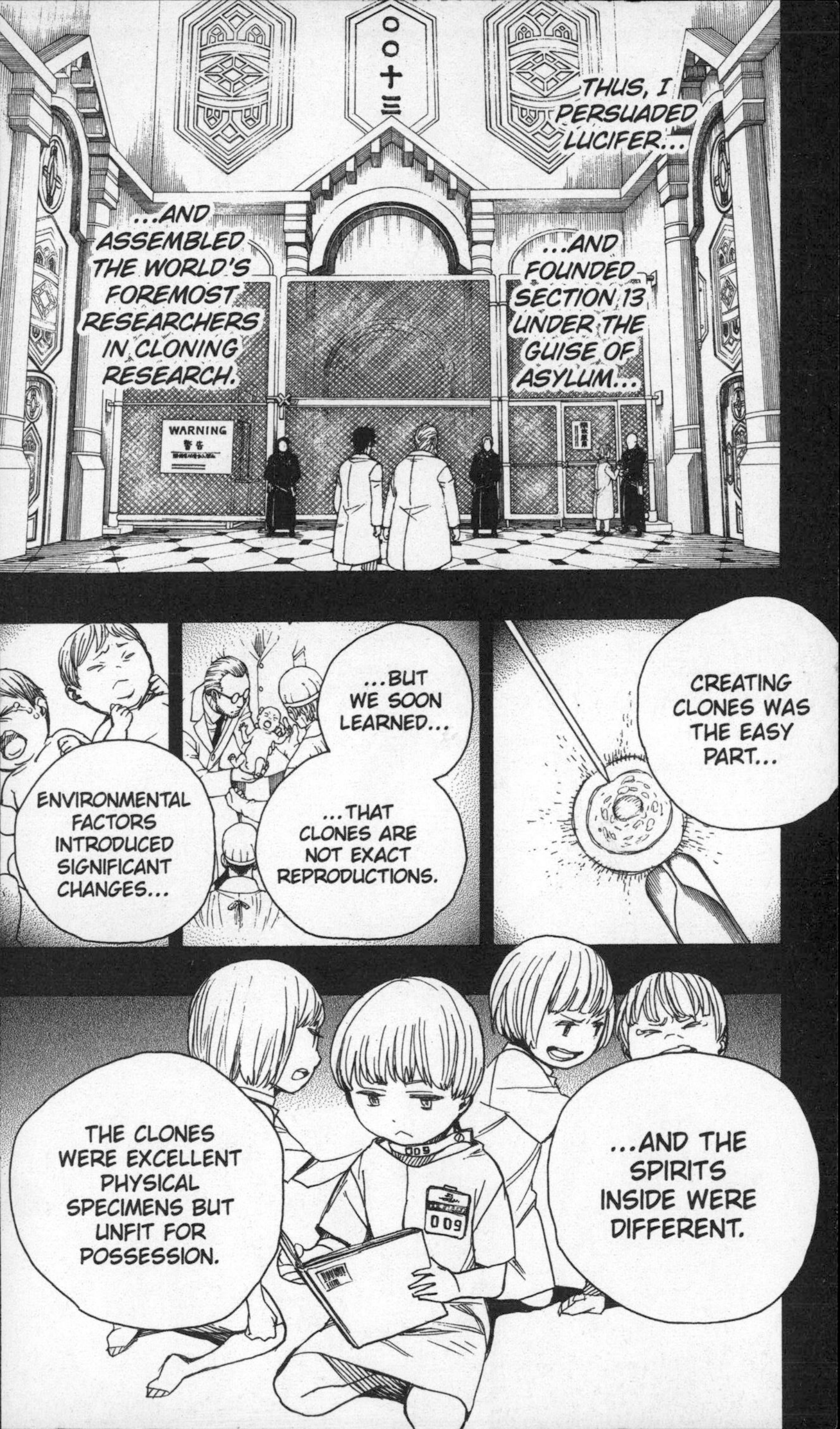
〇〇十三
THUS, I PERSUADED LUCIFER...
...AND FOUNDED SECTION 13 UNDER THE GUISE OF ASYLUM...
...AND ASSEMBLED THE WORLD'S FOREMOST RESEARCHERS IN CLONING RESEARCH.
WARNING
警告
CREATING CLONES WAS THE EASY PART...
...BUT WE SOON LEARNED...
...THAT CLONES ARE NOT EXACT REPRODUCTIONS.
ENVIRONMENTAL FACTORS INTRODUCED SIGNIFICANT CHANGES...
...AND THE SPIRITS INSIDE WERE DIFFERENT.
009
009
THE CLONES WERE EXCELLENT PHYSICAL SPECIMENS BUT UNFIT FOR POSSESSION.

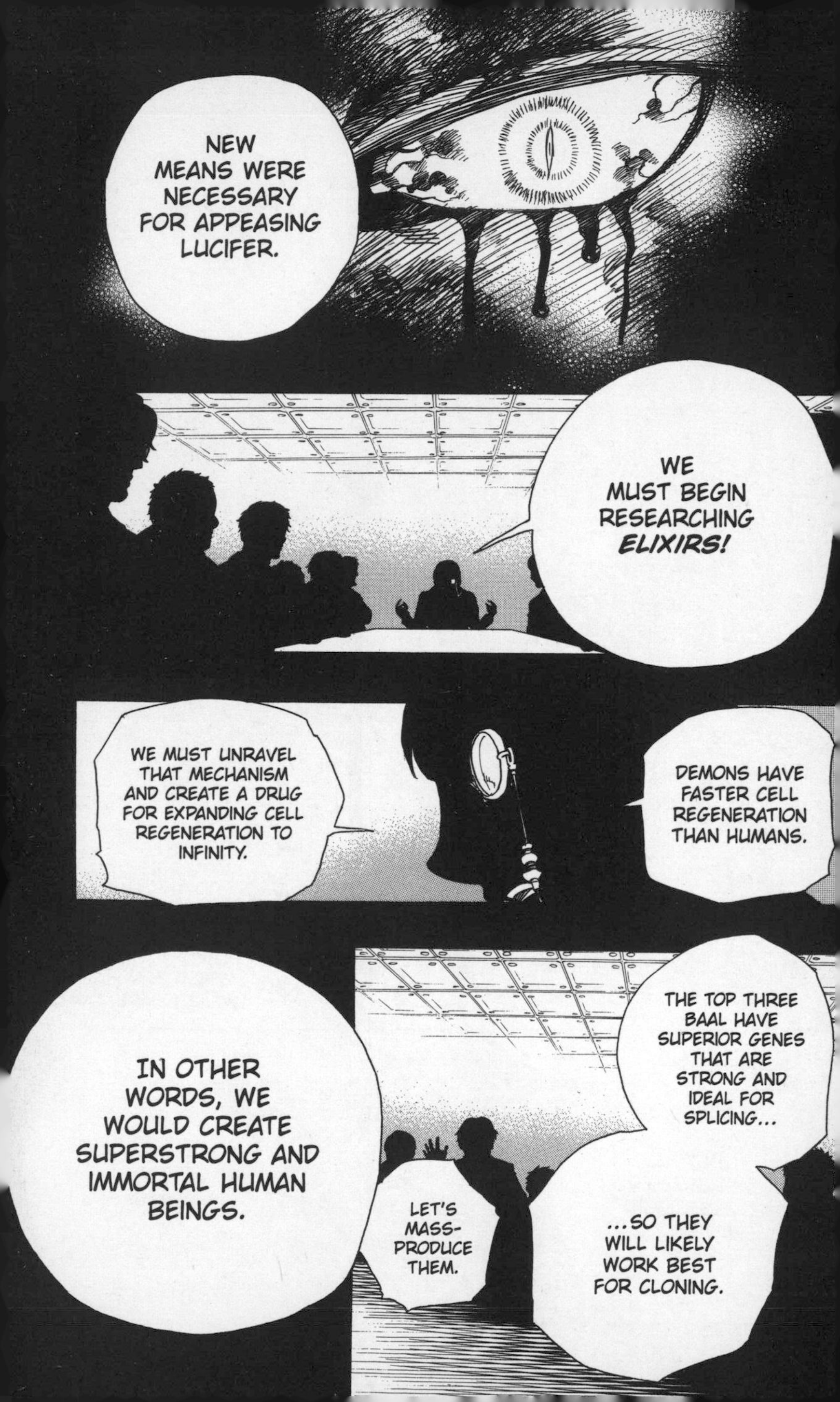
NEW MEANS WERE NECESSARY FOR APPEASING LUCIFER.
WE MUST BEGIN RESEARCHING *ELIXIRS!*
DEMONS HAVE FASTER CELL REGENERATION THAN HUMANS.
WE MUST UNRAVEL THAT MECHANISM AND CREATE A DRUG FOR EXPANDING CELL REGENERATION TO INFINITY.
THE TOP THREE BAAL HAVE SUPERIOR GENES THAT ARE STRONG AND IDEAL FOR SPLICING...
...SO THEY WILL LIKELY WORK BEST FOR CLONING.
LET'S MASS-PRODUCE THEM.
IN OTHER WORDS, WE WOULD CREATE SUPERSTRONG AND IMMORTAL HUMAN BEINGS.

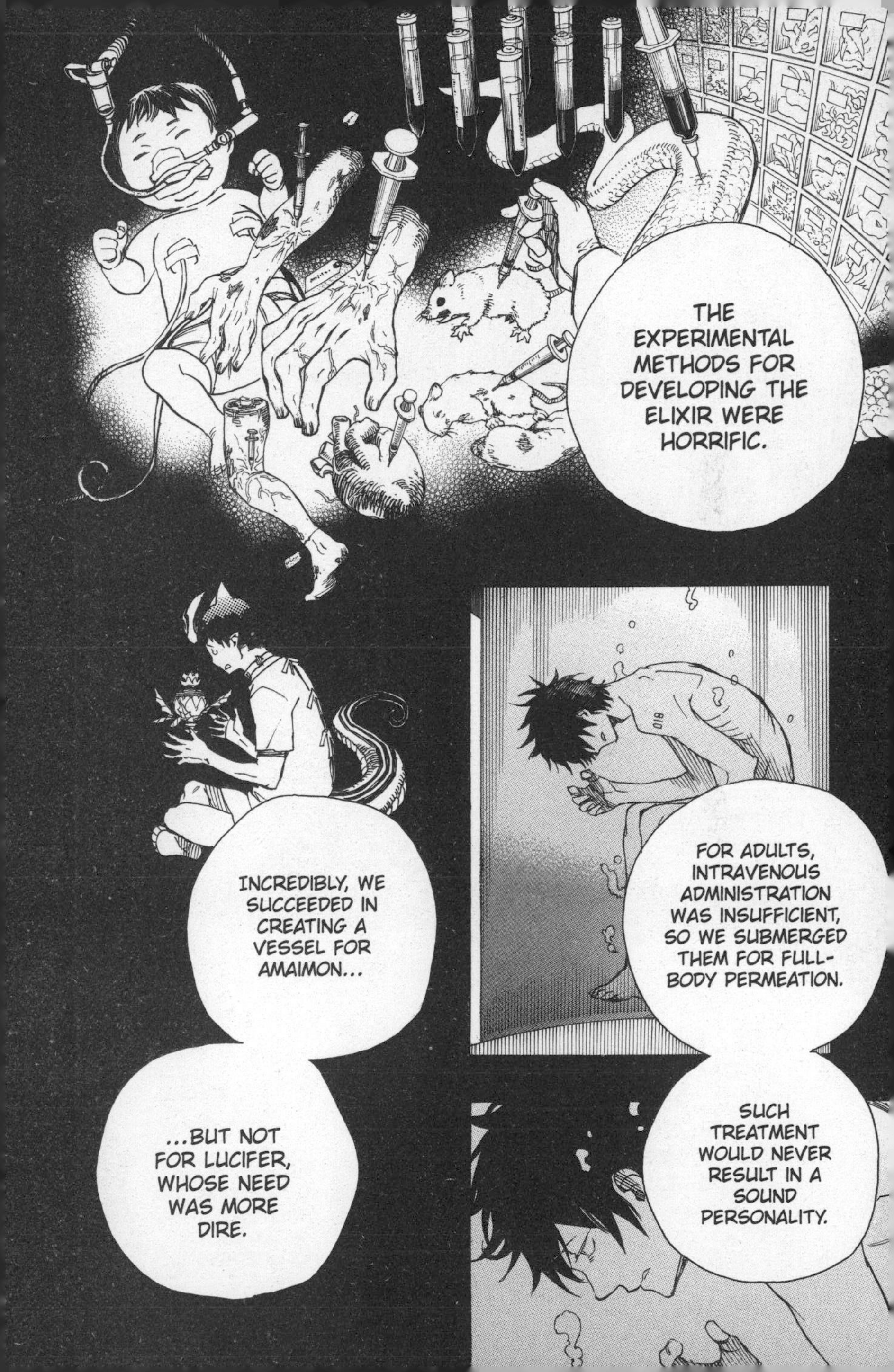
THE EXPERIMENTAL METHODS FOR DEVELOPING THE ELIXIR WERE HORRIFIC.
FOR ADULTS, INTRAVENOUS ADMINISTRATION WAS INSUFFICIENT, SO WE SUBMERGED THEM FOR FULL-BODY PERMEATION.
SUCH TREATMENT WOULD NEVER RESULT IN A SOUND PERSONALITY.
INCREDIBLY, WE SUCCEEDED IN CREATING A VESSEL FOR AMAIMON...
...BUT NOT FOR LUCIFER, WHOSE NEED WAS MORE DIRE.

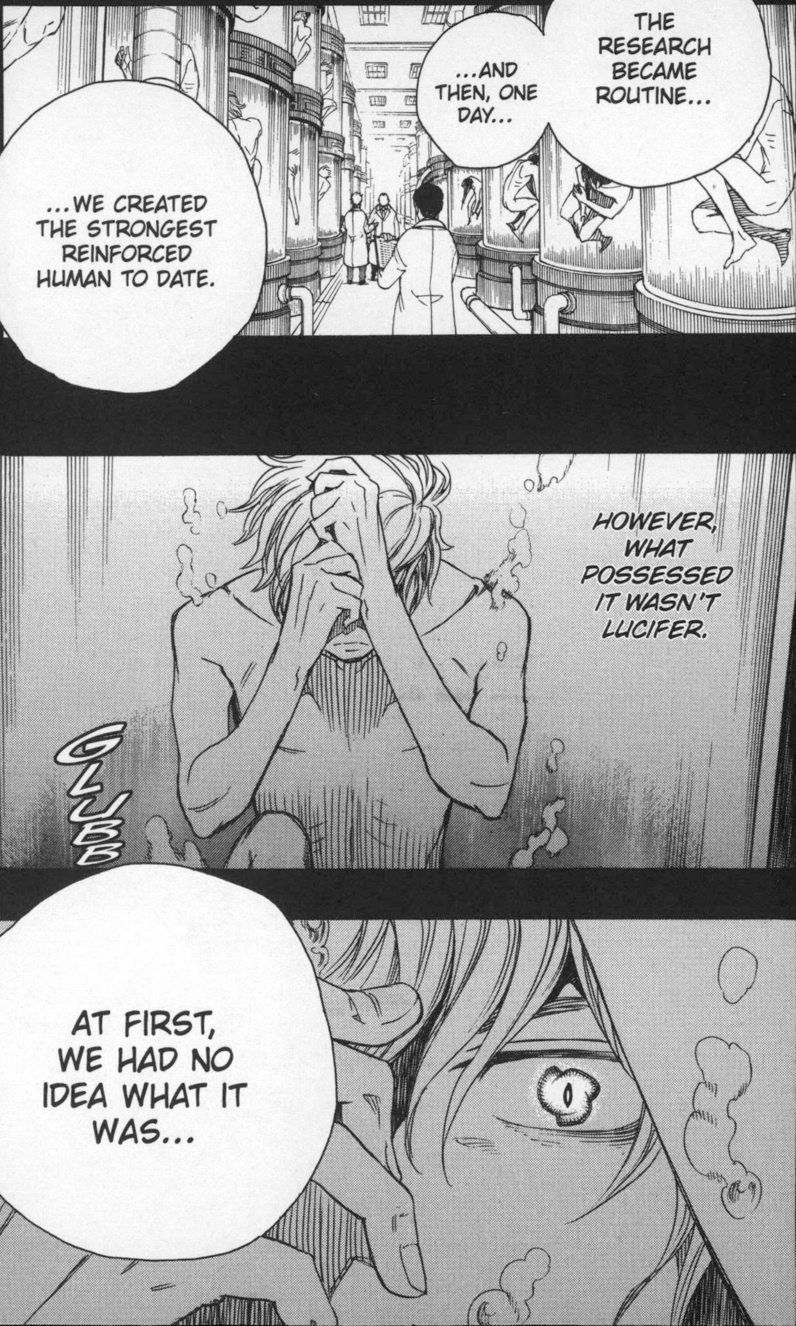
THE RESEARCH BECAME ROUTINE...
...AND THEN, ONE DAY...
...WE CREATED THE STRONGEST REINFORCED HUMAN TO DATE.
HOWEVER, WHAT POSSESSED IT WASN'T LUCIFER.
GLUBB
AT FIRST, WE HAD NO IDEA WHAT IT WAS...

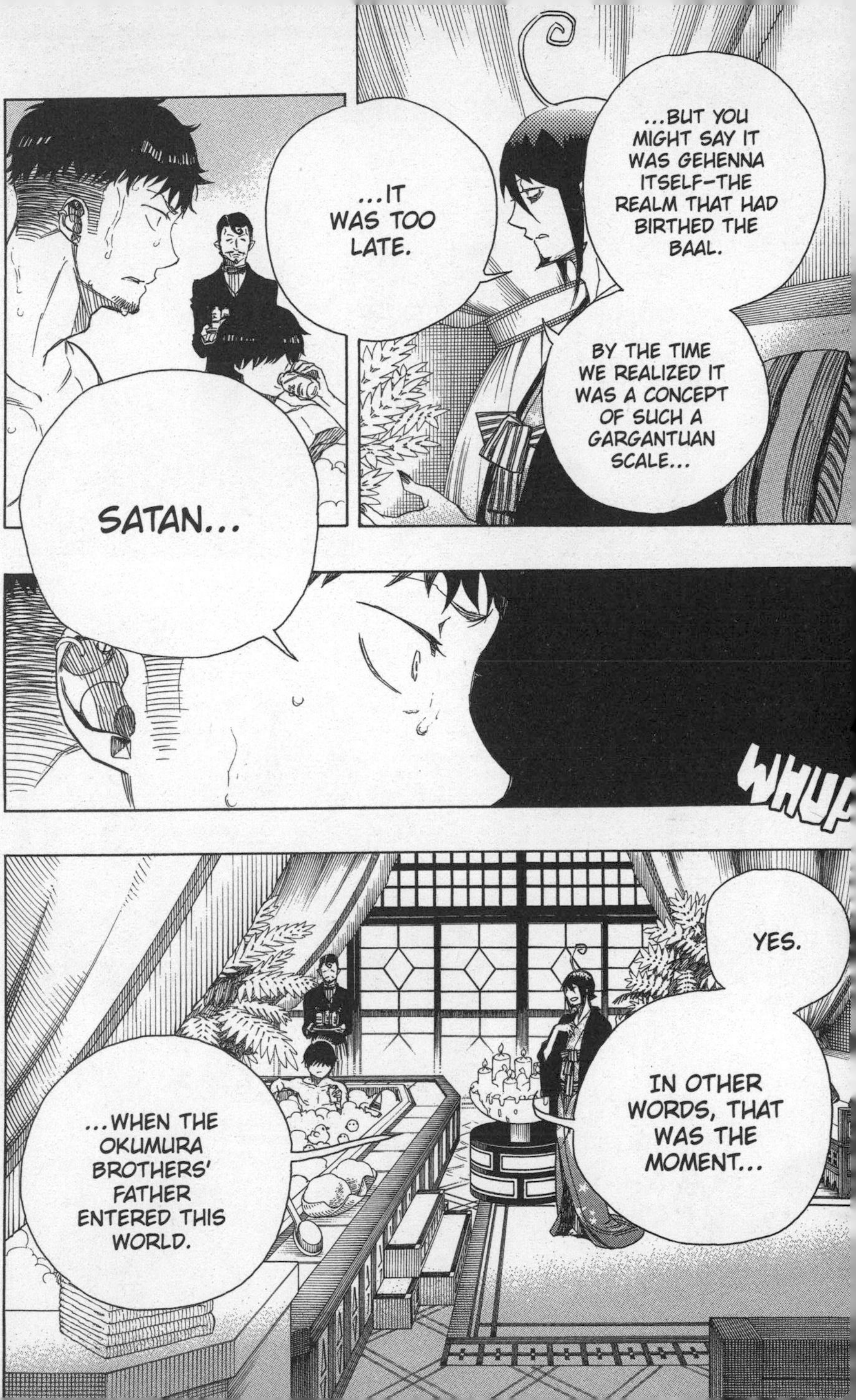
...BUT YOU MIGHT SAY IT WAS GEHENNA ITSELF—THE REALM THAT HAD BIRTHED THE BAAL.
BY THE TIME WE REALIZED IT WAS A CONCEPT OF SUCH A GARGANTUAN SCALE...
...IT WAS TOO LATE.
SATAN...
WHUP
YES.
IN OTHER WORDS, THAT WAS THE MOMENT...
...WHEN THE OKUMURA BROTHERS' FATHER ENTERED THIS WORLD.

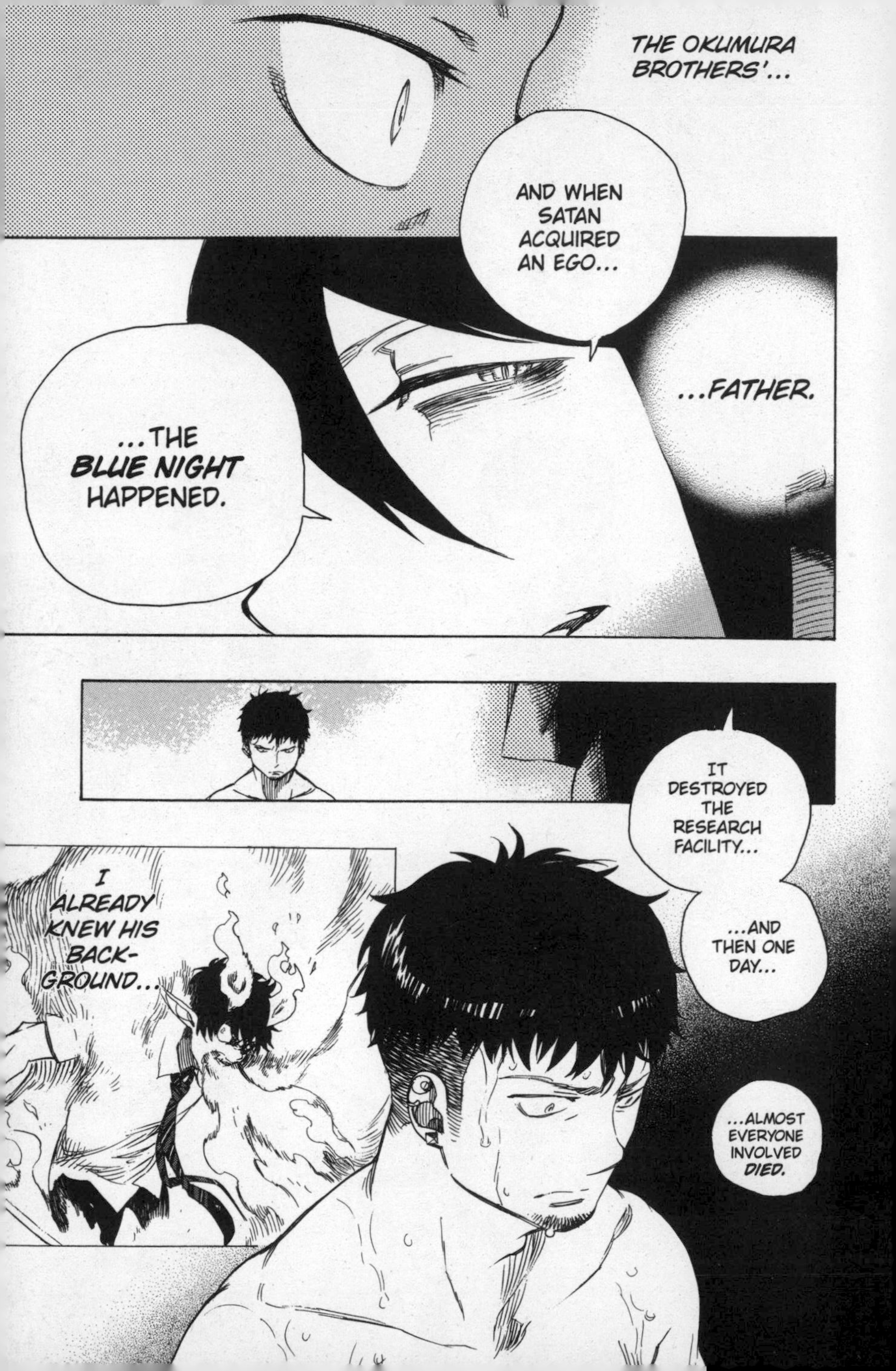
THE OKUMURA BROTHERS'...
AND WHEN SATAN ACQUIRED AN EGO...
...FATHER.
...THE BLUE NIGHT HAPPENED.
IT DESTROYED THE RESEARCH FACILITY...
...AND THEN ONE DAY...
...ALMOST EVERYONE INVOLVED DIED.
I ALREADY KNEW HIS BACK-GROUND...

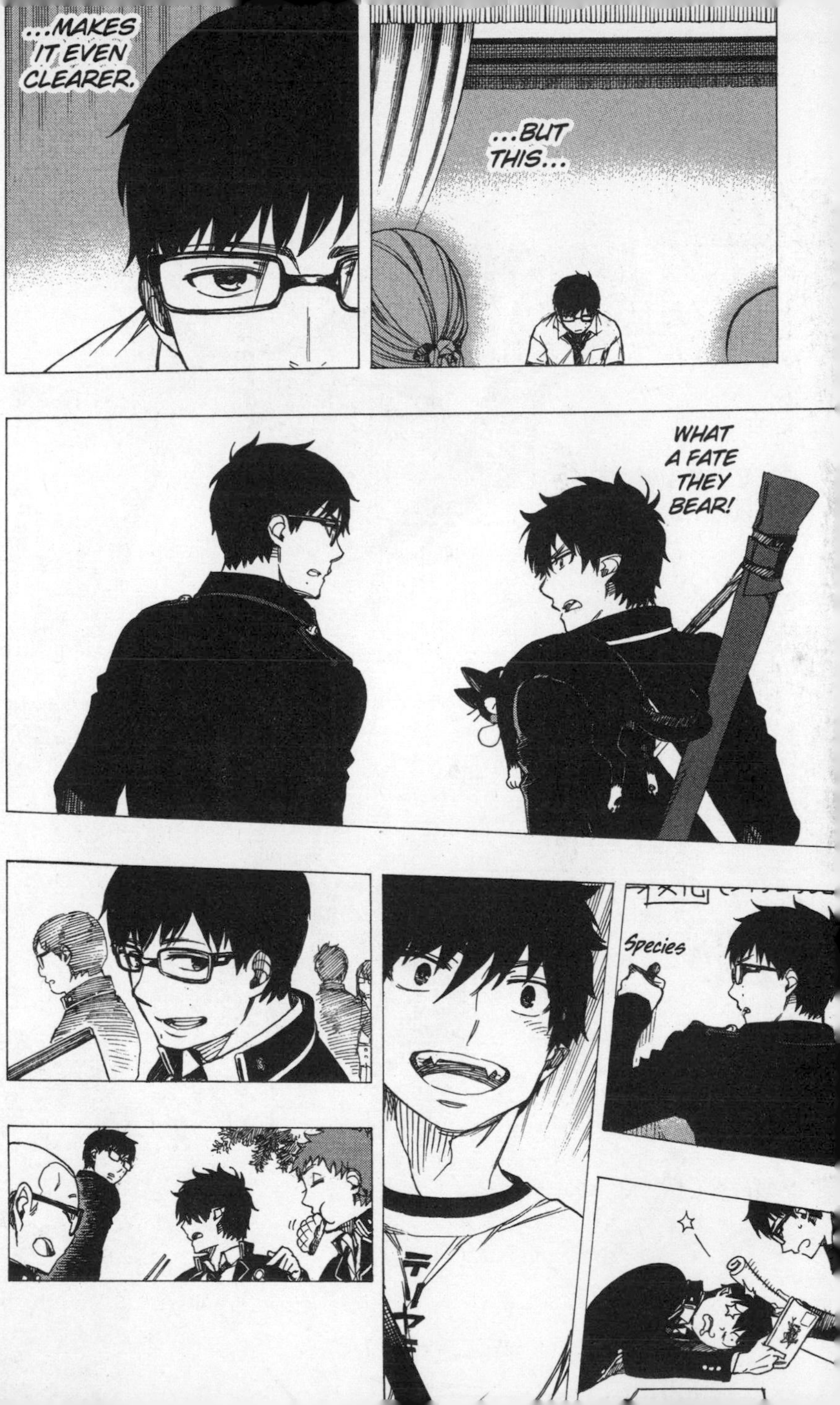
...BUT THIS...
...MAKES IT EVEN CLEARER.
WHAT A FATE THEY BEAR!
Species

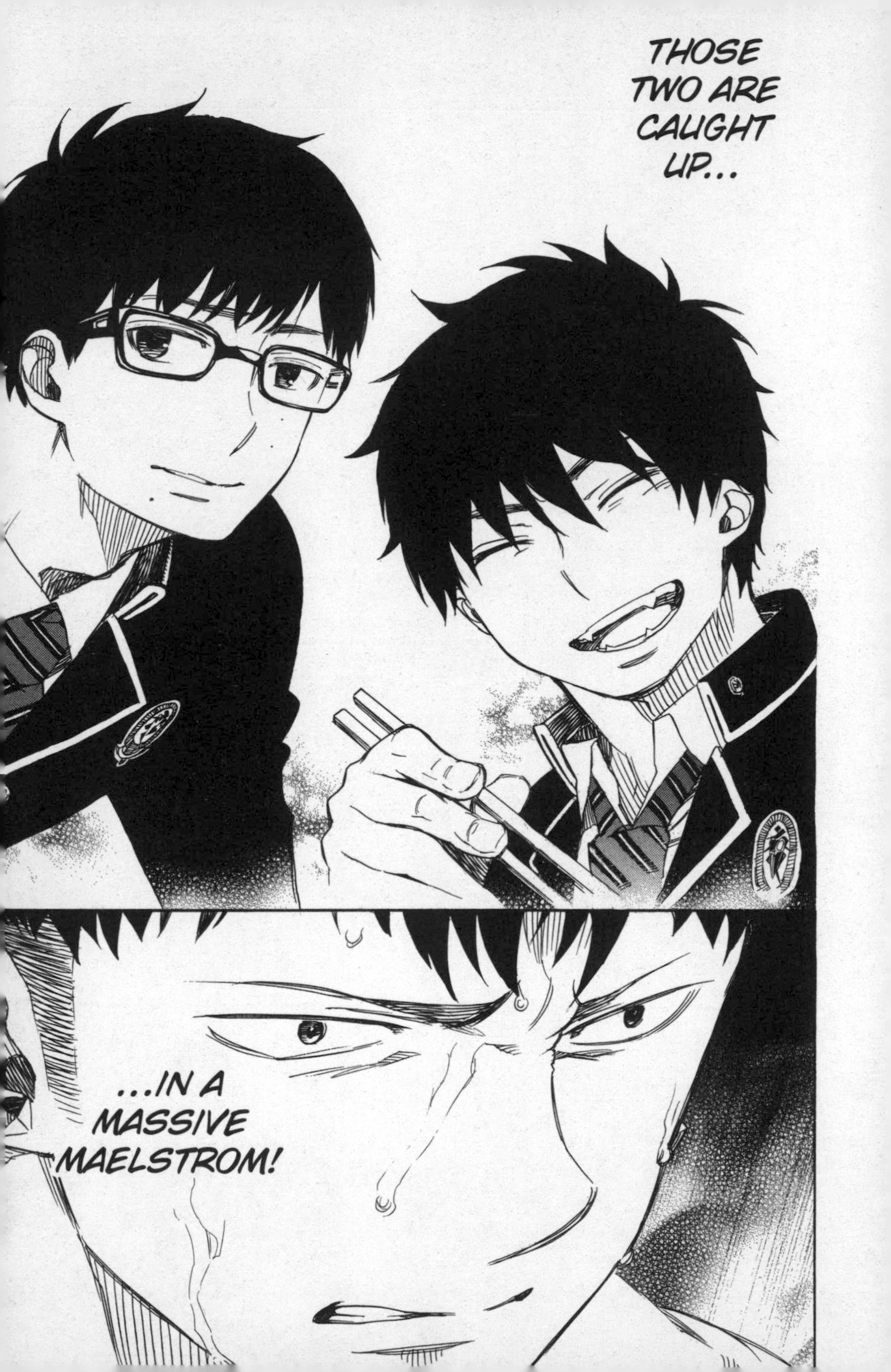
THOSE TWO ARE CAUGHT UP...
...IN A MASSIVE MAELSTROM!

Blue Exorcist Chapter 86: Fruit Branches

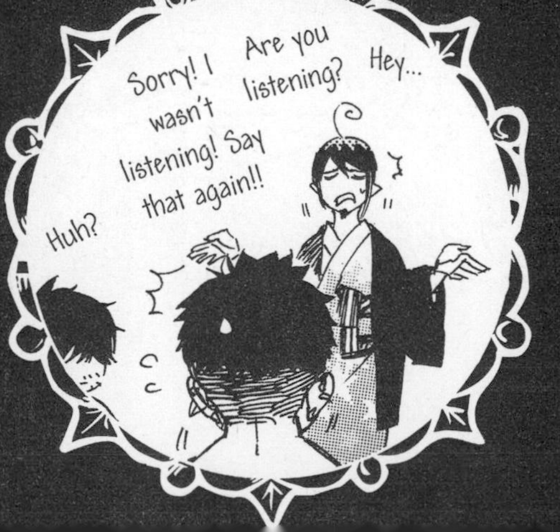

Hey...
Are you listening?
Sorry! I wasn't listening! Say that again!!
Huh?

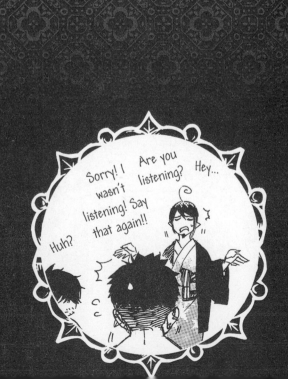

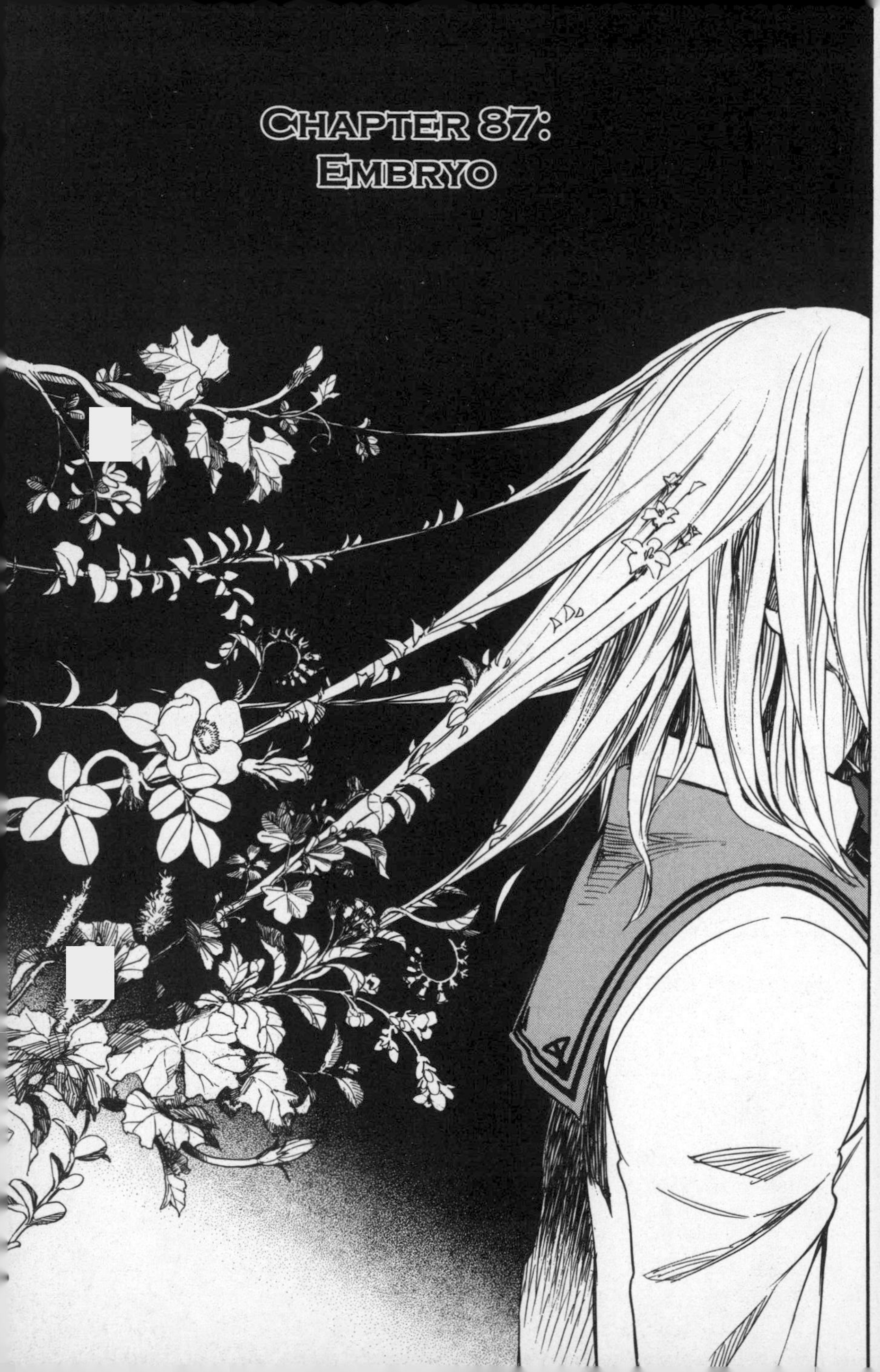
Chapter 87:
Embryo

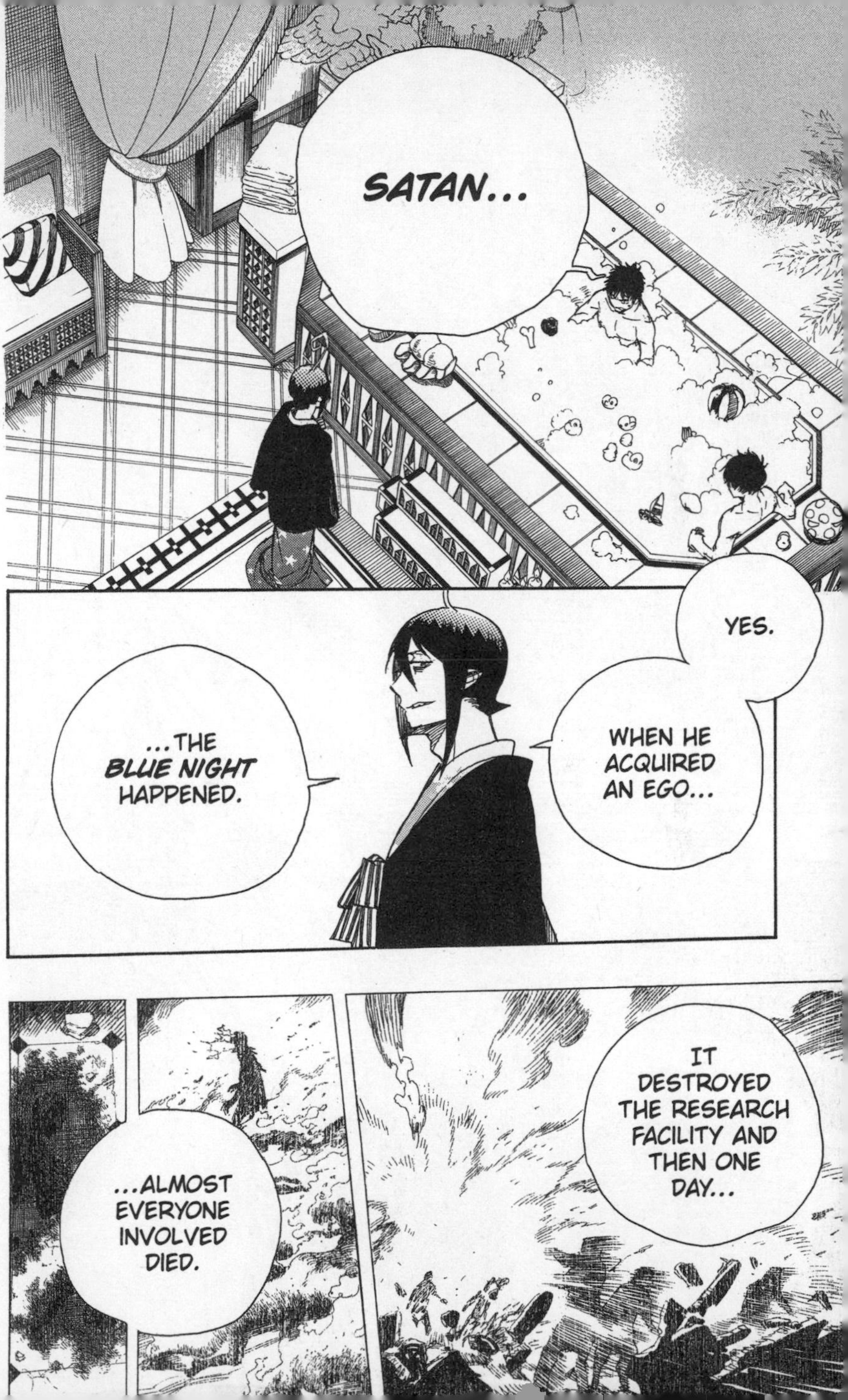
SATAN...
YES.
WHEN HE ACQUIRED AN EGO...
...THE *BLUE NIGHT* HAPPENED.
IT DESTROYED THE RESEARCH FACILITY AND THEN ONE DAY...
...ALMOST EVERYONE INVOLVED DIED.

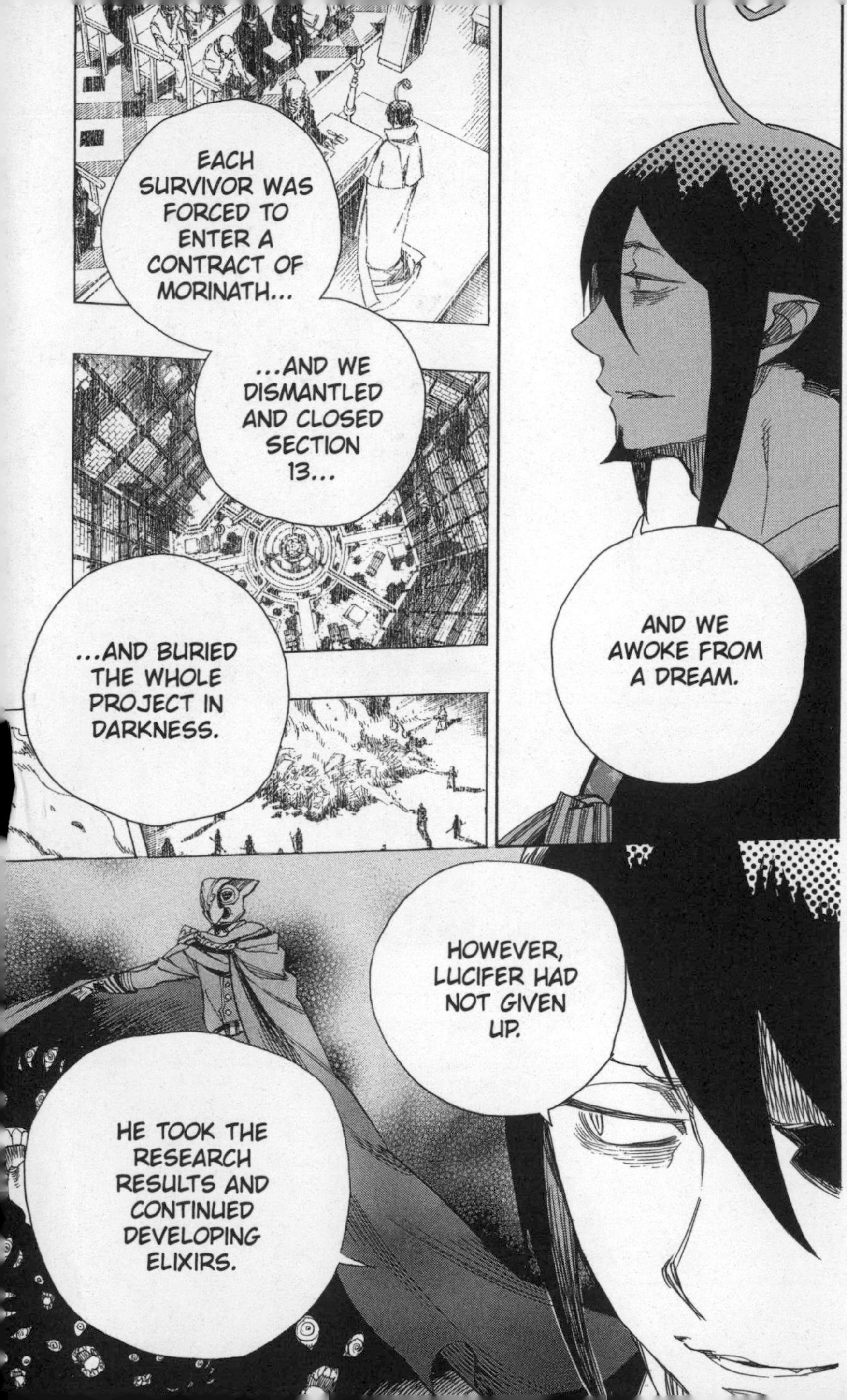
AND WE AWOKE FROM A DREAM.
EACH SURVIVOR WAS FORCED TO ENTER A CONTRACT OF MORINATH...
...AND WE DISMANTLED AND CLOSED SECTION 13...
...AND BURIED THE WHOLE PROJECT IN DARKNESS.
HOWEVER, LUCIFER HAD NOT GIVEN UP.
HE TOOK THE RESEARCH RESULTS AND CONTINUED DEVELOPING ELIXIRS.

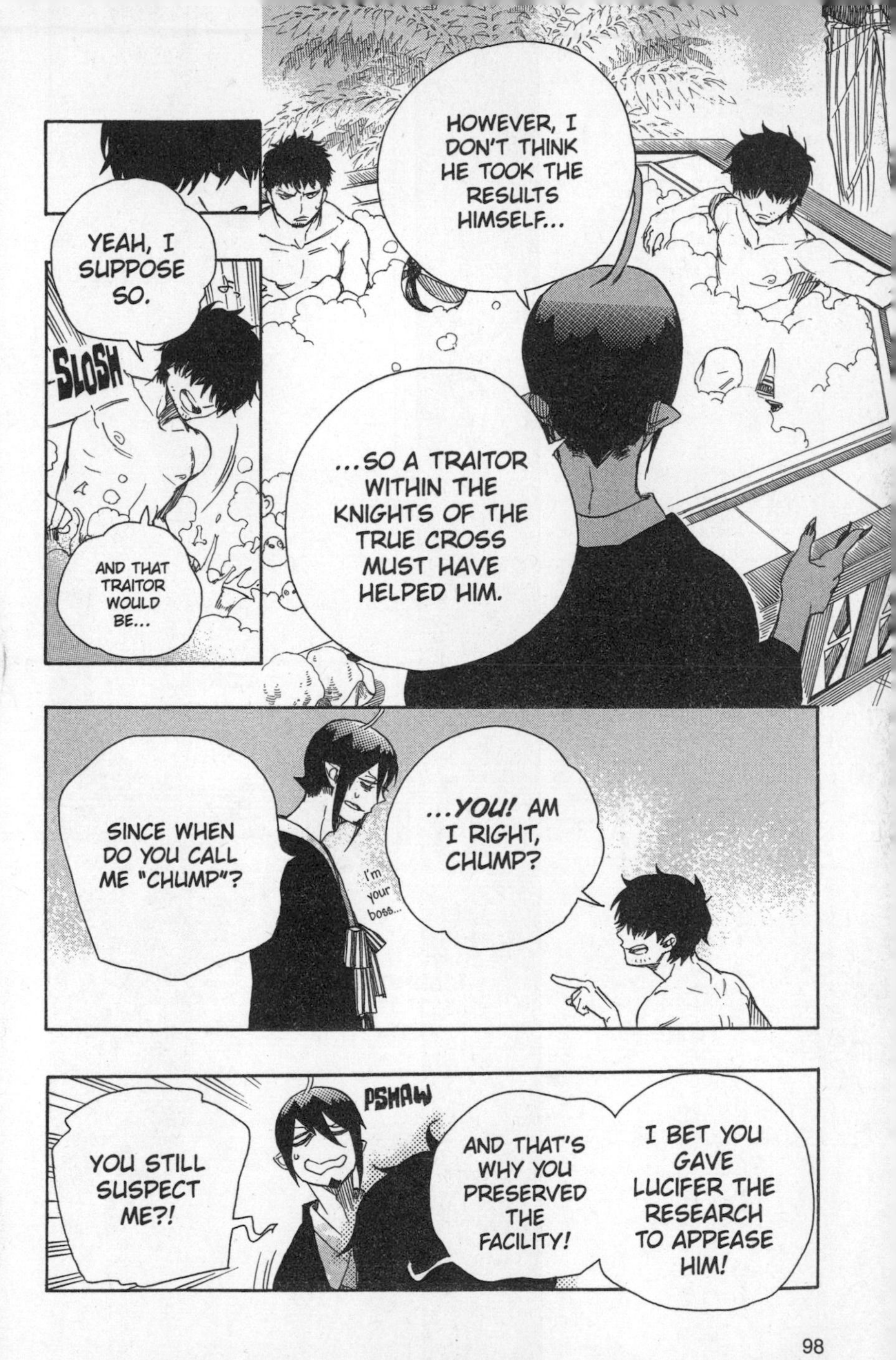
HOWEVER, I DON'T THINK HE TOOK THE RESULTS HIMSELF...
...SO A TRAITOR WITHIN THE KNIGHTS OF THE TRUE CROSS MUST HAVE HELPED HIM.
YEAH, I SUPPOSE SO.
SLOSH
AND THAT TRAITOR WOULD BE...
...*YOU!* AM I RIGHT, CHUMP?
SINCE WHEN DO YOU CALL ME "CHUMP"?
I'm your boss...
I BET YOU GAVE LUCIFER THE RESEARCH TO APPEASE HIM!
AND THAT'S WHY YOU PRESERVED THE FACILITY!
PSHAW
YOU STILL SUSPECT ME?!

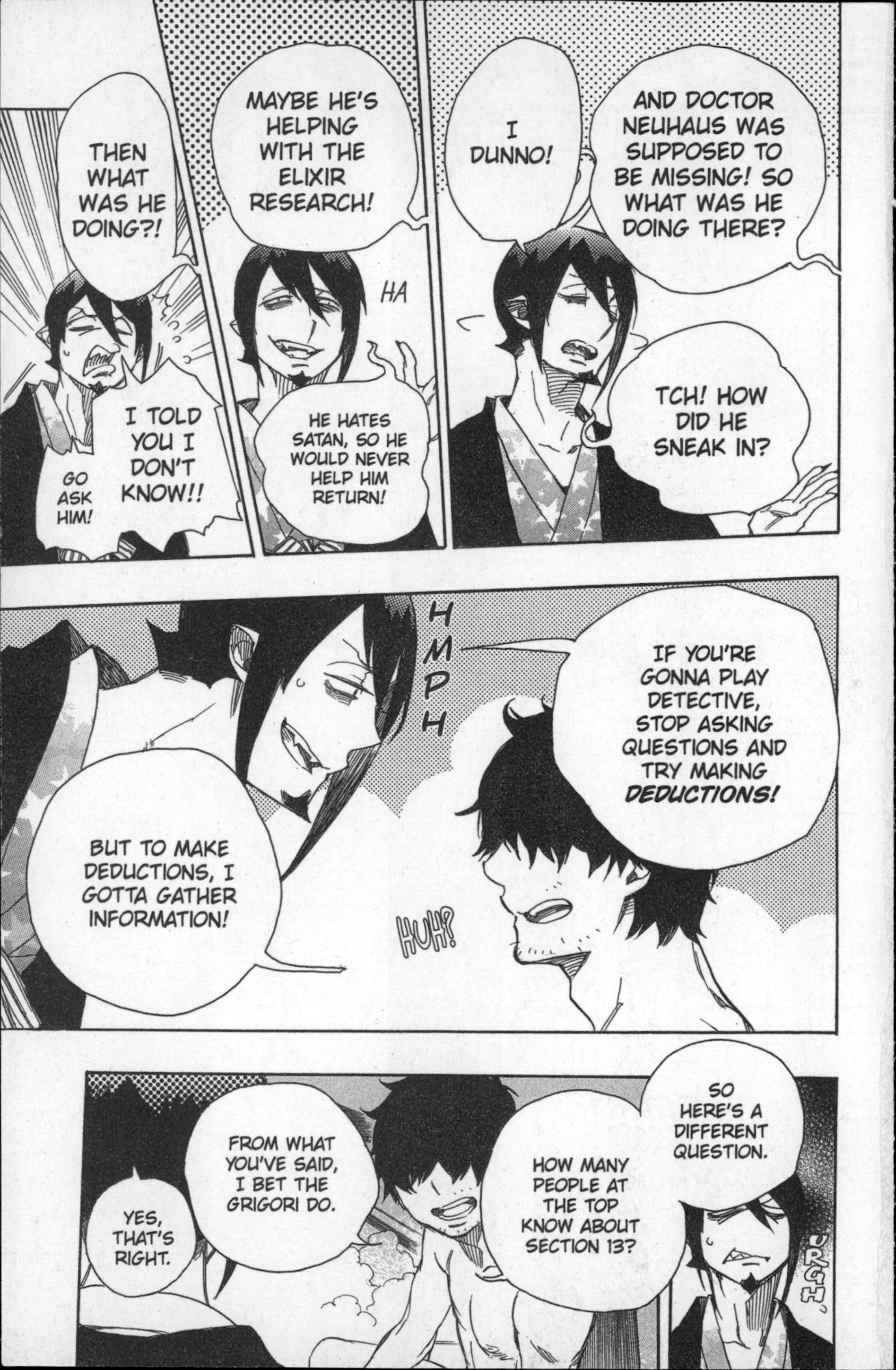
AND DOCTOR NEUHAUS WAS SUPPOSED TO BE MISSING! SO WHAT WAS HE DOING THERE?
I DUNNO!
TCH! HOW DID HE SNEAK IN?
MAYBE HE'S HELPING WITH THE ELIXIR RESEARCH!
HA
HE HATES SATAN, SO HE WOULD NEVER HELP HIM RETURN!
THEN WHAT WAS HE DOING?!
I TOLD YOU I DON'T KNOW!!
GO ASK HIM!
IF YOU'RE GONNA PLAY DETECTIVE, STOP ASKING QUESTIONS AND TRY MAKING DEDUCTIONS!
HMPH
HUH?
BUT TO MAKE DEDUCTIONS, I GOTTA GATHER INFORMATION!
SO HERE'S A DIFFERENT QUESTION.
URGH
HOW MANY PEOPLE AT THE TOP KNOW ABOUT SECTION 13?
FROM WHAT YOU'VE SAID, I BET THE GRIGORI DO.
YES, THAT'S RIGHT.

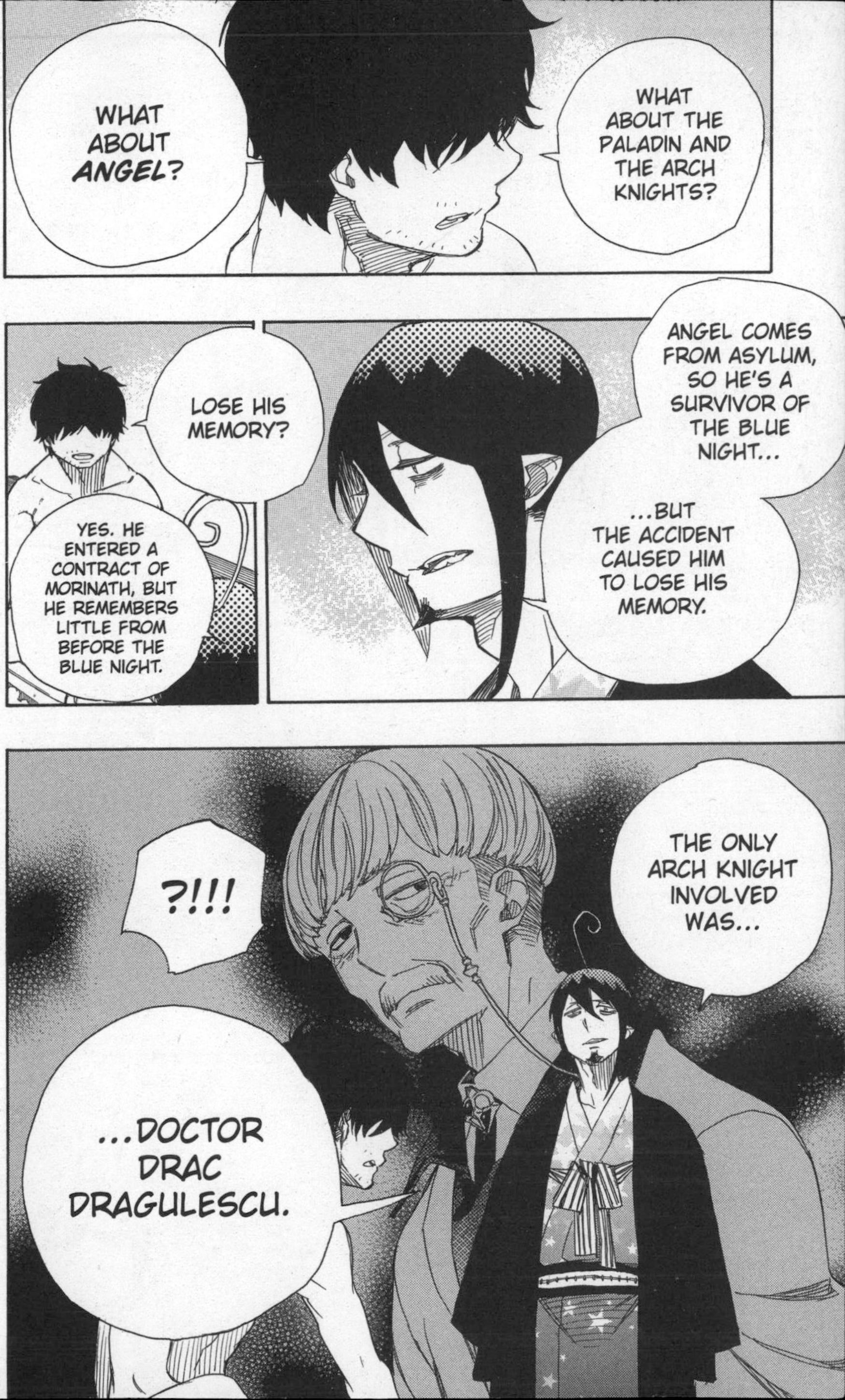
WHAT ABOUT THE PALADIN AND THE ARCH KNIGHTS?
WHAT ABOUT ANGEL?
ANGEL COMES FROM ASYLUM, SO HE'S A SURVIVOR OF THE BLUE NIGHT...
...BUT THE ACCIDENT CAUSED HIM TO LOSE HIS MEMORY.
LOSE HIS MEMORY?
YES. HE ENTERED A CONTRACT OF MORINATH, BUT HE REMEMBERS LITTLE FROM BEFORE THE BLUE NIGHT.
THE ONLY ARCH KNIGHT INVOLVED WAS...
?!!!
...DOCTOR DRAC DRAGULESCU.

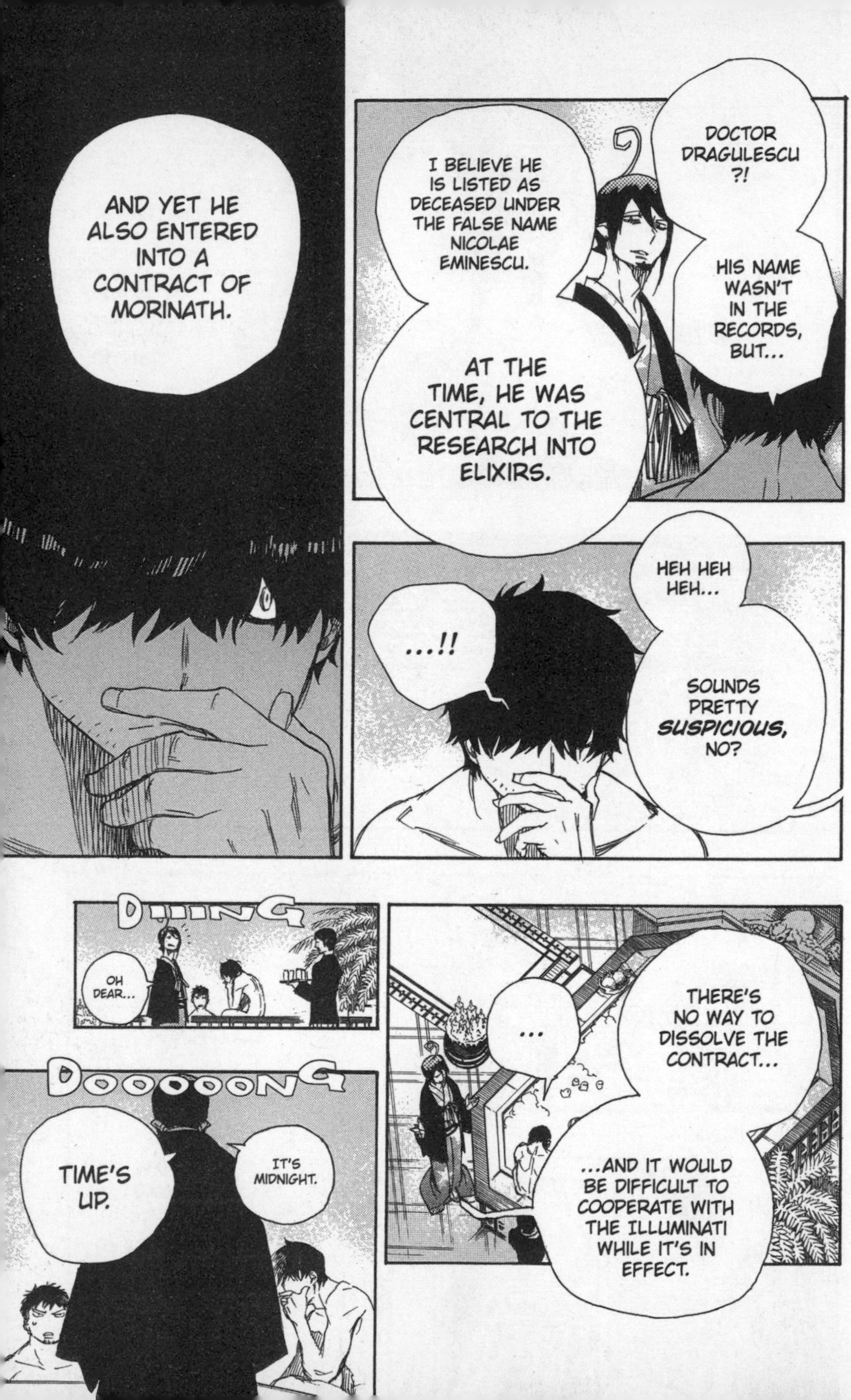
DOCTOR DRAGULESCU ?!
HIS NAME WASN'T IN THE RECORDS, BUT...
I BELIEVE HE IS LISTED AS DECEASED UNDER THE FALSE NAME NICOLAE EMINESCU.
AT THE TIME, HE WAS CENTRAL TO THE RESEARCH INTO ELIXIRS.
HEH HEH HEH...
SOUNDS PRETTY SUSPICIOUS, NO?
...!!
AND YET HE ALSO ENTERED INTO A CONTRACT OF MORINATH.
THERE'S NO WAY TO DISSOLVE THE CONTRACT...
...
...AND IT WOULD BE DIFFICULT TO COOPERATE WITH THE ILLUMINATI WHILE IT'S IN EFFECT.
DIIING
OH DEAR...
DOOOOONG
IT'S MIDNIGHT.
TIME'S UP.

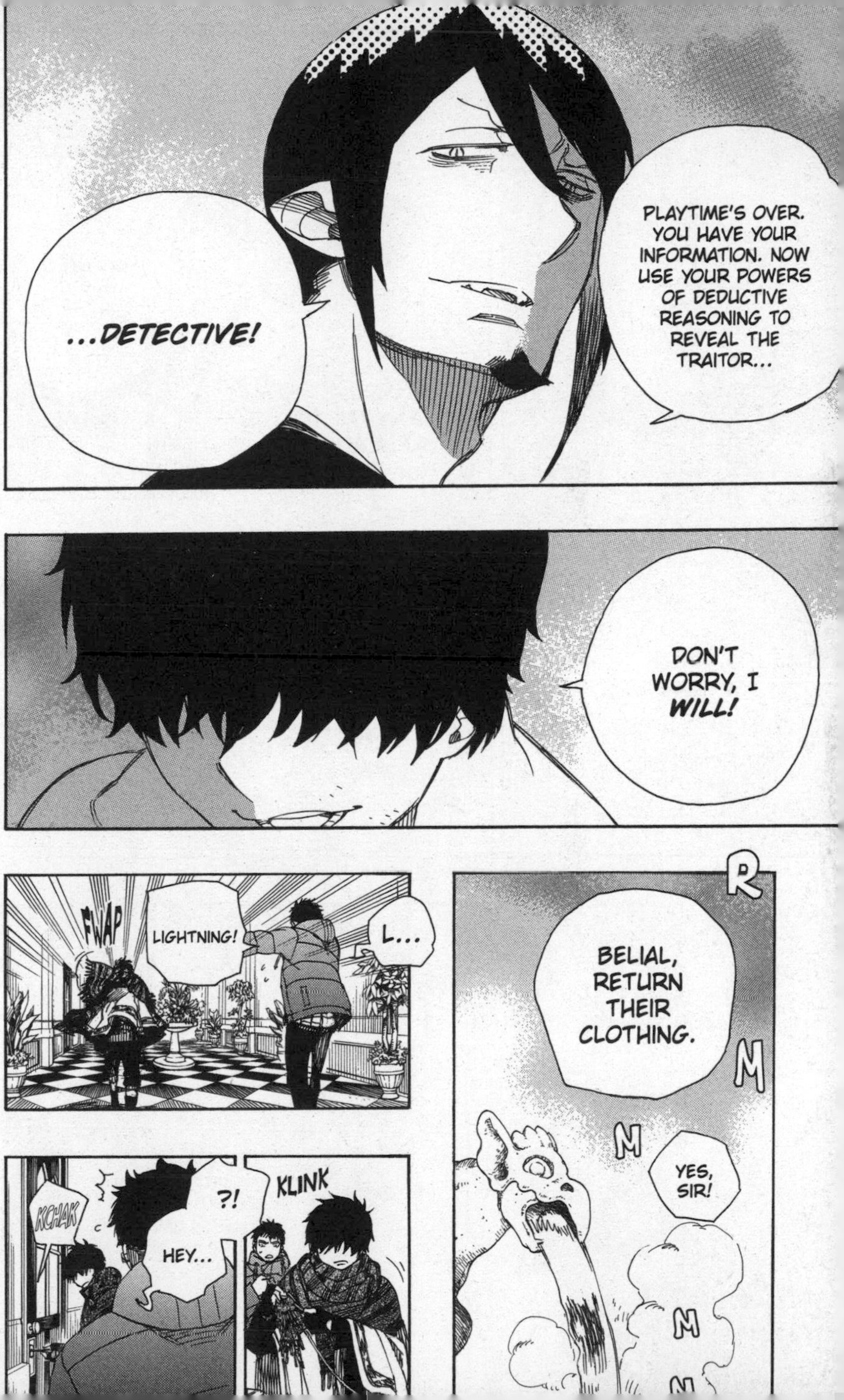
PLAYTIME'S OVER. YOU HAVE YOUR INFORMATION. NOW USE YOUR POWERS OF DEDUCTIVE REASONING TO REVEAL THE TRAITOR...
...DETECTIVE!
DON'T WORRY, I WILL!
RMMMM
BELIAL, RETURN THEIR CLOTHING.
YES, SIR!
L...
LIGHTNING!
FWAP
KLINK
?!
KCHAK
HEY...

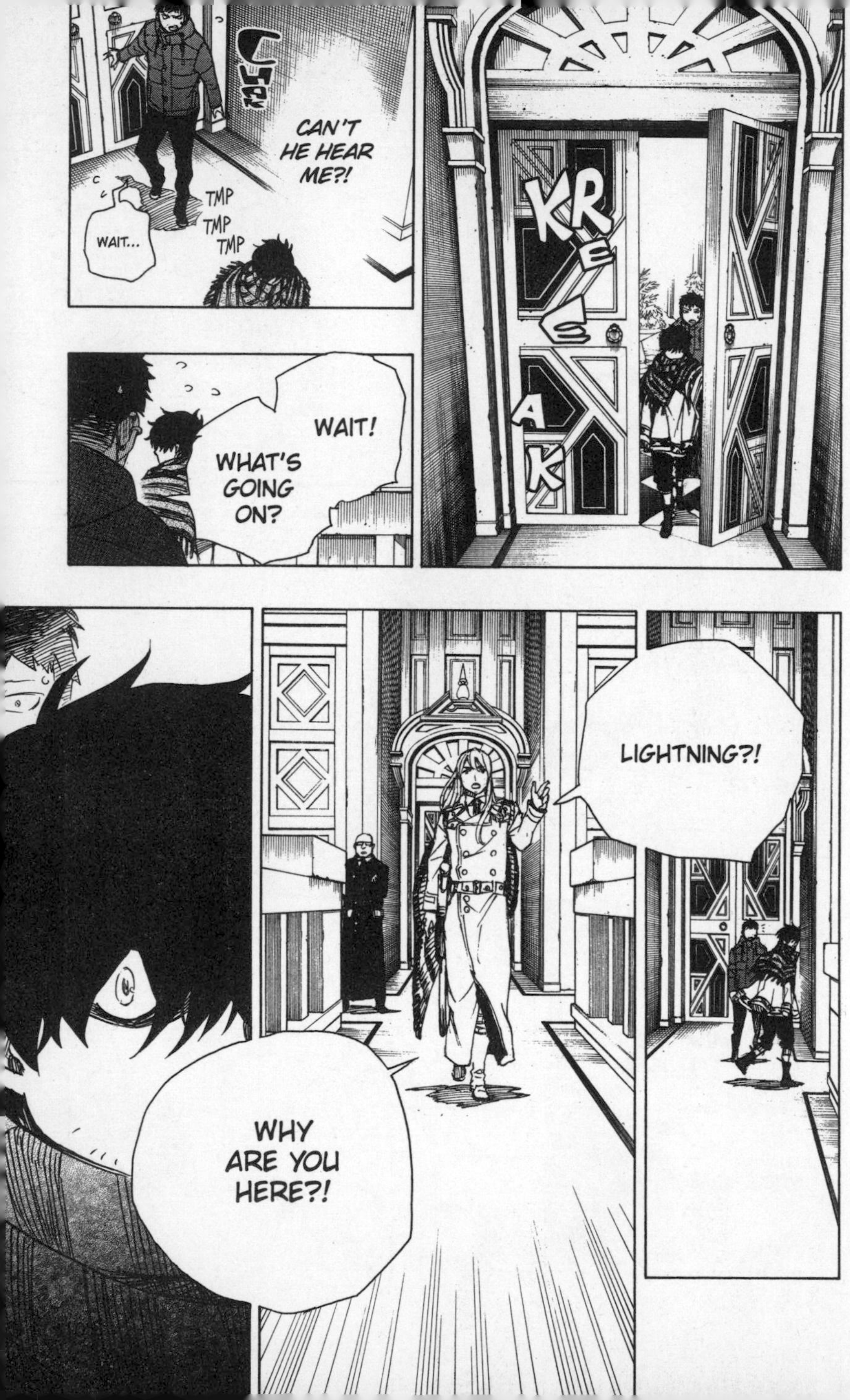
KREEAK
CHAK
CAN'T HE HEAR ME?!
TMP TMP TMP
WAIT...
WAIT! WHAT'S GOING ON?
LIGHTNING?!
WHY ARE YOU HERE?!

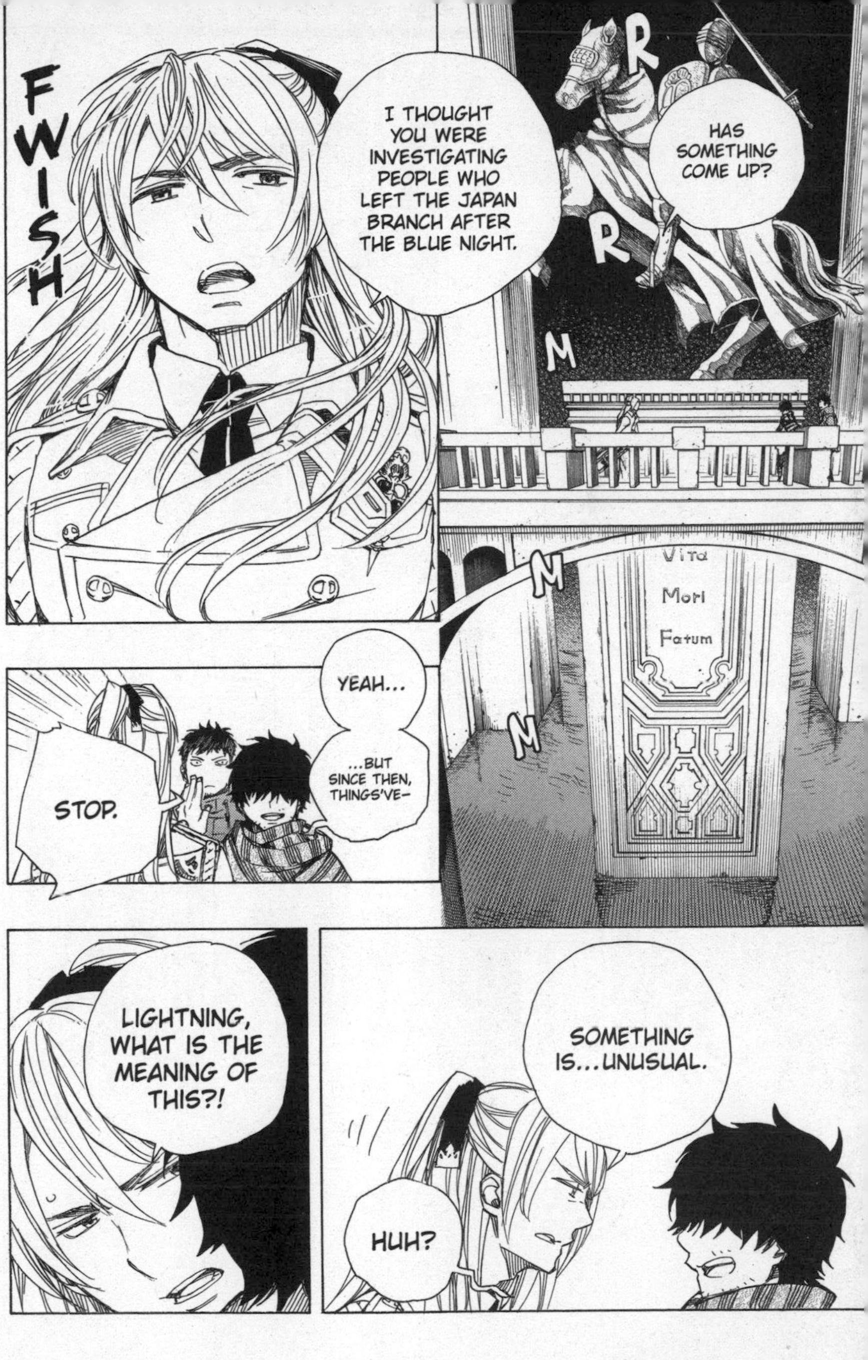
HAS SOMETHING COME UP?
RRMMMM
I THOUGHT YOU WERE INVESTIGATING PEOPLE WHO LEFT THE JAPAN BRANCH AFTER THE BLUE NIGHT.
FWISH
Vita
Mori
Fatum
YEAH...
...BUT SINCE THEN, THINGS'VE-
STOP.
SOMETHING IS...UNUSUAL.
HUH?
LIGHTNING, WHAT IS THE MEANING OF THIS?!

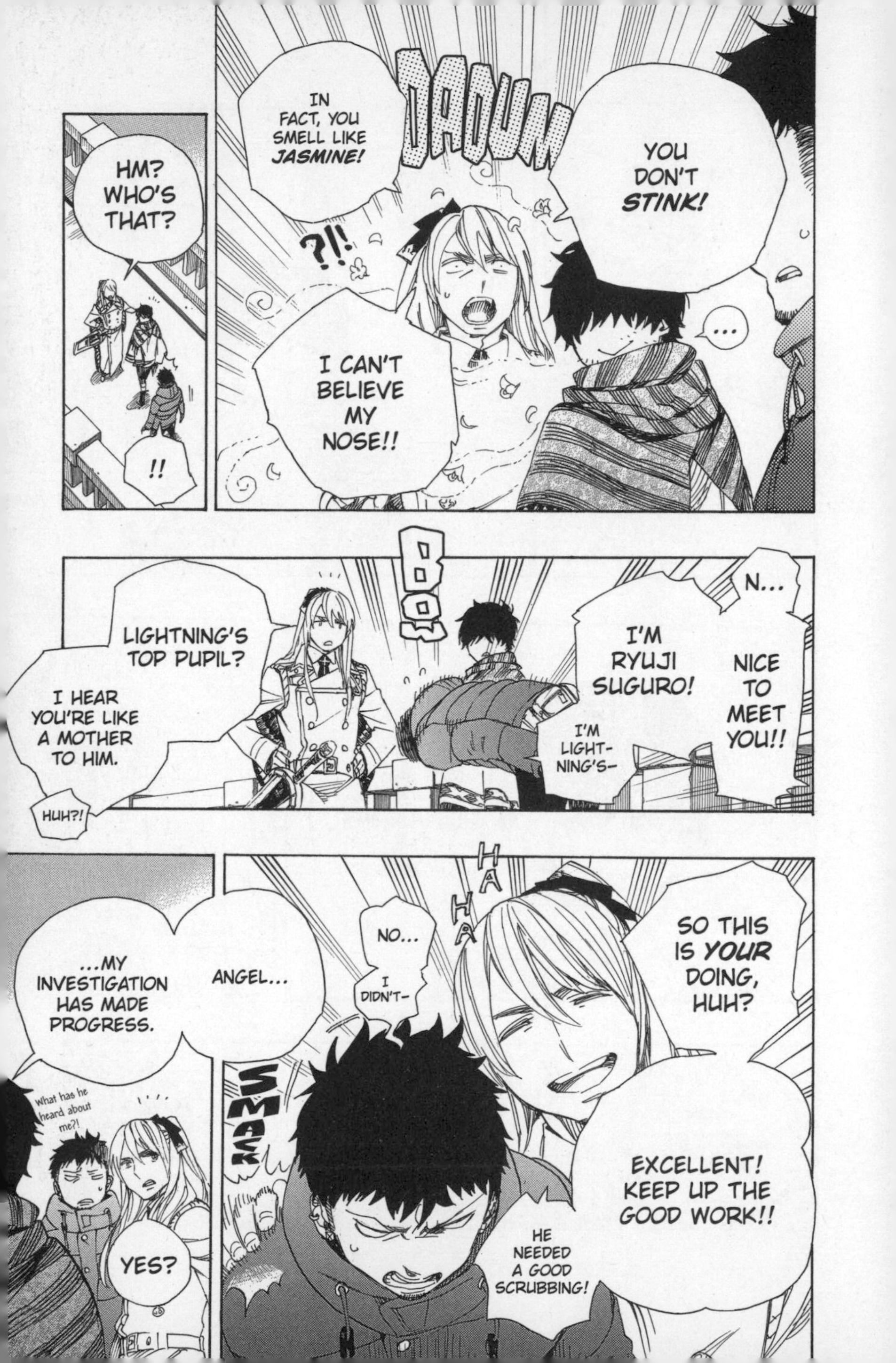
YOU DON'T STINK!
...
DADUM
IN FACT, YOU SMELL LIKE JASMINE!
?!!
I CAN'T BELIEVE MY NOSE!!
HM? WHO'S THAT?
!!
N...
NICE TO MEET YOU!!
I'M RYUJI SUGURO!
I'M LIGHT-NING'S-
BOW
LIGHTNING'S TOP PUPIL?
I HEAR YOU'RE LIKE A MOTHER TO HIM.
HUH?!
HA HA
SO THIS IS YOUR DOING, HUH?
NO...
I DIDN'T-
SMACK
EXCELLENT! KEEP UP THE GOOD WORK!!
HE NEEDED A GOOD SCRUBBING!
ANGEL...
...MY INVESTIGATION HAS MADE PROGRESS.
what has he heard about me?!
YES?

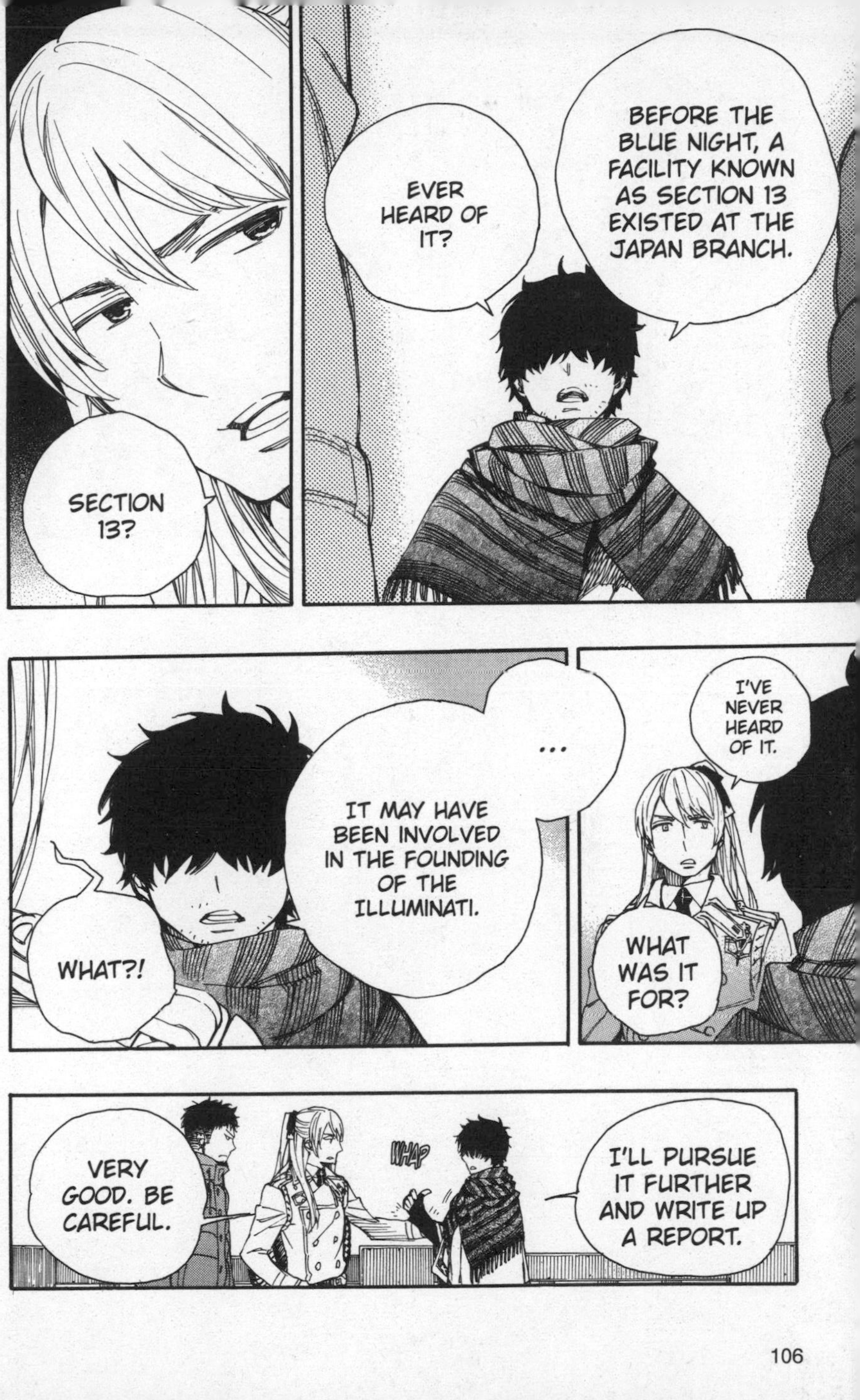
BEFORE THE BLUE NIGHT, A FACILITY KNOWN AS SECTION 13 EXISTED AT THE JAPAN BRANCH.
EVER HEARD OF IT?
SECTION 13?
I'VE NEVER HEARD OF IT.
WHAT WAS IT FOR?
...
IT MAY HAVE BEEN INVOLVED IN THE FOUNDING OF THE ILLUMINATI.
WHAT?!
I'LL PURSUE IT FURTHER AND WRITE UP A REPORT.
WHAP
VERY GOOD. BE CAREFUL.

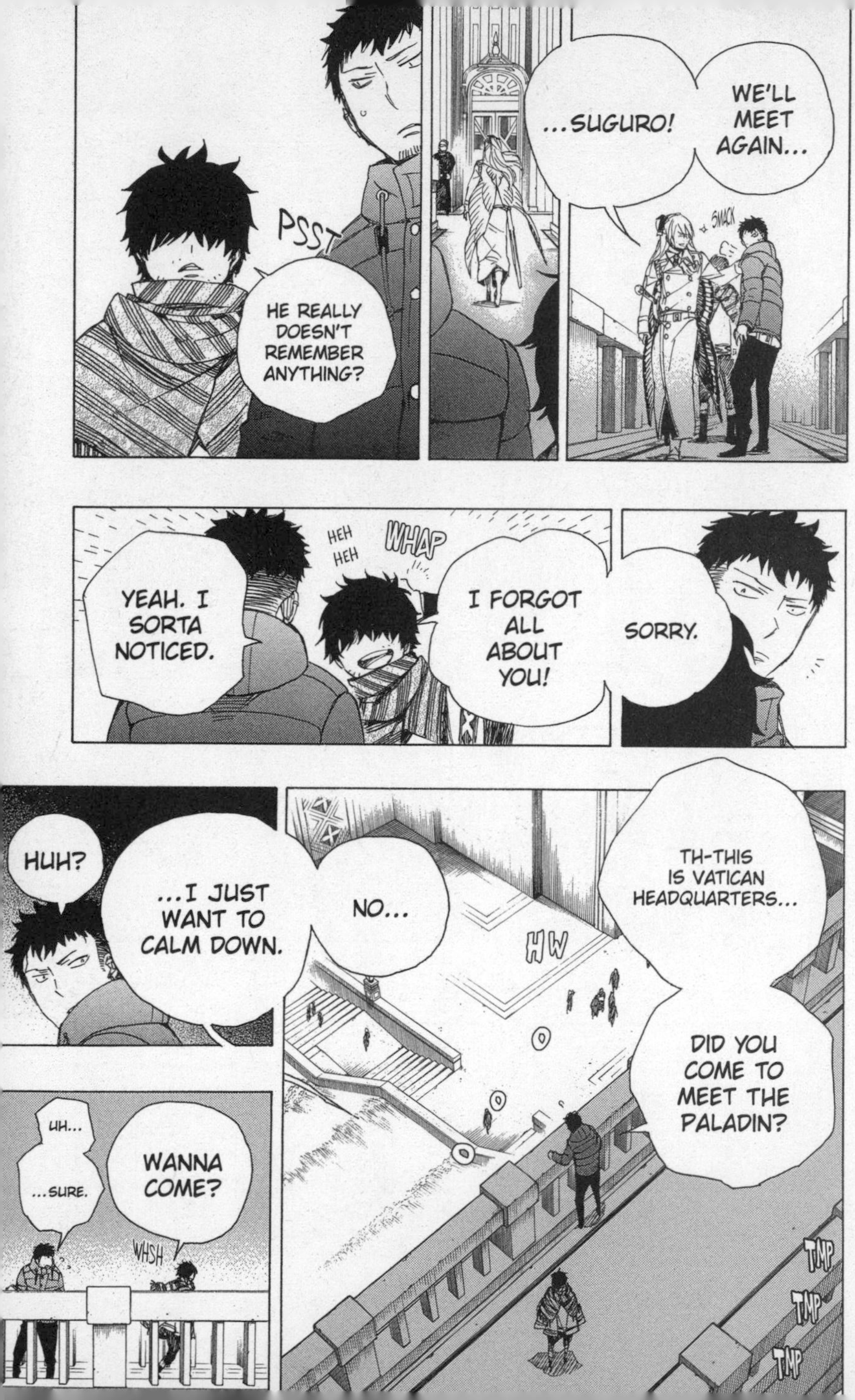

WE'LL MEET AGAIN...
...SUGURO!
SMACK
PSST
HE REALLY DOESN'T REMEMBER ANYTHING?
SORRY.
I FORGOT ALL ABOUT YOU!
WHAP
HEH HEH
YEAH. I SORTA NOTICED.
TH-THIS IS VATICAN HEADQUARTERS...
DID YOU COME TO MEET THE PALADIN?
HW
NO...
TMP
TMP
TMP
...I JUST WANT TO CALM DOWN.
HUH?
WANNA COME?
WHSH
UH...
...SURE.

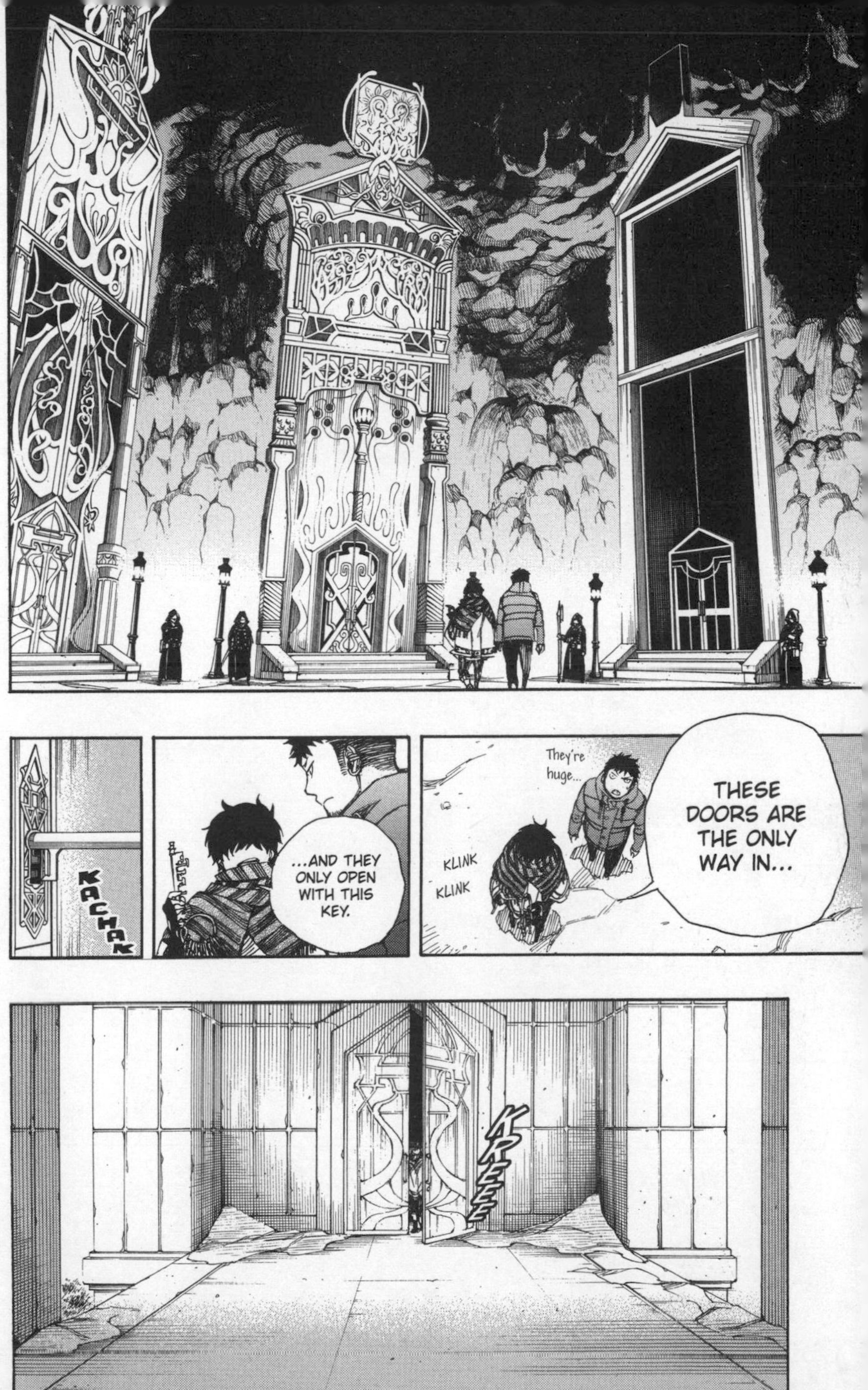
They're huge...
THESE DOORS ARE THE ONLY WAY IN...
KLINK
KLINK
...AND THEY ONLY OPEN WITH THIS KEY.
KACHAK
KREEEE

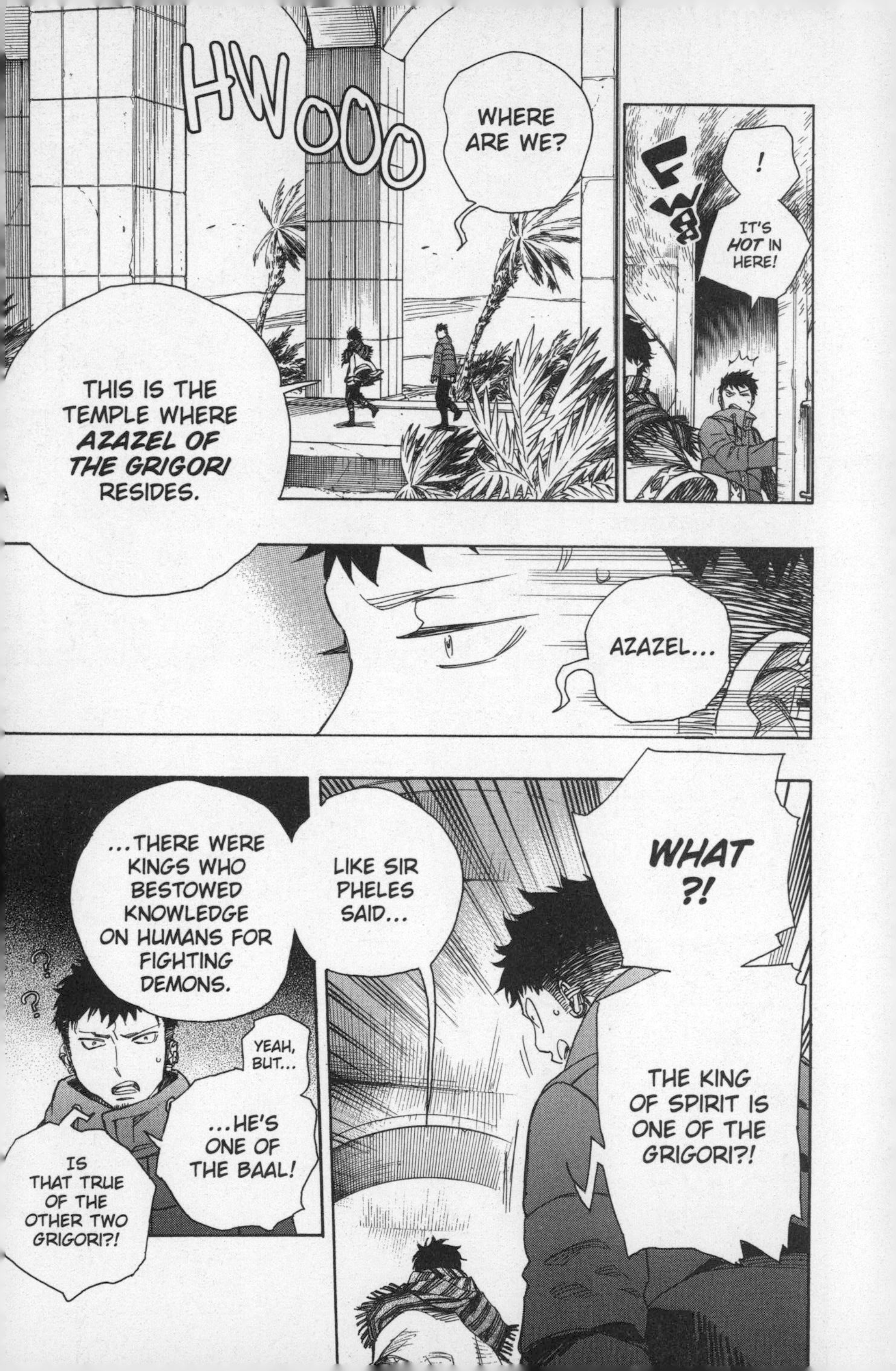
!
IT'S *HOT* IN HERE!
WHERE ARE WE?
HWOOO
THIS IS THE TEMPLE WHERE *AZAZEL OF THE GRIGORI* RESIDES.
AZAZEL...
WHAT?!
THE KING OF SPIRIT IS ONE OF THE GRIGORI?!
LIKE SIR PHELES SAID...
...THERE WERE KINGS WHO BESTOWED KNOWLEDGE ON HUMANS FOR FIGHTING DEMONS.
YEAH, BUT...
...HE'S ONE OF THE BAAL!
IS THAT TRUE OF THE OTHER TWO GRIGORI?!

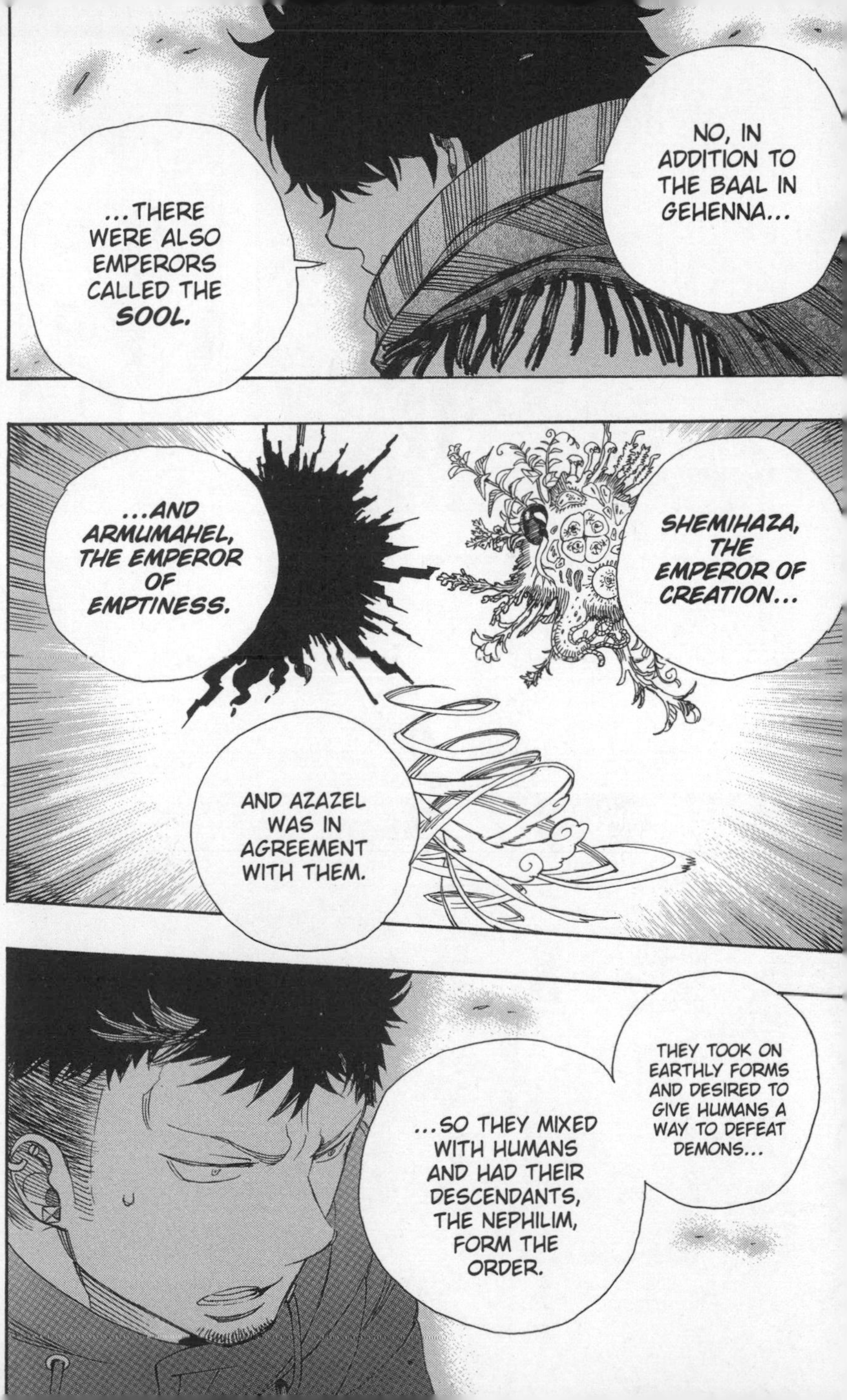
NO, IN ADDITION TO THE BAAL IN GEHENNA...
...THERE WERE ALSO EMPERORS CALLED THE SOOL.
SHEMIHAZA, THE EMPEROR OF CREATION...
...AND ARMUMAHEL, THE EMPEROR OF EMPTINESS.
AND AZAZEL WAS IN AGREEMENT WITH THEM.
THEY TOOK ON EARTHLY FORMS AND DESIRED TO GIVE HUMANS A WAY TO DEFEAT DEMONS...
...SO THEY MIXED WITH HUMANS AND HAD THEIR DESCENDANTS, THE NEPHILIM, FORM THE ORDER.

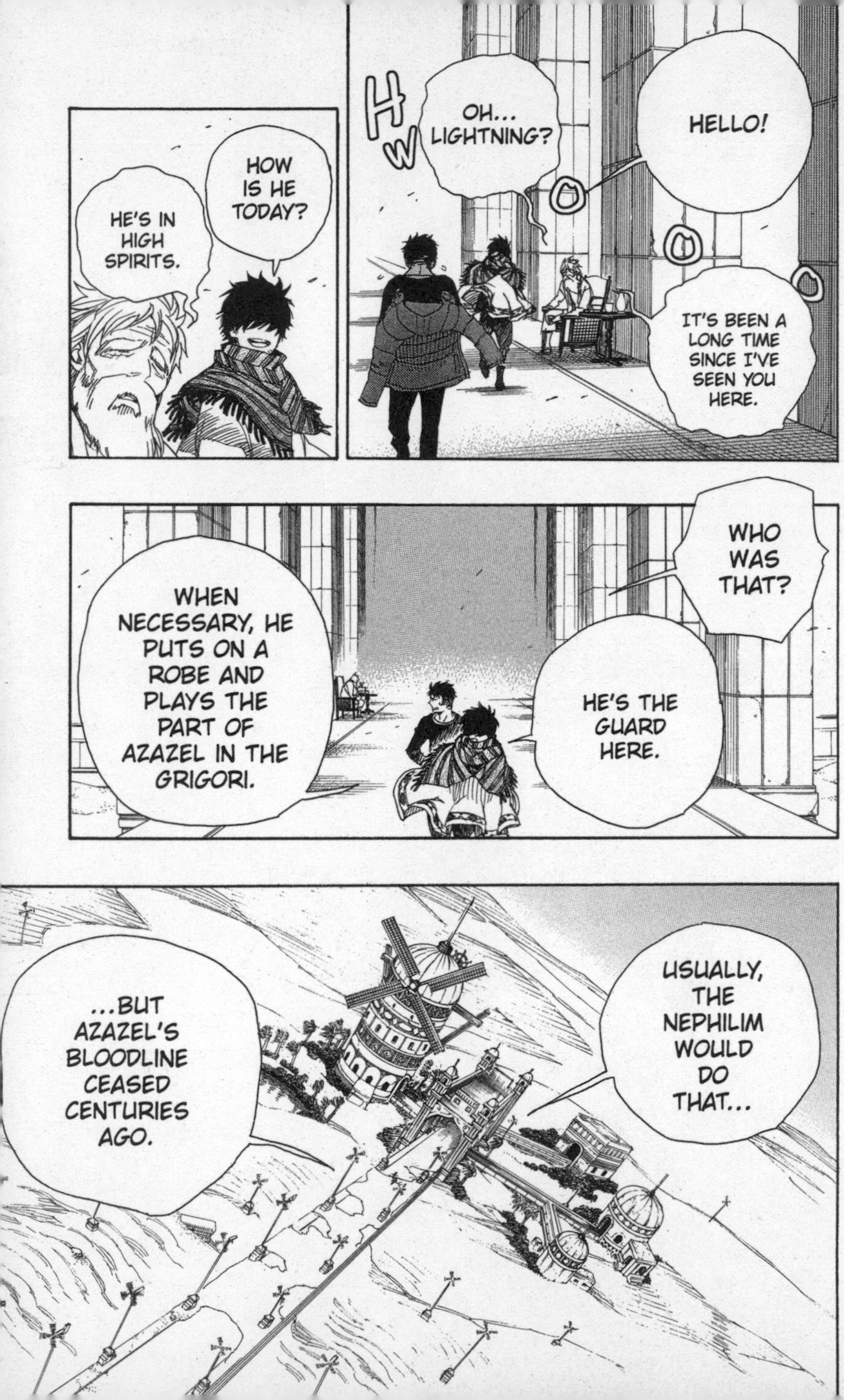
HELLO!
IT'S BEEN A LONG TIME SINCE I'VE SEEN YOU HERE.
OH... LIGHTNING?
HW
HOW IS HE TODAY?
HE'S IN HIGH SPIRITS.
WHO WAS THAT?
HE'S THE GUARD HERE.
WHEN NECESSARY, HE PUTS ON A ROBE AND PLAYS THE PART OF AZAZEL IN THE GRIGORI.
USUALLY, THE NEPHILIM WOULD DO THAT...
...BUT AZAZEL'S BLOODLINE CEASED CENTURIES AGO.

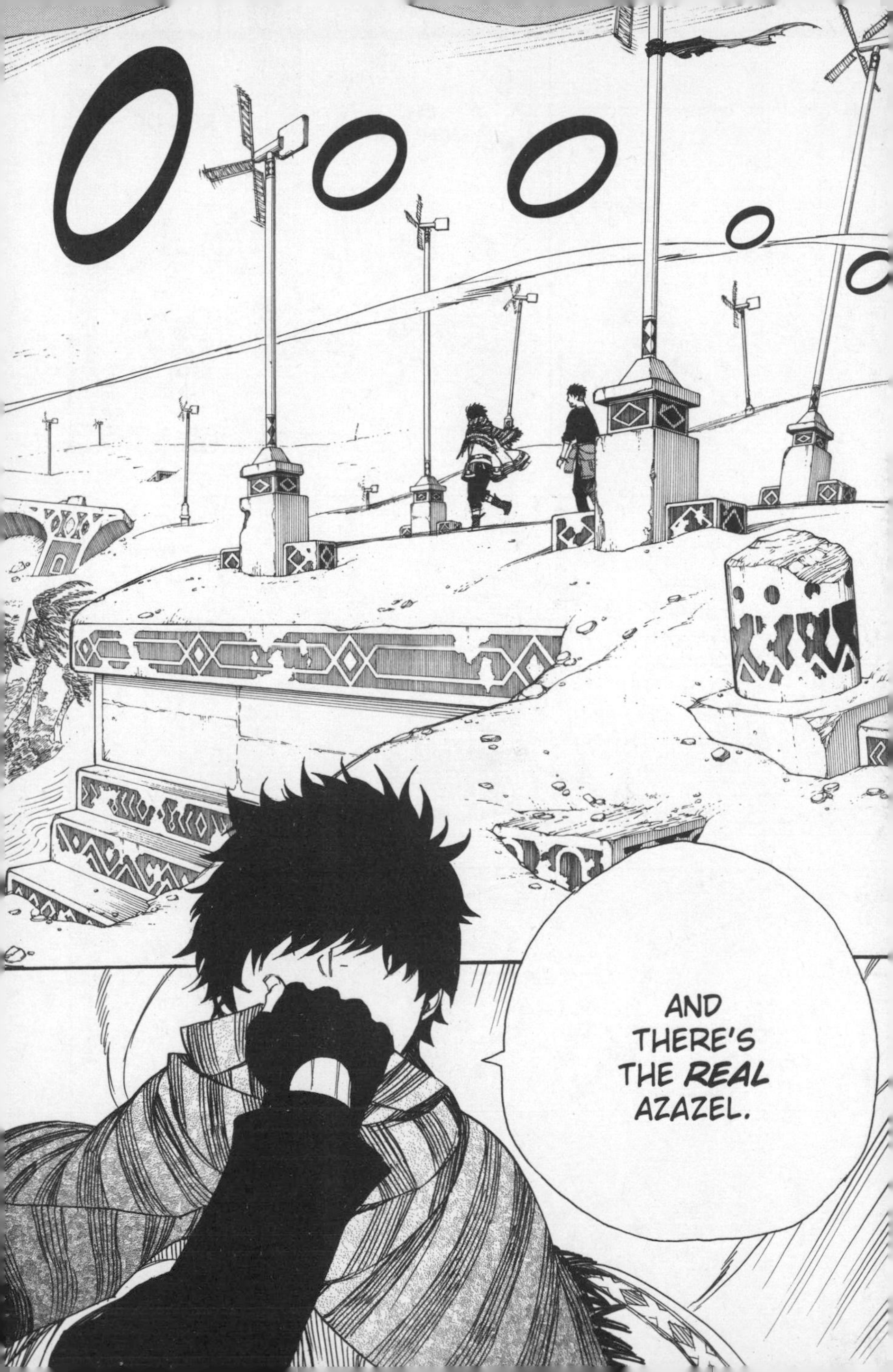
OOOOO
AND THERE'S THE *REAL* AZAZEL.

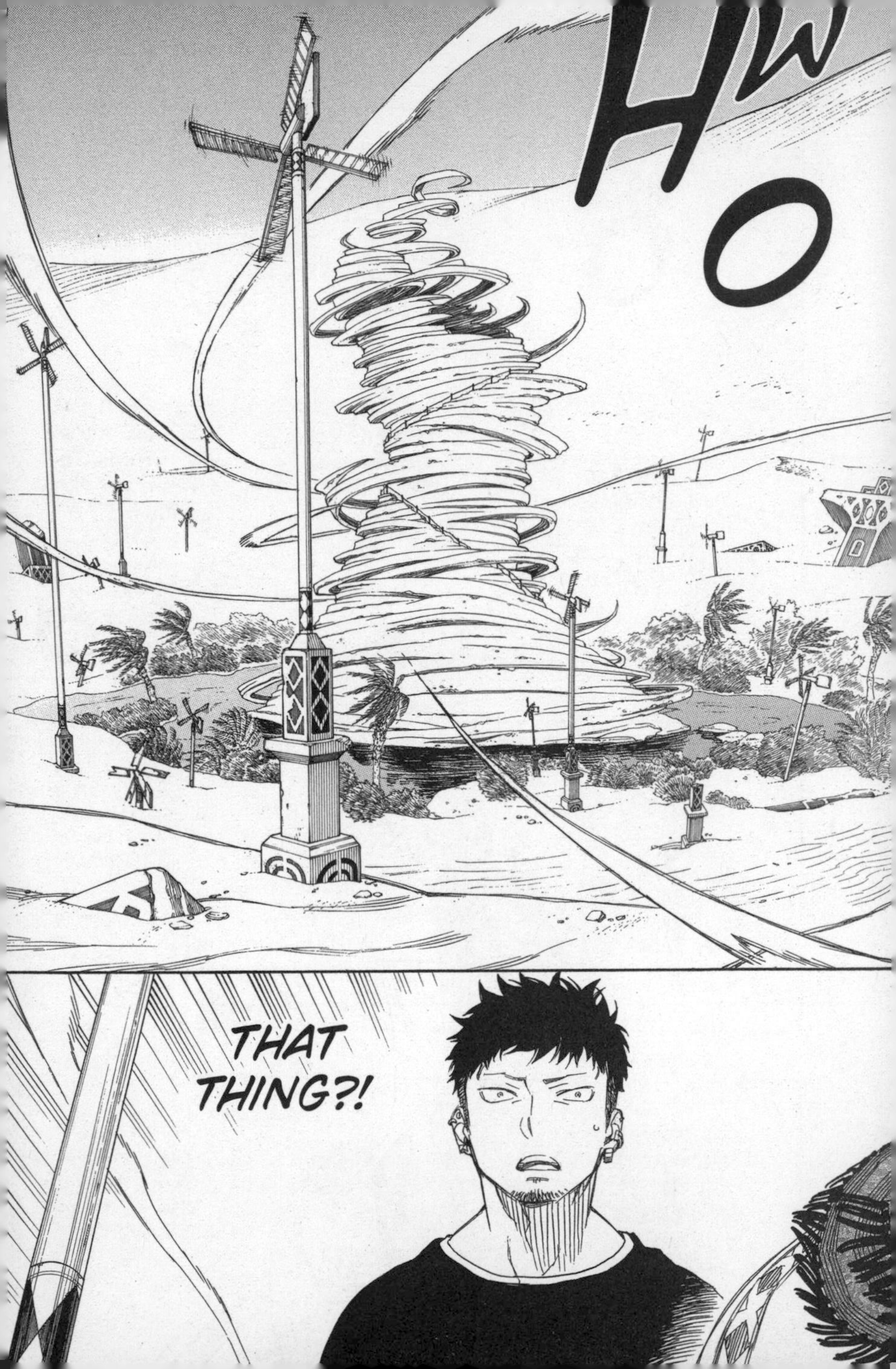
HWO
THAT THING?!

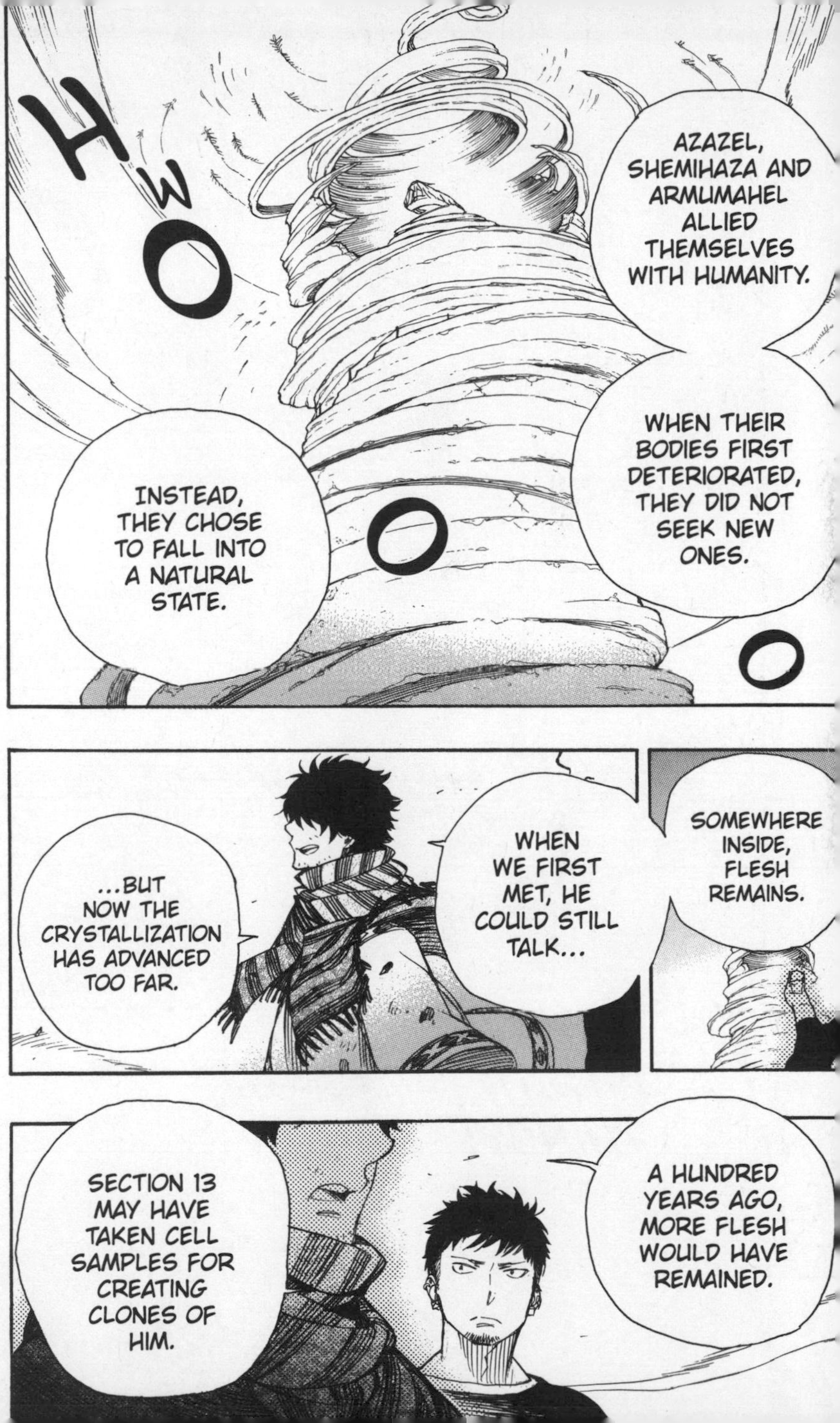
HWOOO
AZAZEL, SHEMIHAZA AND ARMUMAHEL ALLIED THEMSELVES WITH HUMANITY.
WHEN THEIR BODIES FIRST DETERIORATED, THEY DID NOT SEEK NEW ONES.
INSTEAD, THEY CHOSE TO FALL INTO A NATURAL STATE.
SOMEWHERE INSIDE, FLESH REMAINS.
WHEN WE FIRST MET, HE COULD STILL TALK...
...BUT NOW THE CRYSTALLIZATION HAS ADVANCED TOO FAR.
A HUNDRED YEARS AGO, MORE FLESH WOULD HAVE REMAINED.
SECTION 13 MAY HAVE TAKEN CELL SAMPLES FOR CREATING CLONES OF HIM.

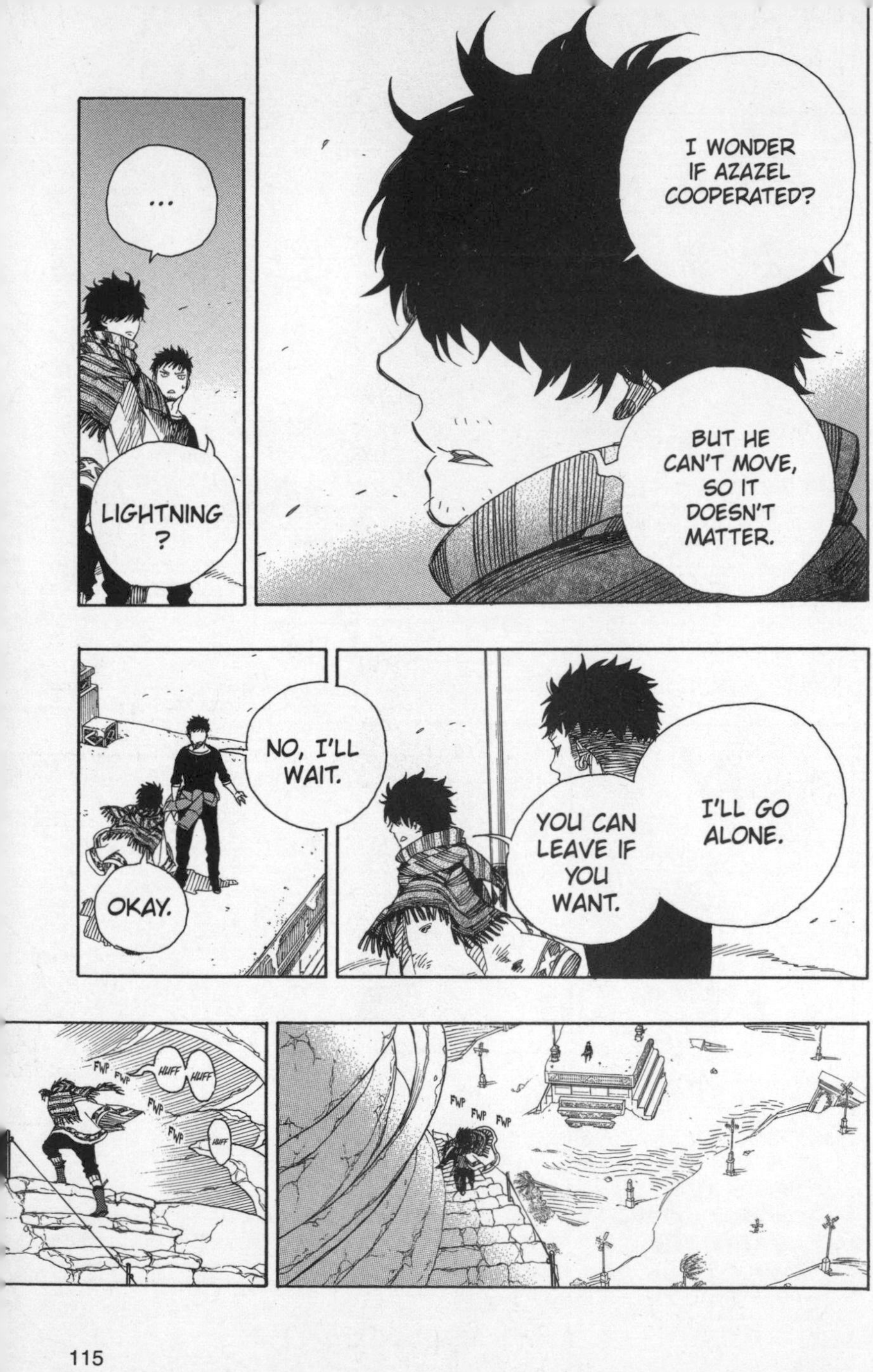
I WONDER IF AZAZEL COOPERATED?
BUT HE CAN'T MOVE, SO IT DOESN'T MATTER.
...
LIGHTNING ?
I'LL GO ALONE.
YOU CAN LEAVE IF YOU WANT.
NO, I'LL WAIT.
OKAY.
FWP FWP FWP
FWP FWP
HUFF HUFF
FWP FWP
HUFF

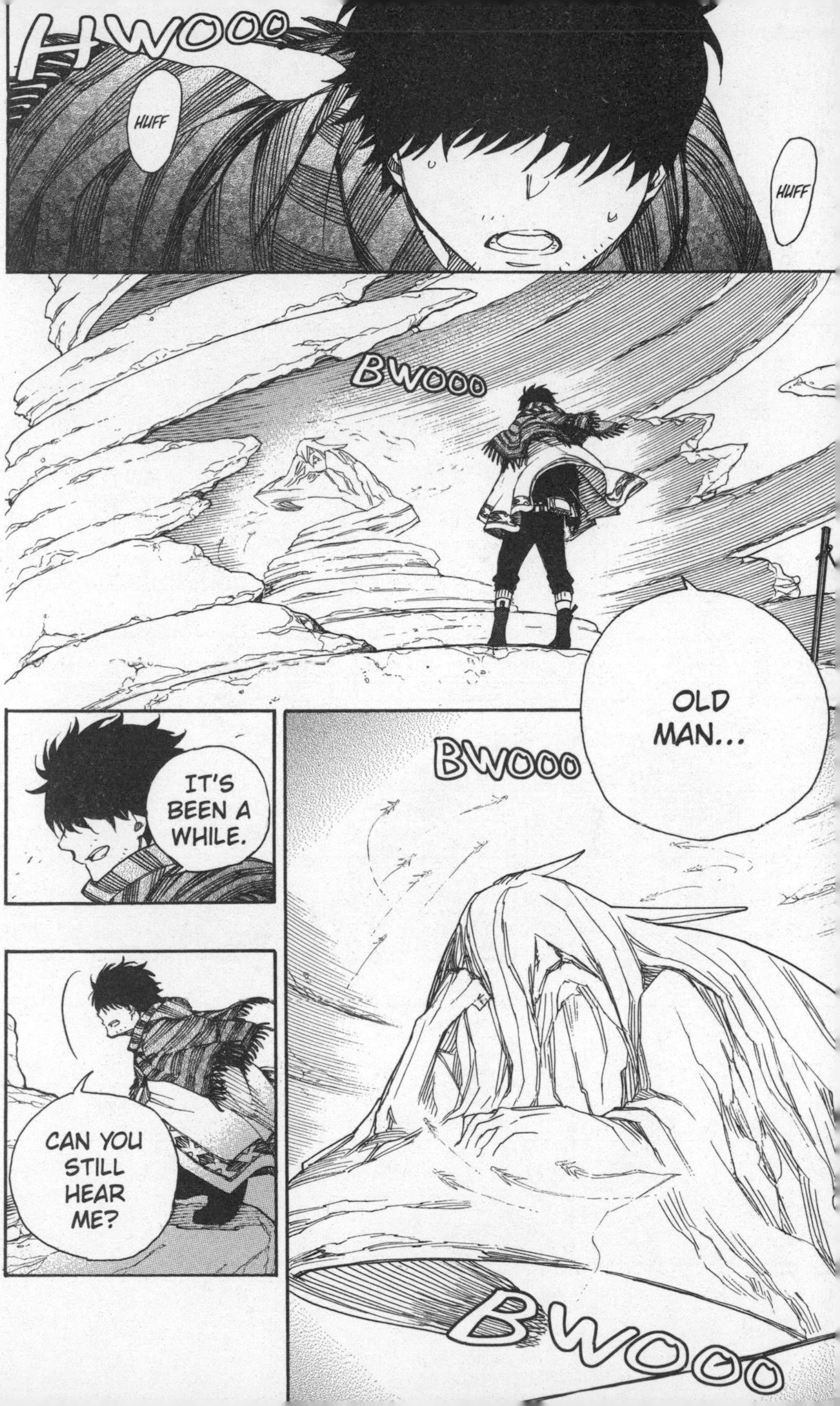
HWOOO
HUFF
HUFF
BWOOO
OLD MAN...
BWOOO
BWOOO
IT'S BEEN A WHILE.
CAN YOU STILL HEAR ME?

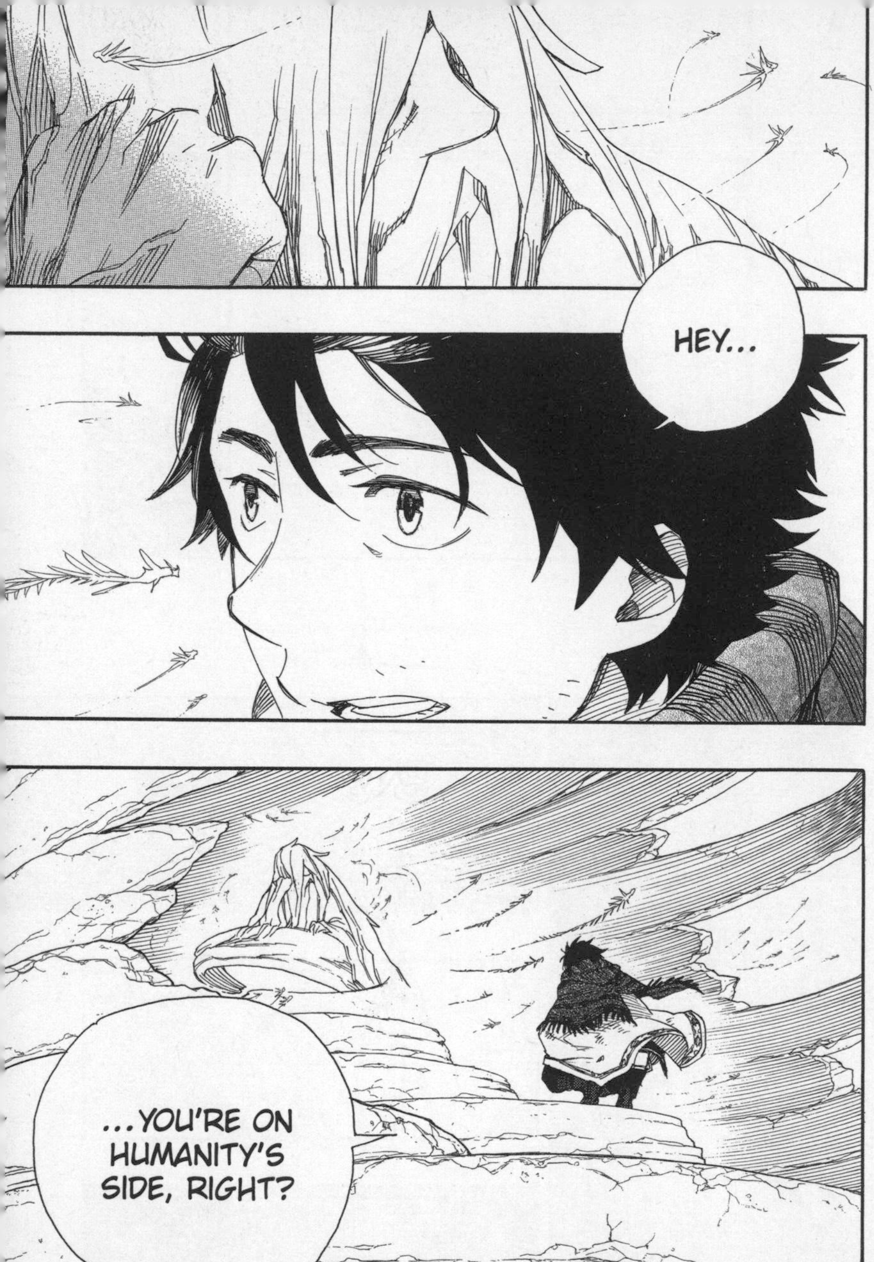
HEY...
...YOU'RE ON HUMANITY'S SIDE, RIGHT?

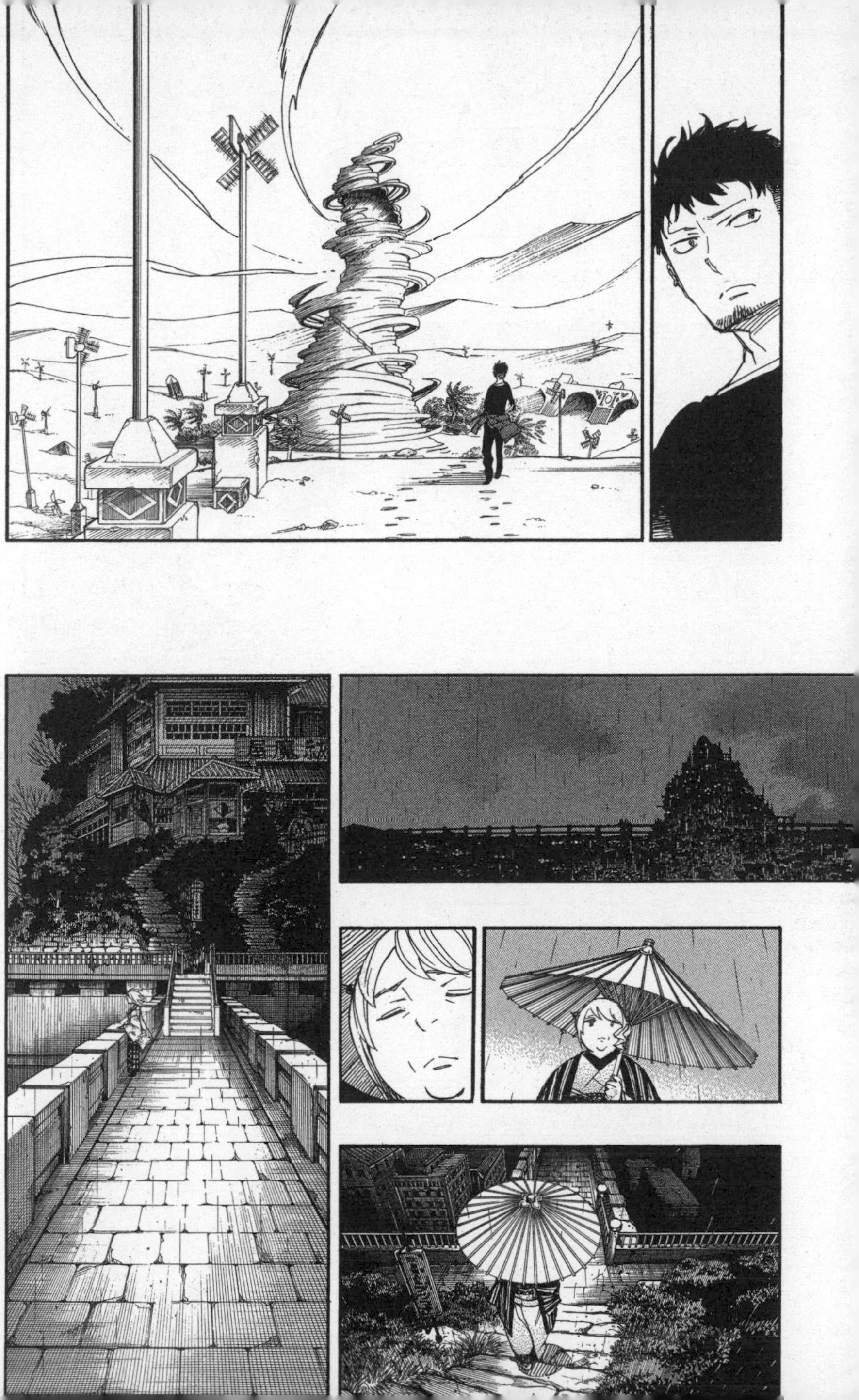

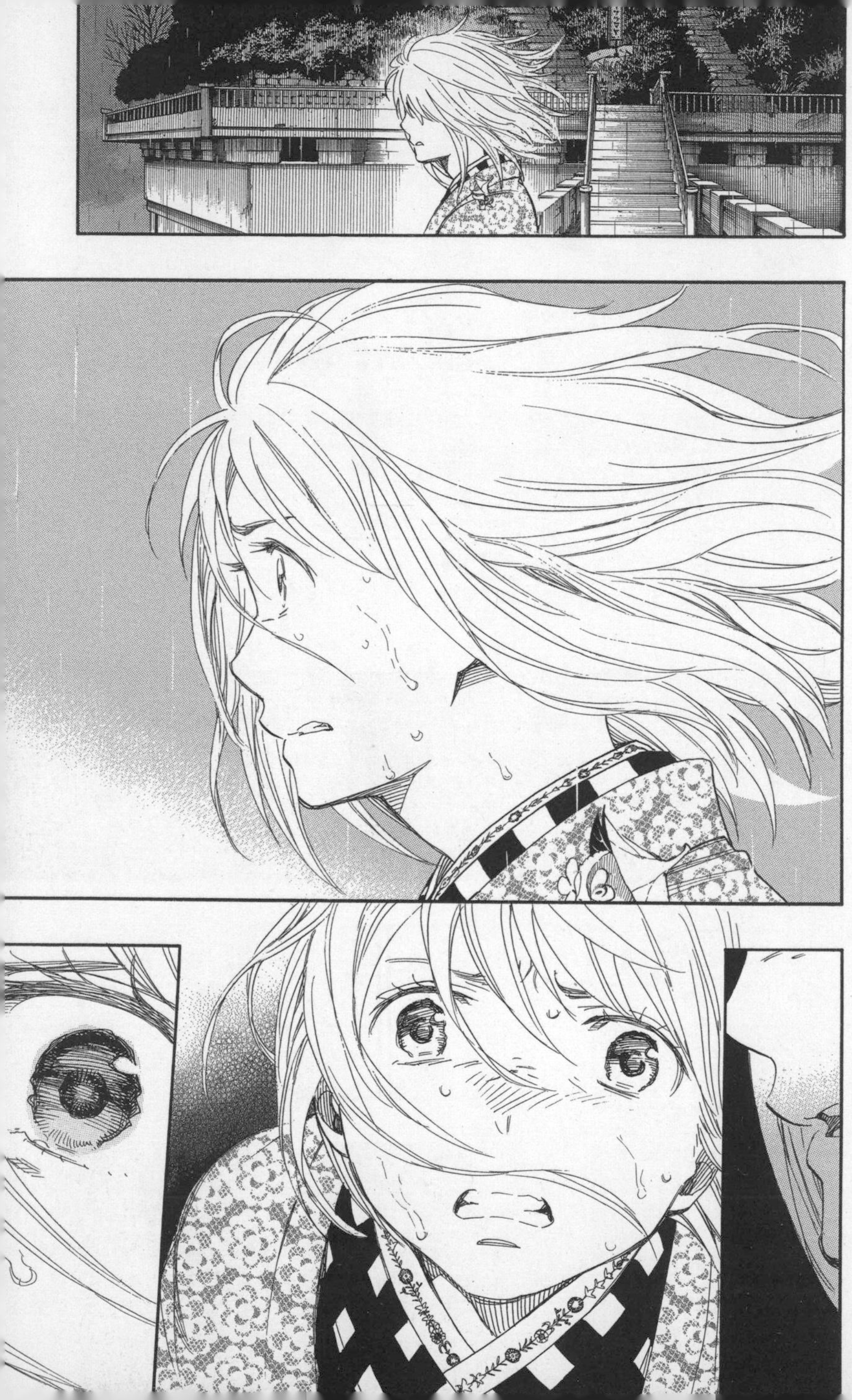

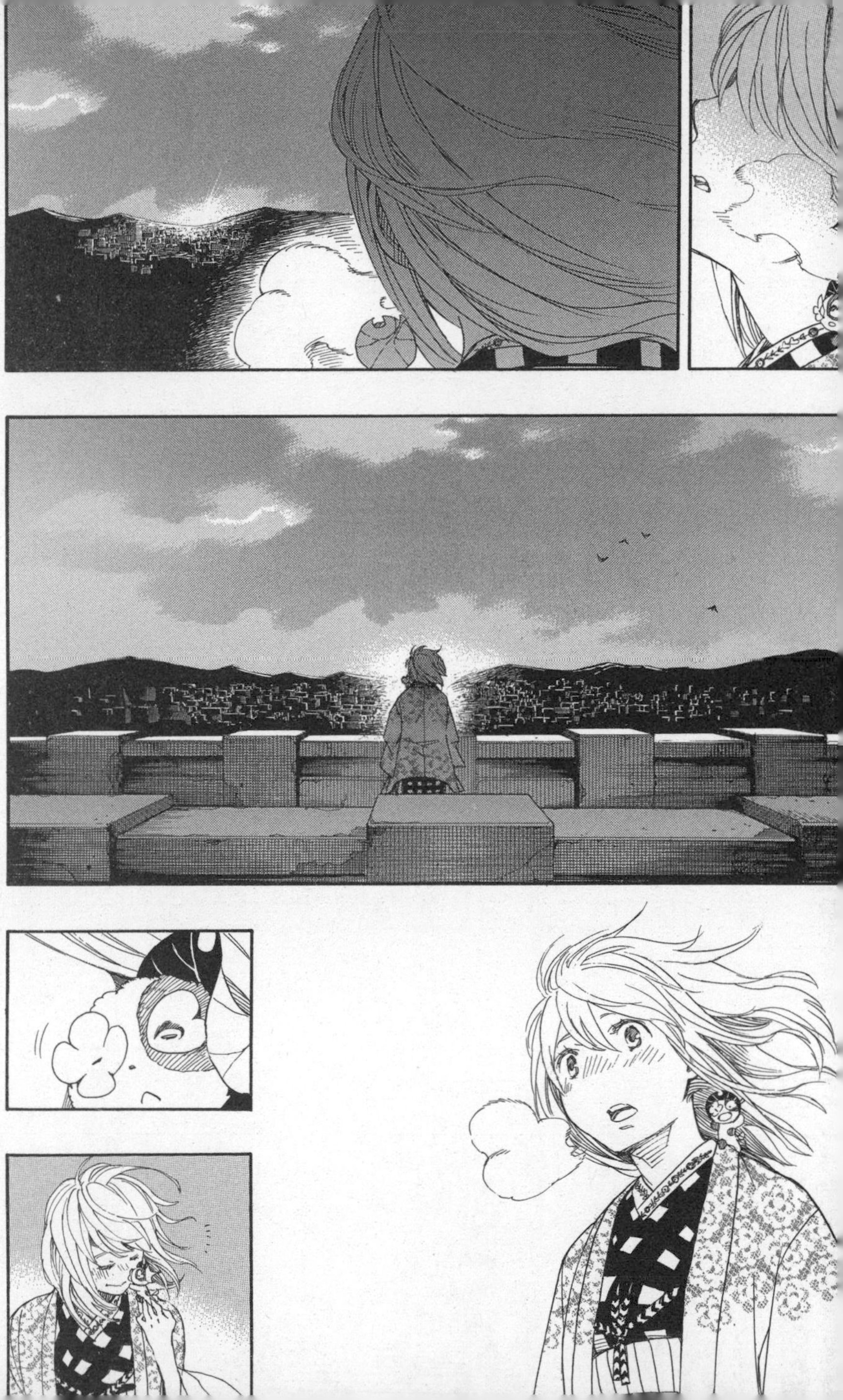

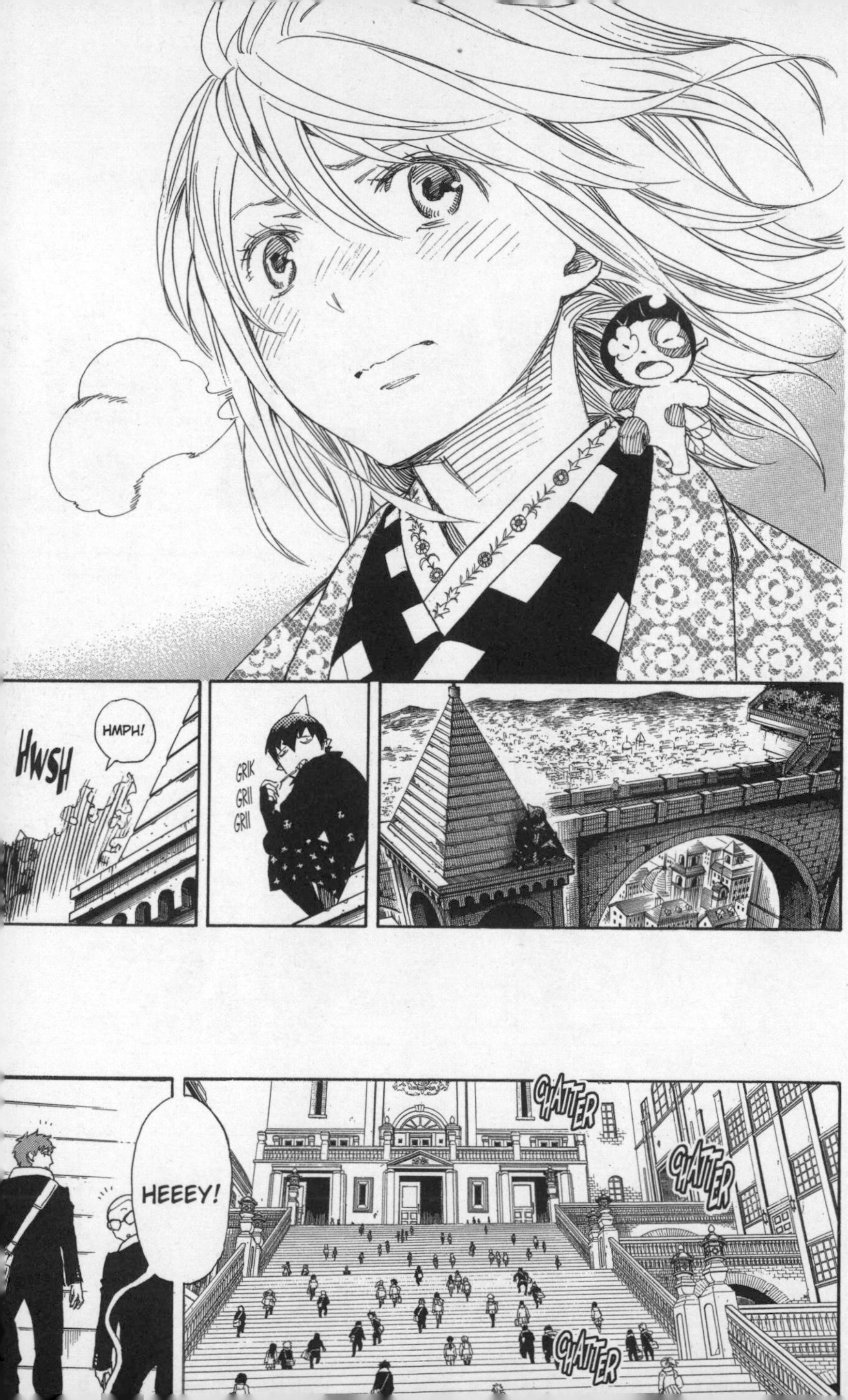
GRIK
GRII
GRII
HMPH!
HWSH
CHATTER
CHATTER
CHATTER
HEEEY!

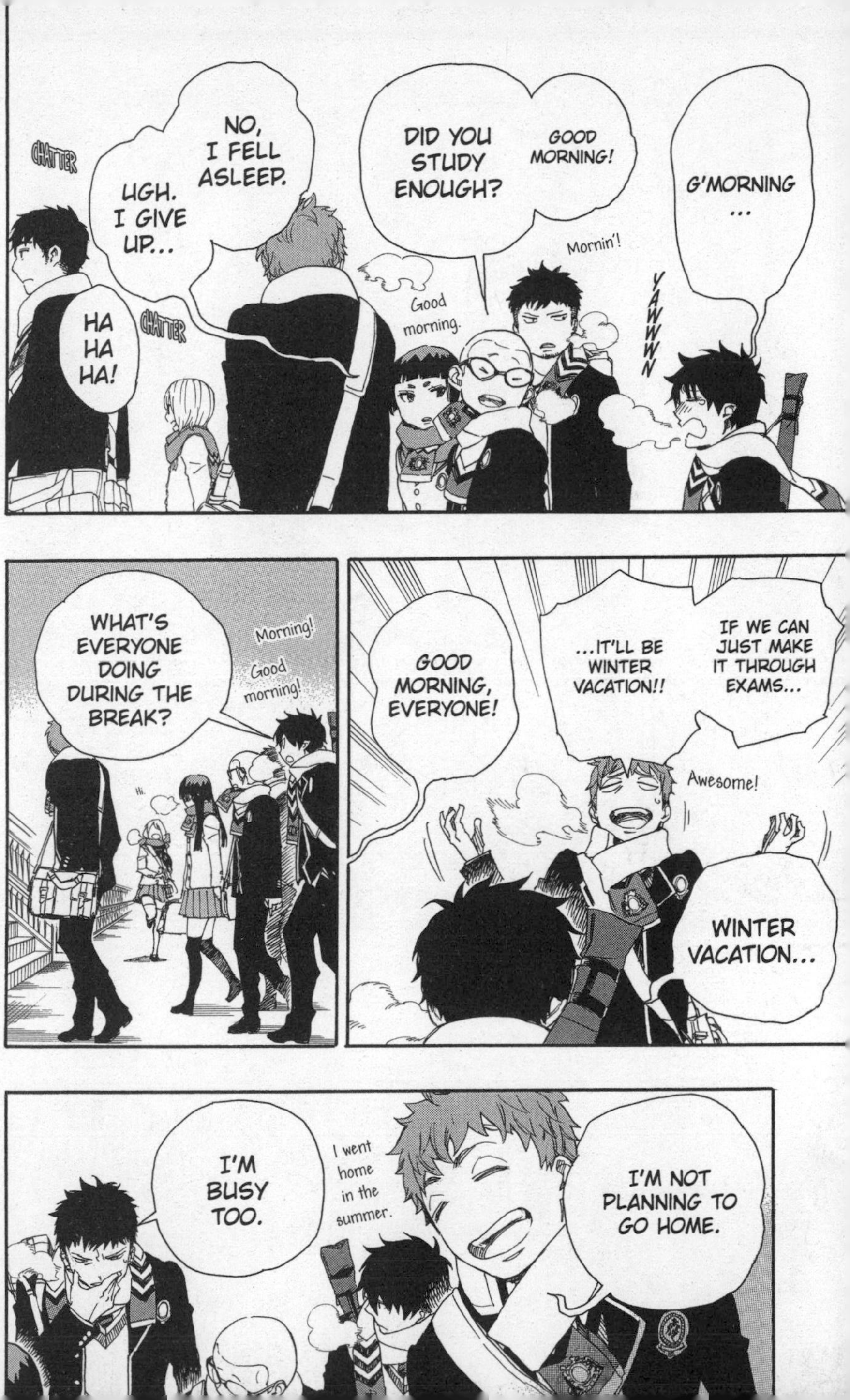
G'MORNING...
YAWWWN
Mornin'!
GOOD MORNING!
DID YOU STUDY ENOUGH?
Good morning.
NO, I FELL ASLEEP.
UGH. I GIVE UP...
CHATTER
HA HA HA!
CHATTER
IF WE CAN JUST MAKE IT THROUGH EXAMS...
...IT'LL BE WINTER VACATION!!
Awesome!
GOOD MORNING, EVERYONE!
WINTER VACATION...
Morning!
Good morning!
WHAT'S EVERYONE DOING DURING THE BREAK?
Hi.
I'M NOT PLANNING TO GO HOME.
I went home in the summer.
I'M BUSY TOO.

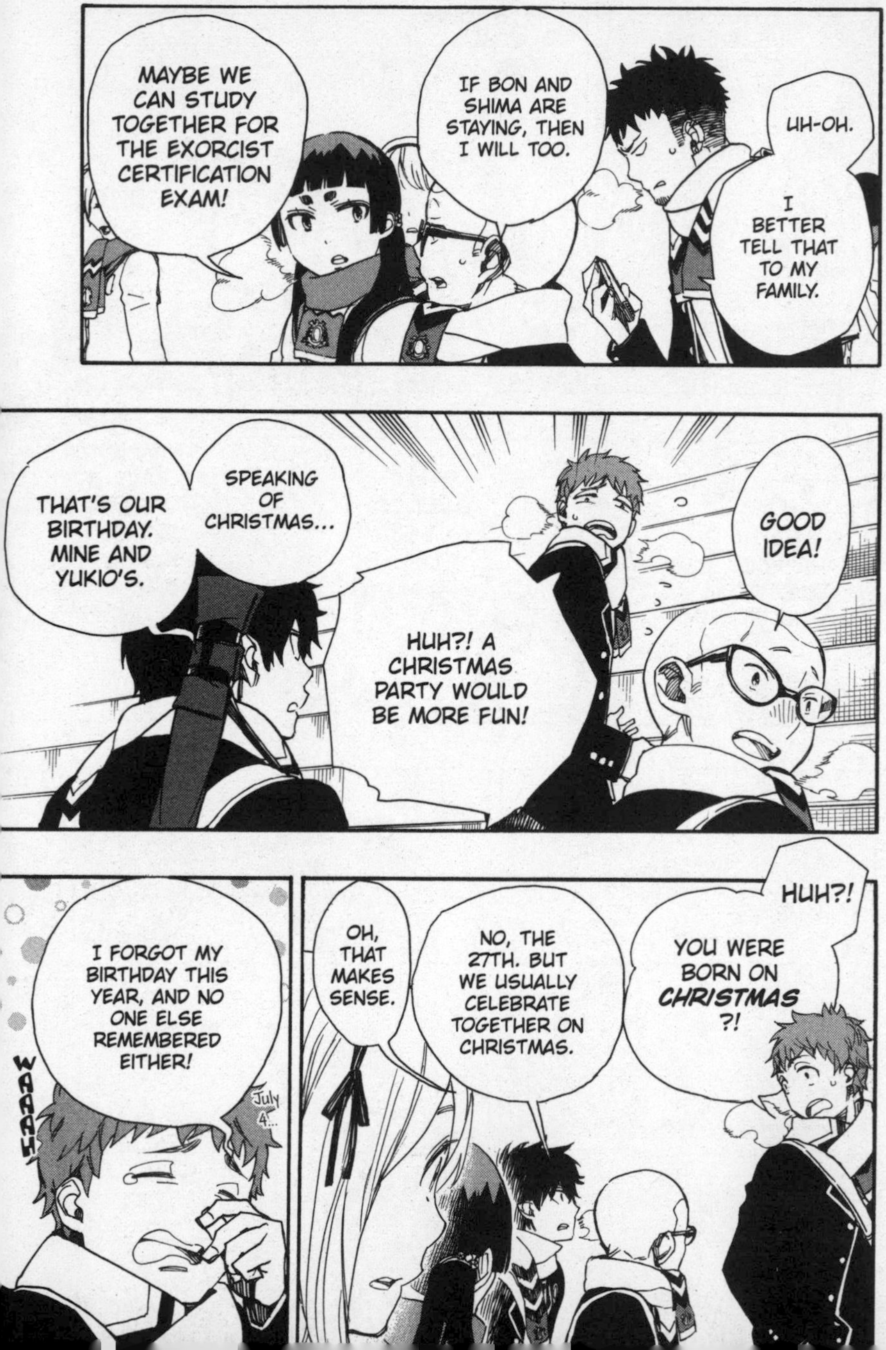
UH-OH.
I BETTER TELL THAT TO MY FAMILY.
IF BON AND SHIMA ARE STAYING, THEN I WILL TOO.
MAYBE WE CAN STUDY TOGETHER FOR THE EXORCIST CERTIFICATION EXAM!
GOOD IDEA!
HUH?! A CHRISTMAS PARTY WOULD BE MORE FUN!
SPEAKING OF CHRISTMAS...
THAT'S OUR BIRTHDAY. MINE AND YUKIO'S.
HUH?!
YOU WERE BORN ON CHRISTMAS?!
NO, THE 27TH. BUT WE USUALLY CELEBRATE TOGETHER ON CHRISTMAS.
OH, THAT MAKES SENSE.
I FORGOT MY BIRTHDAY THIS YEAR, AND NO ONE ELSE REMEMBERED EITHER!
July 4...
WAAAAH!

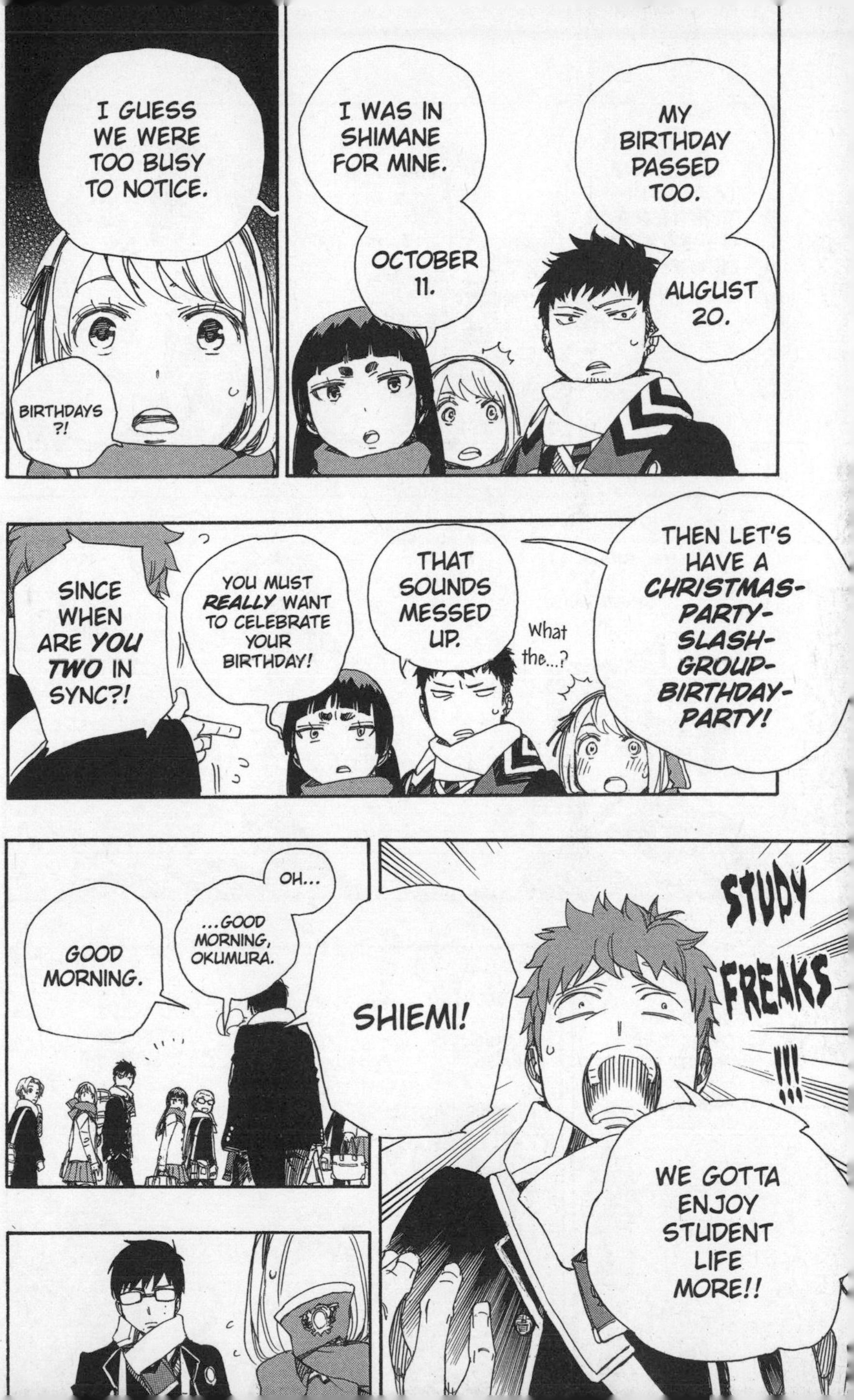
MY BIRTHDAY PASSED TOO.
AUGUST 20.
I WAS IN SHIMANE FOR MINE.
OCTOBER 11.
I GUESS WE WERE TOO BUSY TO NOTICE.
BIRTHDAYS ?!
THEN LET'S HAVE A *CHRISTMAS-PARTY-SLASH-GROUP-BIRTHDAY-PARTY!*
What the...?
THAT SOUNDS MESSED UP.
YOU MUST *REALLY* WANT TO CELEBRATE YOUR BIRTHDAY!
SINCE WHEN ARE *YOU TWO* IN SYNC?!
STUDY FREAKS !!!
WE GOTTA ENJOY STUDENT LIFE MORE!!
SHIEMI!
OH...
...GOOD MORNING, OKUMURA.
GOOD MORNING.

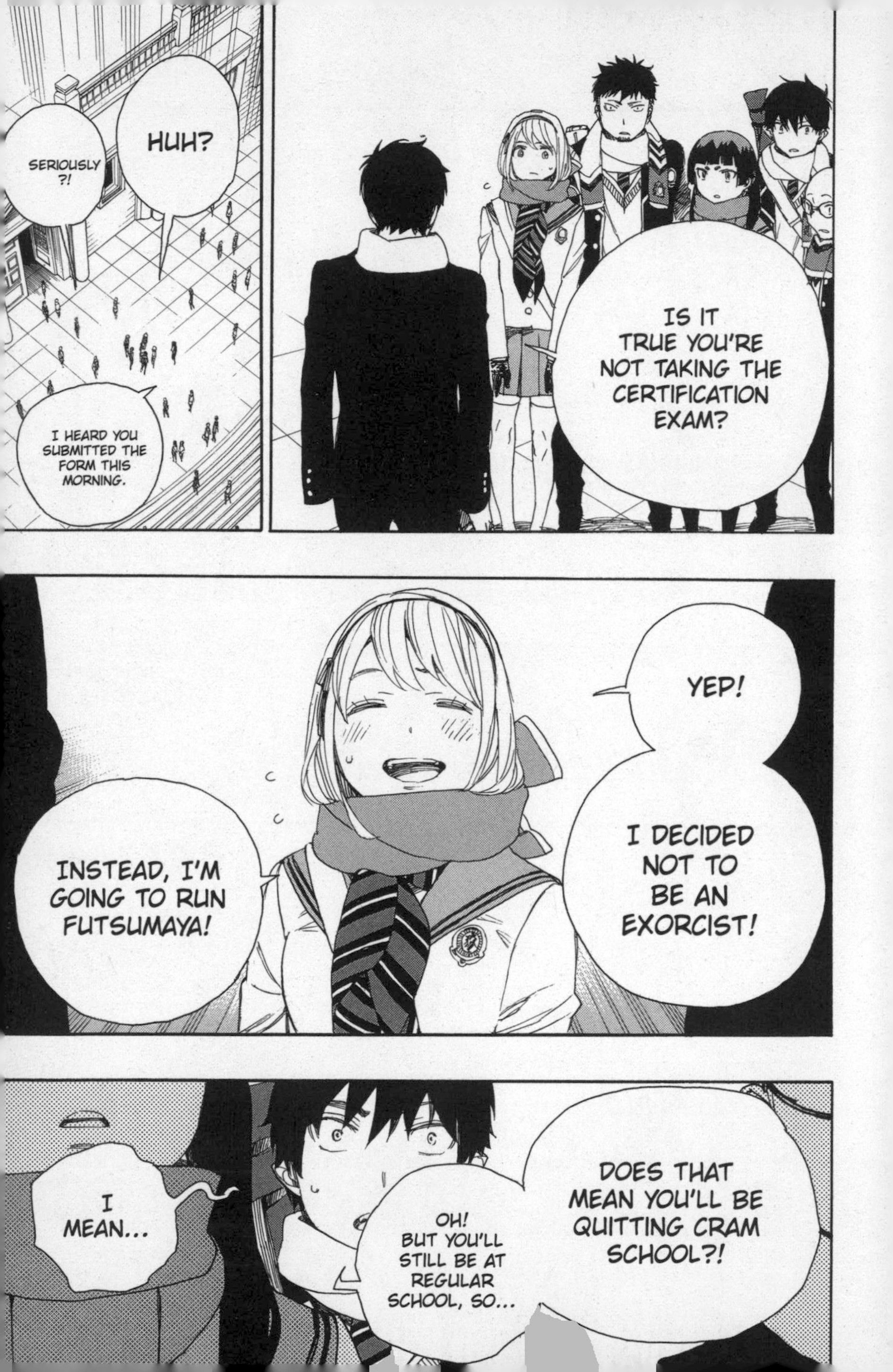
IS IT TRUE YOU'RE NOT TAKING THE CERTIFICATION EXAM?
HUH?
SERIOUSLY ?!
I HEARD YOU SUBMITTED THE FORM THIS MORNING.
YEP!
I DECIDED NOT TO BE AN EXORCIST!
INSTEAD, I'M GOING TO RUN FUTSUMAYA!
DOES THAT MEAN YOU'LL BE QUITTING CRAM SCHOOL?!
OH! BUT YOU'LL STILL BE AT REGULAR SCHOOL, SO...
I MEAN...

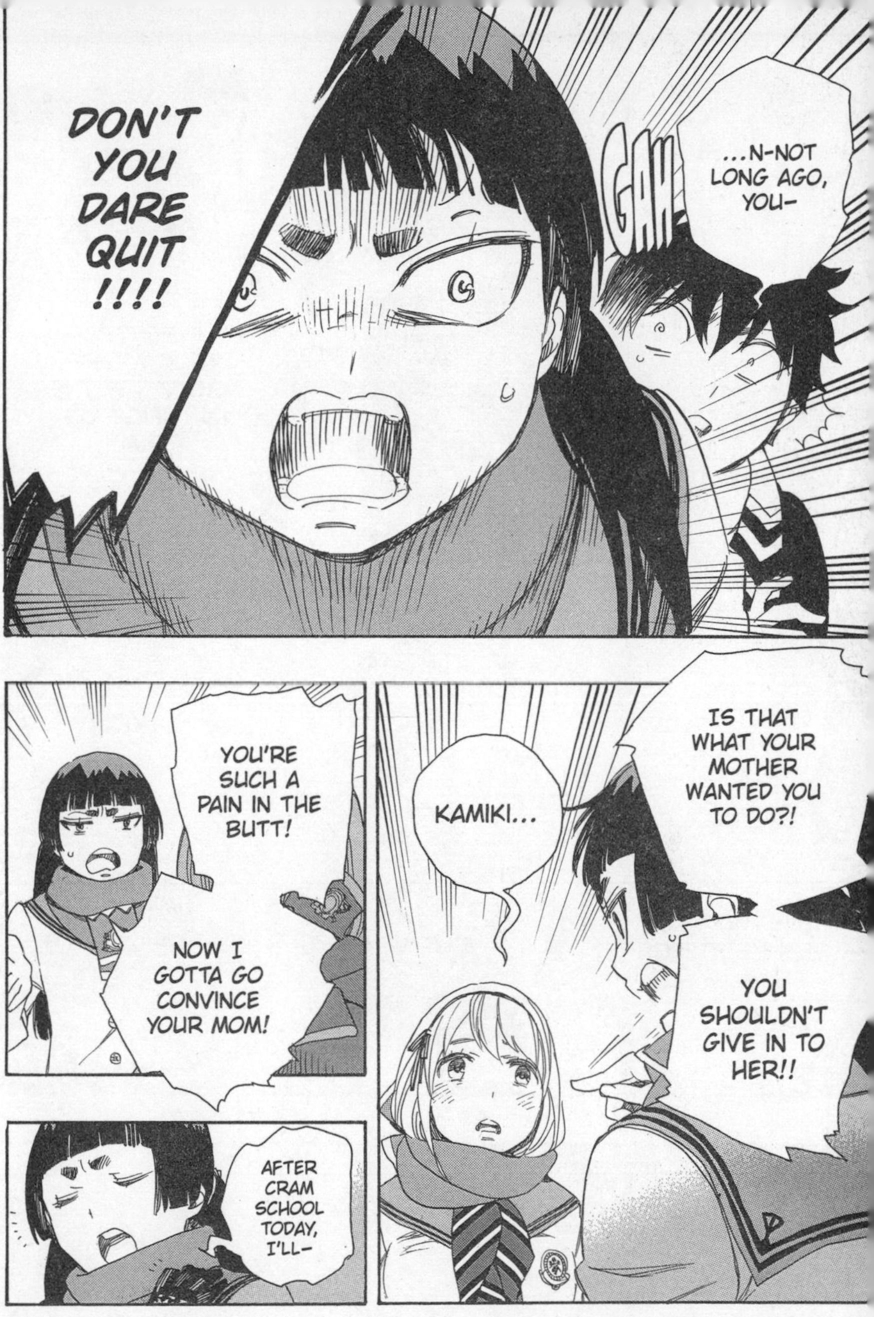
GAH
...N-NOT LONG AGO, YOU-
DON'T YOU DARE QUIT!!!!
IS THAT WHAT YOUR MOTHER WANTED YOU TO DO?!
KAMIKI...
YOU SHOULDN'T GIVE IN TO HER!!
YOU'RE SUCH A PAIN IN THE BUTT!
NOW I GOTTA GO CONVINCE YOUR MOM!
AFTER CRAM SCHOOL TODAY, I'LL-

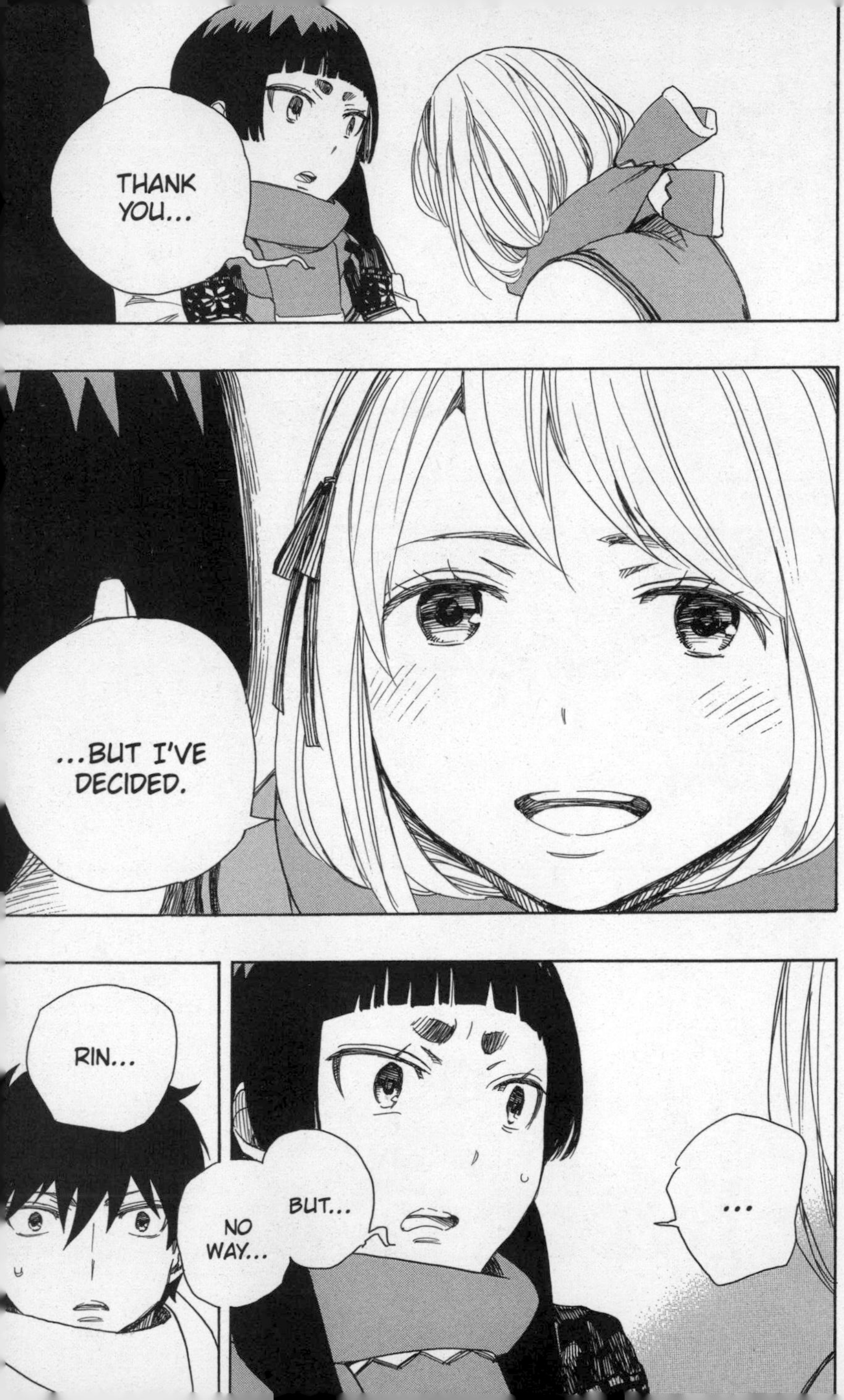
THANK YOU...
...BUT I'VE DECIDED.
...
BUT...
NO WAY...
RIN...

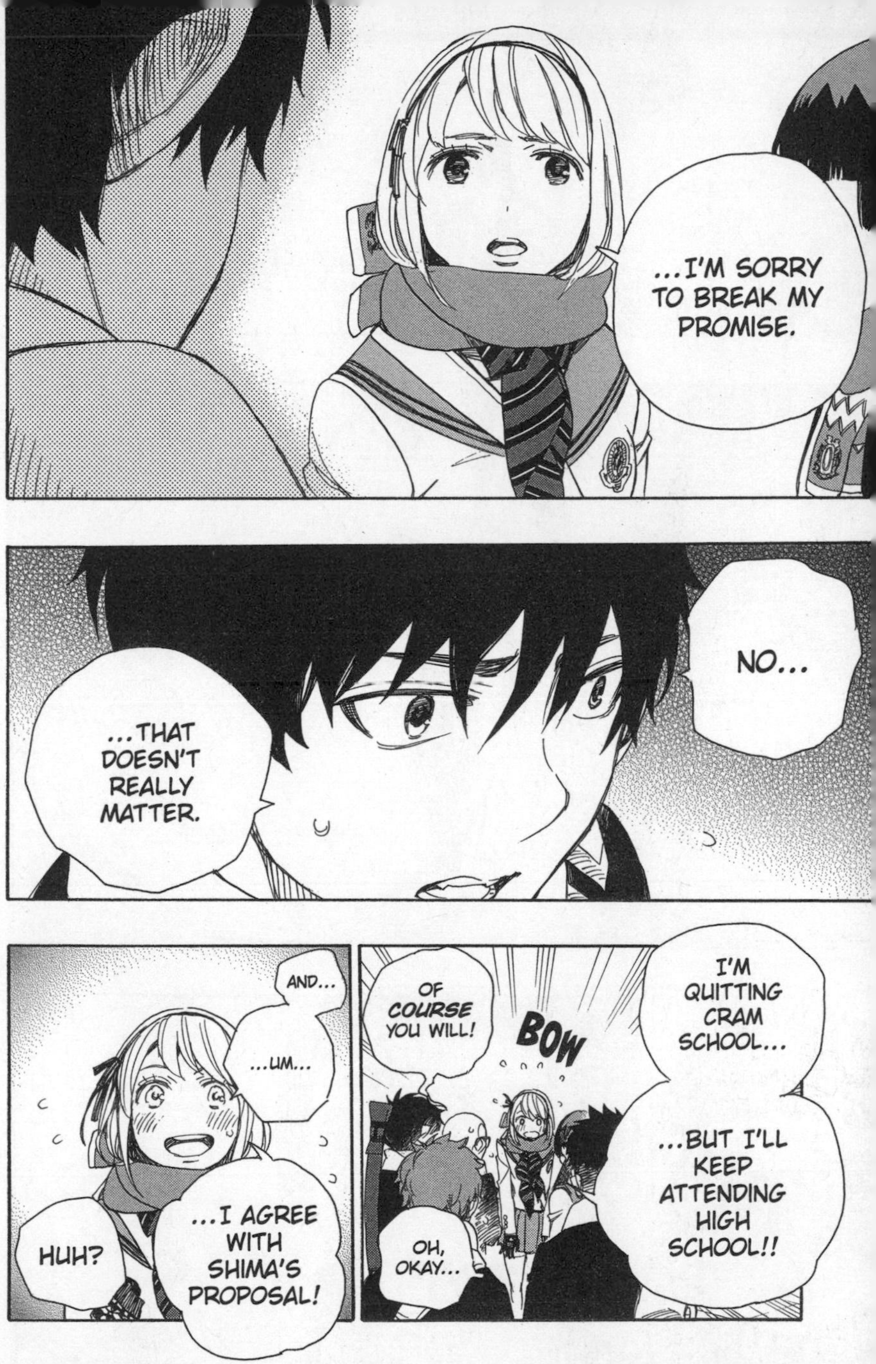
...I'M SORRY TO BREAK MY PROMISE.
NO...
...THAT DOESN'T REALLY MATTER.
I'M QUITTING CRAM SCHOOL...
...BUT I'LL KEEP ATTENDING HIGH SCHOOL!!
BOW
OF COURSE YOU WILL!
OH, OKAY...
AND...
...UM...
...I AGREE WITH SHIMA'S PROPOSAL!
HUH?

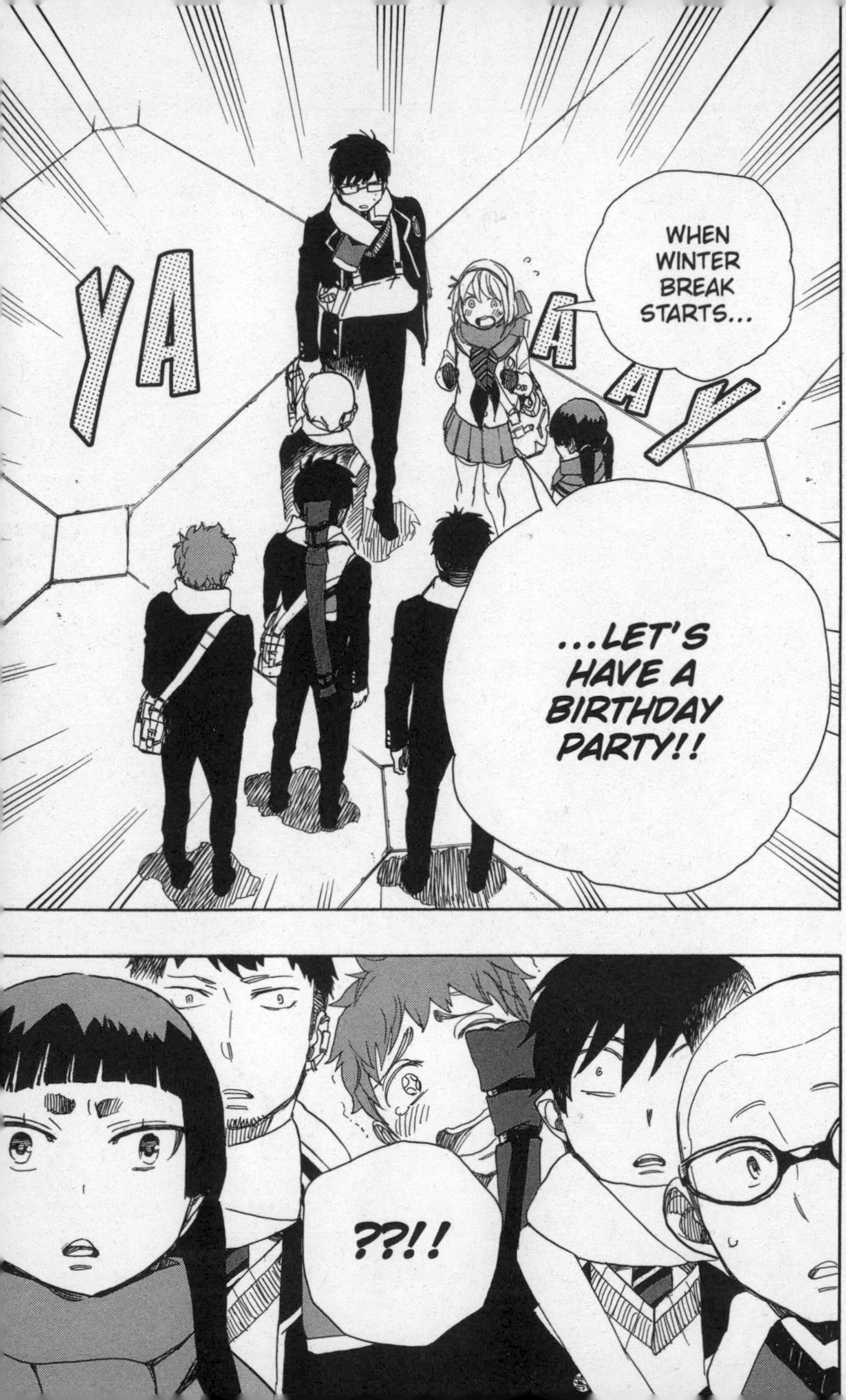
WHEN WINTER BREAK STARTS...
...LET'S HAVE A BIRTHDAY PARTY!!
YAAAAY
??!!

Blue Exorcist Chapter 87: Embryo

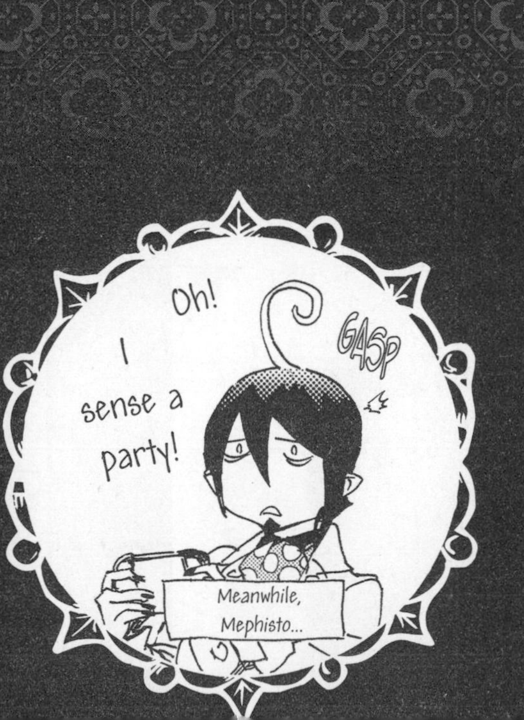
GASP
Oh! I sense a party!
Meanwhile, Mephisto...

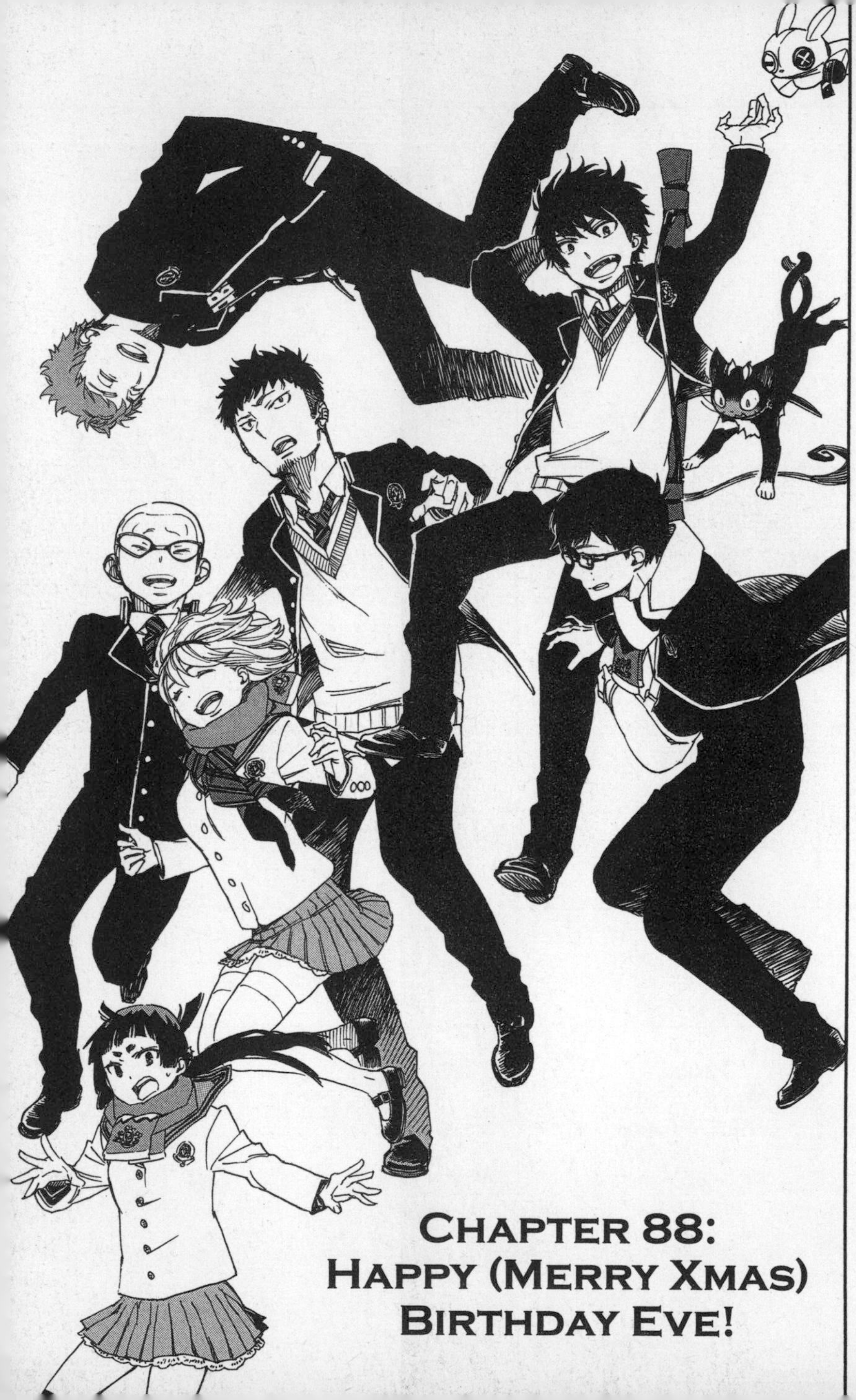

Chapter 88: Happy (Merry Xmas) Birthday Eve!

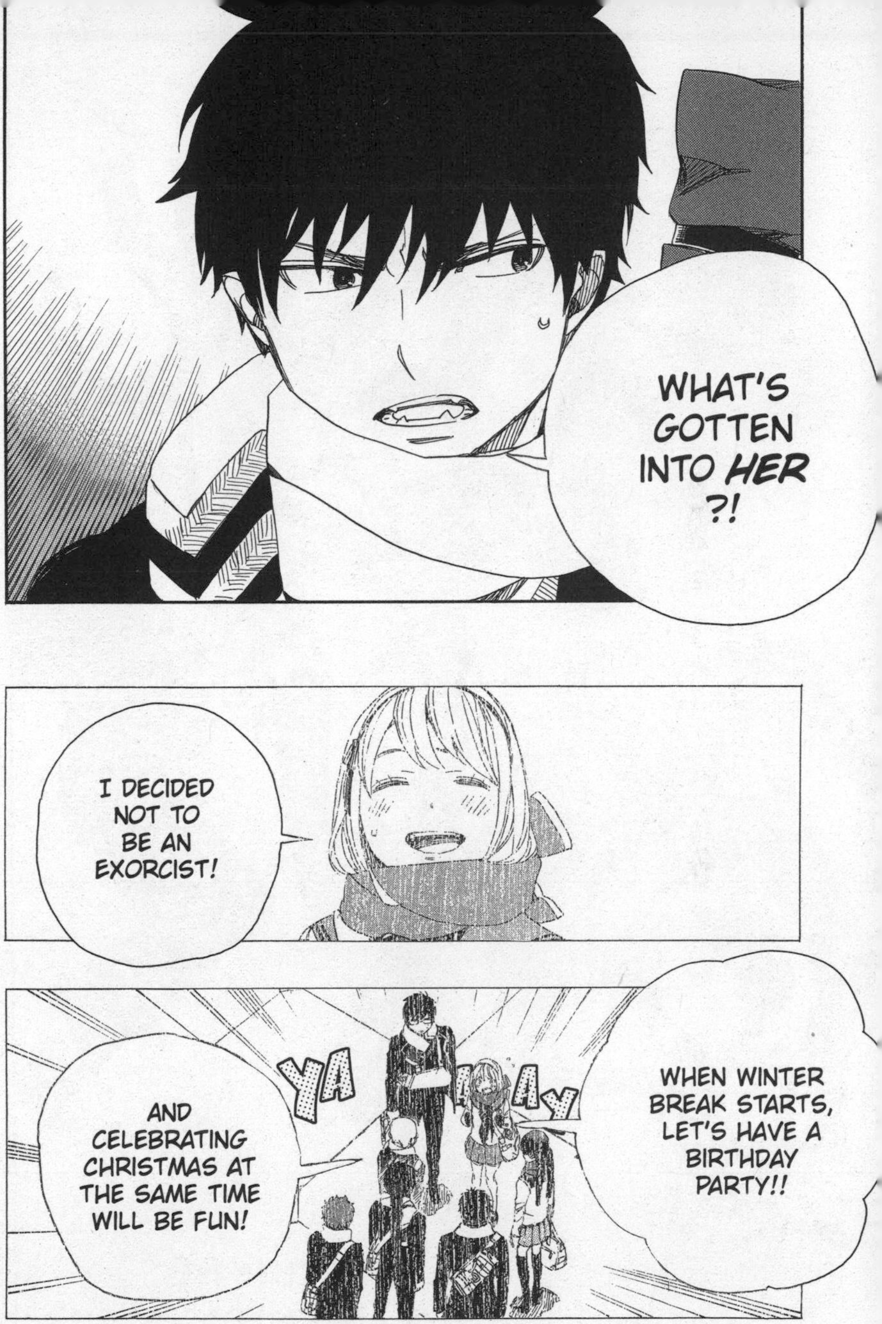
WHAT'S GOTTEN INTO ***HER*** ?!
I DECIDED NOT TO BE AN EXORCIST!
WHEN WINTER BREAK STARTS, LET'S HAVE A BIRTHDAY PARTY!!
YA
AY
AND CELEBRATING CHRISTMAS AT THE SAME TIME WILL BE FUN!

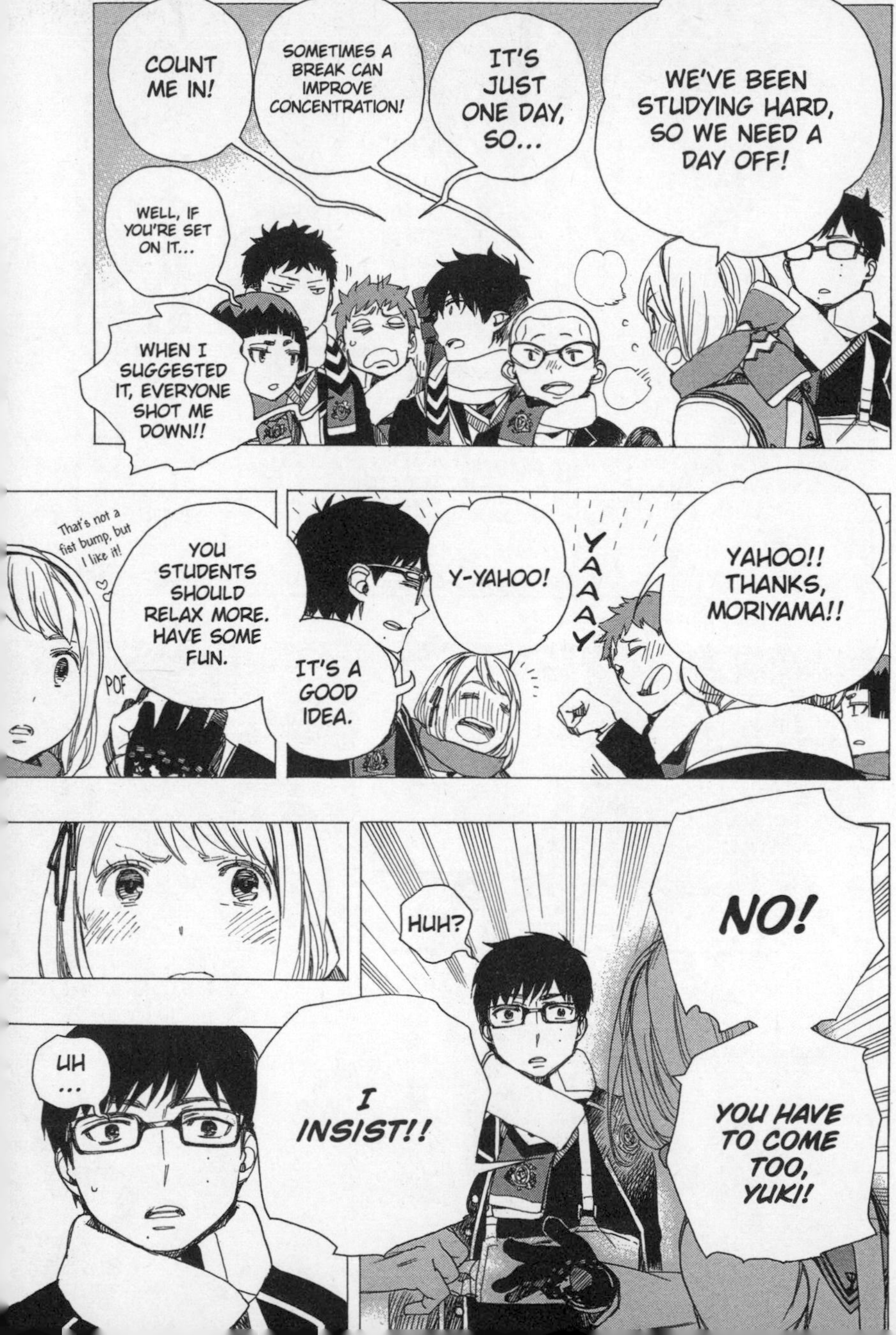

WE'VE BEEN STUDYING HARD, SO WE NEED A DAY OFF!
IT'S JUST ONE DAY, SO...
SOMETIMES A BREAK CAN IMPROVE CONCENTRATION!
COUNT ME IN!
WELL, IF YOU'RE SET ON IT...
WHEN I SUGGESTED IT, EVERYONE SHOT ME DOWN!!
YAHOO!! THANKS, MORIYAMA!!
YAAAY
Y-YAHOO!
IT'S A GOOD IDEA.
YOU STUDENTS SHOULD RELAX MORE. HAVE SOME FUN.
That's not a fist bump, but I like it!
POF
NO!
YOU HAVE TO COME TOO, YUKI!
HUH?
I INSIST!!
UH ...

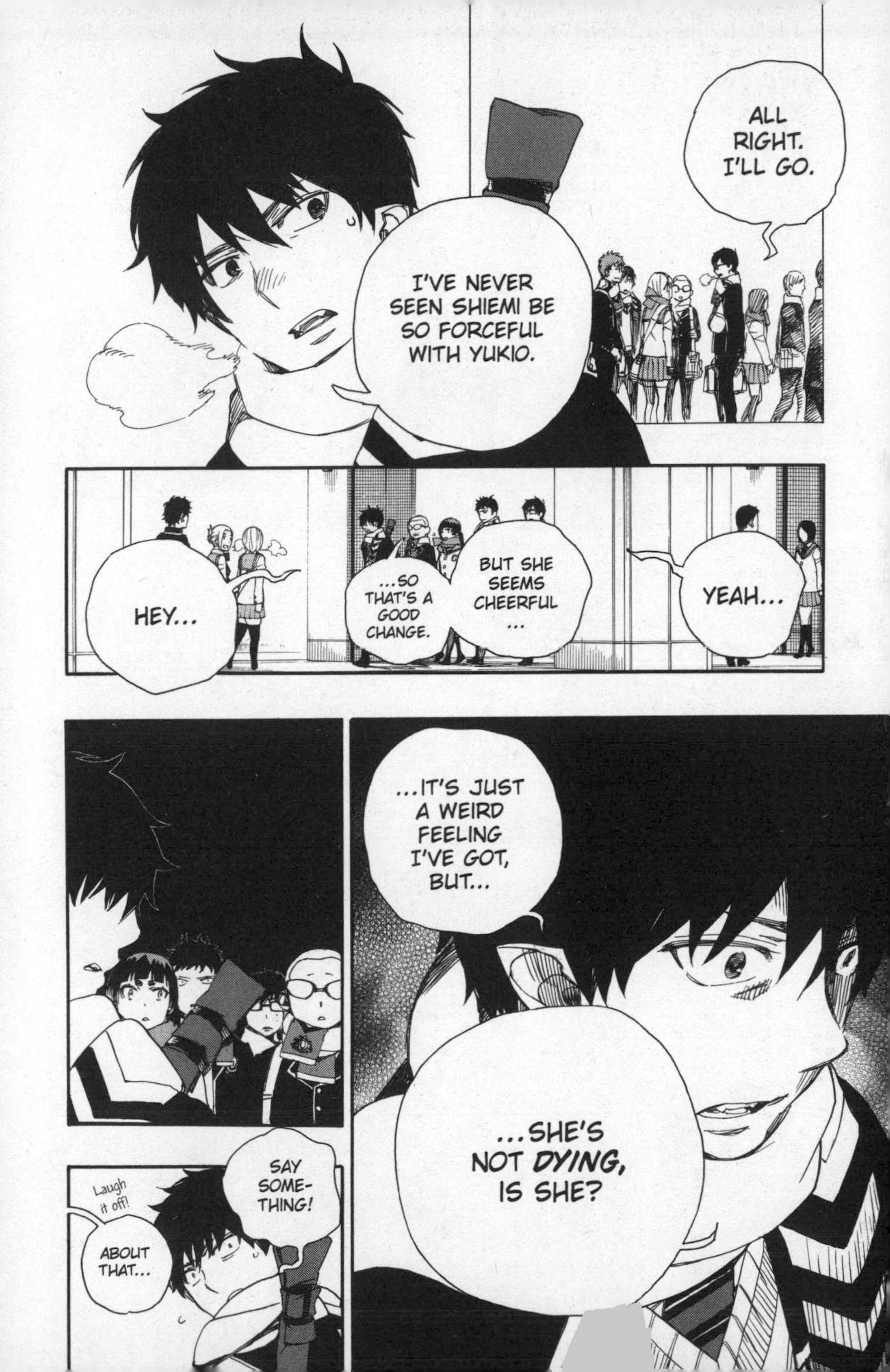
ALL RIGHT. I'LL GO.
I'VE NEVER SEEN SHIEMI BE SO FORCEFUL WITH YUKIO.
YEAH...
BUT SHE SEEMS CHEERFUL ...
...SO THAT'S A GOOD CHANGE.
HEY...
...IT'S JUST A WEIRD FEELING I'VE GOT, BUT...
...SHE'S NOT *DYING*, IS SHE?
SAY SOME-THING!
Laugh it off!
ABOUT THAT...

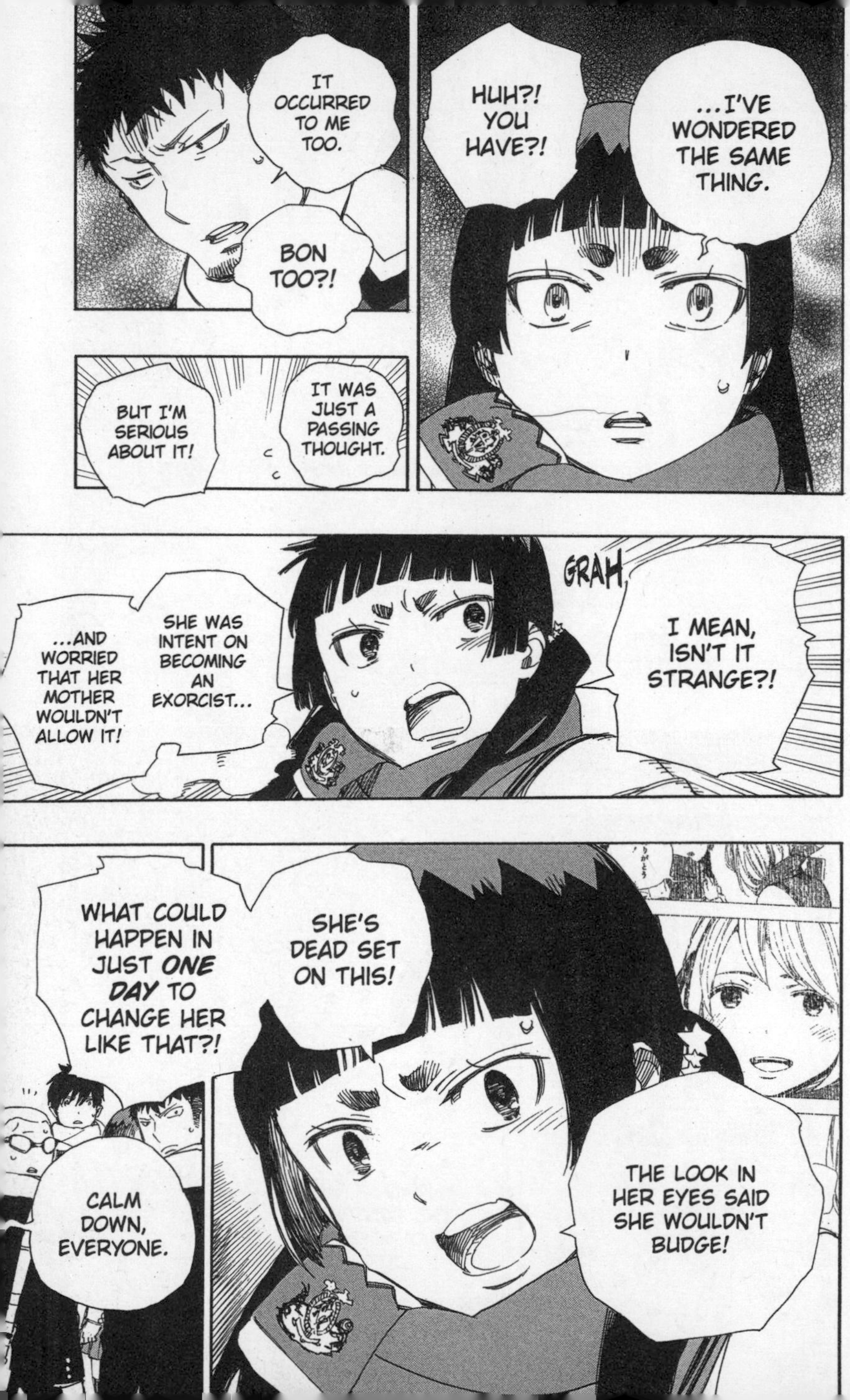
...I'VE WONDERED THE SAME THING.
HUH?! YOU HAVE?!
IT OCCURRED TO ME TOO.
BON TOO?!
IT WAS JUST A PASSING THOUGHT.
BUT I'M SERIOUS ABOUT IT!
GRAH
I MEAN, ISN'T IT STRANGE?!
SHE WAS INTENT ON BECOMING AN EXORCIST...
...AND WORRIED THAT HER MOTHER WOULDN'T ALLOW IT!
SHE'S DEAD SET ON THIS!
THE LOOK IN HER EYES SAID SHE WOULDN'T BUDGE!
WHAT COULD HAPPEN IN JUST ONE DAY TO CHANGE HER LIKE THAT?!
CALM DOWN, EVERYONE.

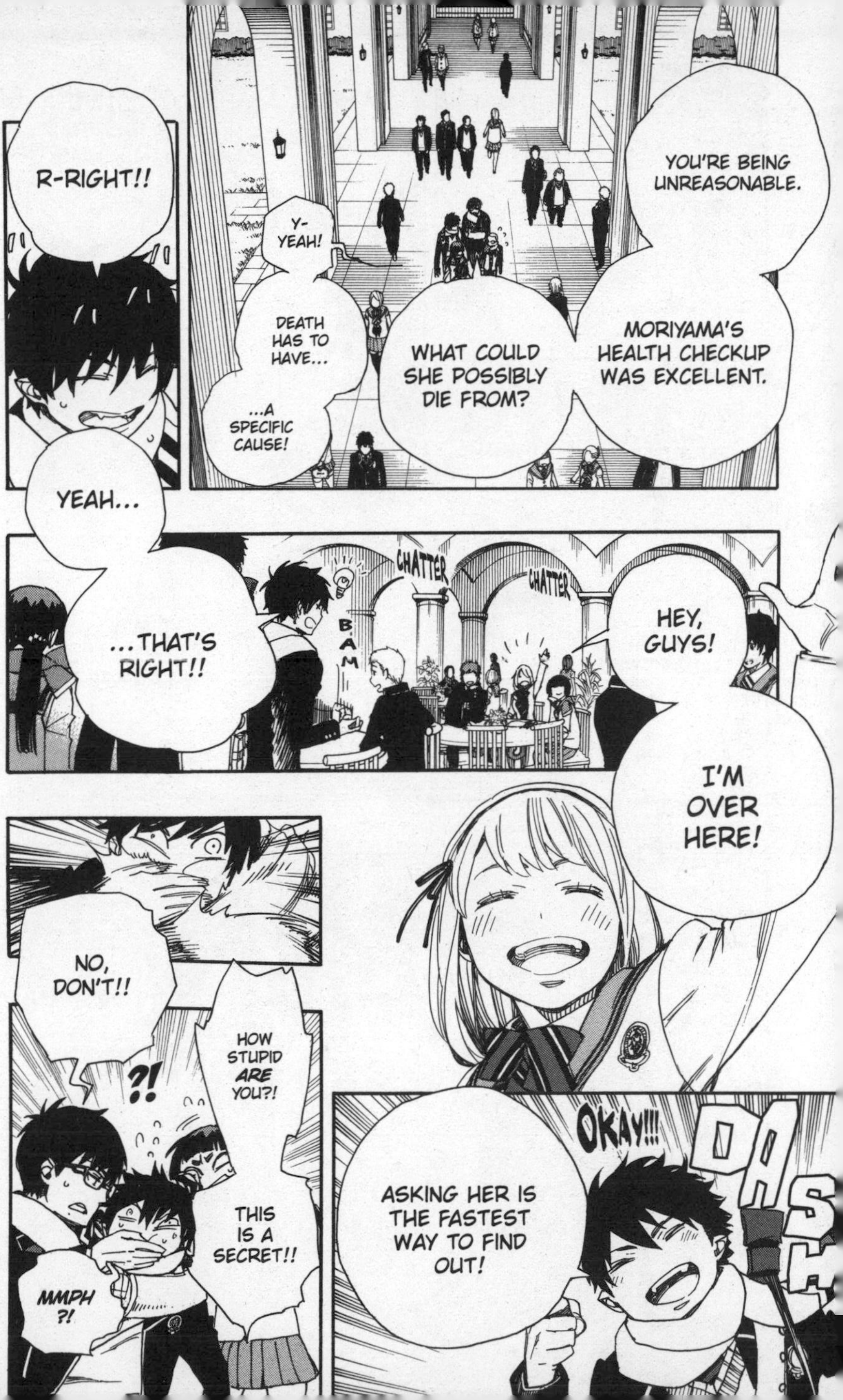
YOU'RE BEING UNREASONABLE.
MORIYAMA'S HEALTH CHECKUP WAS EXCELLENT.
WHAT COULD SHE POSSIBLY DIE FROM?
Y-YEAH!
DEATH HAS TO HAVE...
...A SPECIFIC CAUSE!
R-RIGHT!!
YEAH...
...THAT'S RIGHT!!
HEY, GUYS!
CHATTER
CHATTER
BAM
I'M OVER HERE!
OKAY!!!
DASH
ASKING HER IS THE FASTEST WAY TO FIND OUT!
NO, DON'T!!
?!
HOW STUPID ARE YOU?!
THIS IS A SECRET!!
MMPH ?!

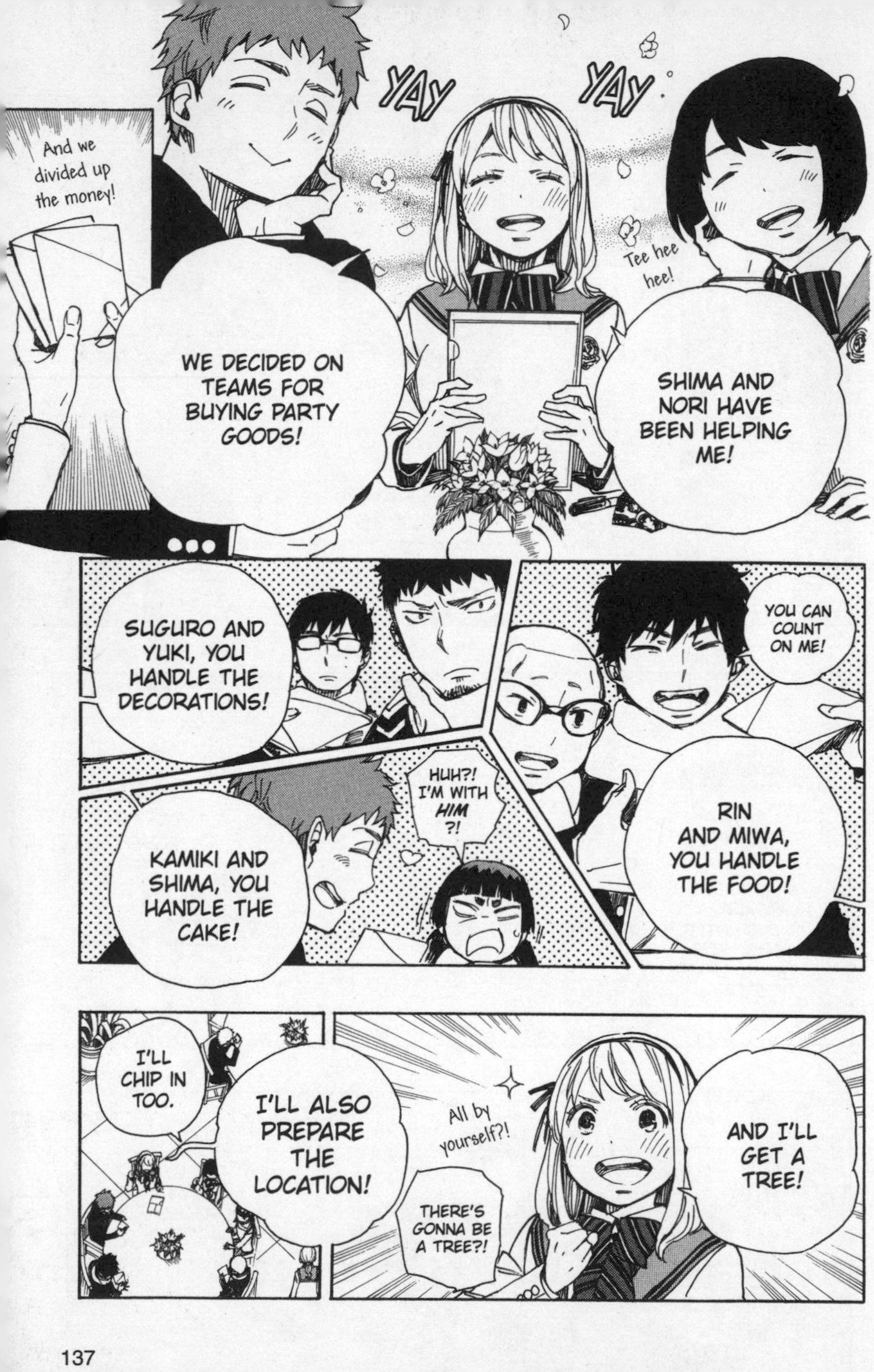
YAY
YAY
Tee hee hee!
SHIMA AND NORI HAVE BEEN HELPING ME!
And we divided up the money!
WE DECIDED ON TEAMS FOR BUYING PARTY GOODS!
...
YOU CAN COUNT ON ME!
RIN AND MIWA, YOU HANDLE THE FOOD!
SUGURO AND YUKI, YOU HANDLE THE DECORATIONS!
HUH?! I'M WITH HIM?!
KAMIKI AND SHIMA, YOU HANDLE THE CAKE!
AND I'LL GET A TREE!
All by yourself?!
THERE'S GONNA BE A TREE?!
I'LL ALSO PREPARE THE LOCATION!
I'LL CHIP IN TOO.

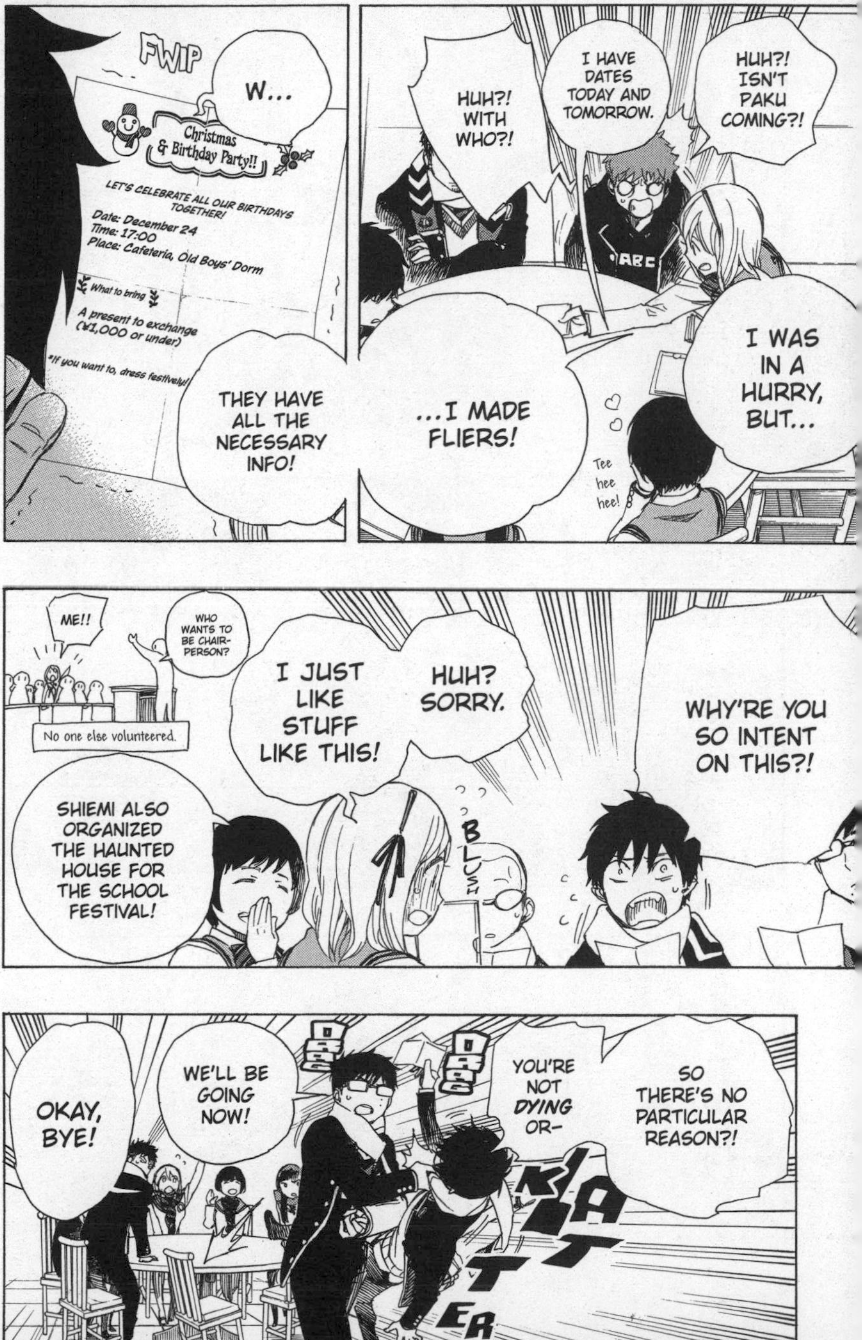
HUH?! ISN'T PAKU COMING?!
I HAVE DATES TODAY AND TOMORROW.
HUH?! WITH WHO?!
I WAS IN A HURRY, BUT...
Tee hee hee!
...I MADE FLIERS!
W...
FWIP
Christmas & Birthday Party!!
LET'S CELEBRATE ALL OUR BIRTHDAYS TOGETHER!
Date: December 24
Time: 17:00
Place: Cafeteria, Old Boys' Dorm
What to bring
A present to exchange (¥1,000 or under)
*If you want to, dress festively!
THEY HAVE ALL THE NECESSARY INFO!
WHY'RE YOU SO INTENT ON THIS?!
BLUSH
HUH? SORRY.
I JUST LIKE STUFF LIKE THIS!
WHO WANTS TO BE CHAIRPERSON?
ME!!
No one else volunteered.
SHIEMI ALSO ORGANIZED THE HAUNTED HOUSE FOR THE SCHOOL FESTIVAL!
SO THERE'S NO PARTICULAR REASON?!
KLATTER
YOU'RE NOT DYING OR—
DRAG
DRAG
WE'LL BE GOING NOW!
OKAY, BYE!

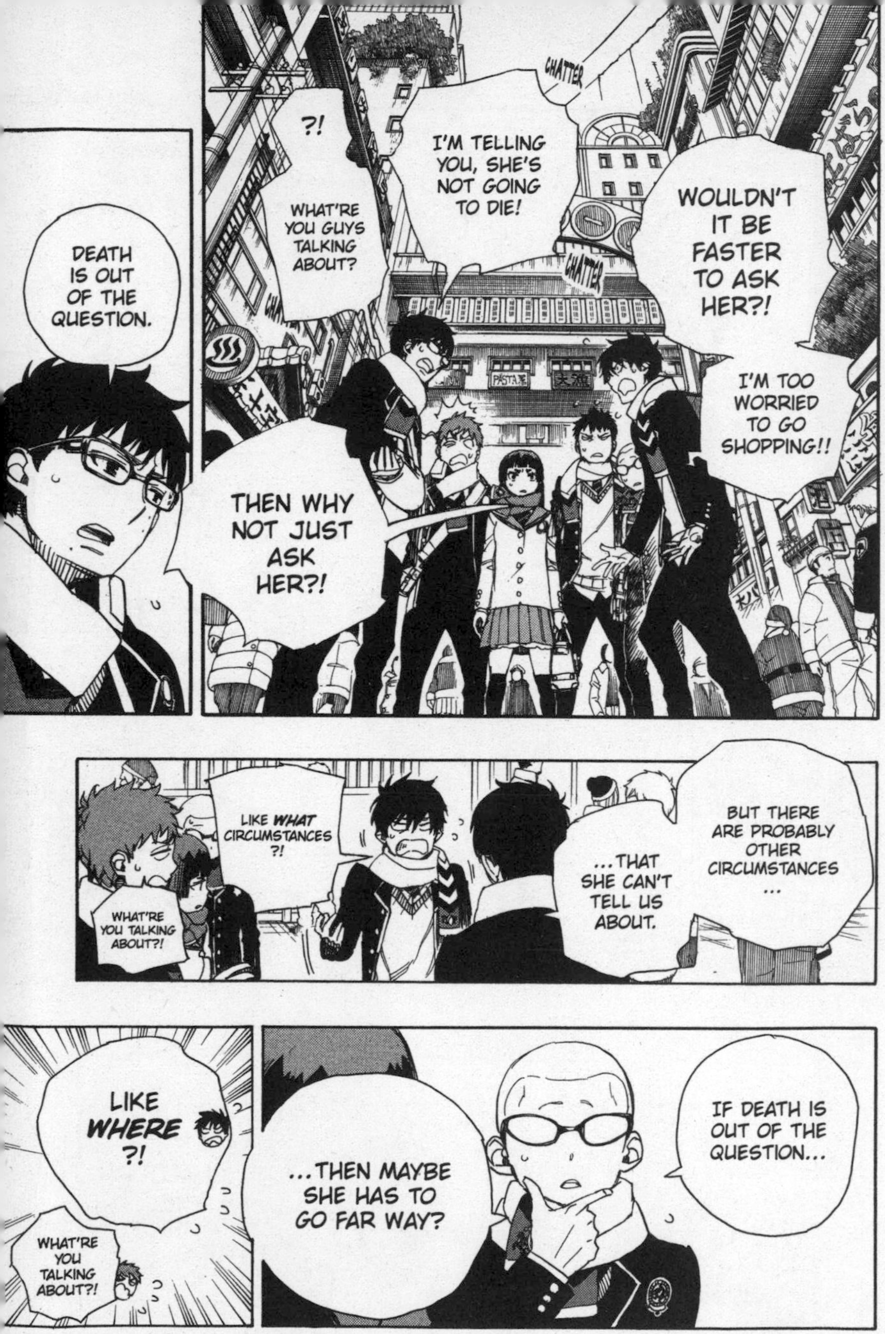

WOULDN'T IT BE FASTER TO ASK HER?!
CHATTER
I'M TELLING YOU, SHE'S NOT GOING TO DIE!
CHATTER
?!
WHAT'RE YOU GUYS TALKING ABOUT?
I'M TOO WORRIED TO GO SHOPPING!!
THEN WHY NOT JUST ASK HER?!
DEATH IS OUT OF THE QUESTION.
BUT THERE ARE PROBABLY OTHER CIRCUMSTANCES...
...THAT SHE CAN'T TELL US ABOUT.
LIKE *WHAT* CIRCUMSTANCES?!
WHAT'RE YOU TALKING ABOUT?!
IF DEATH IS OUT OF THE QUESTION...
...THEN MAYBE SHE HAS TO GO FAR WAY?
LIKE *WHERE*?!
WHAT'RE YOU TALKING ABOUT?!

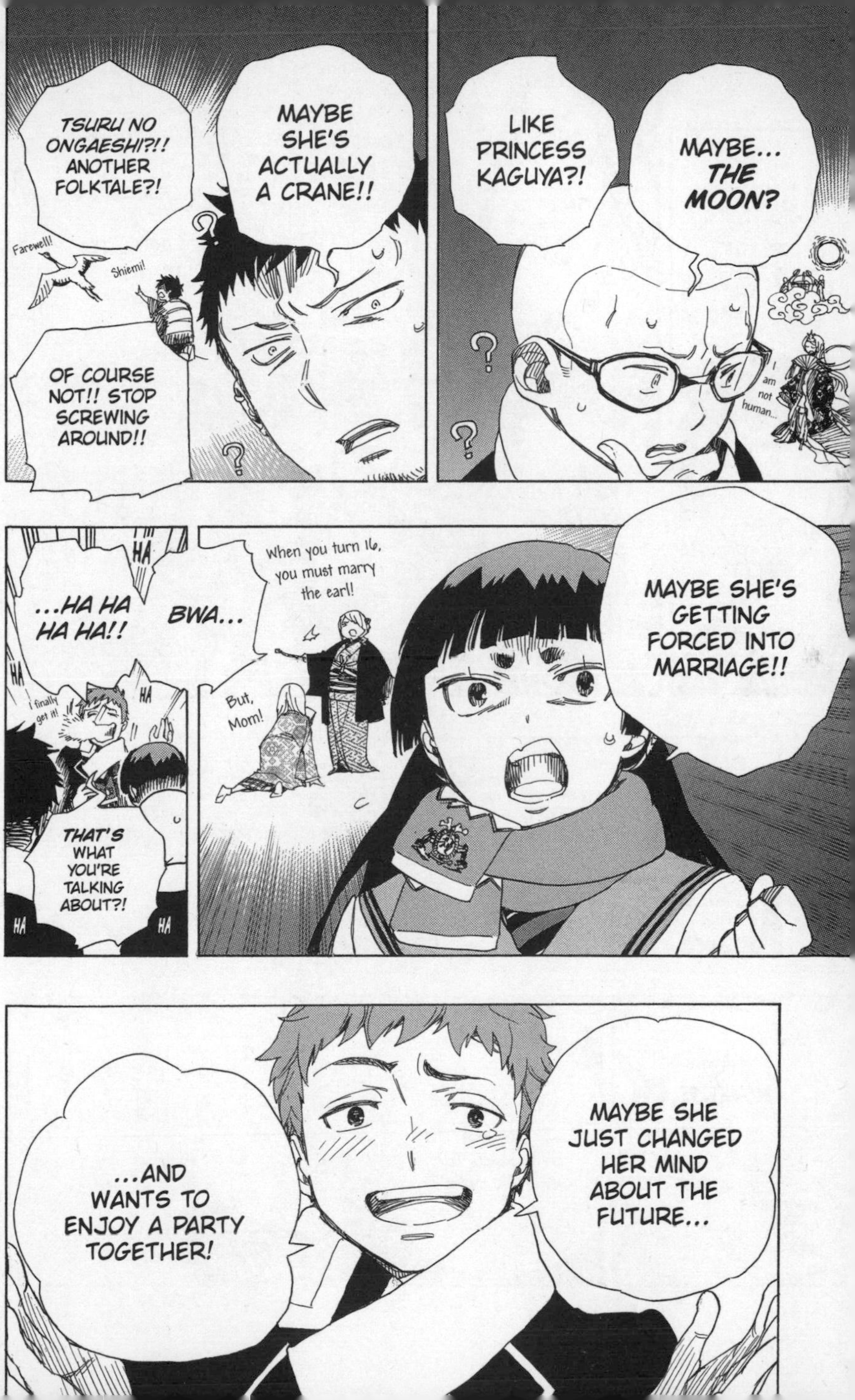
MAYBE... THE MOON?
LIKE PRINCESS KAGUYA?!
I am not human...
MAYBE SHE'S ACTUALLY A CRANE!!
TSURU NO ONGAESHI?!! ANOTHER FOLKTALE?!
Farewell!
Shiemi!
OF COURSE NOT!! STOP SCREWING AROUND!!
MAYBE SHE'S GETTING FORCED INTO MARRIAGE!!
When you turn 16, you must marry the earl!
But, Mom!
BWA...
HA
...HA HA HA HA!!
HA
HA
I finally get it!
THAT'S WHAT YOU'RE TALKING ABOUT?!
HA
HA
MAYBE SHE JUST CHANGED HER MIND ABOUT THE FUTURE...
...AND WANTS TO ENJOY A PARTY TOGETHER!

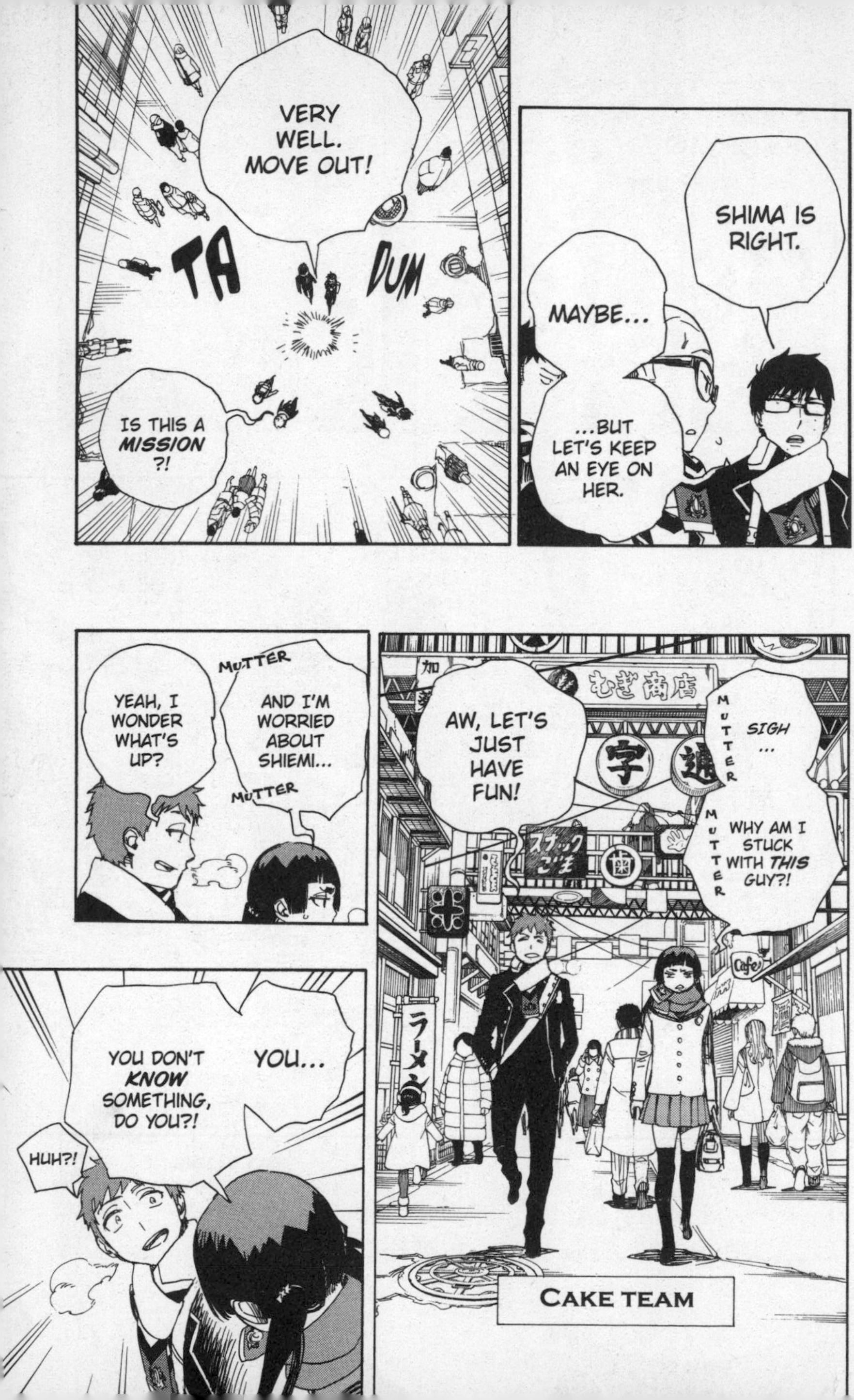

SHIMA IS RIGHT.
MAYBE...
...BUT LET'S KEEP AN EYE ON HER.
VERY WELL. MOVE OUT!
TA
DUM
IS THIS A *MISSION* ?!
AW, LET'S JUST HAVE FUN!
むぎ商店
MUTTER
SIGH...
MUTTER
WHY AM I STUCK WITH *THIS* GUY?!
Cafe
CAKE TEAM
MUTTER
AND I'M WORRIED ABOUT SHIEMI...
MUTTER
YEAH, I WONDER WHAT'S UP?
YOU...
YOU DON'T *KNOW* SOMETHING, DO YOU?!
HUH?!

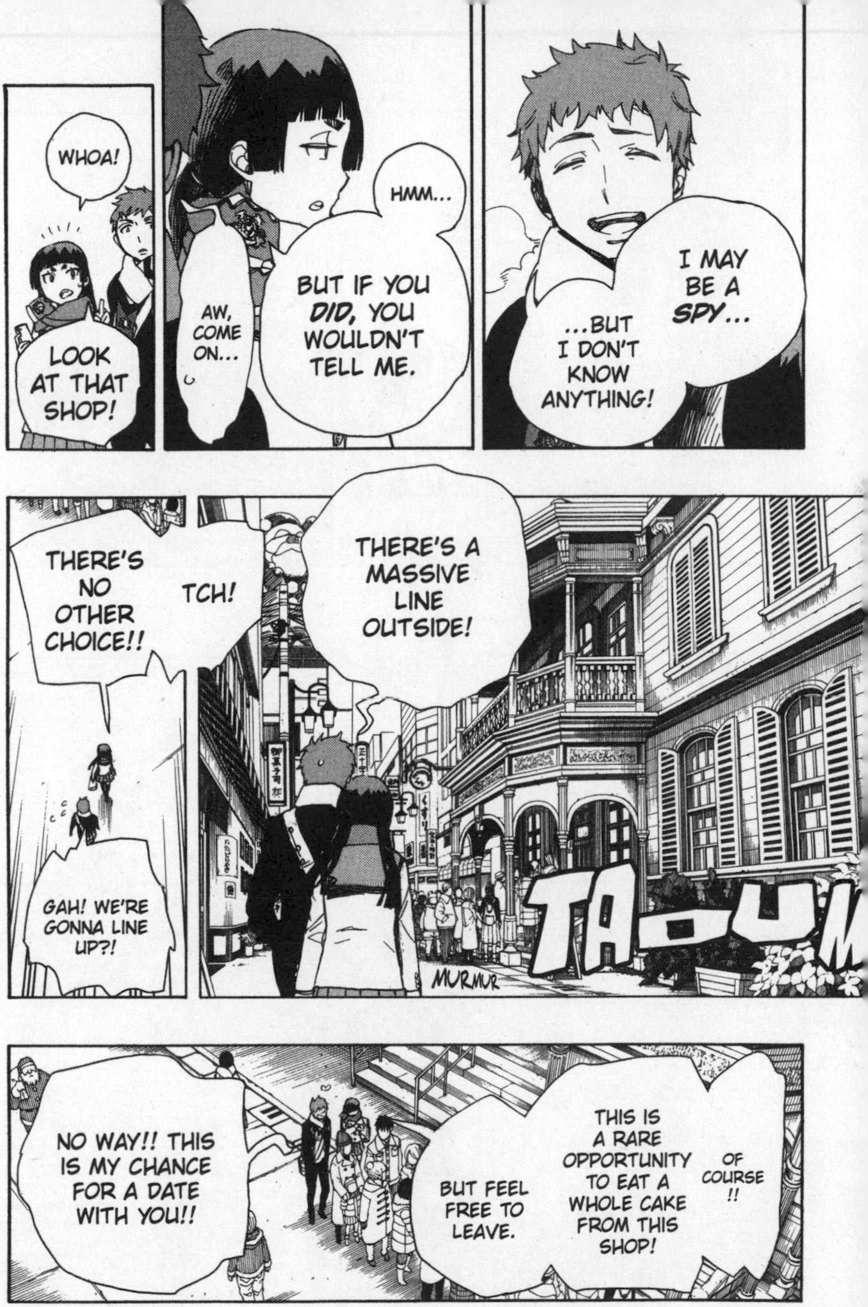
I MAY BE A SPY...
...BUT I DON'T KNOW ANYTHING!
HMM...
BUT IF YOU DID, YOU WOULDN'T TELL ME.
AW, COME ON...
WHOA!
LOOK AT THAT SHOP!
THERE'S A MASSIVE LINE OUTSIDE!
TA-DUM
MURMUR
TCH!
THERE'S NO OTHER CHOICE!!
GAH! WE'RE GONNA LINE UP?!
OF COURSE!!
THIS IS A RARE OPPORTUNITY TO EAT A WHOLE CAKE FROM THIS SHOP!
BUT FEEL FREE TO LEAVE.
NO WAY!! THIS IS MY CHANCE FOR A DATE WITH YOU!!

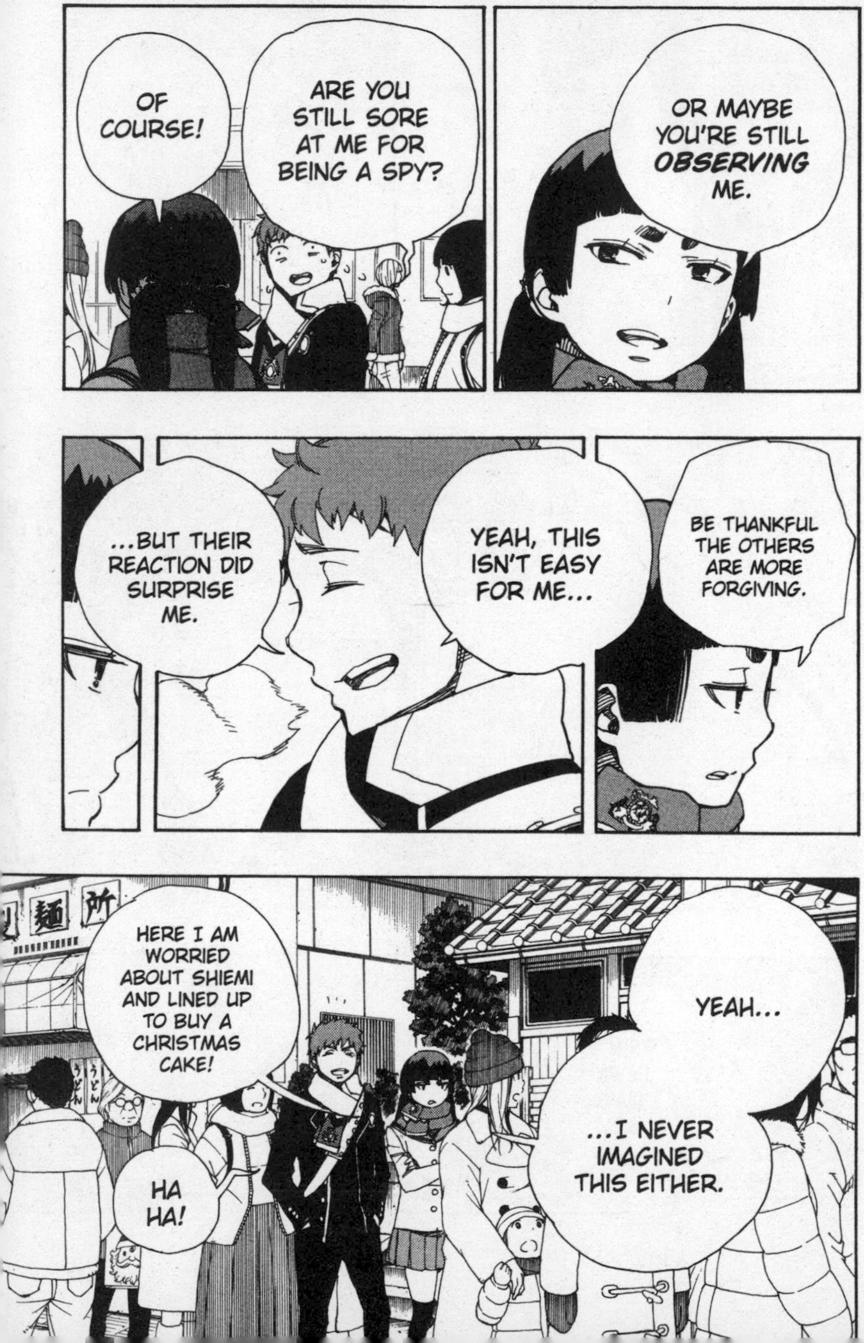
OR MAYBE YOU'RE STILL OBSERVING ME.
ARE YOU STILL SORE AT ME FOR BEING A SPY?
OF COURSE!
BE THANKFUL THE OTHERS ARE MORE FORGIVING.
YEAH, THIS ISN'T EASY FOR ME...
...BUT THEIR REACTION DID SURPRISE ME.
YEAH...
...I NEVER IMAGINED THIS EITHER.
HERE I AM WORRIED ABOUT SHIEMI AND LINED UP TO BUY A CHRISTMAS CAKE!
HA HA!

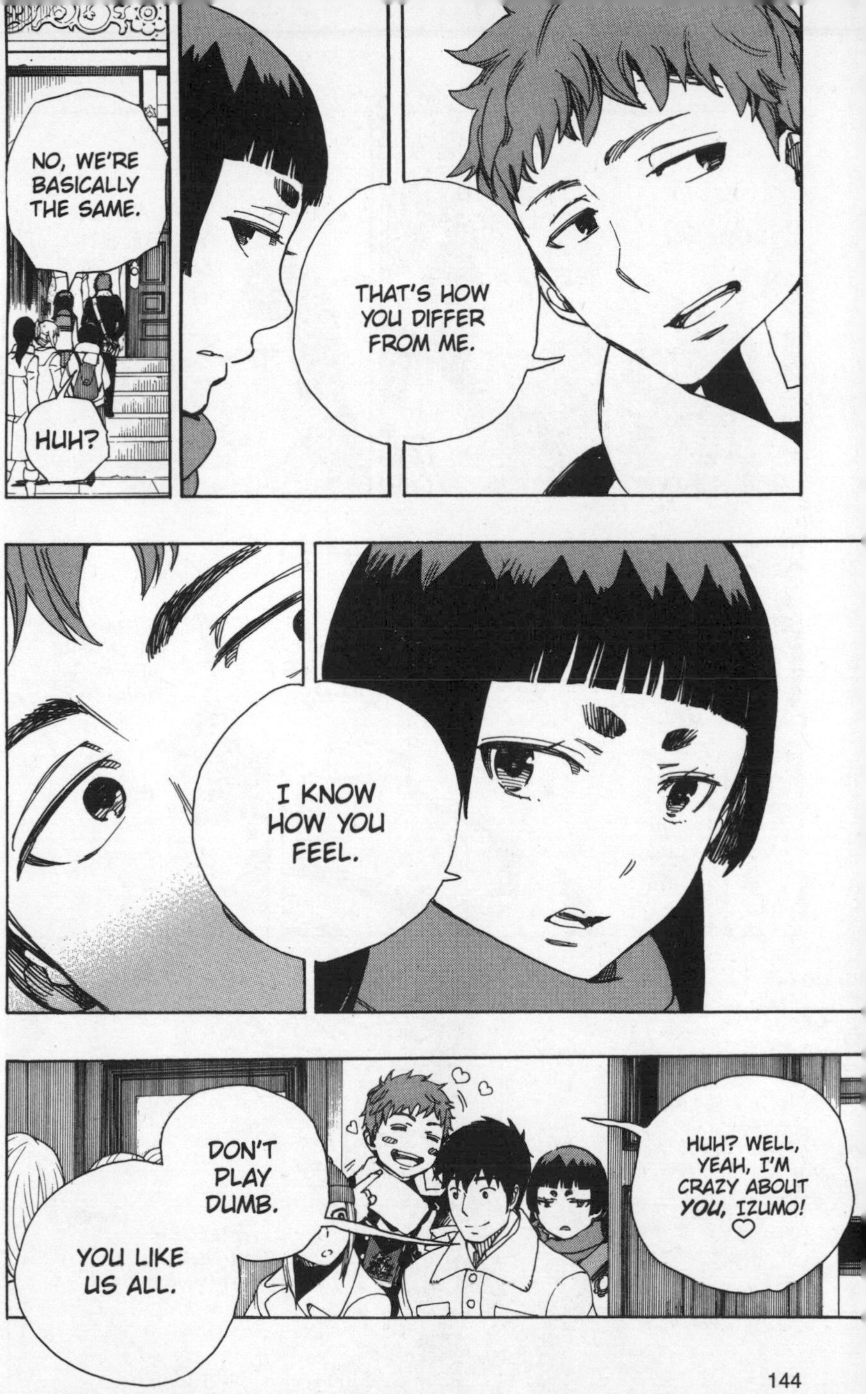
THAT'S HOW YOU DIFFER FROM ME.
NO, WE'RE BASICALLY THE SAME.
HUH?
I KNOW HOW YOU FEEL.
HUH? WELL, YEAH, I'M CRAZY ABOUT *YOU*, IZUMO! ♡
DON'T PLAY DUMB.
YOU LIKE US ALL.

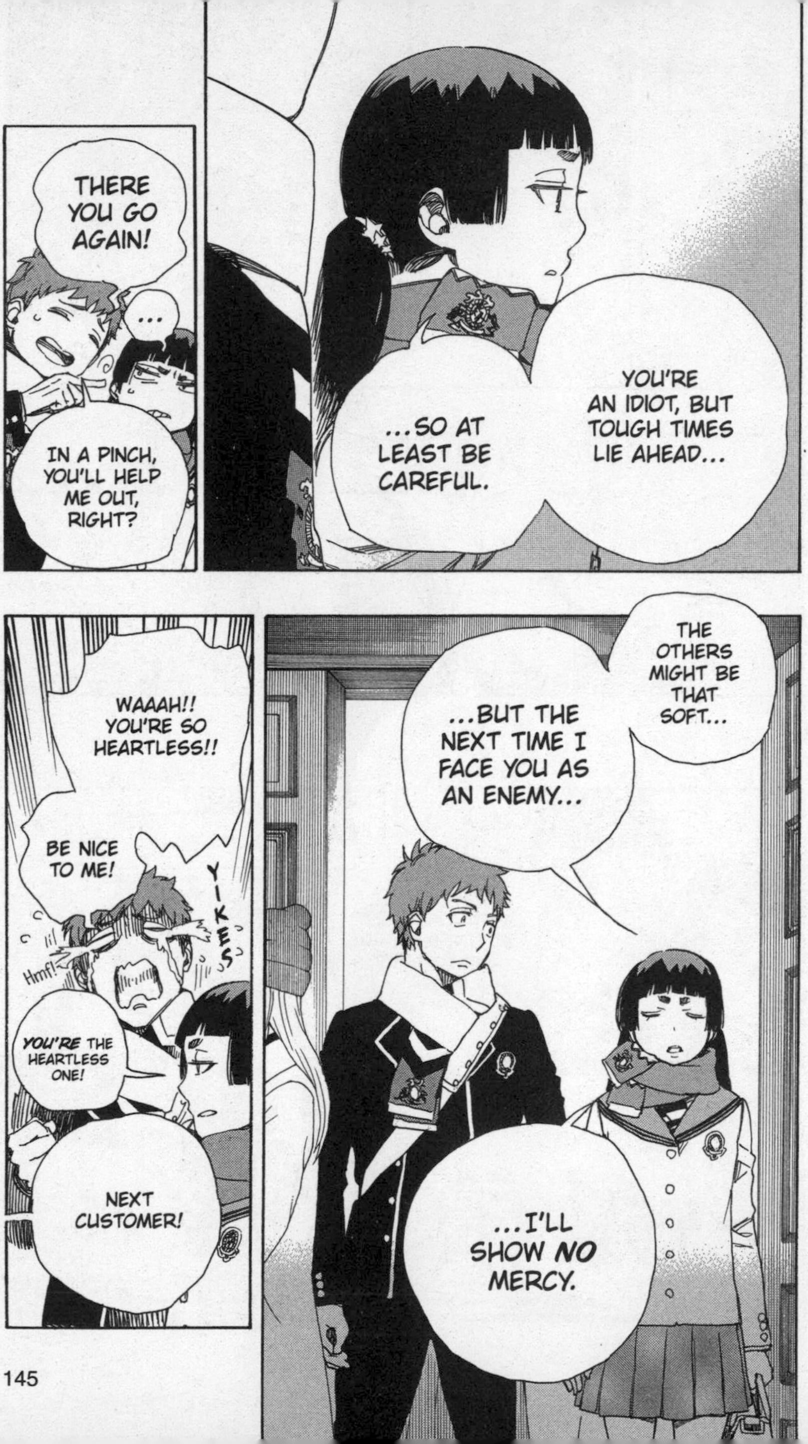
YOU'RE AN IDIOT, BUT TOUGH TIMES LIE AHEAD...
...SO AT LEAST BE CAREFUL.
THERE YOU GO AGAIN!
...
IN A PINCH, YOU'LL HELP ME OUT, RIGHT?
THE OTHERS MIGHT BE THAT SOFT...
...BUT THE NEXT TIME I FACE YOU AS AN ENEMY...
...I'LL SHOW NO MERCY.
WAAAH!! YOU'RE SO HEARTLESS!!
BE NICE TO ME!
YIKES
Hmf!
YOU'RE THE HEARTLESS ONE!
NEXT CUSTOMER!

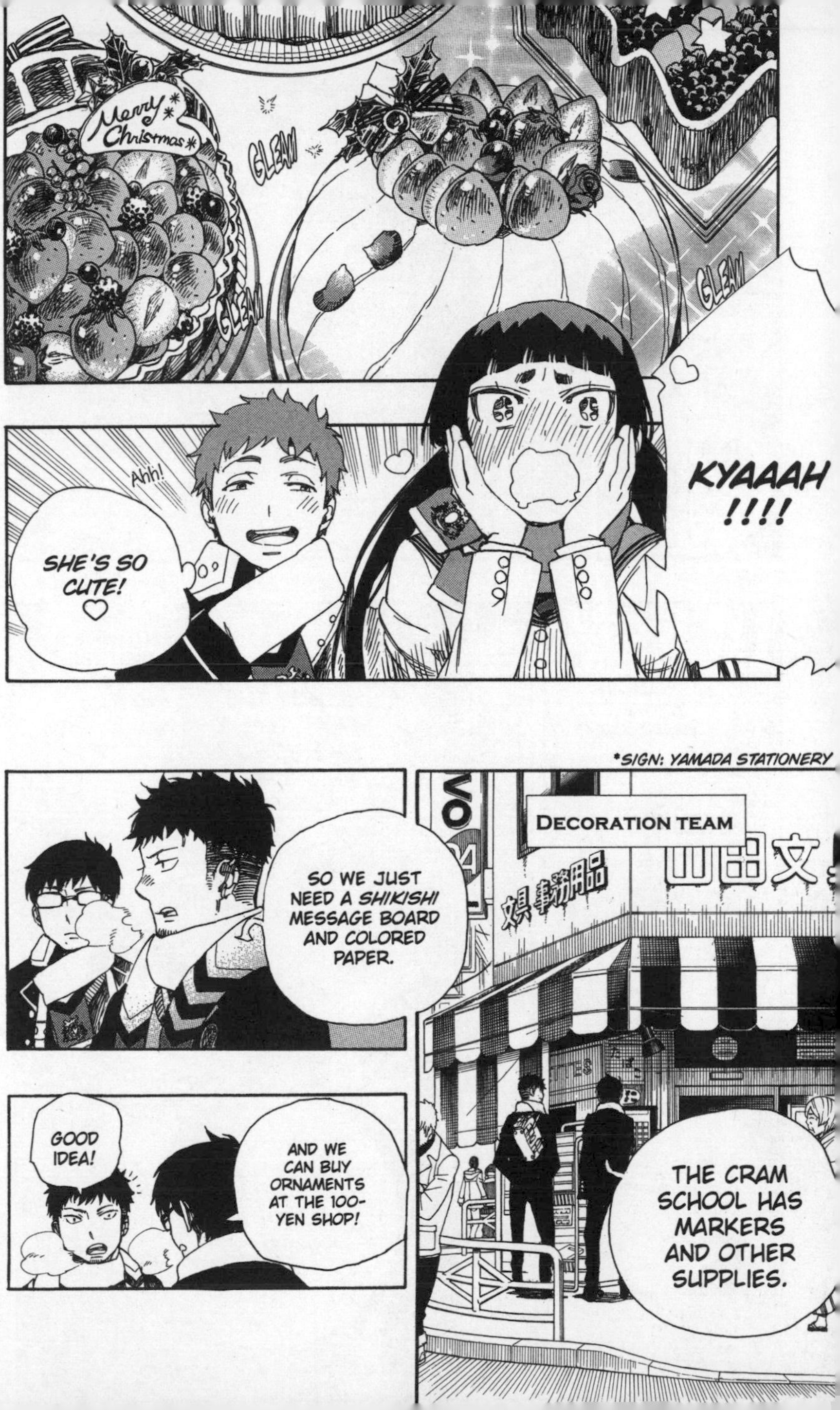
Merry Christmas
GLEAM
GLEAM
GLEAM
KYAAAH !!!!
Ahh!
SHE'S SO CUTE! ♡
*SIGN: YAMADA STATIONERY
Decoration team
THE CRAM SCHOOL HAS MARKERS AND OTHER SUPPLIES.
SO WE JUST NEED A *SHIKISHI* MESSAGE BOARD AND COLORED PAPER.
AND WE CAN BUY ORNAMENTS AT THE 100-YEN SHOP!
GOOD IDEA!

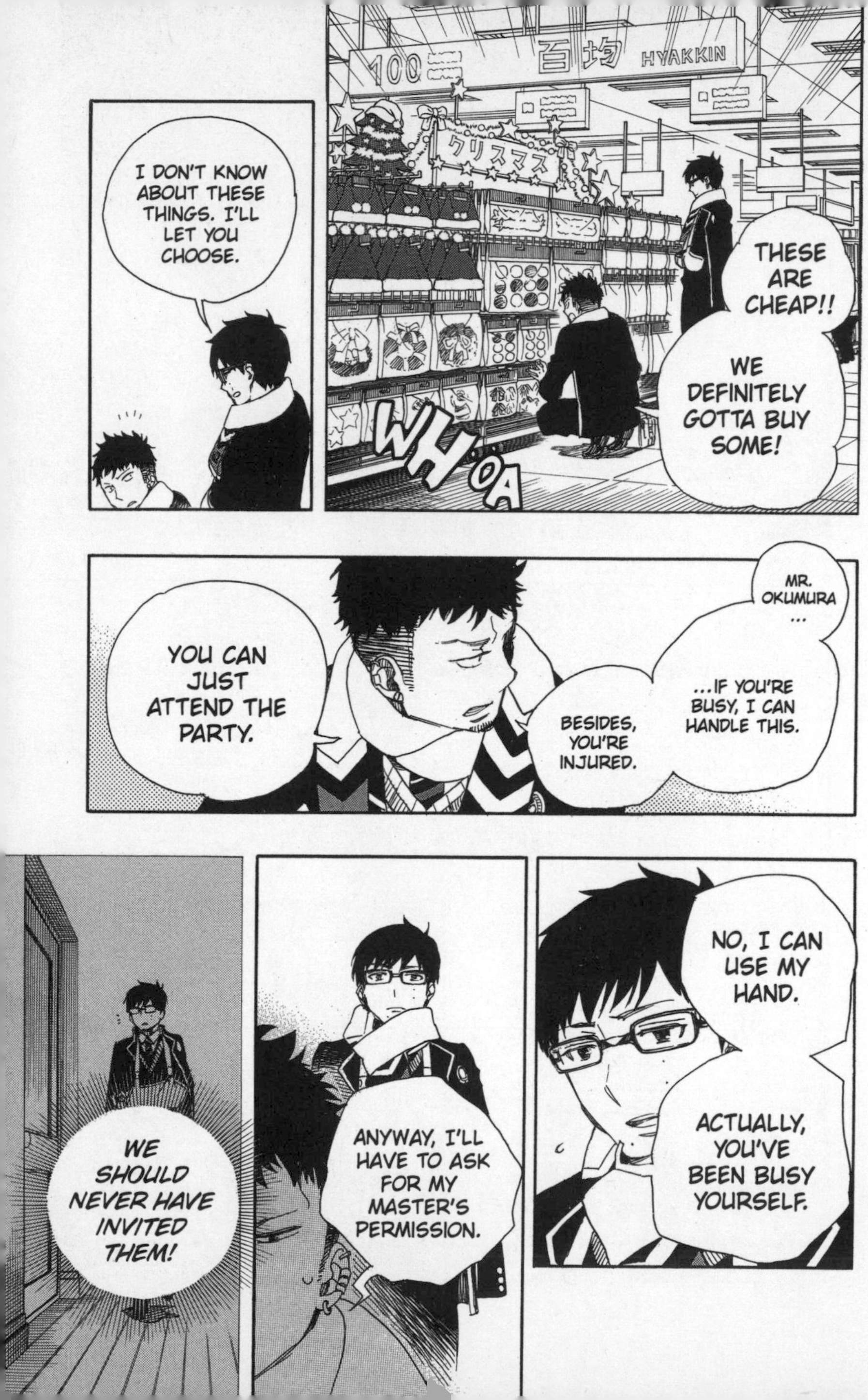
100
百均 HYAKKIN
クリスマス
THESE ARE CHEAP!!
WE DEFINITELY GOTTA BUY SOME!
WHOA
I DON'T KNOW ABOUT THESE THINGS. I'LL LET YOU CHOOSE.
MR. OKUMURA...
...IF YOU'RE BUSY, I CAN HANDLE THIS.
BESIDES, YOU'RE INJURED.
YOU CAN JUST ATTEND THE PARTY.
NO, I CAN USE MY HAND.
ACTUALLY, YOU'VE BEEN BUSY YOURSELF.
ANYWAY, I'LL HAVE TO ASK FOR MY MASTER'S PERMISSION.
WE SHOULD NEVER HAVE INVITED THEM!

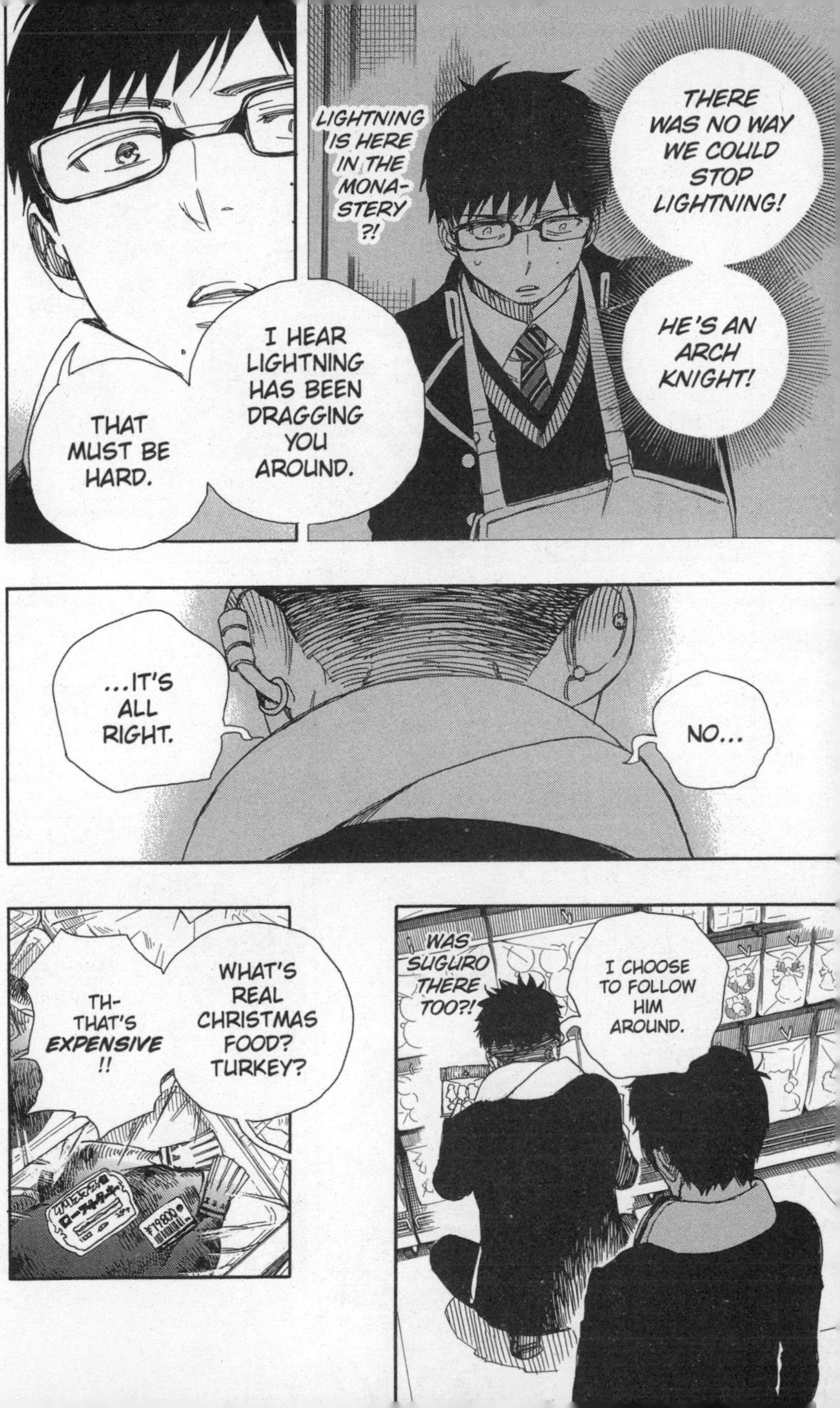
THERE WAS NO WAY WE COULD STOP LIGHTNING!
HE'S AN ARCH KNIGHT!
LIGHTNING IS HERE IN THE MONASTERY?!
I HEAR LIGHTNING HAS BEEN DRAGGING YOU AROUND.
THAT MUST BE HARD.
NO...
...IT'S ALL RIGHT.
I CHOOSE TO FOLLOW HIM AROUND.
WAS SUGURO THERE TOO?!
WHAT'S REAL CHRISTMAS FOOD? TURKEY?
TH-THAT'S EXPENSIVE!!

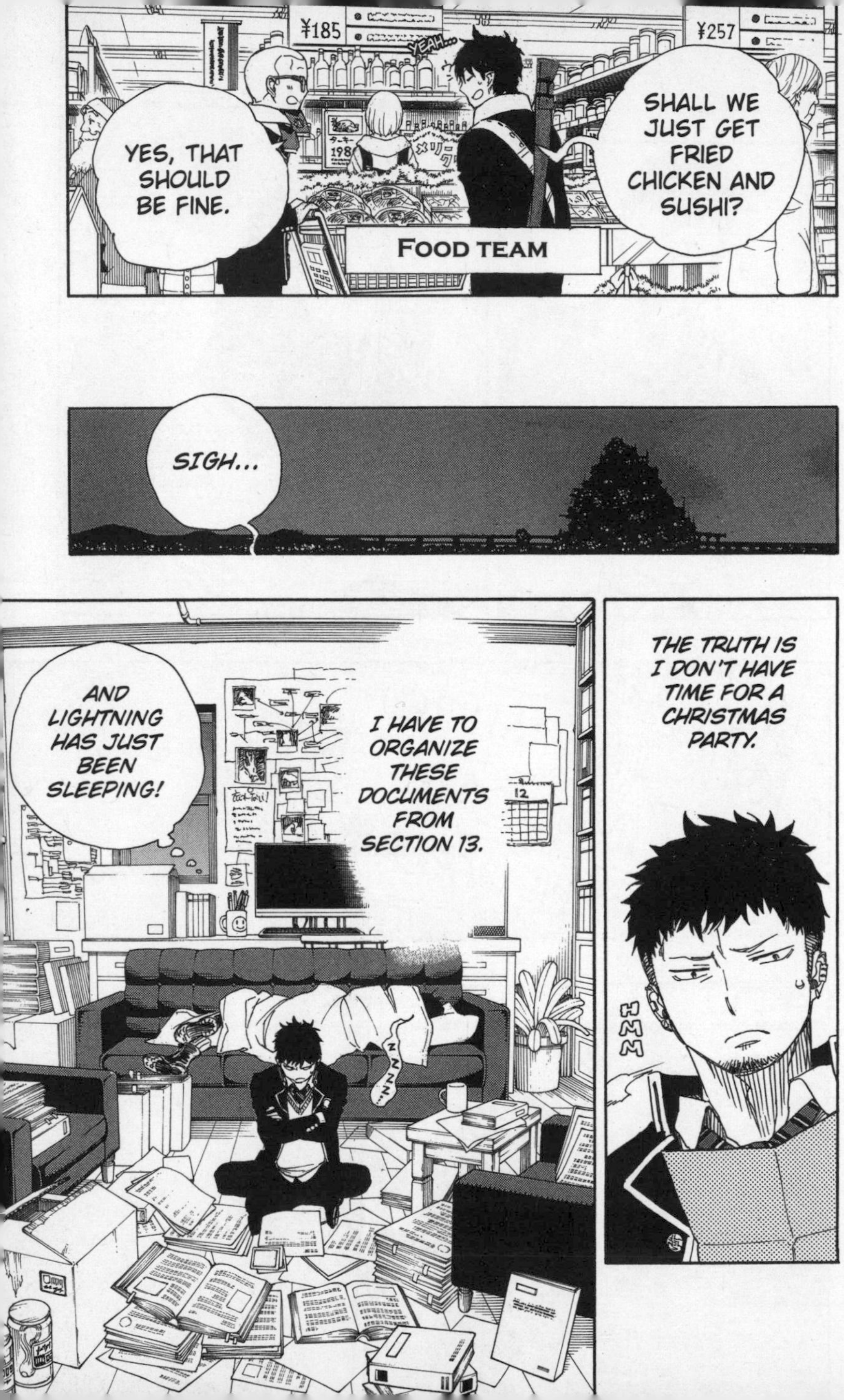
¥257
SHALL WE JUST GET FRIED CHICKEN AND SUSHI?
YEAH...
¥185
YES, THAT SHOULD BE FINE.
FOOD TEAM
SIGH...
THE TRUTH IS I DON'T HAVE TIME FOR A CHRISTMAS PARTY.
HMM
I HAVE TO ORGANIZE THESE DOCUMENTS FROM SECTION 13.
AND LIGHTNING HAS JUST BEEN SLEEPING!
ZZZ...

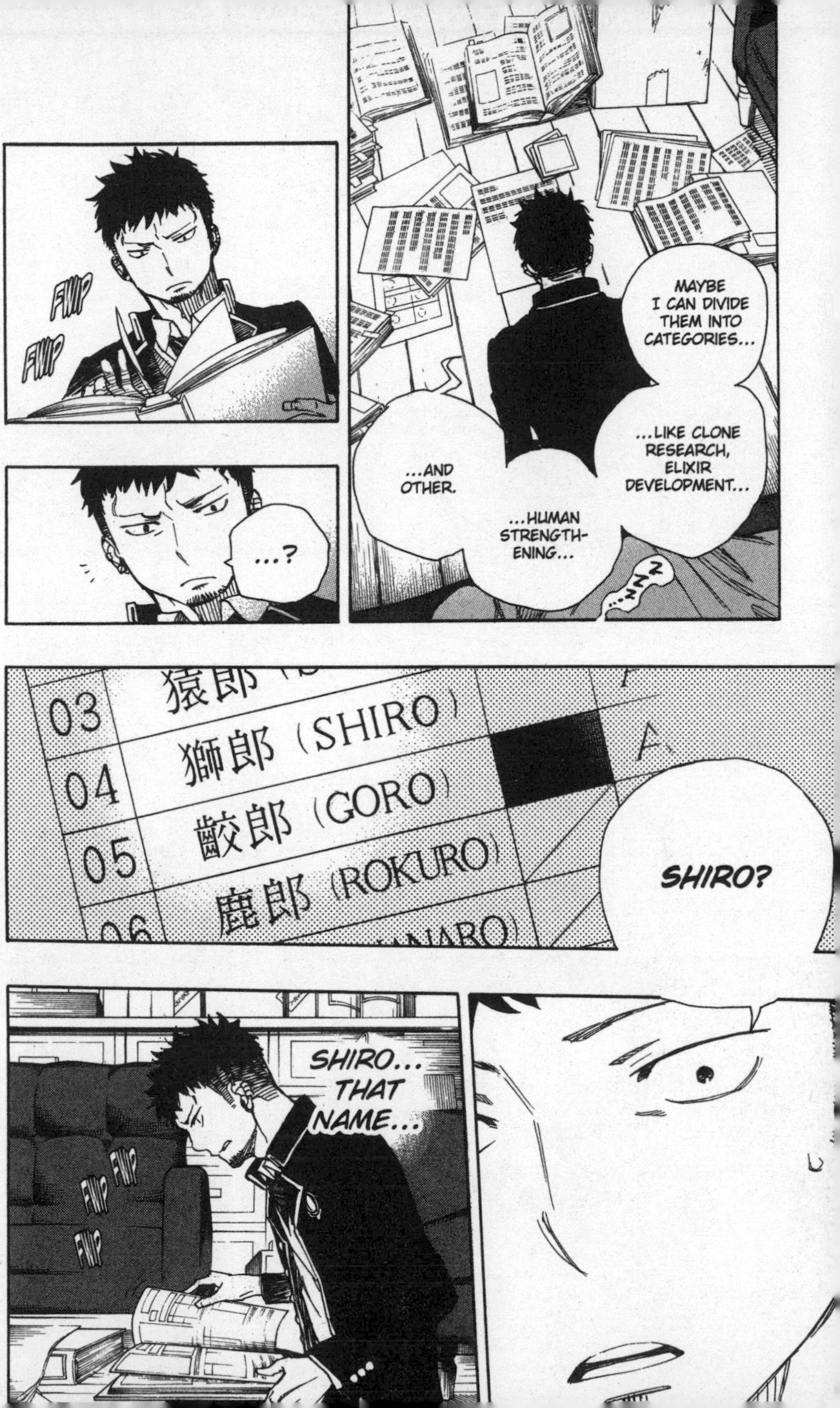
MAYBE I CAN DIVIDE THEM INTO CATEGORIES...
...LIKE CLONE RESEARCH, ELIXIR DEVELOPMENT...
...HUMAN STRENGTH-ENING...
...AND OTHER.
Zzz...
FWIP
FWIP
...?
03
猿郎
獅郎 (SHIRO)
04
A
鮫郎 (GORO)
05
鹿郎 (ROKURO)
SHIRO?
SHIRO... THAT NAME...
FWIP
FWIP
FWIP

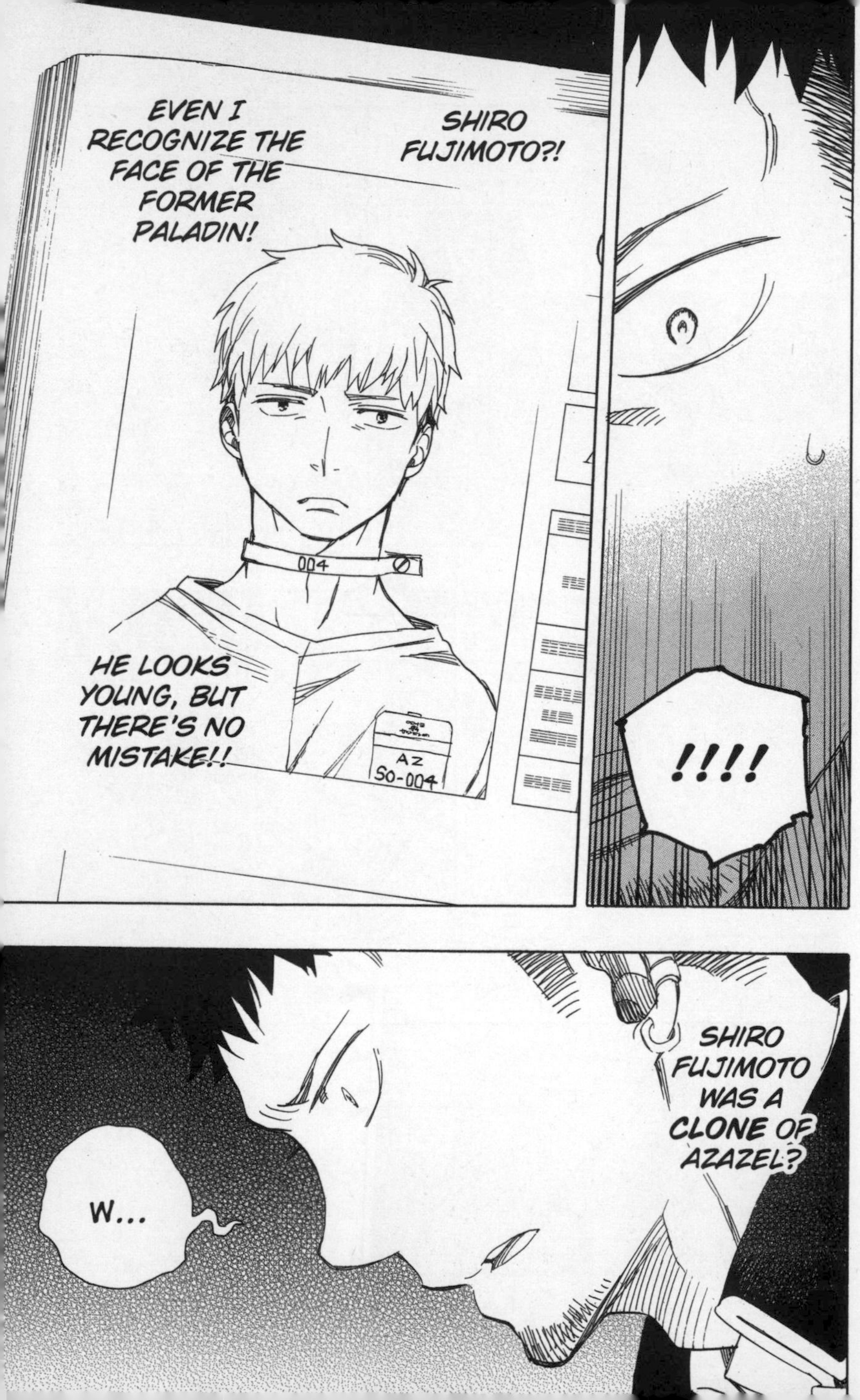
!!!!
SHIRO FUJIMOTO?!
EVEN I RECOGNIZE THE FACE OF THE FORMER PALADIN!
004
AZ
SO-004
HE LOOKS YOUNG, BUT THERE'S NO MISTAKE!!
SHIRO FUJIMOTO WAS A CLONE OF AZAZEL?
W...

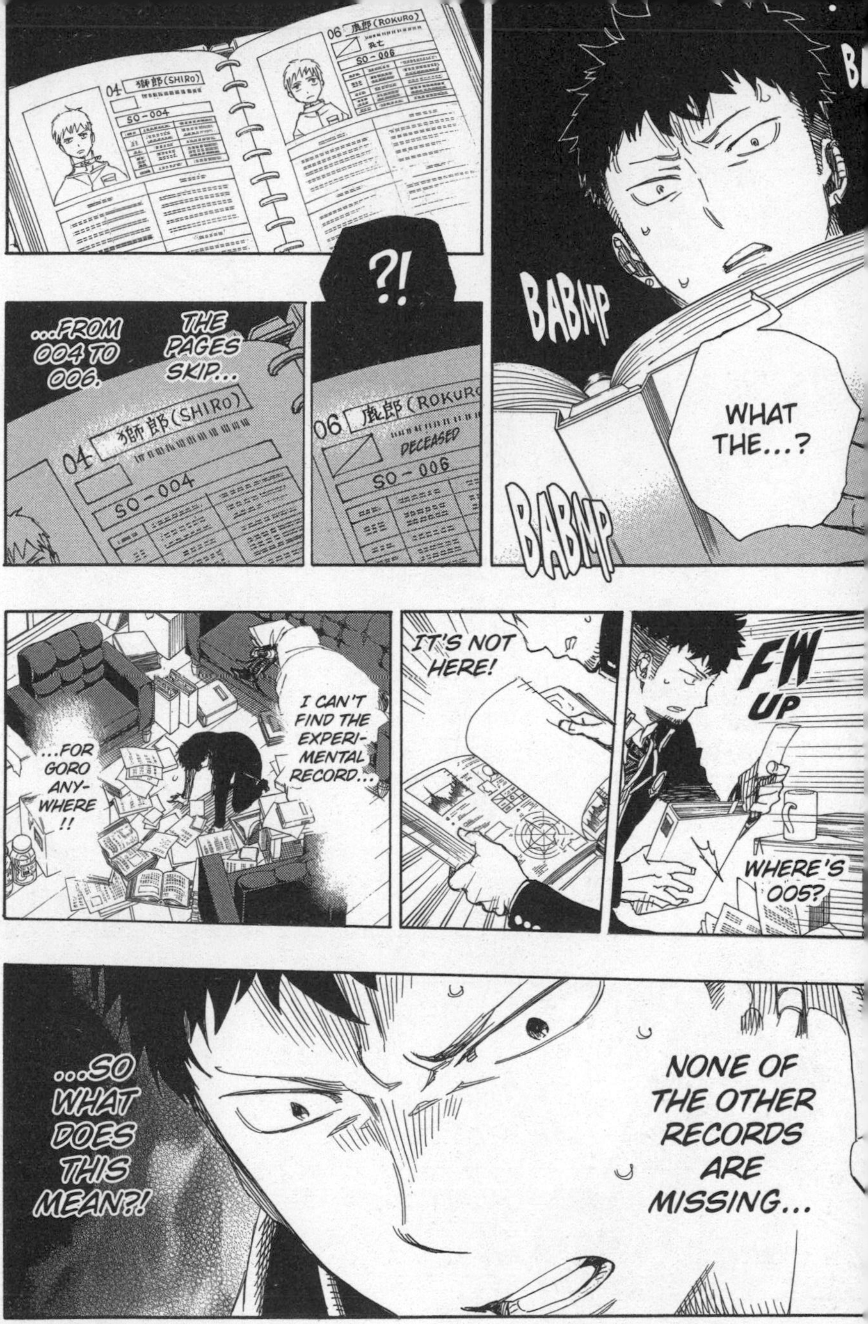
BABMP
BABMP
WHAT THE...?
04 獅郎 (SHIRO)
SO-004
06 鹿郎 (ROKURO)
SO-006
?!
06 鹿郎 (ROKURO
DECEASED
SO-006
THE PAGES SKIP...
...FROM 004 TO 006.
04 獅郎 (SHIRO)
SO-004
FWUP
WHERE'S 005?
IT'S NOT HERE!
I CAN'T FIND THE EXPERI-MENTAL RECORD...
...FOR GORO ANY-WHERE!!
NONE OF THE OTHER RECORDS ARE MISSING...
...SO WHAT DOES THIS MEAN?!

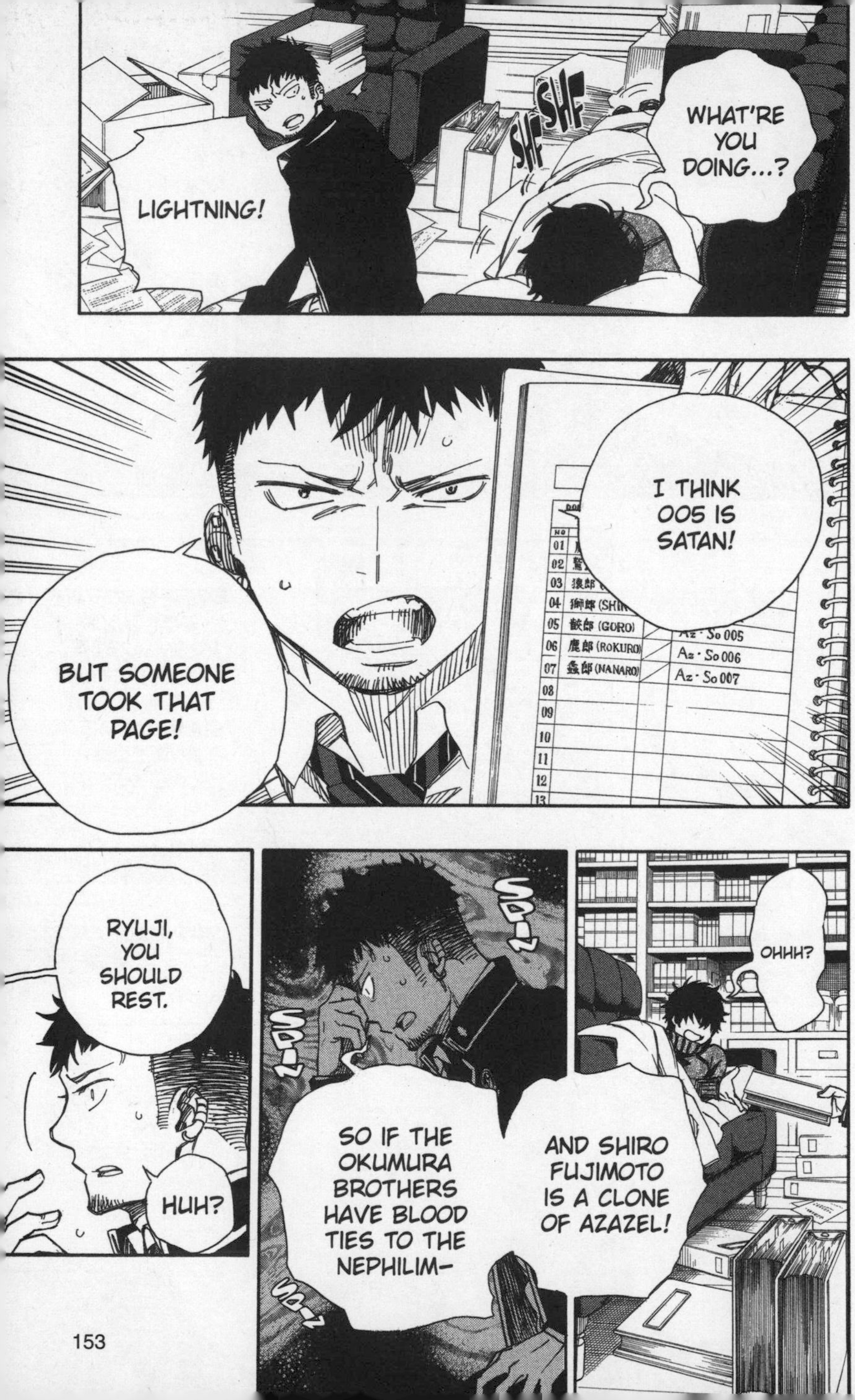
WHAT'RE YOU DOING...?
SHF SHF
LIGHTNING!
I THINK 005 IS SATAN!
BUT SOMEONE TOOK THAT PAGE!
(GORO) Az · So 005
(ROKURO) Az · So 006
(NANARO) Az · So 007
OHHH?
SO IF THE OKUMURA BROTHERS HAVE BLOOD TIES TO THE NEPHILIM-
AND SHIRO FUJIMOTO IS A CLONE OF AZAZEL!
RYUJI, YOU SHOULD REST.
HUH?

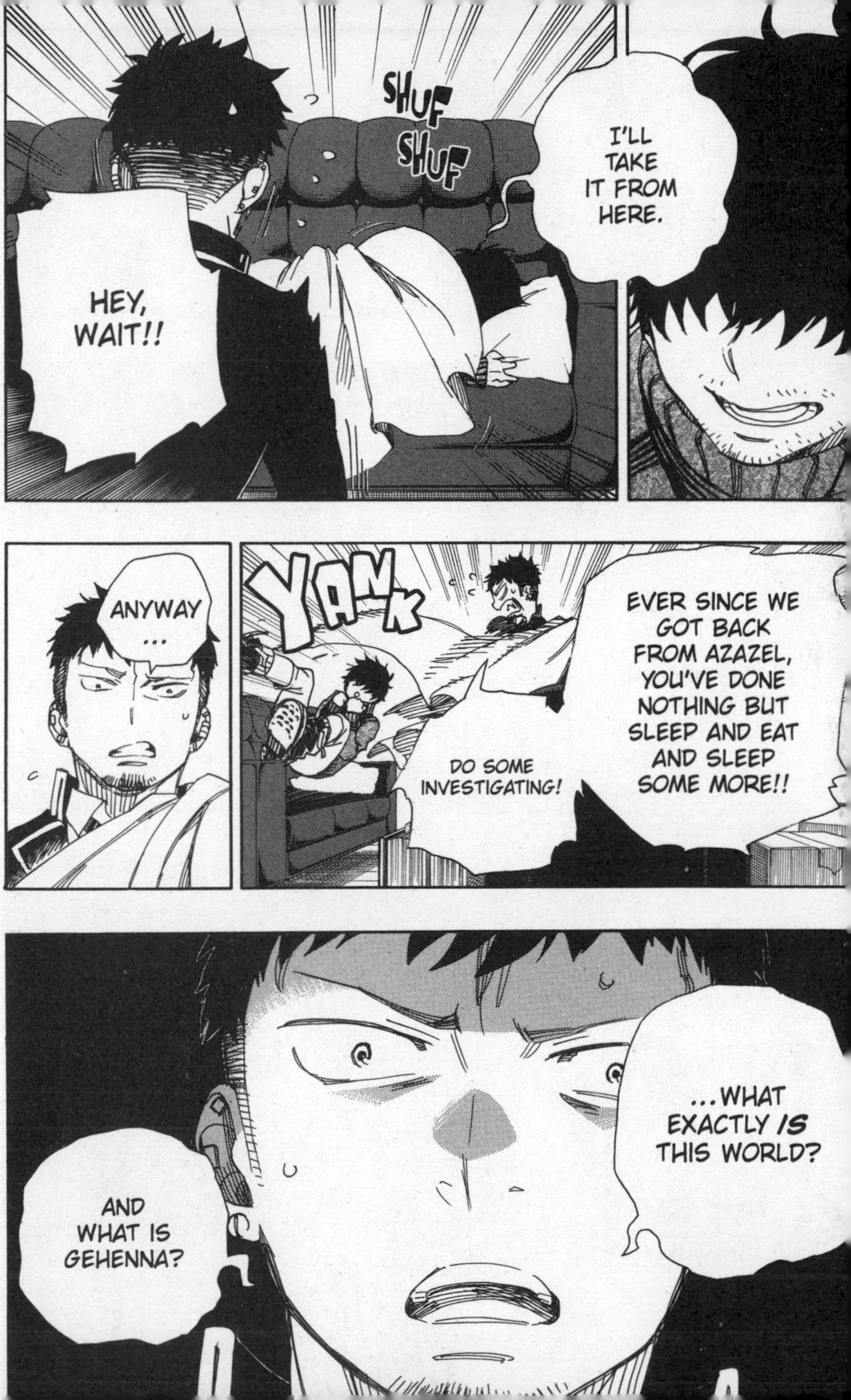
I'LL TAKE IT FROM HERE.
SHUF SHUF
HEY, WAIT!!
EVER SINCE WE GOT BACK FROM AZAZEL, YOU'VE DONE NOTHING BUT SLEEP AND EAT AND SLEEP SOME MORE!!
YANK
DO SOME INVESTIGATING!
ANYWAY ...
...WHAT EXACTLY IS THIS WORLD?
AND WHAT IS GEHENNA?

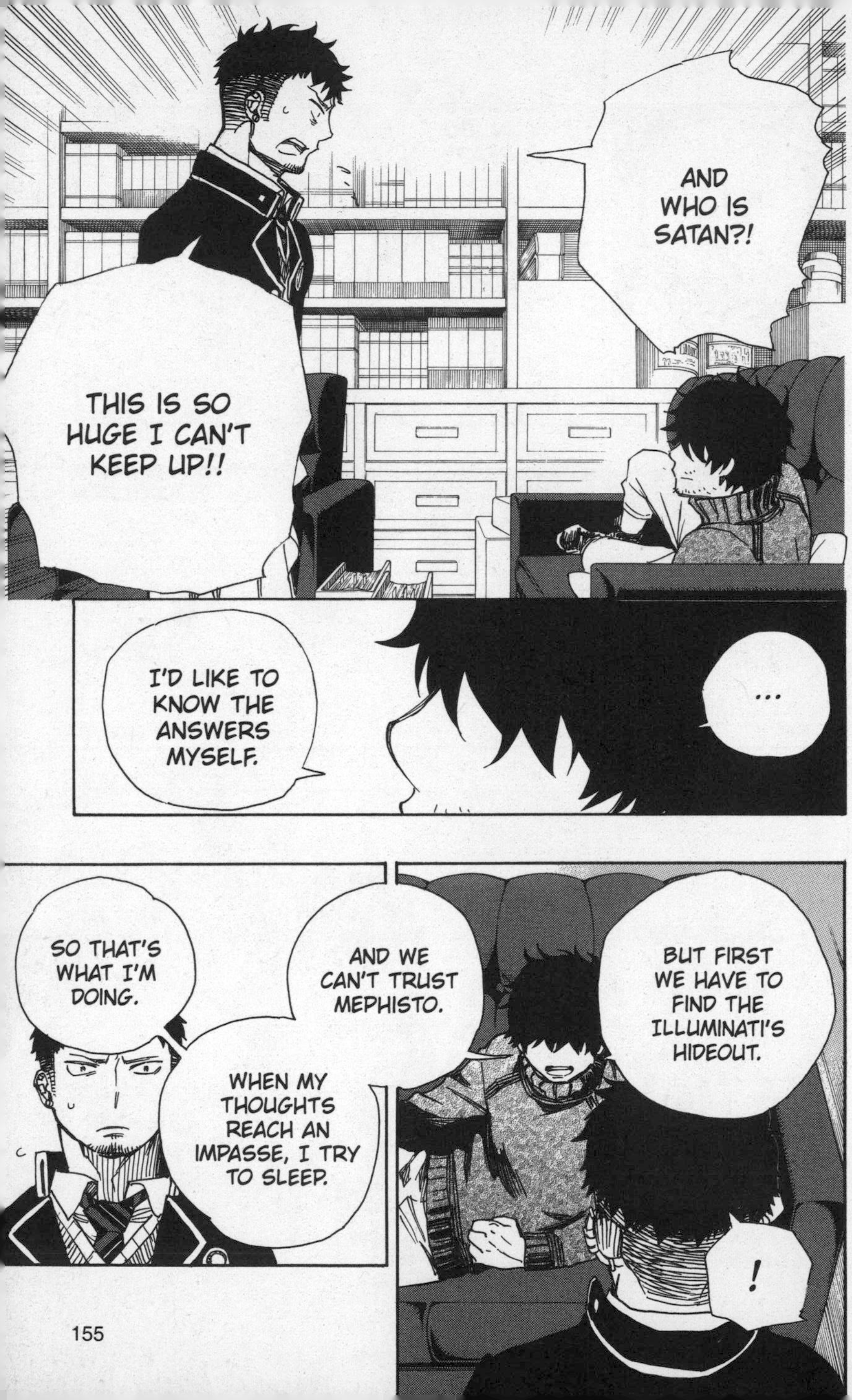
AND WHO IS SATAN?!
THIS IS SO HUGE I CAN'T KEEP UP!!
...
I'D LIKE TO KNOW THE ANSWERS MYSELF.
BUT FIRST WE HAVE TO FIND THE ILLUMINATI'S HIDEOUT.
AND WE CAN'T TRUST MEPHISTO.
!
SO THAT'S WHAT I'M DOING.
WHEN MY THOUGHTS REACH AN IMPASSE, I TRY TO SLEEP.

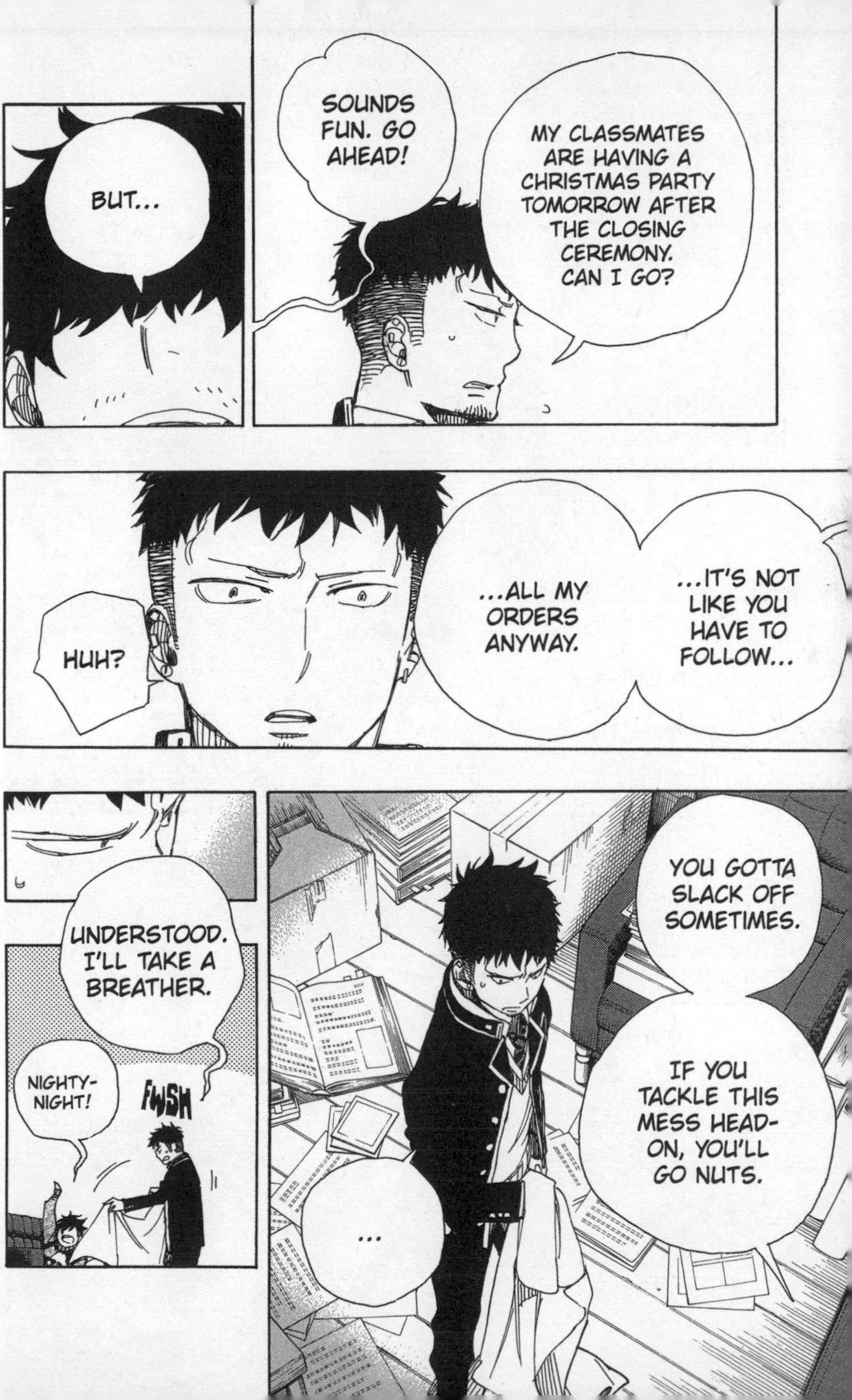
MY CLASSMATES ARE HAVING A CHRISTMAS PARTY TOMORROW AFTER THE CLOSING CEREMONY. CAN I GO?
SOUNDS FUN. GO AHEAD!
BUT...
...IT'S NOT LIKE YOU HAVE TO FOLLOW...
...ALL MY ORDERS ANYWAY.
HUH?
YOU GOTTA SLACK OFF SOMETIMES.
IF YOU TACKLE THIS MESS HEAD-ON, YOU'LL GO NUTS.
...
UNDERSTOOD. I'LL TAKE A BREATHER.
FWSH
NIGHTY-NIGHT!

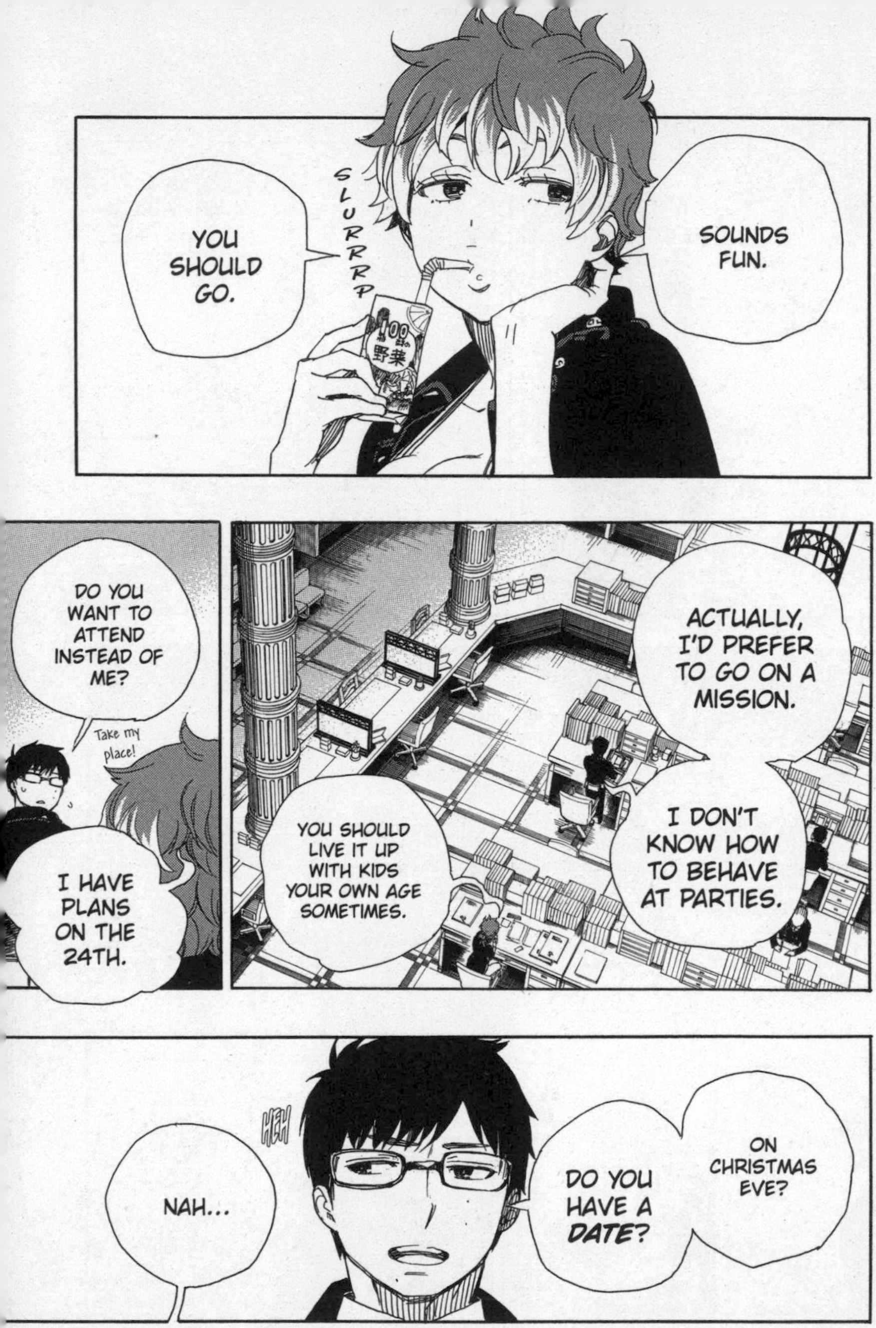

SOUNDS FUN.
SLURRRP
YOU SHOULD GO.
ACTUALLY, I'D PREFER TO GO ON A MISSION.
I DON'T KNOW HOW TO BEHAVE AT PARTIES.
YOU SHOULD LIVE IT UP WITH KIDS YOUR OWN AGE SOMETIMES.
DO YOU WANT TO ATTEND INSTEAD OF ME?
Take my place!
I HAVE PLANS ON THE 24TH.
ON CHRISTMAS EVE?
DO YOU HAVE A *DATE*?
HEH
NAH...

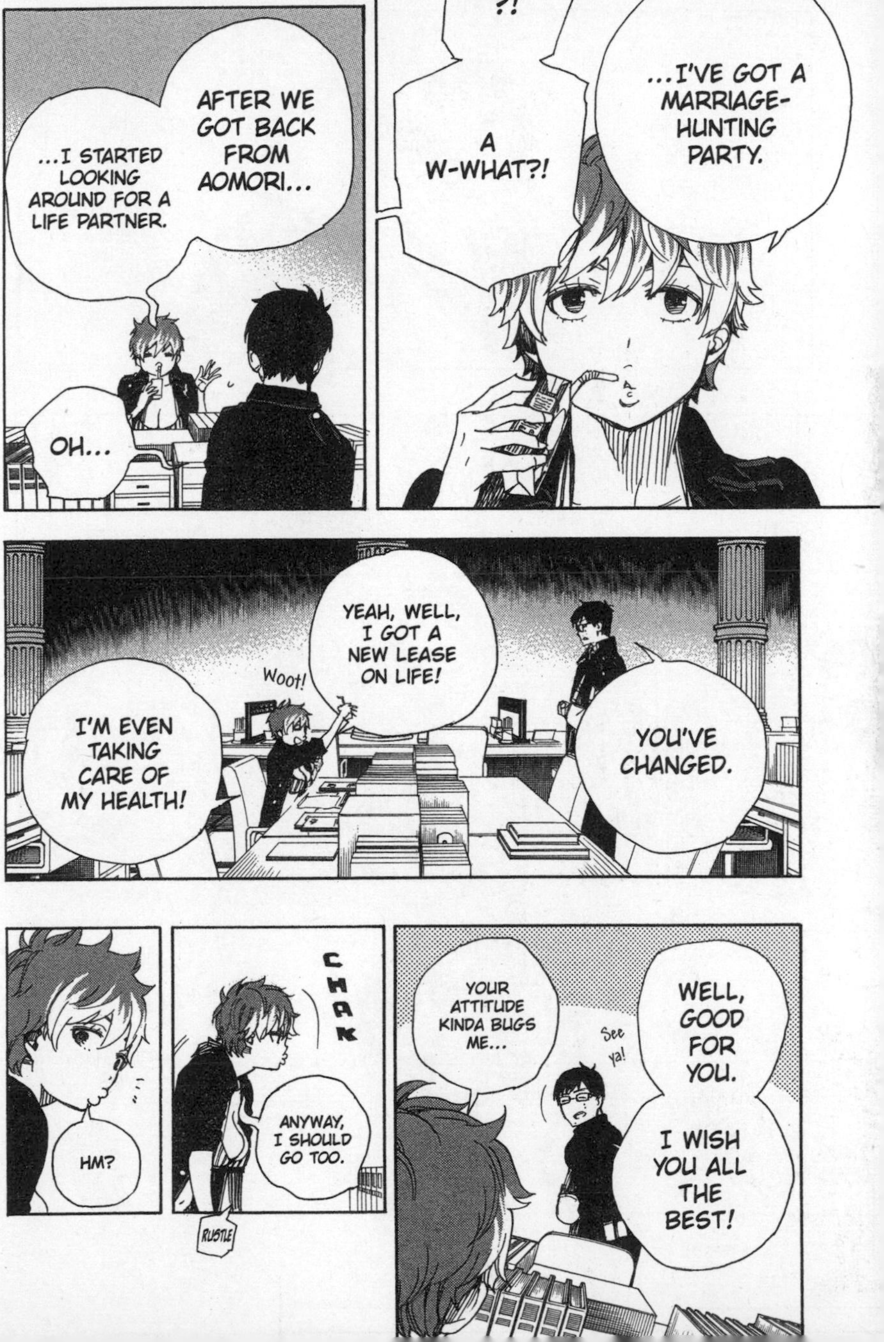

...I'VE GOT A MARRIAGE-HUNTING PARTY.
?!
A W-WHAT?!
AFTER WE GOT BACK FROM AOMORI...
...I STARTED LOOKING AROUND FOR A LIFE PARTNER.
OH...
YOU'VE CHANGED.
YEAH, WELL, I GOT A NEW LEASE ON LIFE!
Woot!
I'M EVEN TAKING CARE OF MY HEALTH!
WELL, GOOD FOR YOU.
I WISH YOU ALL THE BEST!
See ya!
YOUR ATTITUDE KINDA BUGS ME...
CHAK
ANYWAY, I SHOULD GO TOO.
RUSTLE
HM?

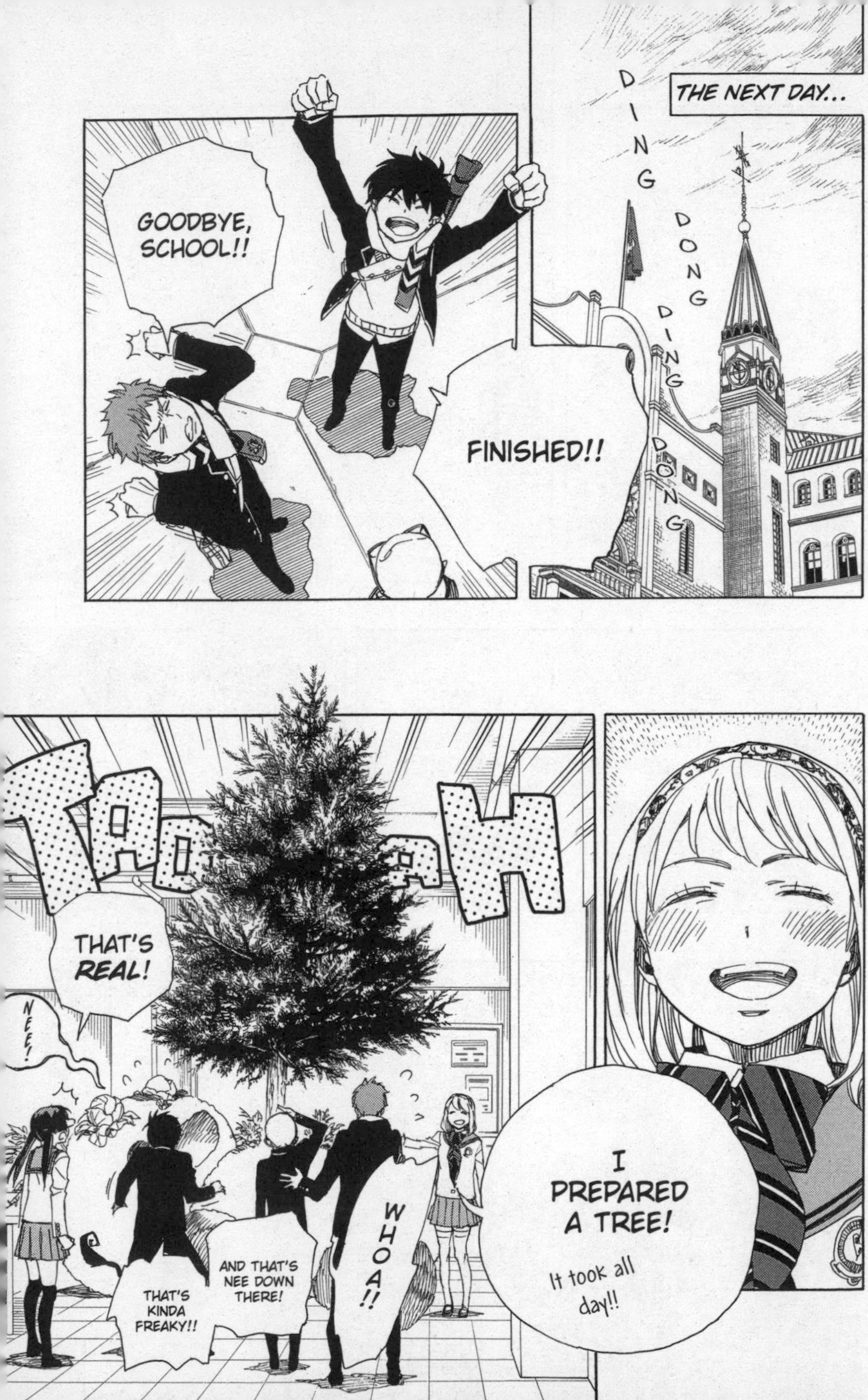
THE NEXT DAY...
DING DONG DING DONG
FINISHED!!
GOODBYE, SCHOOL!!
I PREPARED A TREE!
It took all day!!
THAT'S REAL!
NEE!
WHOA!!
AND THAT'S NEE DOWN THERE!
THAT'S KINDA FREAKY!!

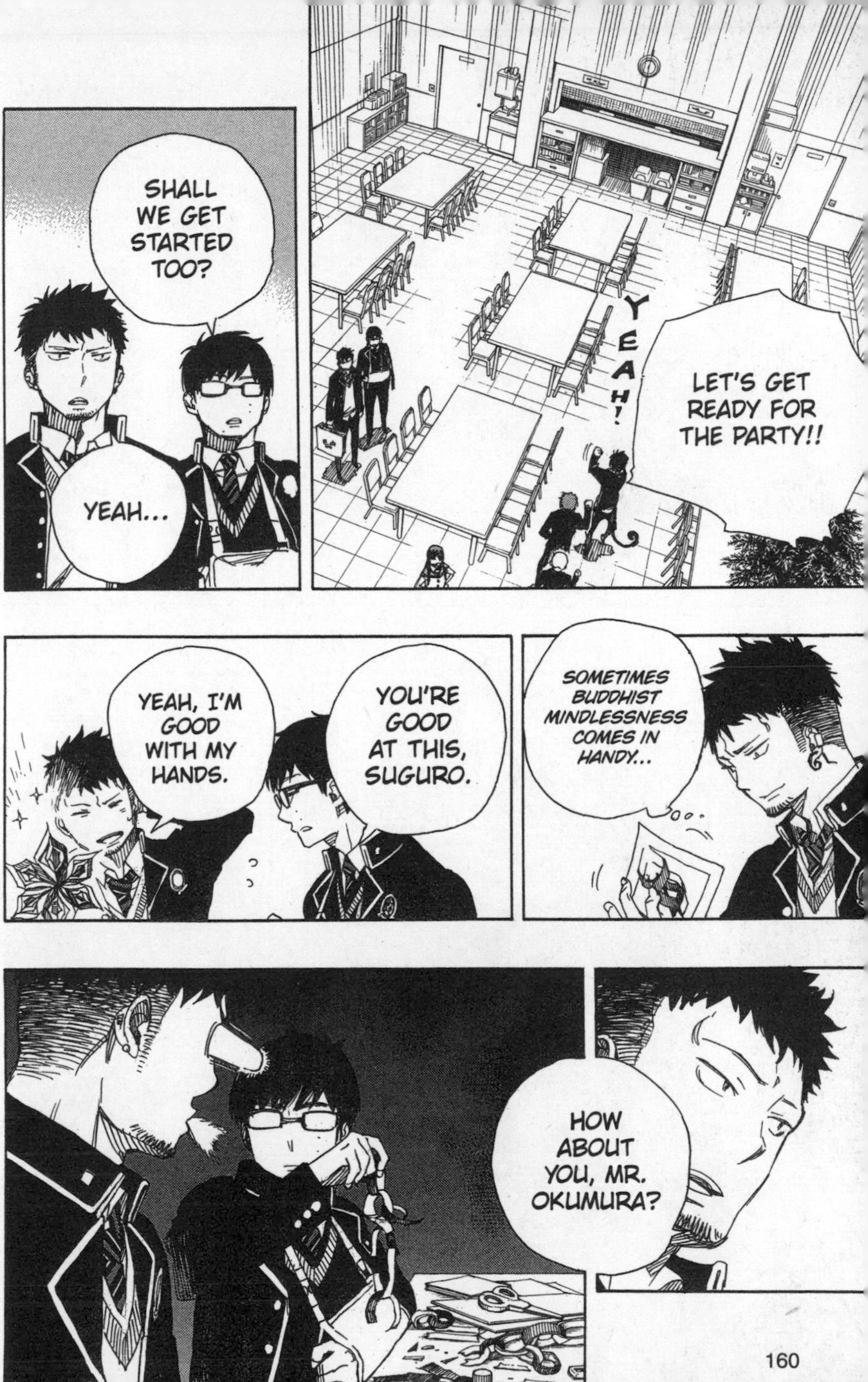
LET'S GET READY FOR THE PARTY!!
YEAH!
SHALL WE GET STARTED TOO?
YEAH...
SOMETIMES BUDDHIST MINDLESSNESS COMES IN HANDY...
YOU'RE GOOD AT THIS, SUGURO.
YEAH, I'M GOOD WITH MY HANDS.
HOW ABOUT YOU, MR. OKUMURA?

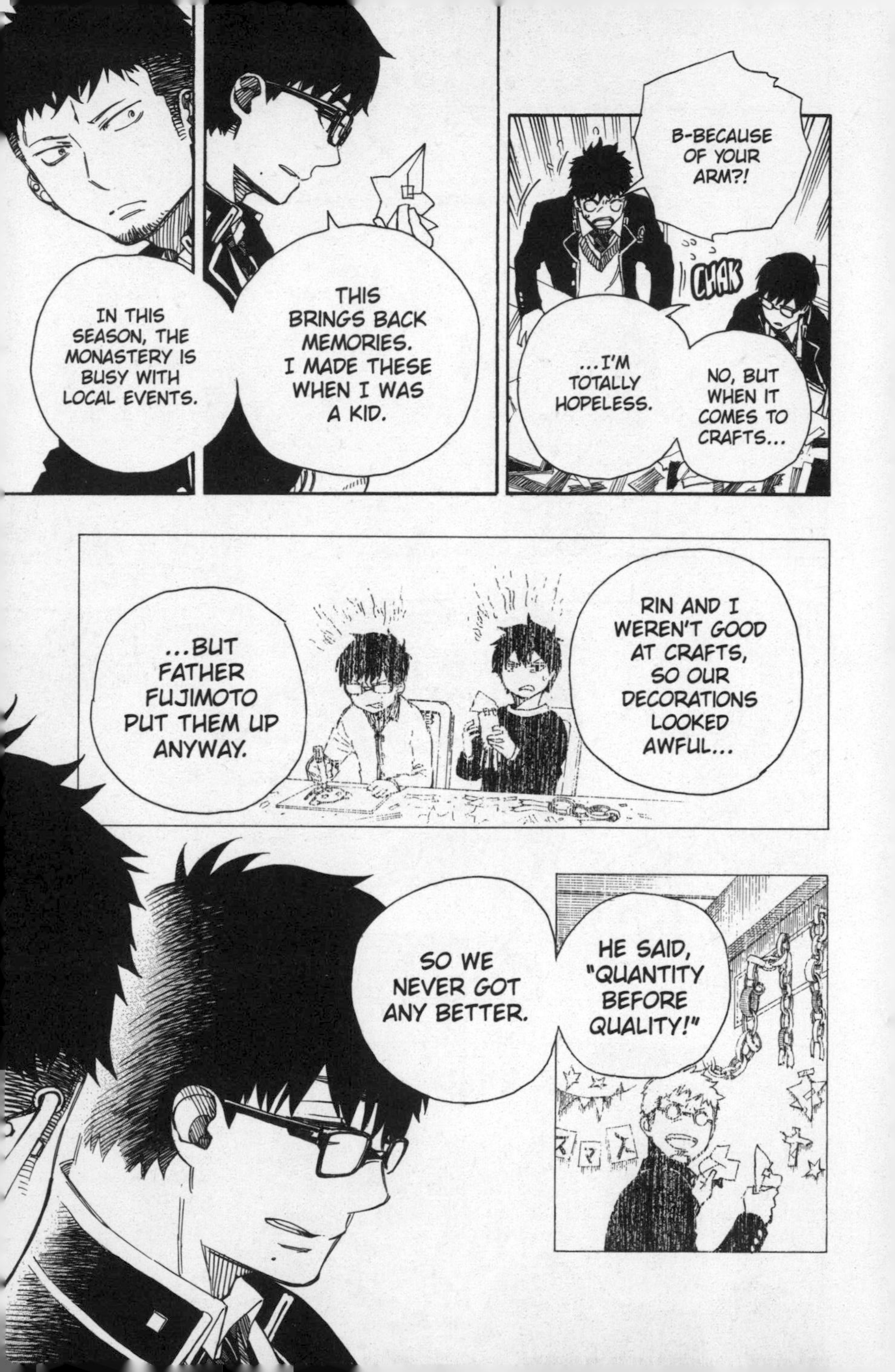
B-BECAUSE OF YOUR ARM?!
CHAK
NO, BUT WHEN IT COMES TO CRAFTS...
...I'M TOTALLY HOPELESS.
THIS BRINGS BACK MEMORIES. I MADE THESE WHEN I WAS A KID.
IN THIS SEASON, THE MONASTERY IS BUSY WITH LOCAL EVENTS.
RIN AND I WEREN'T GOOD AT CRAFTS, SO OUR DECORATIONS LOOKED AWFUL...
...BUT FATHER FUJIMOTO PUT THEM UP ANYWAY.
HE SAID, "QUANTITY BEFORE QUALITY!"
SO WE NEVER GOT ANY BETTER.

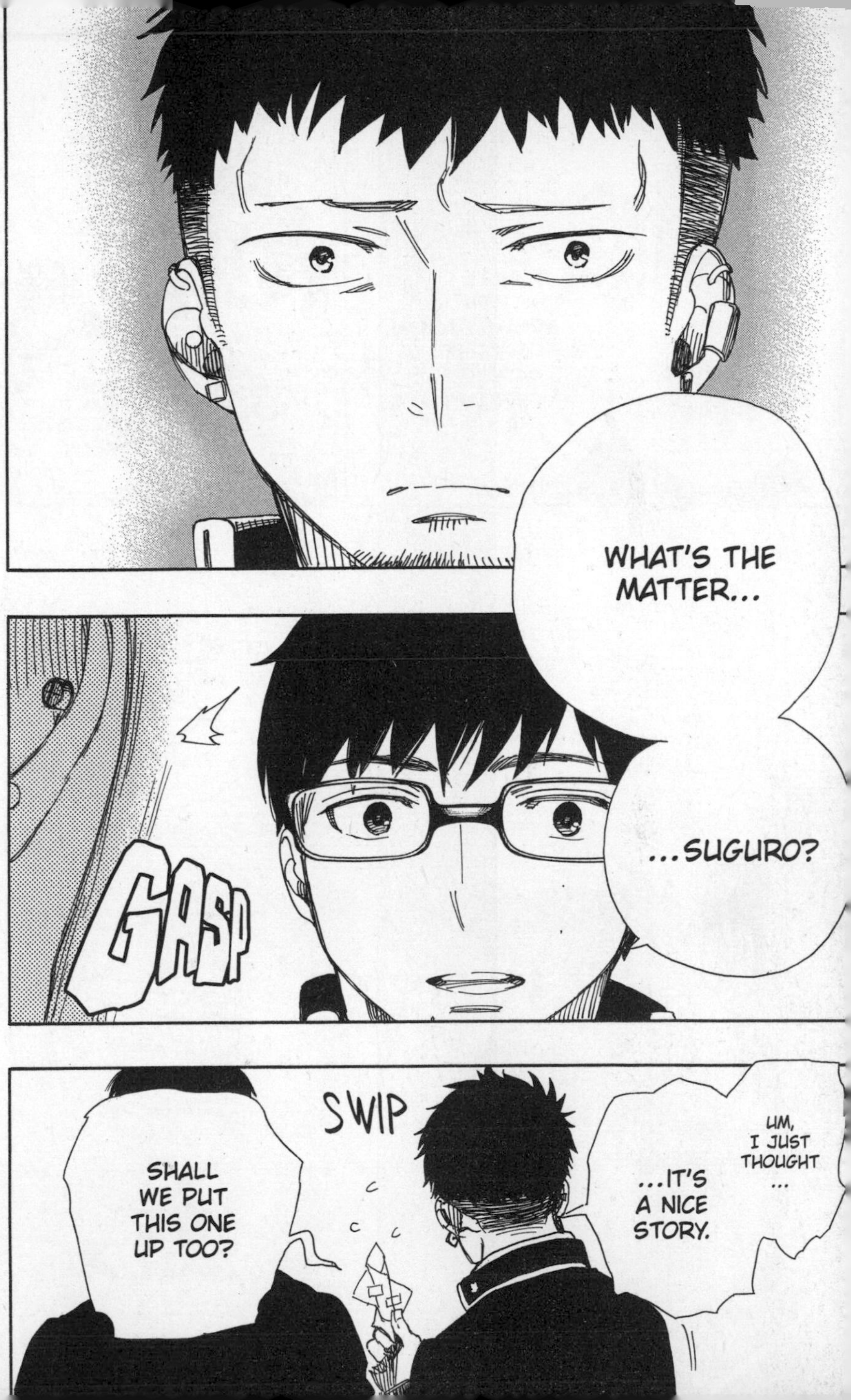
WHAT'S THE MATTER...
...SUGURO?
GASP
UM, I JUST THOUGHT ...
...IT'S A NICE STORY.
SWIP
SHALL WE PUT THIS ONE UP TOO?

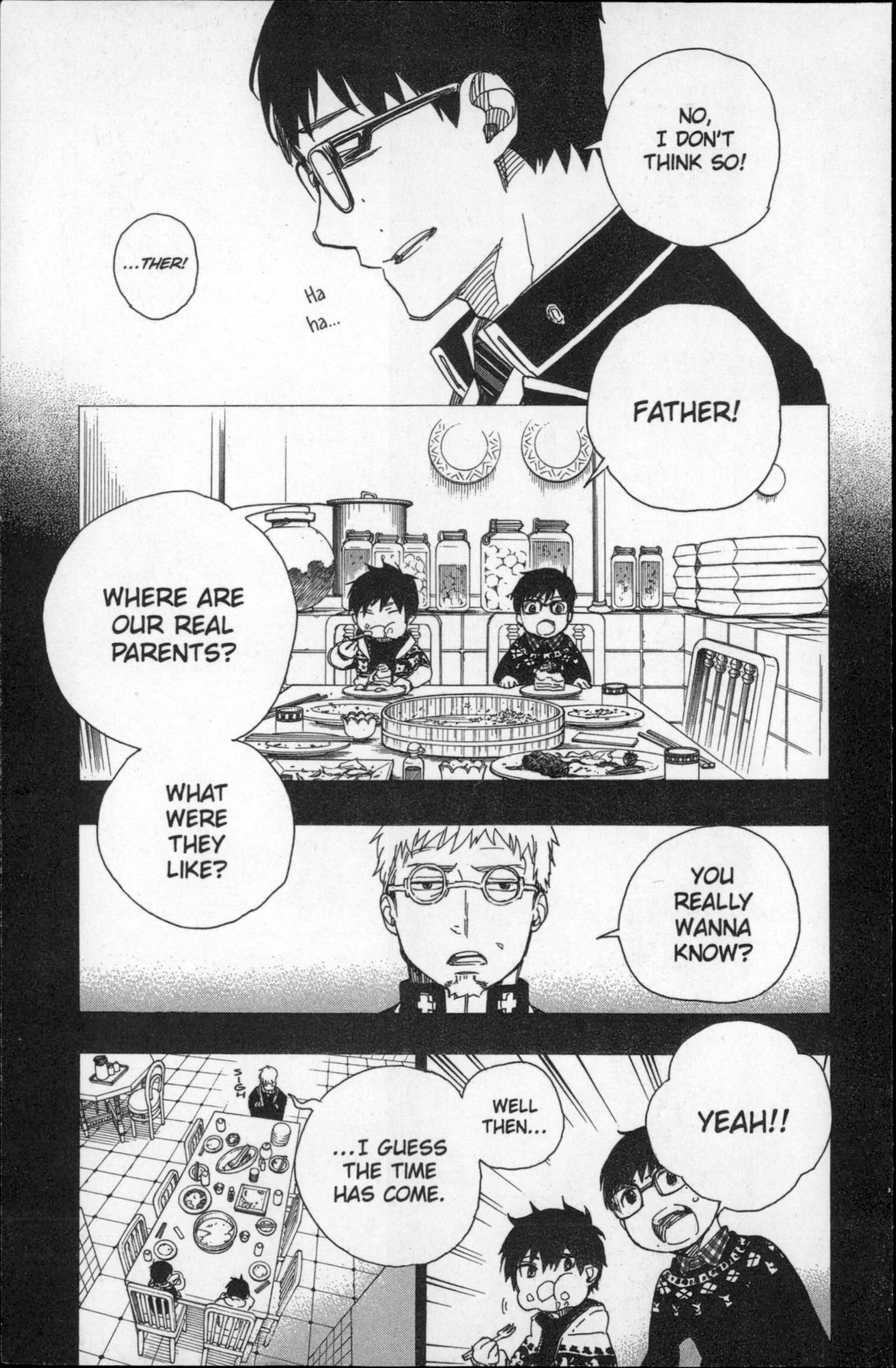
NO, I DON'T THINK SO!
...THER!
Ha ha...
FATHER!
WHERE ARE OUR REAL PARENTS?
WHAT WERE THEY LIKE?
YOU REALLY WANNA KNOW?
YEAH!!
WELL THEN...
...I GUESS THE TIME HAS COME.
SIGH

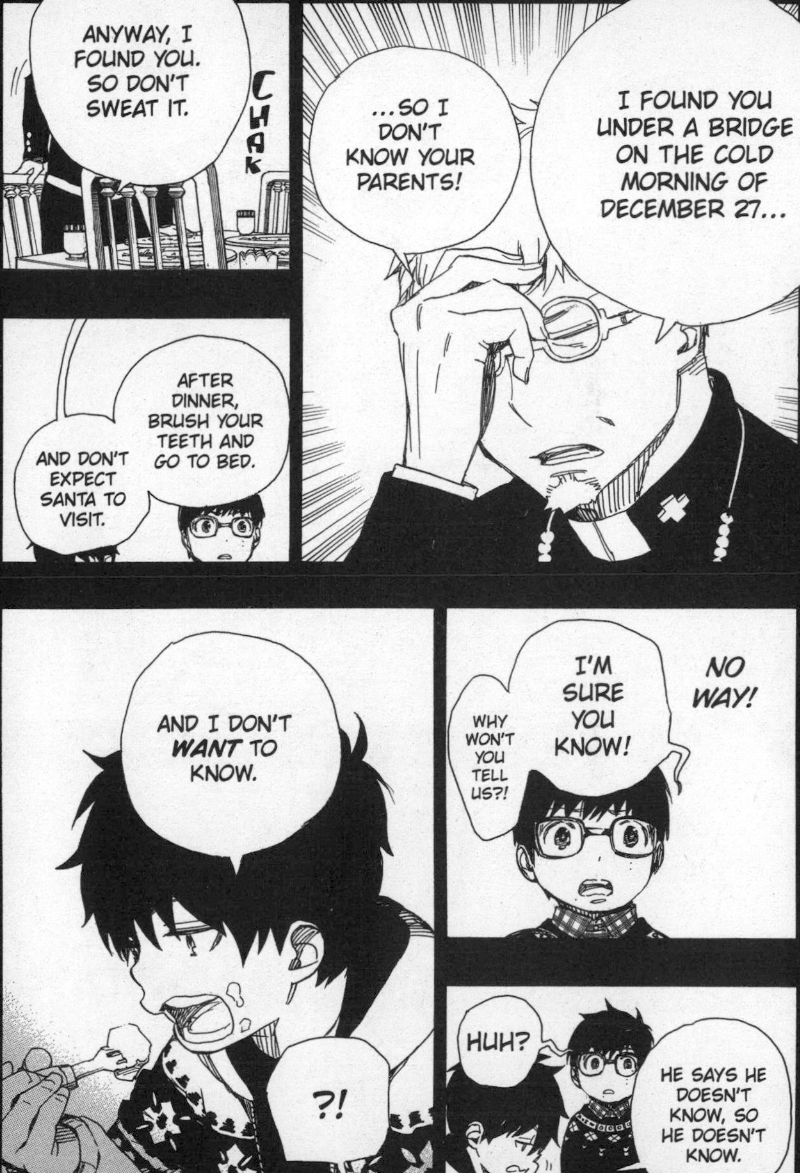
I FOUND YOU UNDER A BRIDGE ON THE COLD MORNING OF DECEMBER 27…
…SO I DON'T KNOW YOUR PARENTS!
ANYWAY, I FOUND YOU. SO DON'T SWEAT IT.
CHAK
AFTER DINNER, BRUSH YOUR TEETH AND GO TO BED.
AND DON'T EXPECT SANTA TO VISIT.
NO WAY!
I'M SURE YOU KNOW!
WHY WON'T YOU TELL US?!
HE SAYS HE DOESN'T KNOW, SO HE DOESN'T KNOW.
HUH?
AND I DON'T *WANT* TO KNOW.
?!

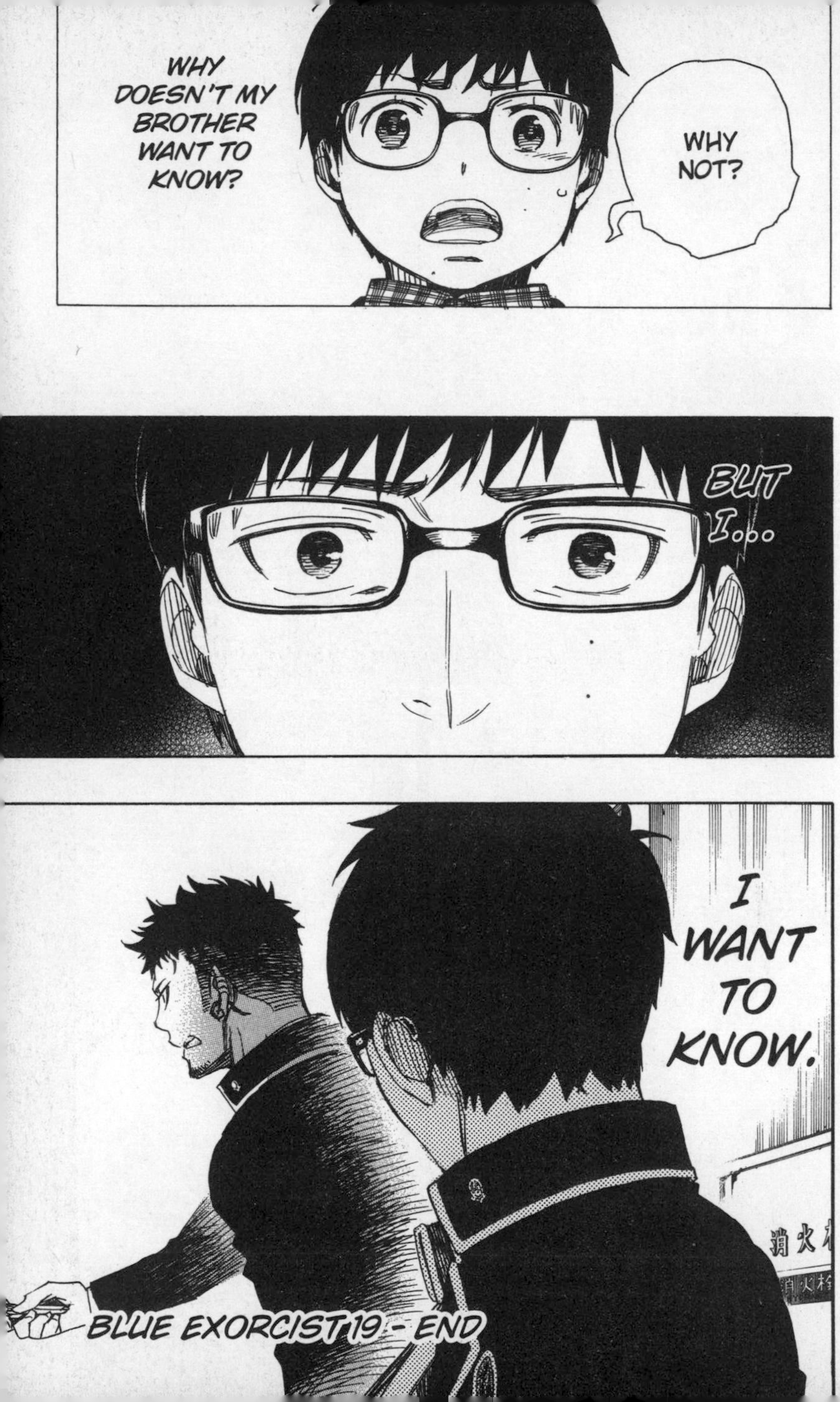
WHY NOT?
WHY DOESN'T MY BROTHER WANT TO KNOW?
BUT I...
I WANT TO KNOW.
BLUE EXORCIST 19 - END

Blue Exorcist Chapter 88: Happy (Merry Xmas) Birthday Eve!

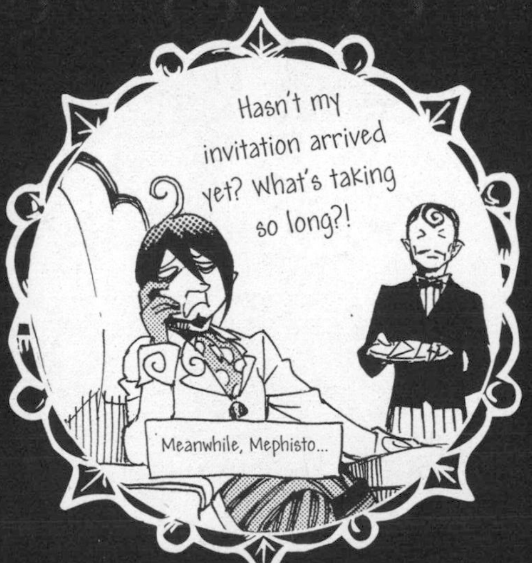
Hasn't my invitation arrived yet? What's taking so long?!
Meanwhile, Mephisto...

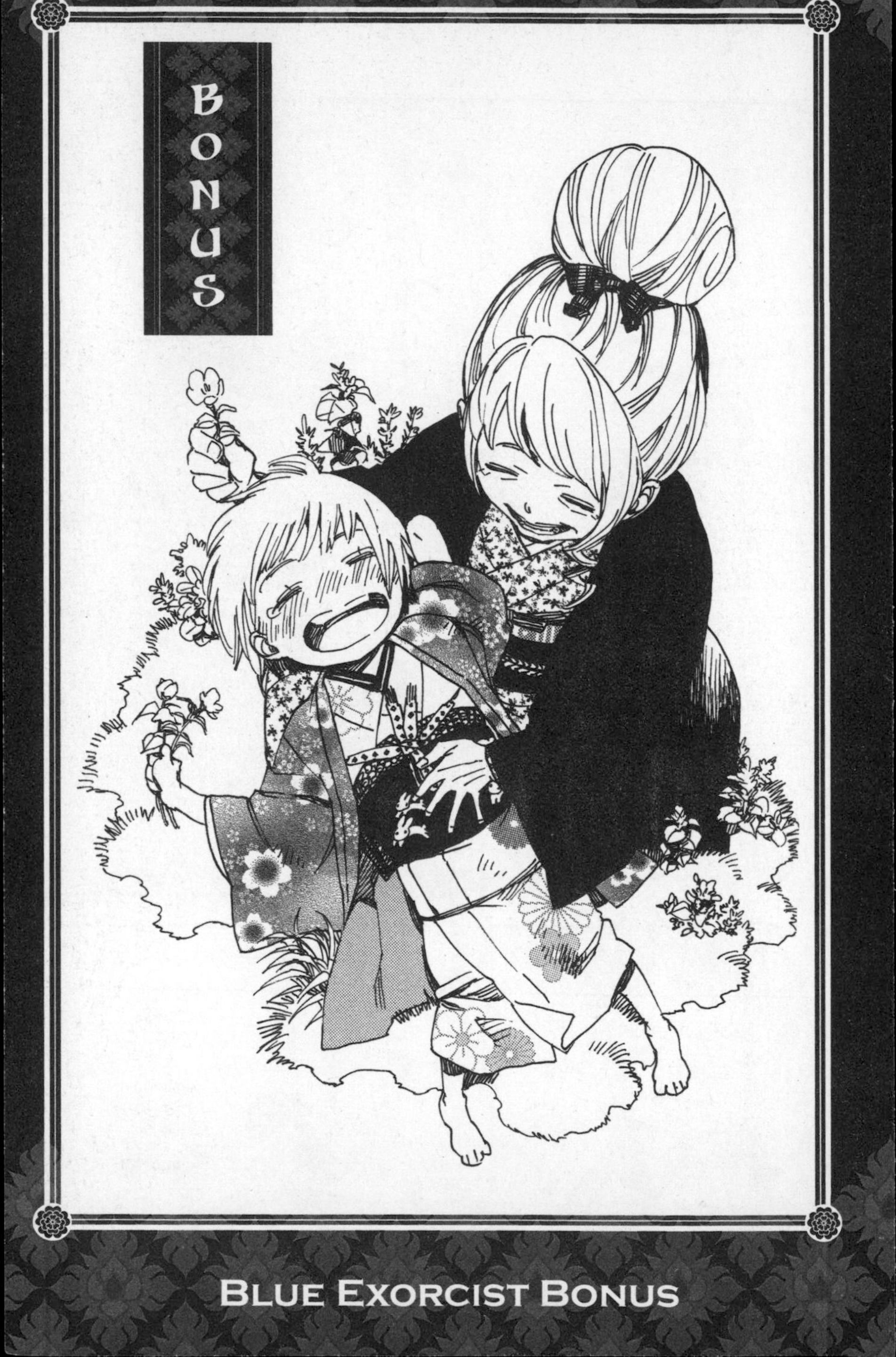
BONUS

BLUE EXORCIST BONUS

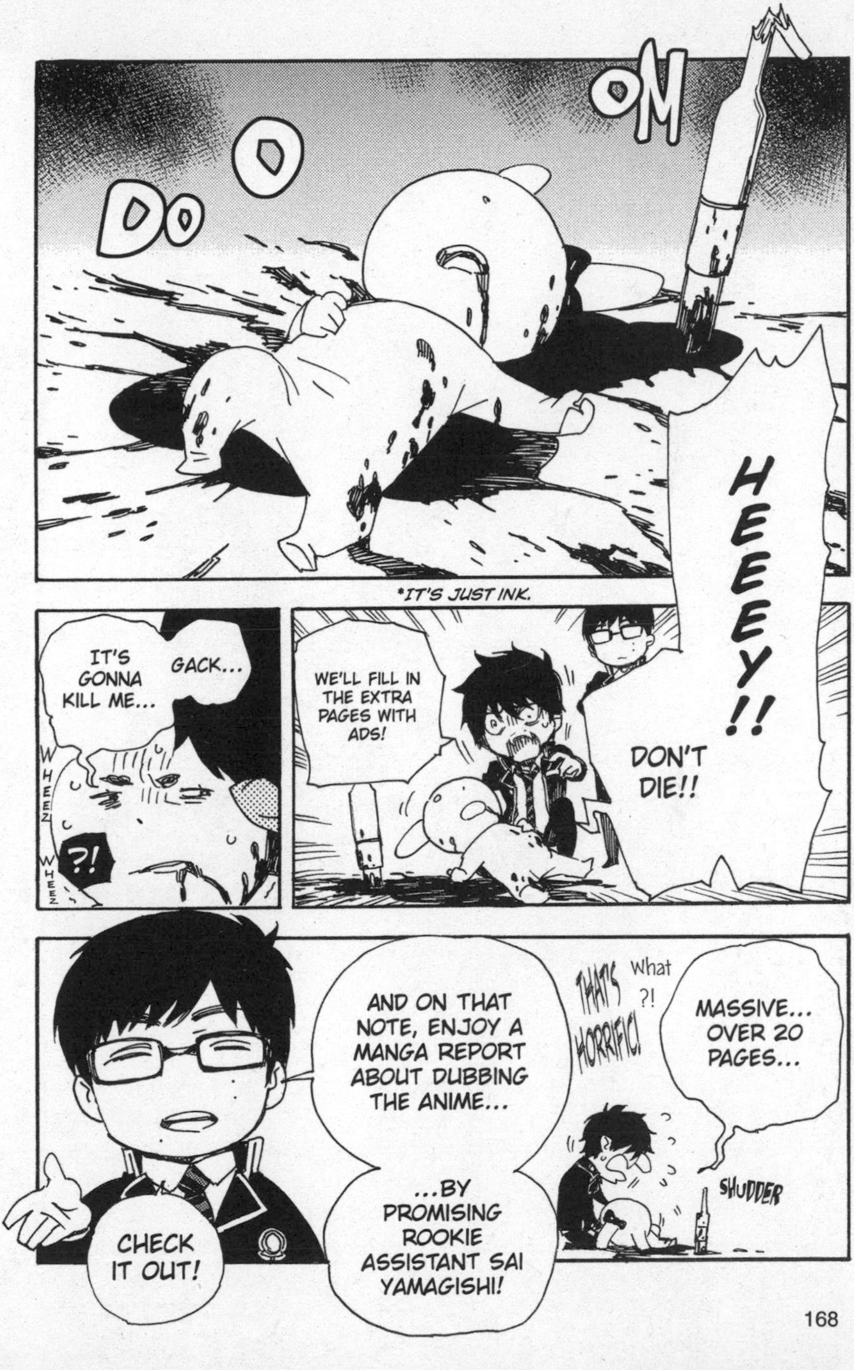
DOOOM
*IT'S JUST INK.
HEEEY!!
DON'T DIE!!
WE'LL FILL IN THE EXTRA PAGES WITH ADS!
GACK...
IT'S GONNA KILL ME...
WHEEZ
WHEEZ
?!
MASSIVE... OVER 20 PAGES...
What ?!
THAT'S HORRIFIC!
SHUDDER
AND ON THAT NOTE, ENJOY A MANGA REPORT ABOUT DUBBING THE ANIME...
...BY PROMISING ROOKIE ASSISTANT SAI YAMAGISHI!
CHECK IT OUT!

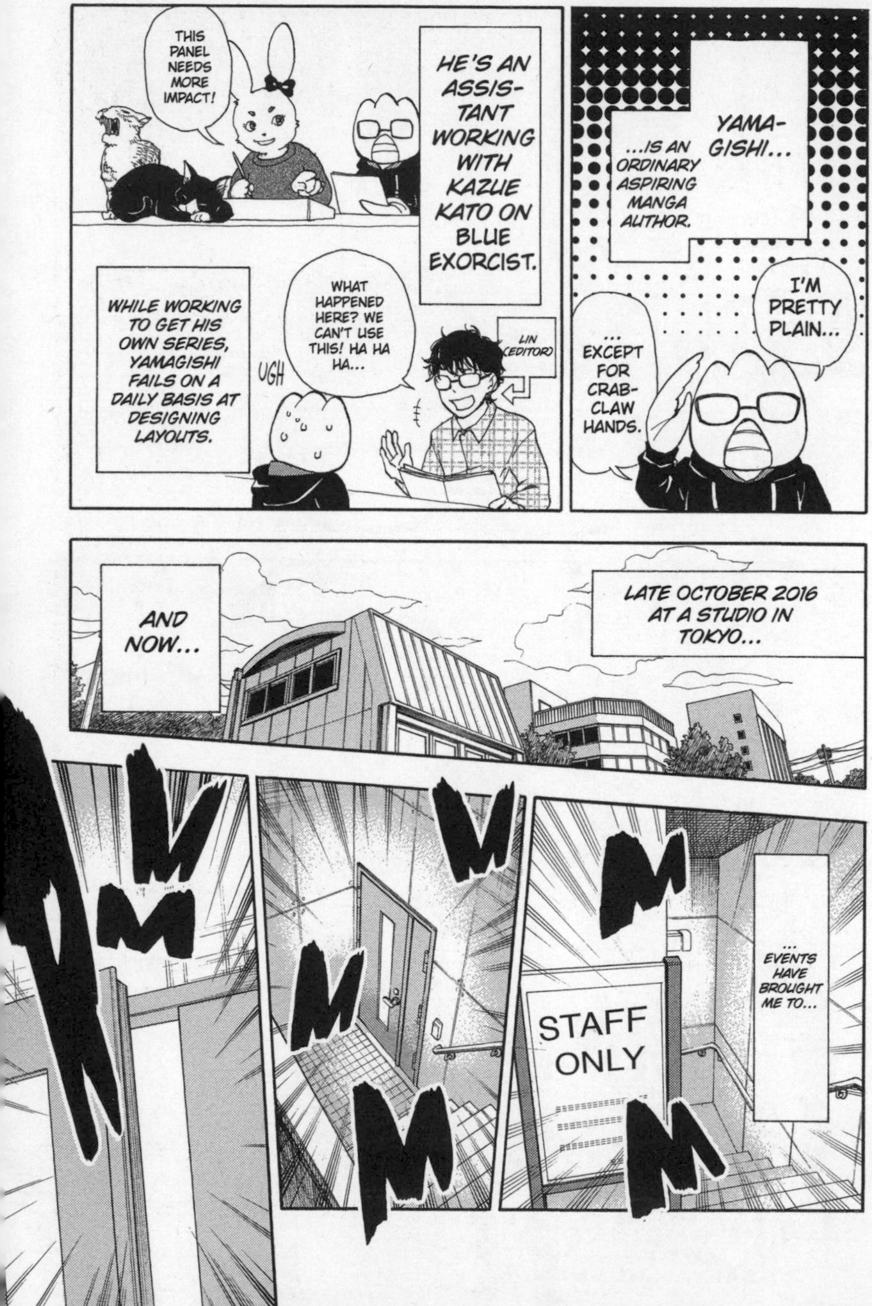

YAMAGISHI...
...IS AN ORDINARY ASPIRING MANGA AUTHOR.
I'M PRETTY PLAIN...
...EXCEPT FOR CRAB-CLAW HANDS.
HE'S AN ASSISTANT WORKING WITH KAZUE KATO ON BLUE EXORCIST.
THIS PANEL NEEDS MORE IMPACT!
LIN (EDITOR)
WHAT HAPPENED HERE? WE CAN'T USE THIS! HA HA HA...
UGH
WHILE WORKING TO GET HIS OWN SERIES, YAMAGISHI FAILS ON A DAILY BASIS AT DESIGNING LAYOUTS.
LATE OCTOBER 2016 AT A STUDIO IN TOKYO...
AND NOW...
...EVENTS HAVE BROUGHT ME TO...
STAFF ONLY
MMM
MMM
MMM

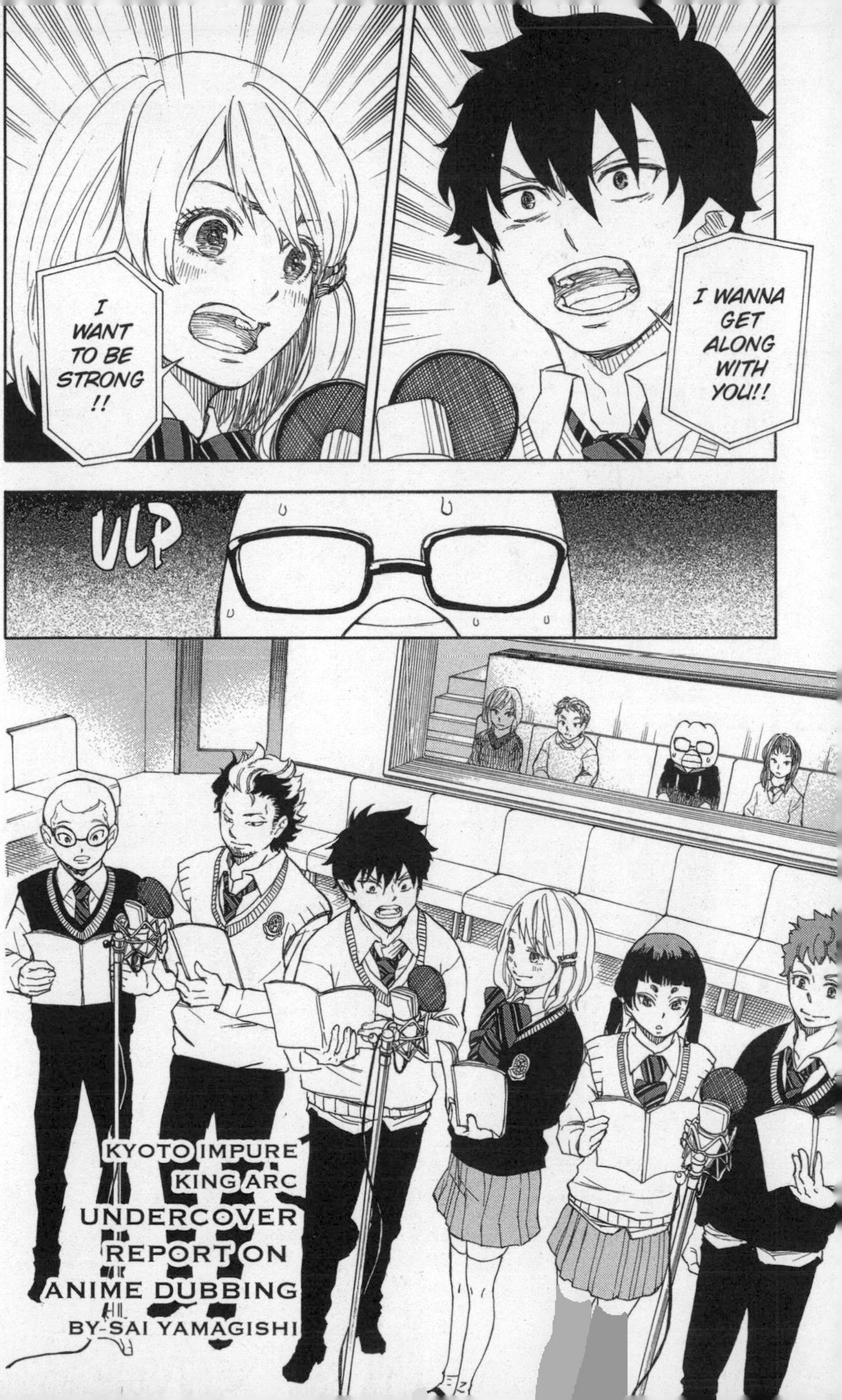
I WANNA GET ALONG WITH YOU!!
I WANT TO BE STRONG!!
ULP
KYOTO IMPURE KING ARC
UNDERCOVER REPORT ON ANIME DUBBING
BY SAI YAMAGISHI

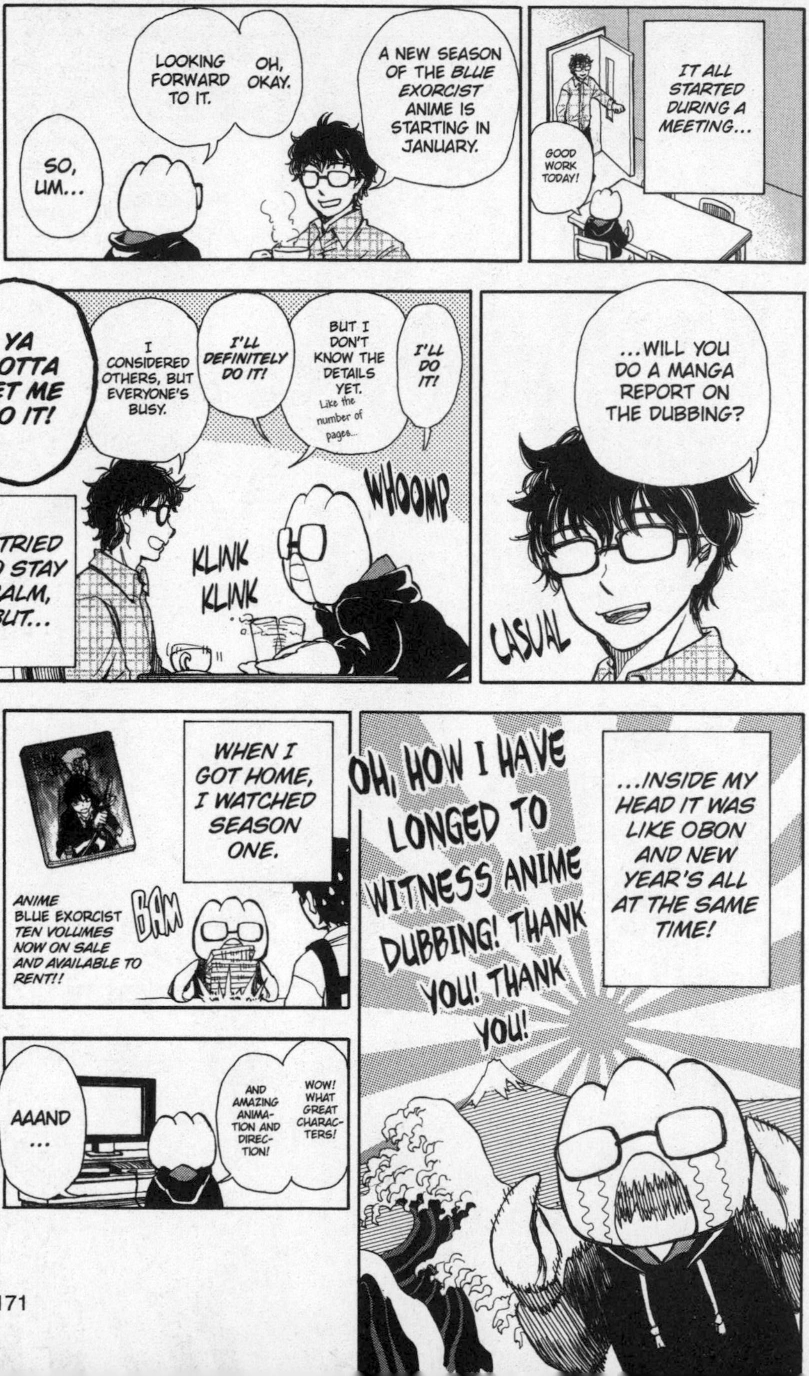
IT ALL STARTED DURING A MEETING...
GOOD WORK TODAY!
A NEW SEASON OF THE BLUE EXORCIST ANIME IS STARTING IN JANUARY.
OH, OKAY.
LOOKING FORWARD TO IT.
SO, UM...
...WILL YOU DO A MANGA REPORT ON THE DUBBING?
CASUAL
I'LL DO IT!
BUT I DON'T KNOW THE DETAILS YET. Like the number of pages...
I'LL DEFINITELY DO IT!
I CONSIDERED OTHERS, BUT EVERYONE'S BUSY.
YA GOTTA LET ME DO IT!
WHOOMP
KLINK KLINK
I TRIED TO STAY CALM, BUT...
...INSIDE MY HEAD IT WAS LIKE OBON AND NEW YEAR'S ALL AT THE SAME TIME!
OH, HOW I HAVE LONGED TO WITNESS ANIME DUBBING! THANK YOU! THANK YOU!
WHEN I GOT HOME, I WATCHED SEASON ONE.
BAM
ANIME BLUE EXORCIST TEN VOLUMES NOW ON SALE AND AVAILABLE TO RENT!!
WOW! WHAT GREAT CHARACTERS!
AND AMAZING ANIMATION AND DIRECTION!
AAAND...

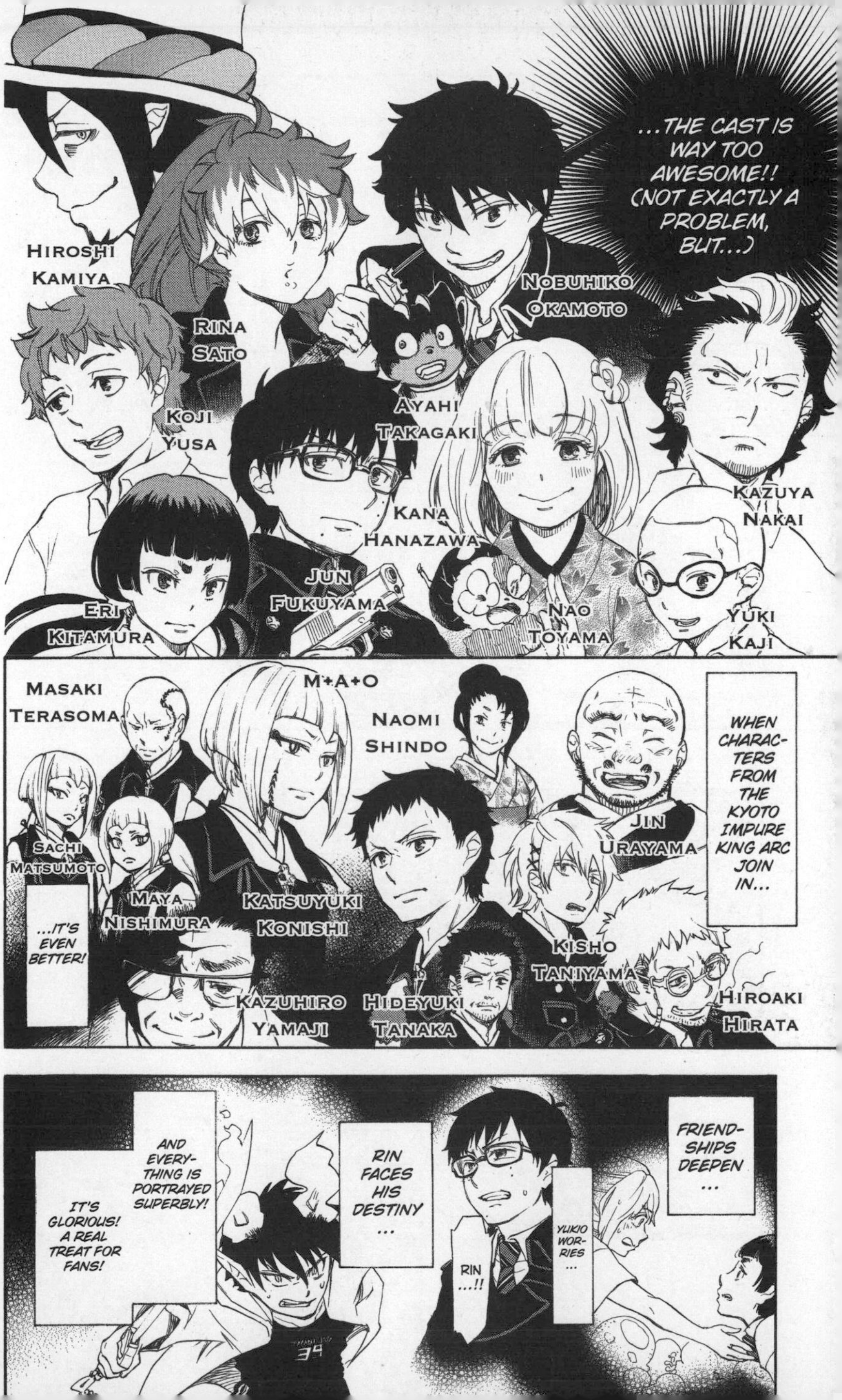
...THE CAST IS WAY TOO AWESOME!! (NOT EXACTLY A PROBLEM, BUT...)
NOBUHIKO OKAMOTO
KAZUYA NAKAI
AYAHI TAKAGAKI
RINA SATO
HIROSHI KAMIYA
KOJI YUSA
KANA HANAZAWA
YUKI KAJI
NAO TOYAMA
JUN FUKUYAMA
ERI KITAMURA
WHEN CHARAC-TERS FROM THE KYOTO IMPURE KING ARC JOIN IN...
NAOMI SHINDO
M+A+O
MASAKI TERASOMA
JIN URAYAMA
KISHO TANIYAMA
HIROAKI HIRATA
HIDEYUKI TANAKA
KATSUYUKI KONISHI
MAYA NISHIMURA
SACHI MATSUMOTO
KAZUHIRO YAMAJI
...IT'S EVEN BETTER!
FRIEND-SHIPS DEEPEN...
YUKIO WOR-RIES...
RIN ...!!
RIN FACES HIS DESTINY...
AND EVERY-THING IS PORTRAYED SUPERBLY!
IT'S GLORIOUS! A REAL TREAT FOR FANS!

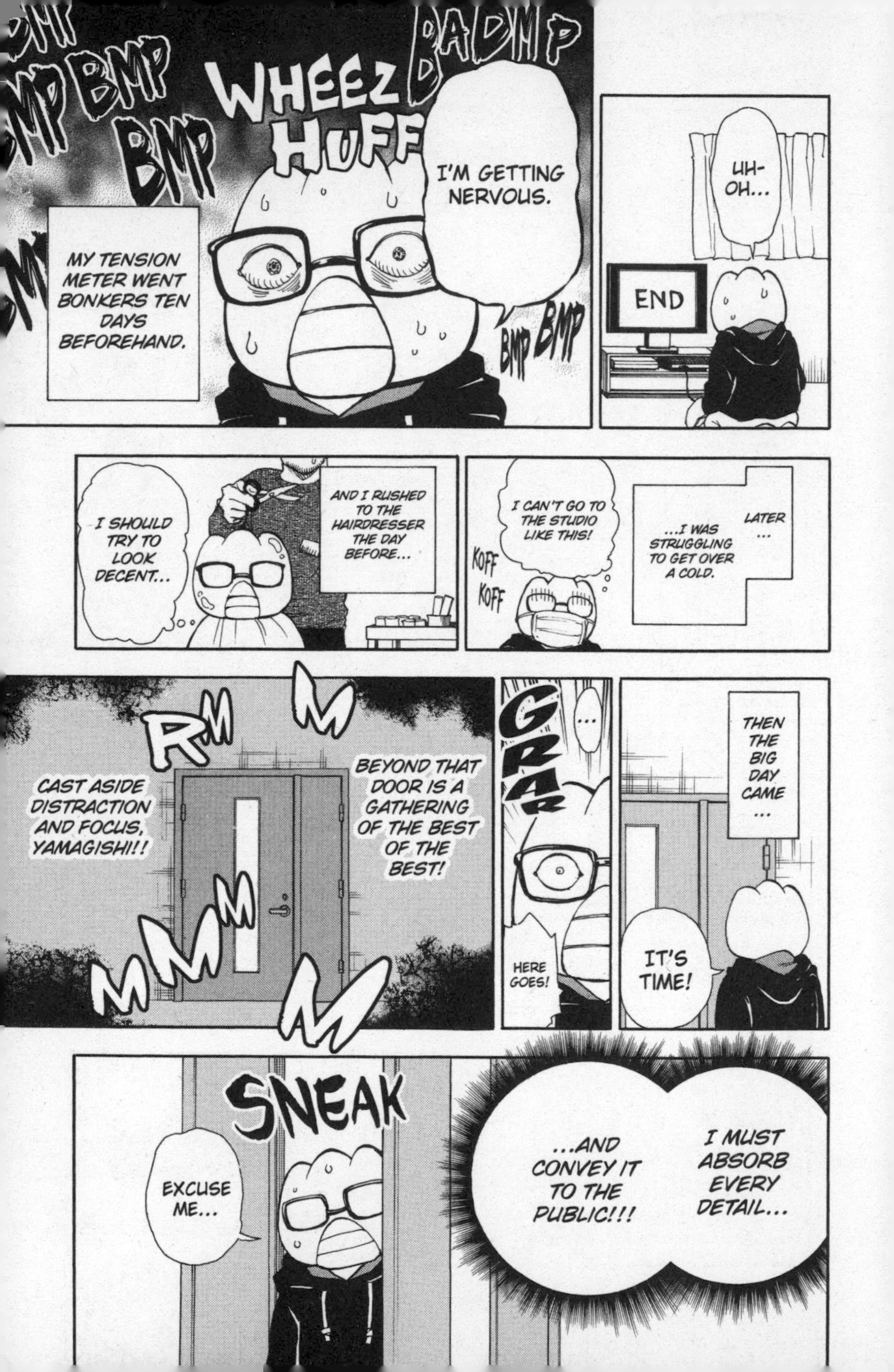
UH-OH...
END
BADMP
I'M GETTING NERVOUS.
WHEEZ HUFF
BMP BMP BMP
BMP BMP
MY TENSION METER WENT BONKERS TEN DAYS BEFOREHAND.
LATER...
...I WAS STRUGGLING TO GET OVER A COLD.
I CAN'T GO TO THE STUDIO LIKE THIS!
KOFF KOFF
AND I RUSHED TO THE HAIRDRESSER THE DAY BEFORE...
I SHOULD TRY TO LOOK DECENT...
THEN THE BIG DAY CAME...
IT'S TIME!
...
GRAR
HERE GOES!
RMMMMMM
BEYOND THAT DOOR IS A GATHERING OF THE BEST OF THE BEST!
CAST ASIDE DISTRACTION AND FOCUS, YAMAGISHI!!
I MUST ABSORB EVERY DETAIL...
...AND CONVEY IT TO THE PUBLIC!!!
SNEAK
EXCUSE ME...

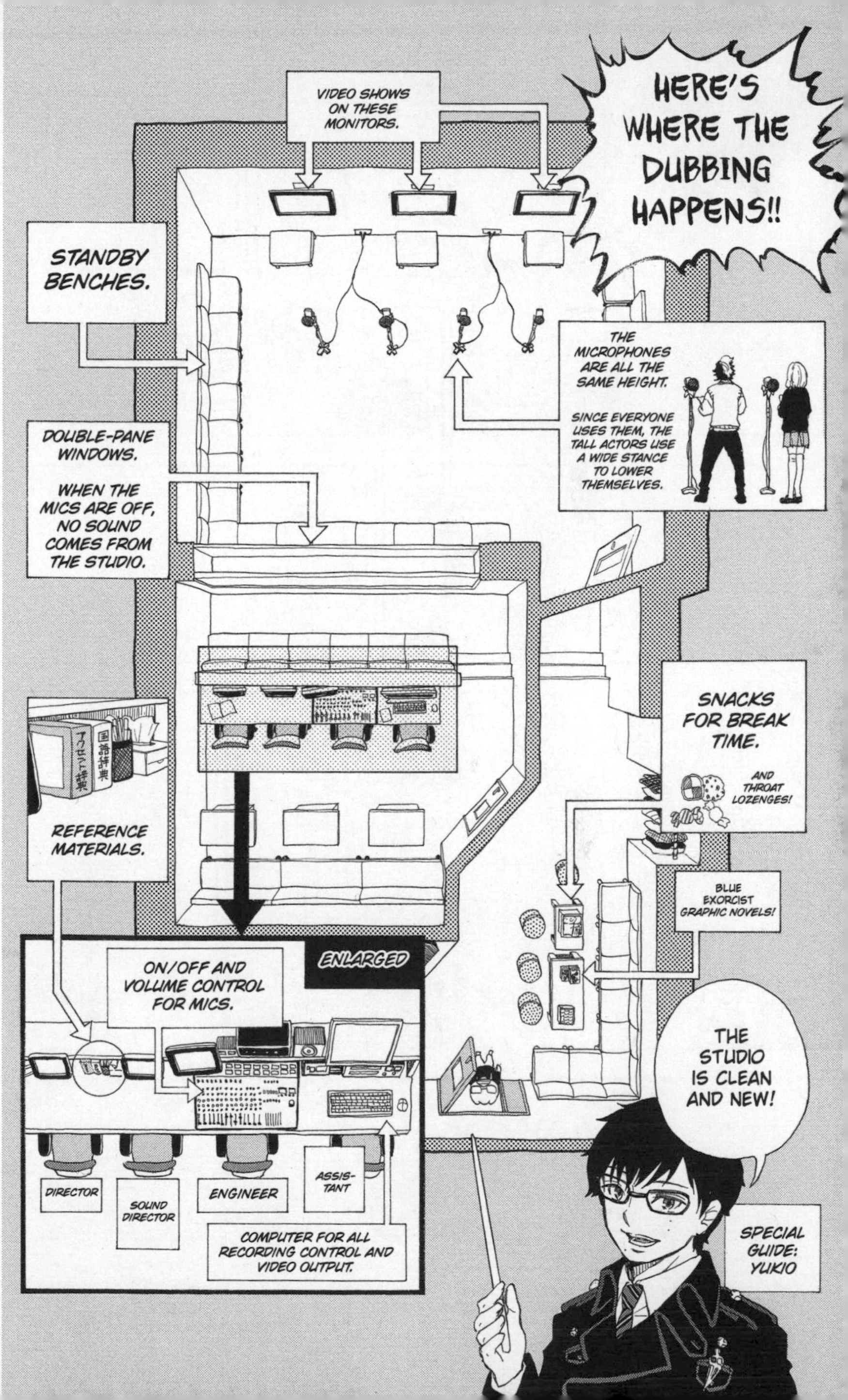
HERE'S WHERE THE DUBBING HAPPENS!!
VIDEO SHOWS ON THESE MONITORS.
STANDBY BENCHES.
THE MICROPHONES ARE ALL THE SAME HEIGHT.
SINCE EVERYONE USES THEM, THE TALL ACTORS USE A WIDE STANCE TO LOWER THEMSELVES.
DOUBLE-PANE WINDOWS.
WHEN THE MICS ARE OFF, NO SOUND COMES FROM THE STUDIO.
SNACKS FOR BREAK TIME.
AND THROAT LOZENGES!
国語辞典
アクセント辞典
REFERENCE MATERIALS.
BLUE EXORCIST GRAPHIC NOVELS!
ENLARGED
ON/OFF AND VOLUME CONTROL FOR MICS.
DIRECTOR
SOUND DIRECTOR
ENGINEER
ASSIS-TANT
COMPUTER FOR ALL RECORDING CONTROL AND VIDEO OUTPUT.
THE STUDIO IS CLEAN AND NEW!
SPECIAL GUIDE: YUKIO

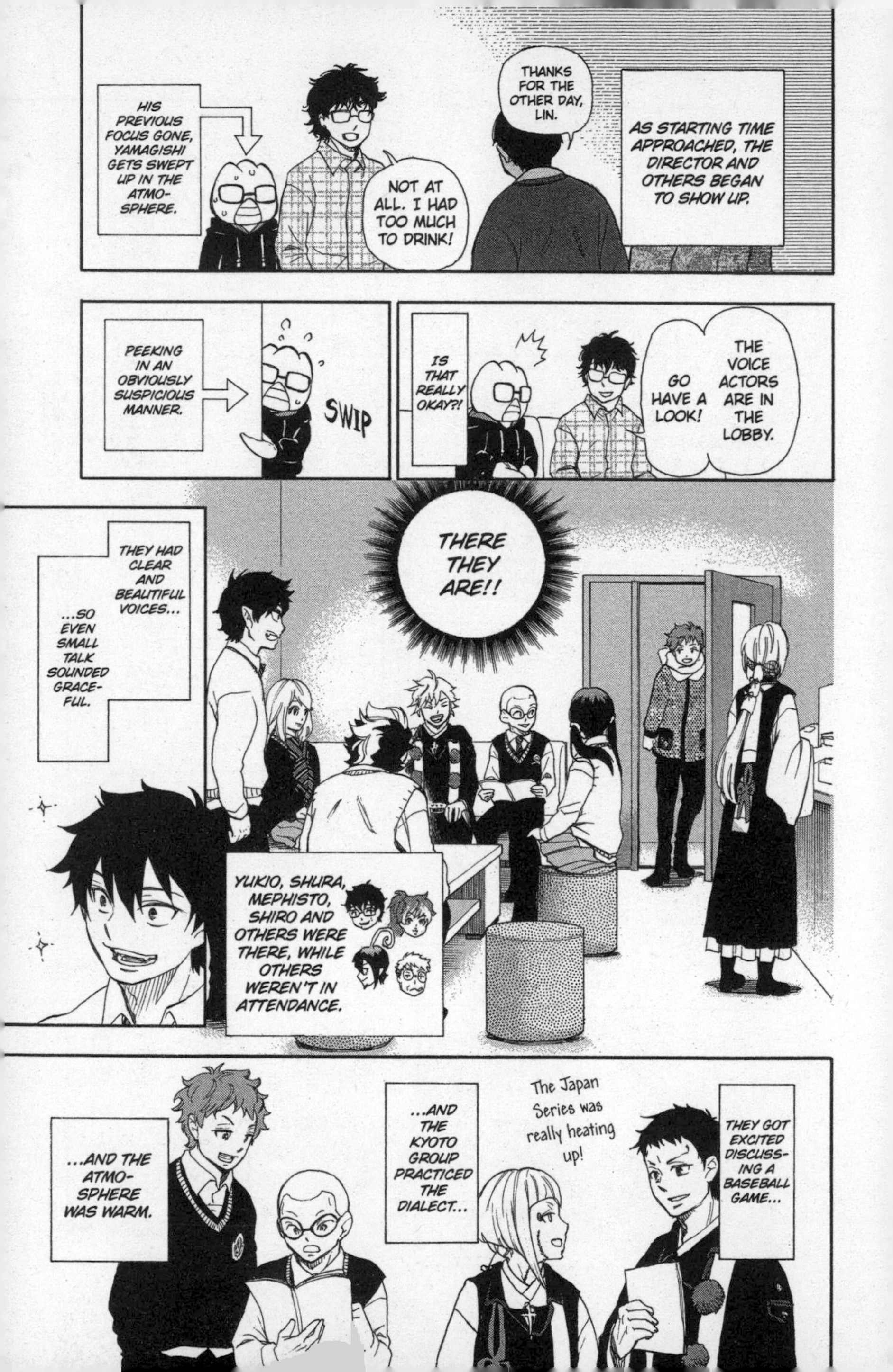
AS STARTING TIME APPROACHED, THE DIRECTOR AND OTHERS BEGAN TO SHOW UP.
THANKS FOR THE OTHER DAY, LIN.
NOT AT ALL. I HAD TOO MUCH TO DRINK!
HIS PREVIOUS FOCUS GONE, YAMAGISHI GETS SWEPT UP IN THE ATMOSPHERE.
THE VOICE ACTORS ARE IN THE LOBBY.
GO HAVE A LOOK!
IS THAT REALLY OKAY?!
PEEKING IN AN OBVIOUSLY SUSPICIOUS MANNER.
SWIP
THERE THEY ARE!!
THEY HAD CLEAR AND BEAUTIFUL VOICES...
...SO EVEN SMALL TALK SOUNDED GRACEFUL.
YUKIO, SHURA, MEPHISTO, SHIRO AND OTHERS WERE THERE, WHILE OTHERS WEREN'T IN ATTENDANCE.
THEY GOT EXCITED DISCUSSING A BASEBALL GAME...
The Japan Series was really heating up!
...AND THE KYOTO GROUP PRACTICED THE DIALECT...
...AND THE ATMOSPHERE WAS WARM.

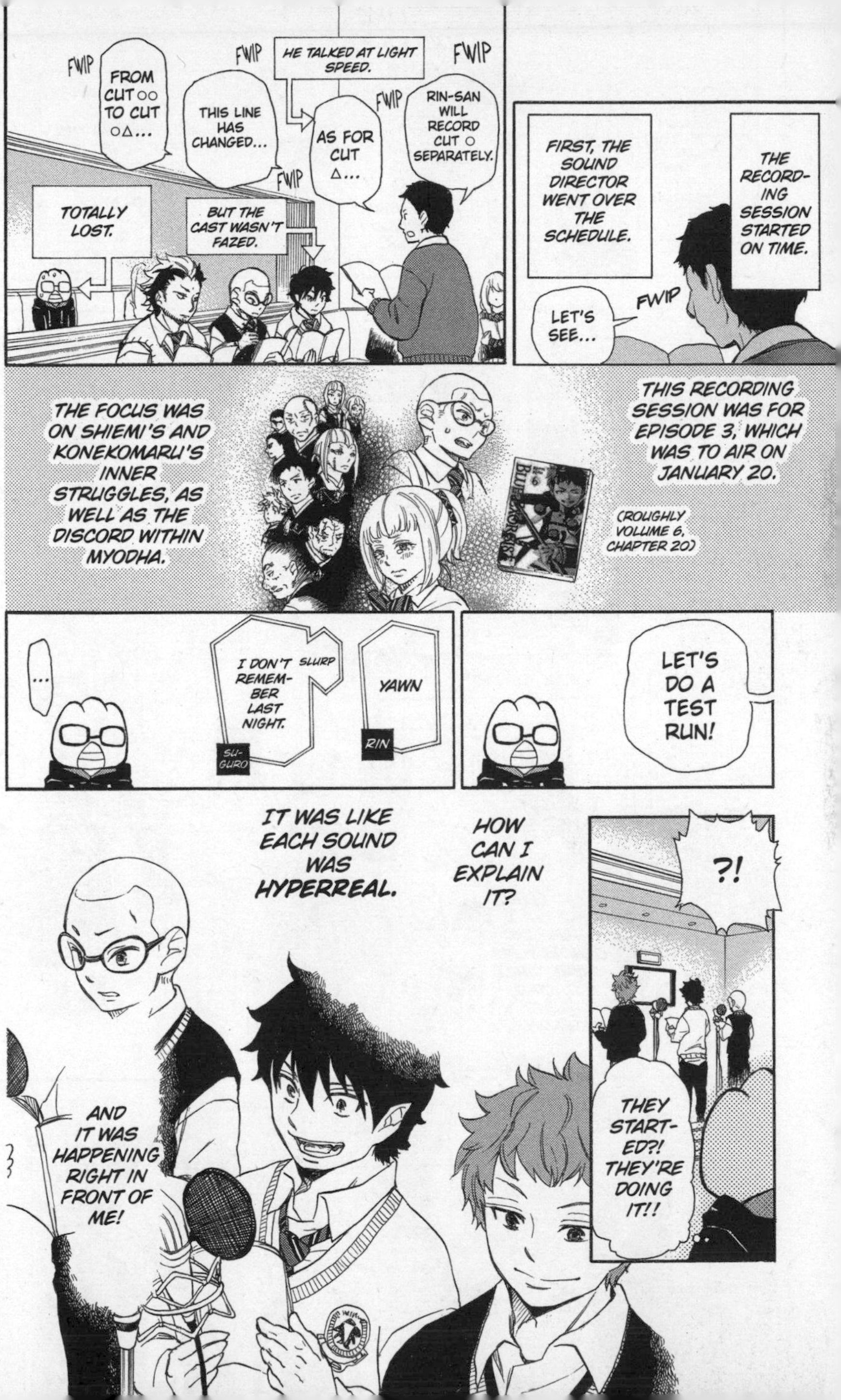
THE RECORDING SESSION STARTED ON TIME.
FIRST, THE SOUND DIRECTOR WENT OVER THE SCHEDULE.
FWIP
LET'S SEE...
FWIP
RIN-SAN WILL RECORD CUT ○ SEPARATELY.
HE TALKED AT LIGHT SPEED.
FWIP
AS FOR CUT △...
FWIP
FWIP
THIS LINE HAS CHANGED...
FWIP
FROM CUT ○○ TO CUT ○△...
BUT THE CAST WASN'T FAZED.
TOTALLY LOST.
THIS RECORDING SESSION WAS FOR EPISODE 3, WHICH WAS TO AIR ON JANUARY 20.
(ROUGHLY VOLUME 6, CHAPTER 20)
THE FOCUS WAS ON SHIEMI'S AND KONEKOMARU'S INNER STRUGGLES, AS WELL AS THE DISCORD WITHIN MYODHA.
LET'S DO A TEST RUN!
YAWN
RIN
I DON'T REMEMBER LAST NIGHT.
SLURP
SUGURO
...
?!
THEY STARTED?! THEY'RE DOING IT!!
HOW CAN I EXPLAIN IT?
IT WAS LIKE EACH SOUND WAS HYPERREAL.
AND IT WAS HAPPENING RIGHT IN FRONT OF ME!

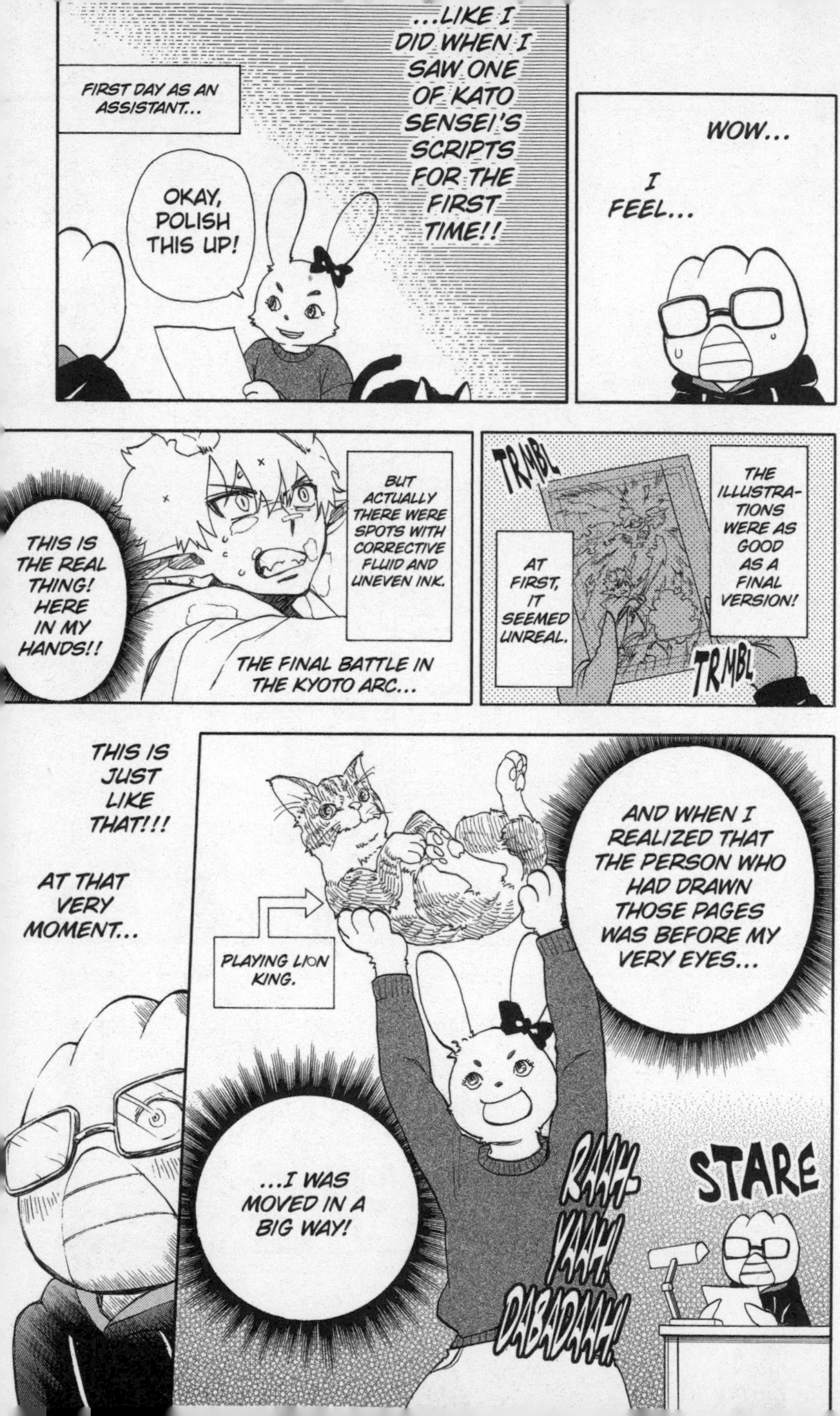
WOW...
I FEEL...
...LIKE I DID WHEN I SAW ONE OF KATO SENSEI'S SCRIPTS FOR THE FIRST TIME!!
FIRST DAY AS AN ASSISTANT...
OKAY, POLISH THIS UP!
TRMBL
THE ILLUSTRATIONS WERE AS GOOD AS A FINAL VERSION!
AT FIRST, IT SEEMED UNREAL.
TRMBL
BUT ACTUALLY THERE WERE SPOTS WITH CORRECTIVE FLUID AND UNEVEN INK.
THIS IS THE REAL THING! HERE IN MY HANDS!!
THE FINAL BATTLE IN THE KYOTO ARC...
AND WHEN I REALIZED THAT THE PERSON WHO HAD DRAWN THOSE PAGES WAS BEFORE MY VERY EYES...
STARE
PLAYING LION KING.
RAAAH-YAAAH! DABADAAAH!
...I WAS MOVED IN A BIG WAY!
THIS IS JUST LIKE THAT!!!
AT THAT VERY MOMENT...

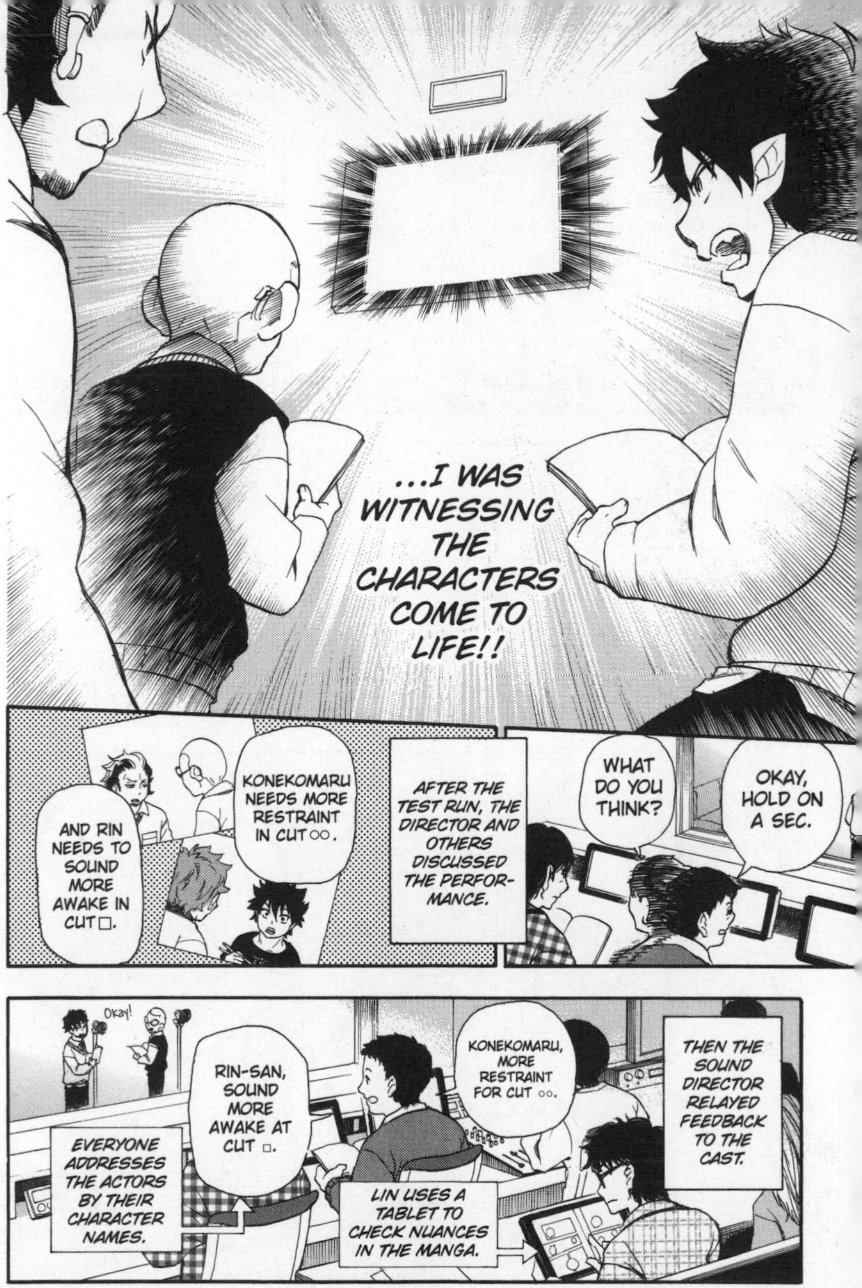
...I WAS WITNESSING THE CHARACTERS COME TO LIFE!!
OKAY, HOLD ON A SEC.
WHAT DO YOU THINK?
AFTER THE TEST RUN, THE DIRECTOR AND OTHERS DISCUSSED THE PERFORMANCE.
KONEKOMARU NEEDS MORE RESTRAINT IN CUT○○.
AND RIN NEEDS TO SOUND MORE AWAKE IN CUT□.
THEN THE SOUND DIRECTOR RELAYED FEEDBACK TO THE CAST.
KONEKOMARU, MORE RESTRAINT FOR CUT ○○.
RIN-SAN, SOUND MORE AWAKE AT CUT □.
Okay!
LIN USES A TABLET TO CHECK NUANCES IN THE MANGA.
EVERYONE ADDRESSES THE ACTORS BY THEIR CHARACTER NAMES.

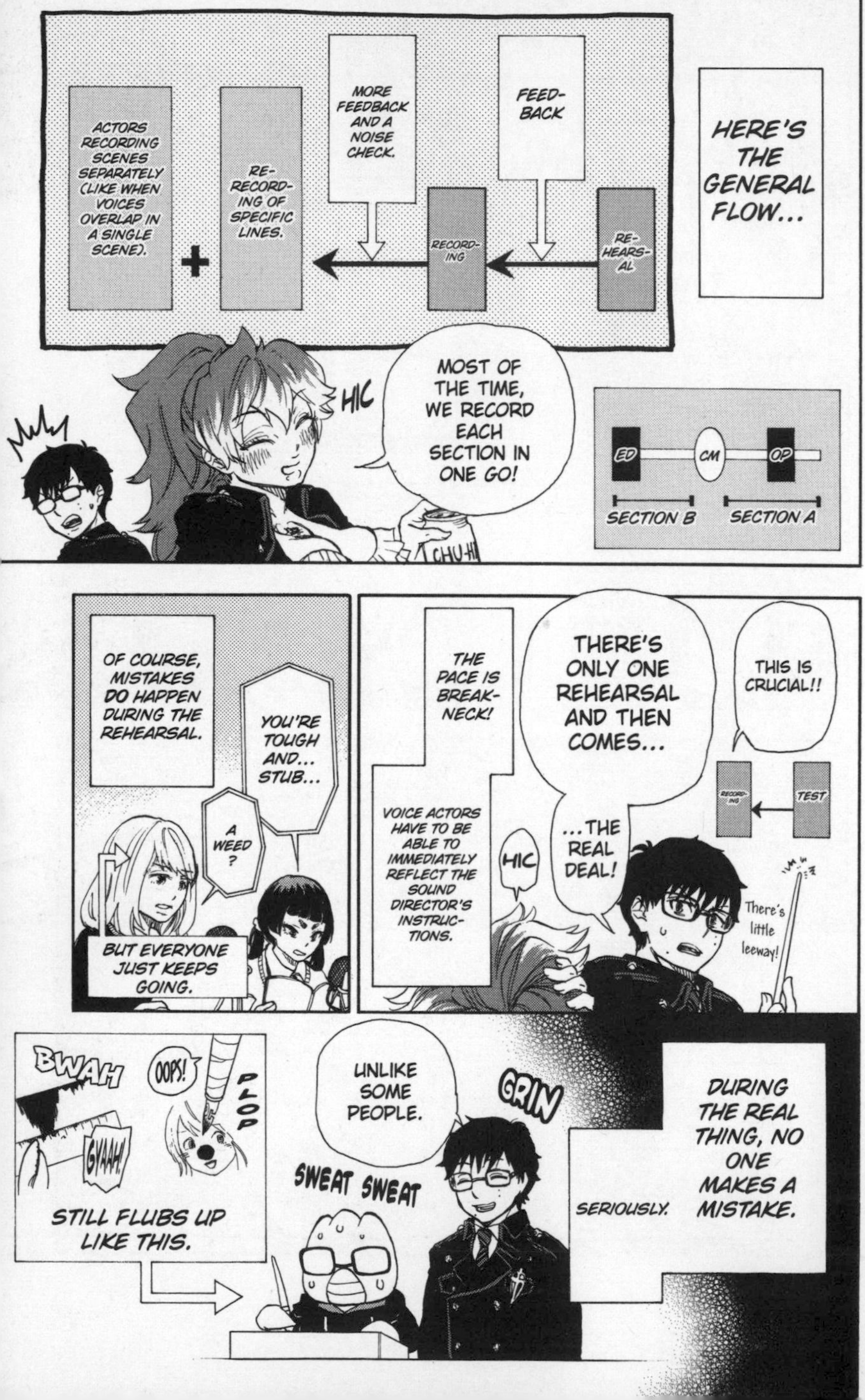

HERE'S THE GENERAL FLOW...
REHEARSAL
FEEDBACK
RECORDING
MORE FEEDBACK AND A NOISE CHECK.
RE-RECORDING OF SPECIFIC LINES.
+
ACTORS RECORDING SCENES SEPARATELY (LIKE WHEN VOICES OVERLAP IN A SINGLE SCENE).
OP
CM
ED
SECTION A
SECTION B
MOST OF THE TIME, WE RECORD EACH SECTION IN ONE GO!
HIC
CHU-HI
THIS IS CRUCIAL!!
TEST
RECORDING
THERE'S ONLY ONE REHEARSAL AND THEN COMES...
...THE REAL DEAL!
There's little leeway!
HIC
THE PACE IS BREAKNECK!
VOICE ACTORS HAVE TO BE ABLE TO IMMEDIATELY REFLECT THE SOUND DIRECTOR'S INSTRUCTIONS.
OF COURSE, MISTAKES DO HAPPEN DURING THE REHEARSAL.
YOU'RE TOUGH AND... STUB...
A WEED?
BUT EVERYONE JUST KEEPS GOING.
DURING THE REAL THING, NO ONE MAKES A MISTAKE.
SERIOUSLY.
GRIN
UNLIKE SOME PEOPLE.
SWEAT SWEAT
PLOP
OOPS!
BWAH
GYAAH!
STILL FLUBS UP LIKE THIS.

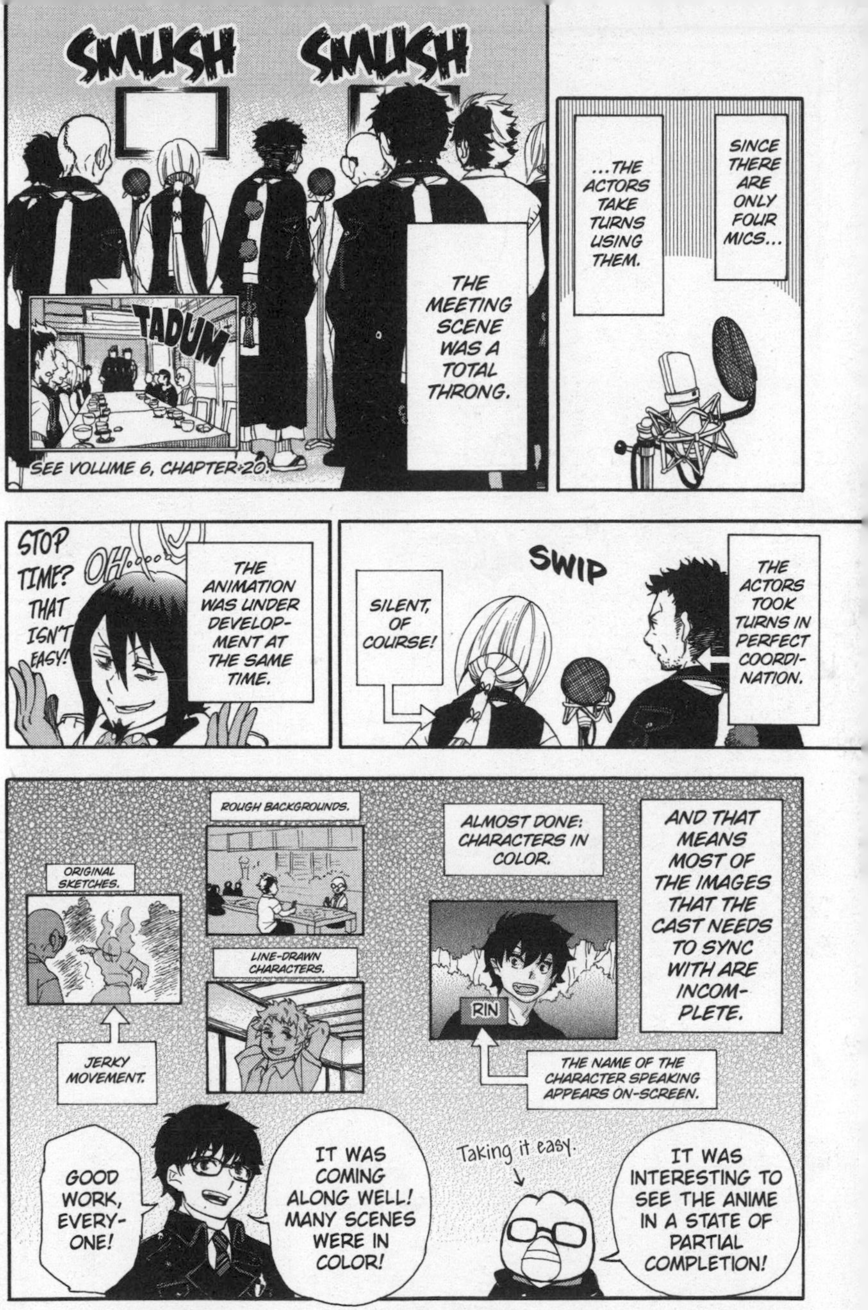
SINCE THERE ARE ONLY FOUR MICS...
...THE ACTORS TAKE TURNS USING THEM.
SMUSH
SMUSH
THE MEETING SCENE WAS A TOTAL THRONG.
TADUM
SEE VOLUME 6, CHAPTER 20.
THE ACTORS TOOK TURNS IN PERFECT COORDINATION.
SWIP
SILENT, OF COURSE!
THE ANIMATION WAS UNDER DEVELOPMENT AT THE SAME TIME.
OH.....
STOP TIME? THAT ISN'T EASY!
AND THAT MEANS MOST OF THE IMAGES THAT THE CAST NEEDS TO SYNC WITH ARE INCOMPLETE.
ALMOST DONE: CHARACTERS IN COLOR.
RIN
THE NAME OF THE CHARACTER SPEAKING APPEARS ON-SCREEN.
ROUGH BACKGROUNDS.
LINE-DRAWN CHARACTERS.
ORIGINAL SKETCHES.
JERKY MOVEMENT.
IT WAS INTERESTING TO SEE THE ANIME IN A STATE OF PARTIAL COMPLETION!
Taking it easy.
IT WAS COMING ALONG WELL! MANY SCENES WERE IN COLOR!
GOOD WORK, EVERYONE!

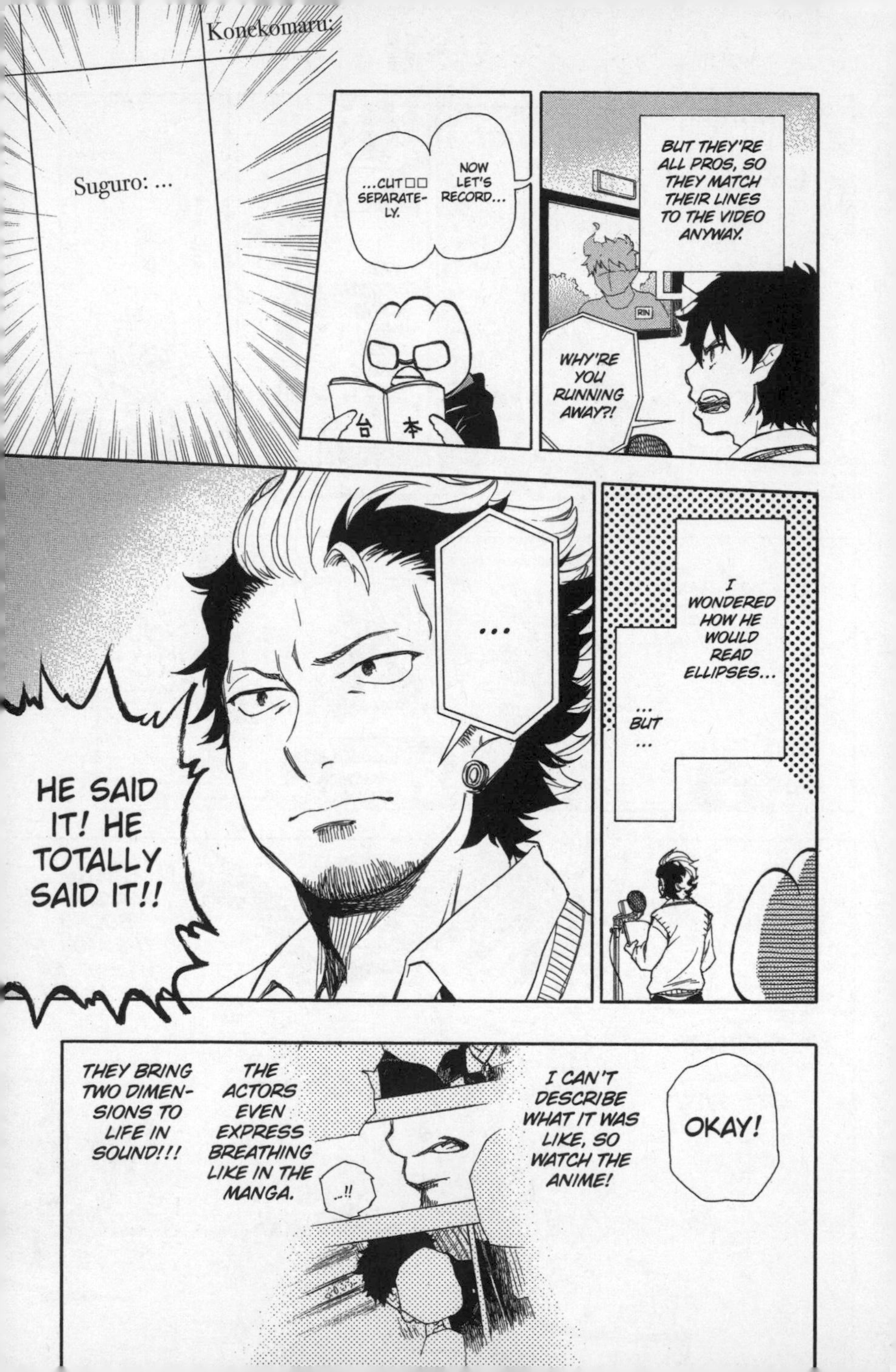
BUT THEY'RE ALL PROS, SO THEY MATCH THEIR LINES TO THE VIDEO ANYWAY.
RIN
WHY'RE YOU RUNNING AWAY?!
NOW LET'S RECORD...
...CUT□□ SEPARATELY.
台本
Konekomaru:
Suguro: ...
I WONDERED HOW HE WOULD READ ELLIPSES...
...BUT...
...
HE SAID IT! HE TOTALLY SAID IT!!
OKAY!
I CAN'T DESCRIBE WHAT IT WAS LIKE, SO WATCH THE ANIME!
...!!
THE ACTORS EVEN EXPRESS BREATHING LIKE IN THE MANGA.
THEY BRING TWO DIMENSIONS TO LIFE IN SOUND!!!

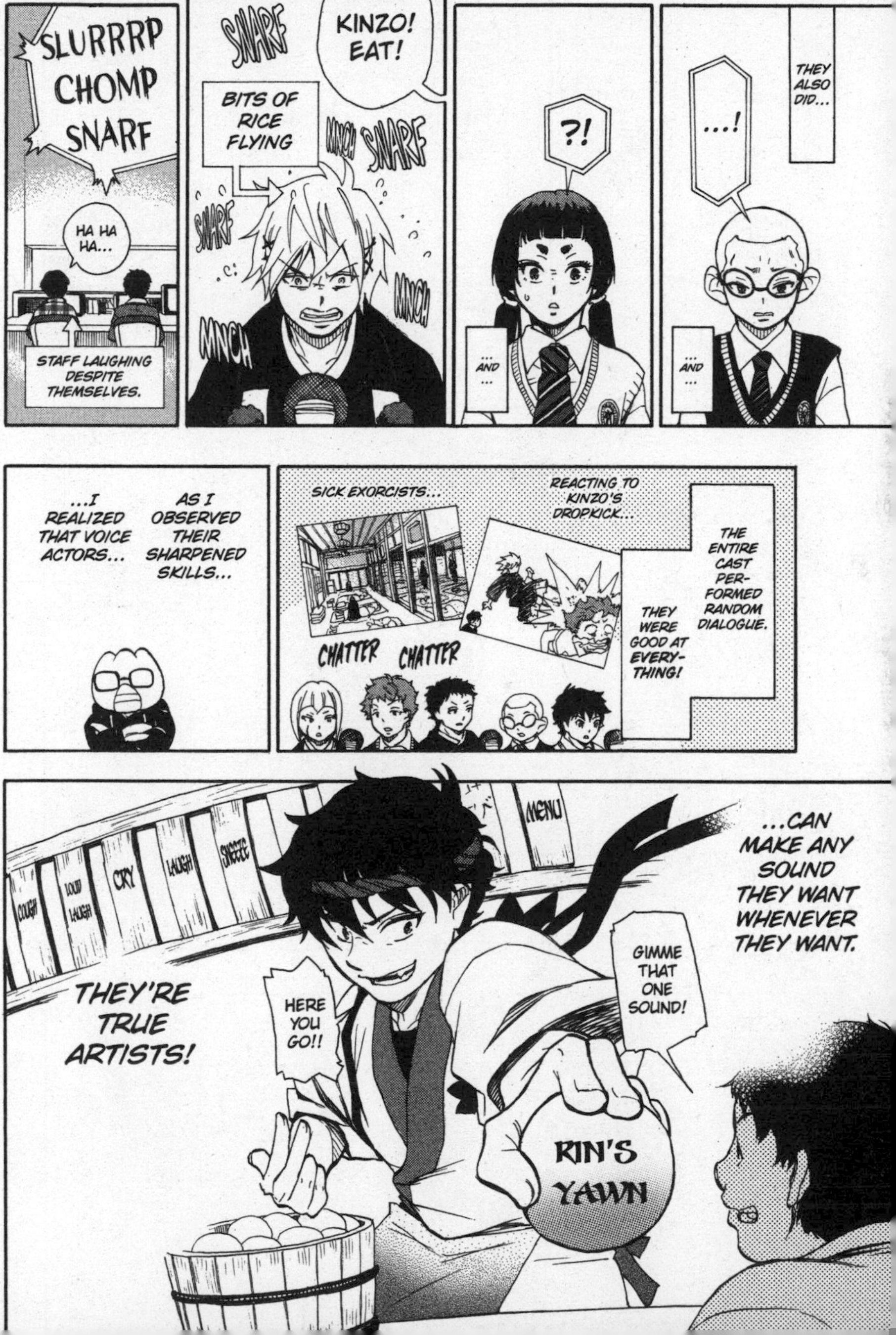
THEY ALSO DID...
...!
...AND...
?!
...AND...
KINZO! EAT!
SNARF
MNCH SNARF
BITS OF RICE FLYING
SNARF
MNCH
MNCH
SLURRRP CHOMP SNARF
HA HA HA...
STAFF LAUGHING DESPITE THEMSELVES.
THE ENTIRE CAST PERFORMED RANDOM DIALOGUE.
THEY WERE GOOD AT EVERYTHING!
REACTING TO KINZO'S DROPKICK...
SICK EXORCISTS...
CHATTER CHATTER
AS I OBSERVED THEIR SHARPENED SKILLS...
...I REALIZED THAT VOICE ACTORS...
...CAN MAKE ANY SOUND THEY WANT WHENEVER THEY WANT.
MENU
LAUGH
CRY
LOUD LAUGH
COUGH
GIMME THAT ONE SOUND!
HERE YOU GO!!
THEY'RE TRUE ARTISTS!
RIN'S YAWN

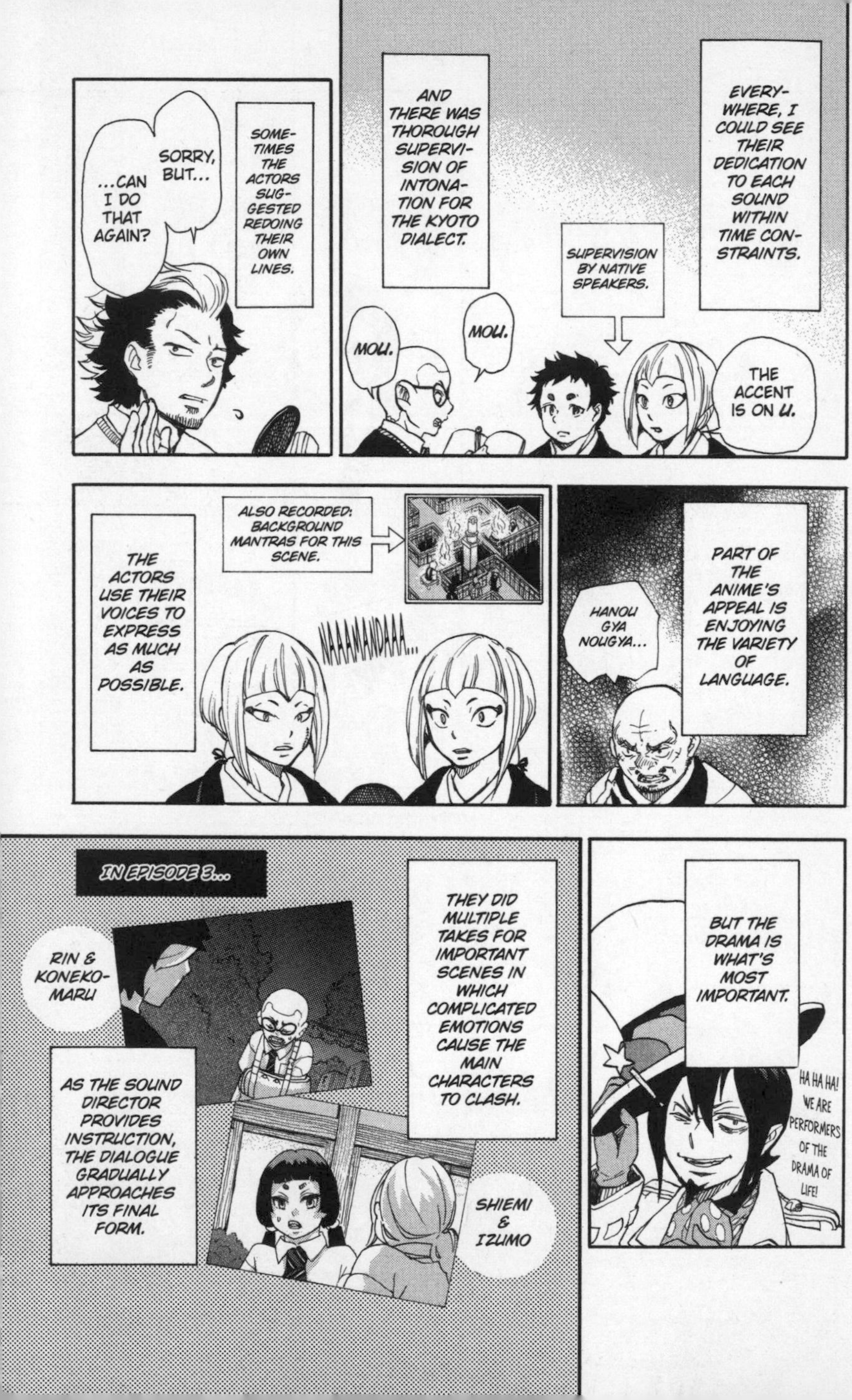
EVERYWHERE, I COULD SEE THEIR DEDICATION TO EACH SOUND WITHIN TIME CONSTRAINTS.
AND THERE WAS THOROUGH SUPERVISION OF INTONATION FOR THE KYOTO DIALECT.
SUPERVISION BY NATIVE SPEAKERS.
THE ACCENT IS ON U.
MOU.
MOU.
SOMETIMES THE ACTORS SUGGESTED REDOING THEIR OWN LINES.
SORRY, BUT...
...CAN I DO THAT AGAIN?
PART OF THE ANIME'S APPEAL IS ENJOYING THE VARIETY OF LANGUAGE.
HANOU GYA NOUGYA...
ALSO RECORDED: BACKGROUND MANTRAS FOR THIS SCENE.
THE ACTORS USE THEIR VOICES TO EXPRESS AS MUCH AS POSSIBLE.
NAAAMANDAAA...
BUT THE DRAMA IS WHAT'S MOST IMPORTANT.
HA HA HA! WE ARE PERFORMERS OF THE DRAMA OF LIFE!
IN EPISODE 3...
THEY DID MULTIPLE TAKES FOR IMPORTANT SCENES IN WHICH COMPLICATED EMOTIONS CAUSE THE MAIN CHARACTERS TO CLASH.
RIN & KONEKOMARU
AS THE SOUND DIRECTOR PROVIDES INSTRUCTION, THE DIALOGUE GRADUALLY APPROACHES ITS FINAL FORM.
SHIEMI & IZUMO

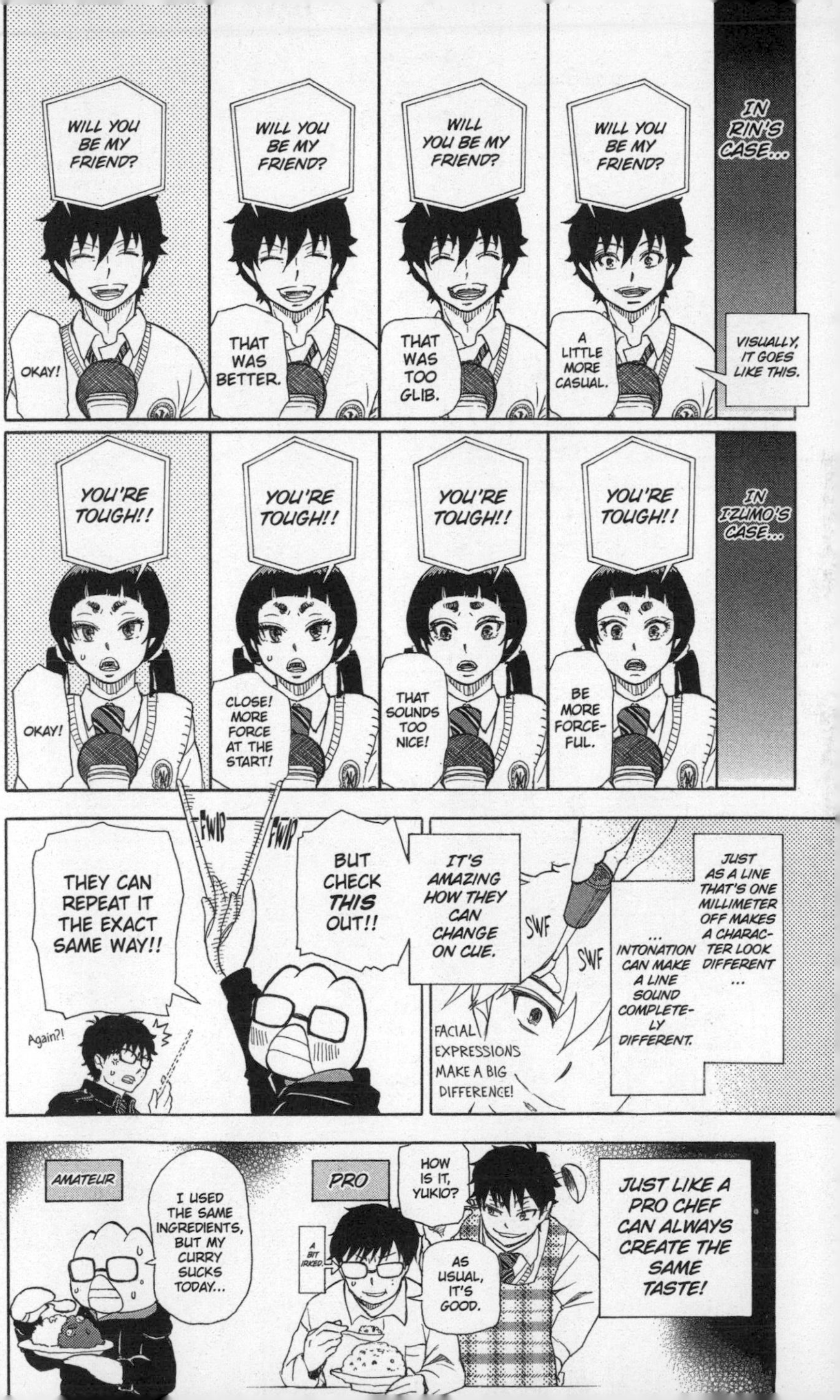
IN RIN'S CASE...
VISUALLY, IT GOES LIKE THIS.
WILL YOU BE MY FRIEND?
A LITTLE MORE CASUAL.
WILL YOU BE MY FRIEND?
THAT WAS TOO GLIB.
WILL YOU BE MY FRIEND?
THAT WAS BETTER.
WILL YOU BE MY FRIEND?
OKAY!
IN IZUMO'S CASE...
YOU'RE TOUGH!!
BE MORE FORCE-FUL.
YOU'RE TOUGH!!
THAT SOUNDS TOO NICE!
YOU'RE TOUGH!!
CLOSE! MORE FORCE AT THE START!
YOU'RE TOUGH!!
OKAY!
JUST AS A LINE THAT'S ONE MILLIMETER OFF MAKES A CHARAC-TER LOOK DIFFERENT...
...INTONATION CAN MAKE A LINE SOUND COMPLETE-LY DIFFERENT.
IT'S AMAZING HOW THEY CAN CHANGE ON CUE.
S'WF
S'WF
FACIAL EXPRESSIONS MAKE A BIG DIFFERENCE!
FWIP
FWIP
BUT CHECK THIS OUT!!
THEY CAN REPEAT IT THE EXACT SAME WAY!!
Again?!
JUST LIKE A PRO CHEF CAN ALWAYS CREATE THE SAME TASTE!
HOW IS IT, YUKIO?
PRO
AS USUAL, IT'S GOOD.
A BIT IRKED.
I USED THE SAME INGREDIENTS, BUT MY CURRY SUCKS TODAY...
AMATEUR

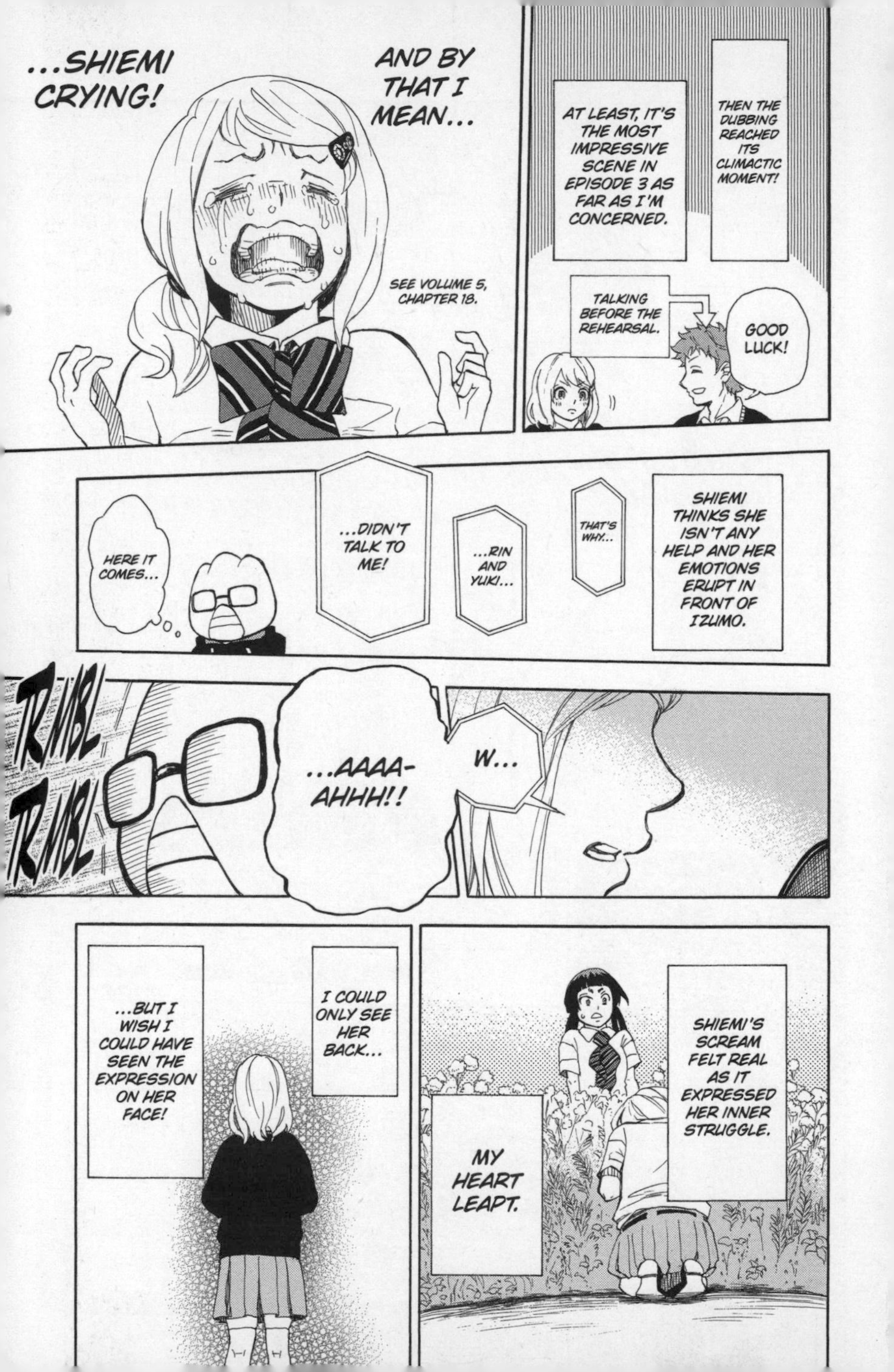
THEN THE DUBBING REACHED ITS CLIMACTIC MOMENT!
AT LEAST, IT'S THE MOST IMPRESSIVE SCENE IN EPISODE 3 AS FAR AS I'M CONCERNED.
GOOD LUCK!
TALKING BEFORE THE REHEARSAL.
AND BY THAT I MEAN...
...SHIEMI CRYING!
SEE VOLUME 5, CHAPTER 18.
SHIEMI THINKS SHE ISN'T ANY HELP AND HER EMOTIONS ERUPT IN FRONT OF IZUMO.
THAT'S WHY...
...RIN AND YUKI...
...DIDN'T TALK TO ME!
HERE IT COMES...
W...
...AAAA-AHHH!!
TRMBL
TRMBL
SHIEMI'S SCREAM FELT REAL AS IT EXPRESSED HER INNER STRUGGLE.
MY HEART LEAPT.
I COULD ONLY SEE HER BACK...
...BUT I WISH I COULD HAVE SEEN THE EXPRESSION ON HER FACE!

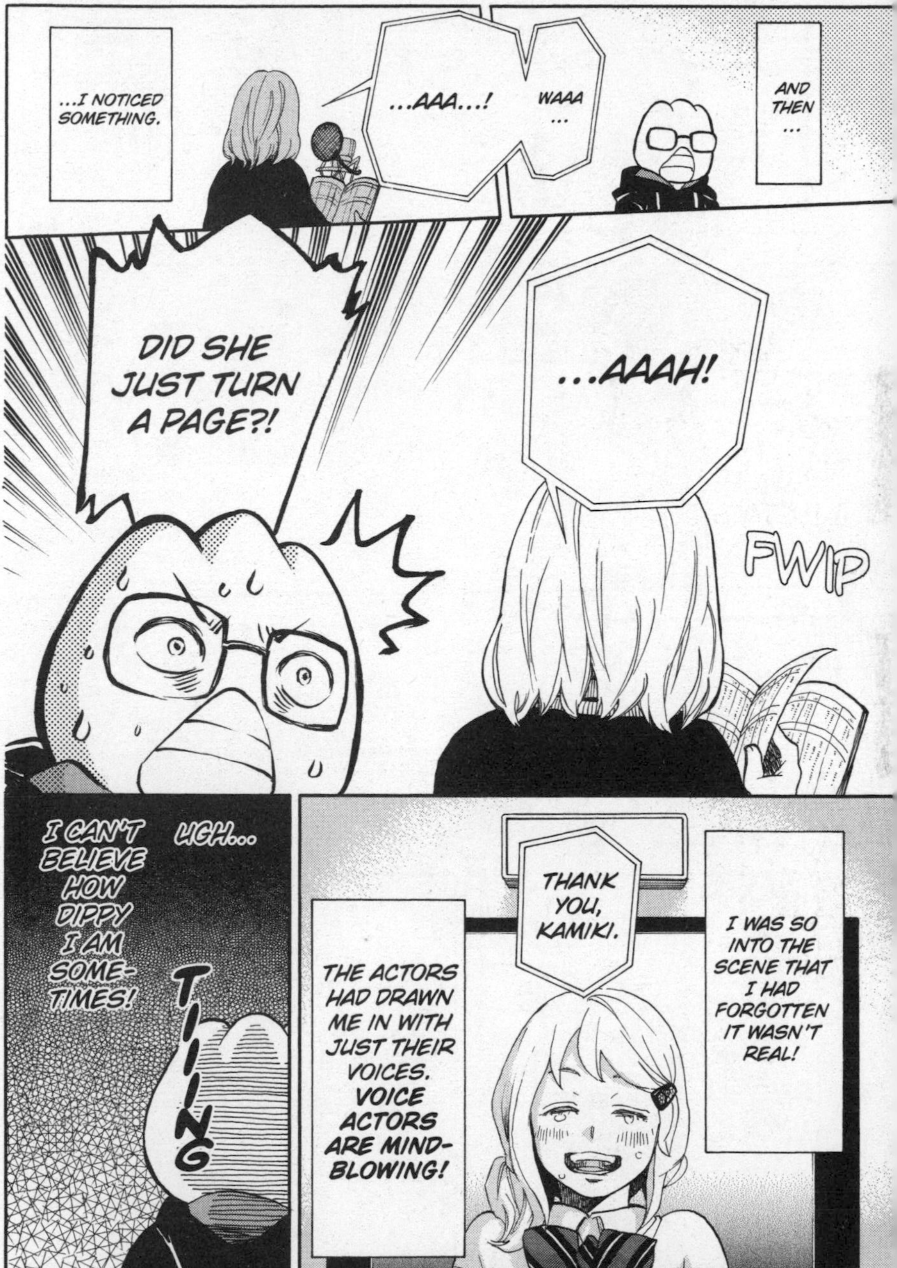

AND THEN ...
WAAA ...
...AAA...!
...I NOTICED SOMETHING.
...AAAH!
FWIP
DID SHE JUST TURN A PAGE?!
I WAS SO INTO THE SCENE THAT I HAD FORGOTTEN IT WASN'T REAL!
THANK YOU, KAMIKI.
THE ACTORS HAD DRAWN ME IN WITH JUST THEIR VOICES. VOICE ACTORS ARE MIND-BLOWING!
UGH...
I CAN'T BELIEVE HOW DIPPY I AM SOME-TIMES!
TIIING

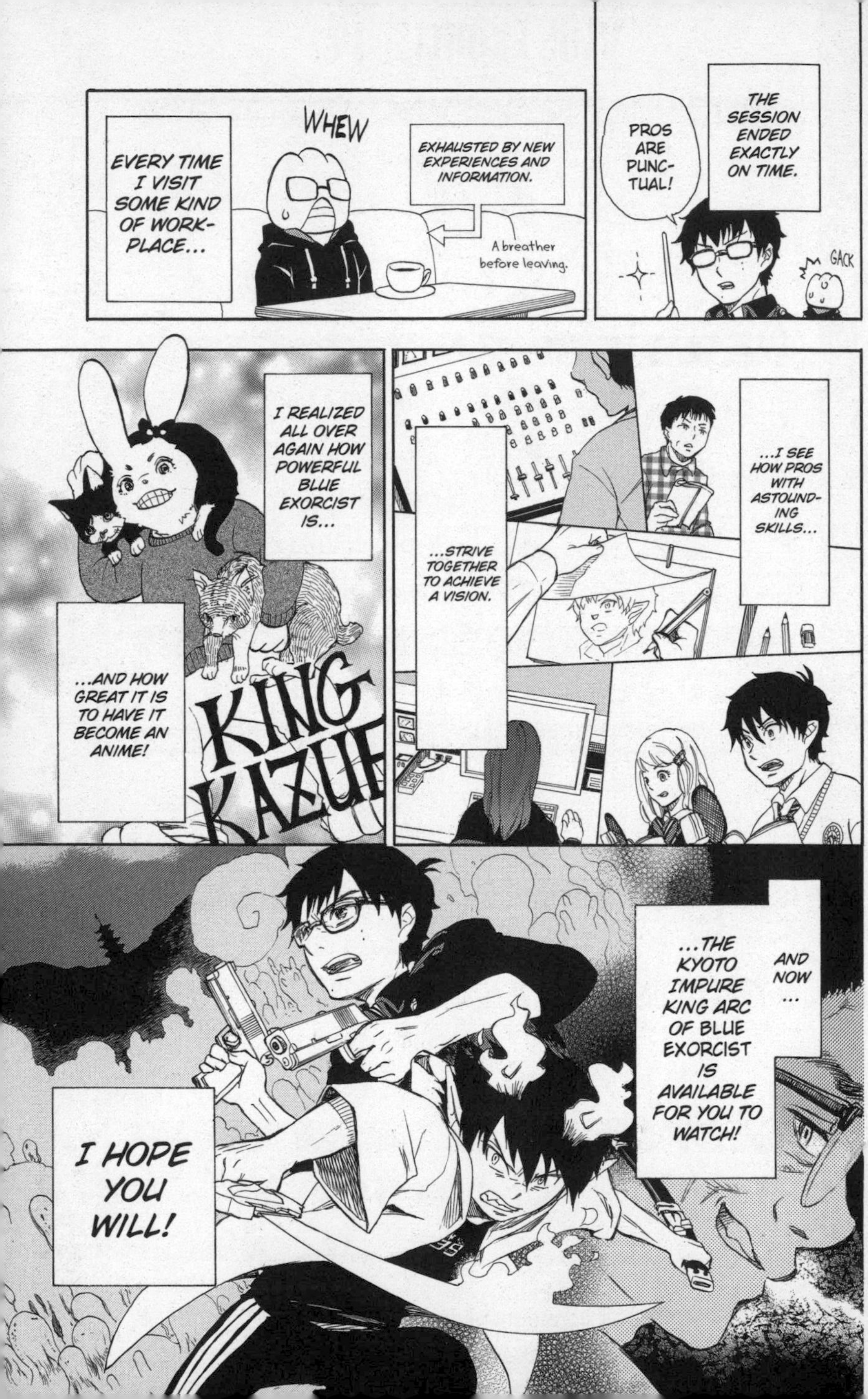
THE SESSION ENDED EXACTLY ON TIME.
PROS ARE PUNCTUAL!
GACK
EVERY TIME I VISIT SOME KIND OF WORKPLACE...
WHEW
EXHAUSTED BY NEW EXPERIENCES AND INFORMATION.
A breather before leaving.
...I SEE HOW PROS WITH ASTOUNDING SKILLS...
...STRIVE TOGETHER TO ACHIEVE A VISION.
I REALIZED ALL OVER AGAIN HOW POWERFUL BLUE EXORCIST IS...
...AND HOW GREAT IT IS TO HAVE IT BECOME AN ANIME!
KING
KAZU
AND NOW...
...THE KYOTO IMPURE KING ARC OF BLUE EXORCIST IS AVAILABLE FOR YOU TO WATCH!
I HOPE YOU WILL!

BLUE EXORCIST 19

Art Staff

GOTTA AVOID THE FLU!
Miyuki Shibuya

I'M PROTECTING MYSELF!
Erika Uemura

SORRY. I'M SICK AS A DOG!
Ryoji Hayashi

KOFF KOFF KOFF KOFF
Mari Oda

Art Assistants

HUH? INFLUENZA?!
Yamanaka-san

HUH?!
Yanagimoto-san

I THOUGHT I HAD THE FLU, BUT IT WAS A COLD!
Yamagishi-san

OOH! SCARY!
Yoshiyama-kun

HUH?!
Obata-san

Composition Assistant

WHEW! THAT WAS HARD!
Minoru Sasaki

Editors

I'LL KEEP ON SELLIN'!
Shihei Lin

LIN-SAN'S AMAZING!
Tadahiro Fukushima

Thank you, Lin!!

LIN WAS EDITOR FOR NINE YEARS! NOW HE PASSES THE BATON TO FUKUSHIMA!! GOOD LUCK!!

Graphic Novel Editor

UH...OKAY. GOT IT.
Ryusuke Kuroki

Graphic Novel Design

RENEWAL !!!
Shimada Hideaki

Daiju Asami (L.S.D.)

Manga

THE FLU'S SCARY! I'M SCARED OF IT!
Kazue Kato

(In no particular order)
(Note: The caricatures and statements are from memory!)

Next is volume 20 at last!!
The story is gonna move big-time, so check it out!!

The Hierarchy of Gehenna

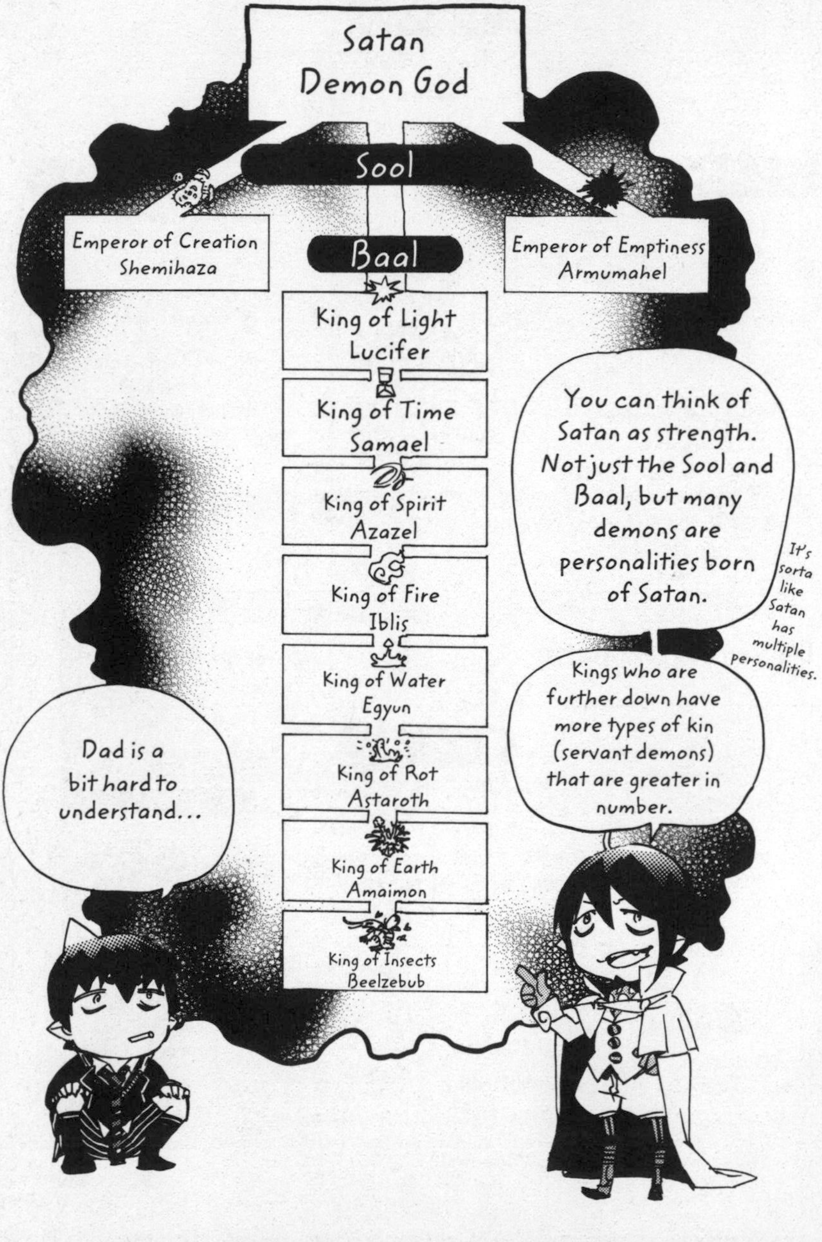
Satan
Demon God
Sool
Emperor of Creation
Shemihaza
Baal
Emperor of Emptiness
Armumahel
King of Light
Lucifer
King of Time
Samael
King of Spirit
Azazel
King of Fire
Iblis
King of Water
Egyun
King of Rot
Astaroth
King of Earth
Amaimon
King of Insects
Beelzebub
You can think of Satan as strength. Not just the Sool and Baal, but many demons are personalities born of Satan.
It's sorta like Satan has multiple personalities.
Kings who are further down have more types of kin (servant demons) that are greater in number.
Dad is a bit hard to understand...

Gehenna Power Flowchart

Third Power

Demon God
Satan
(corporeal)

Lucifer's Faction

King of Light Lucifer
(corporeal)

King of Fire Iblis
(corporeal)
King of Water Egyun
(corporeal)
King of Rot Astaroth
(corporeal)

Demon supremacists

OPPOSED TO

Samael's Faction

Emperor of Creation Shemihaza
(crystallized)
Emperor of Emptiness Armumahel
(crystallized)

King of Time Samael
(corporeal)
King of Spirits Azazel
(crystallized)

Defend humanity

Neutral

King of Earth Amaimon
(corporeal)

King of Insects Beelzebub
(corporeal)

Cooperating

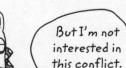

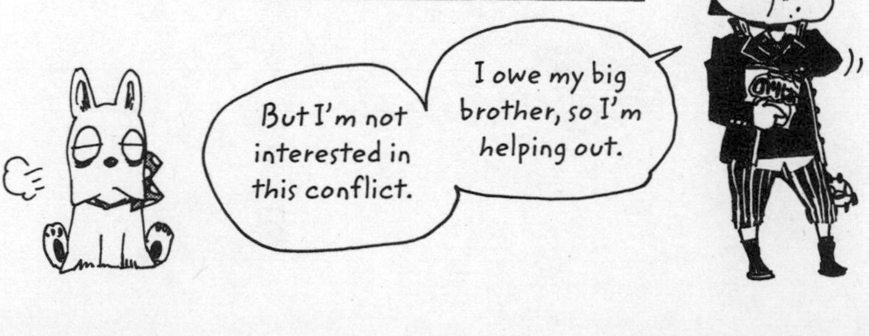

I owe my big brother, so I'm helping out.
But I'm not interested in this conflict.

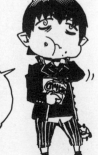

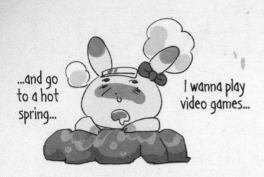

I wanna play video games...
...and go to a hot spring...

Kazue Kato

The rabbit is tired,
so she took a dip in a hot spring.

In this volume,
the interlude continues
with scenes from a school life
full of horror and suspense!

Enjoy volume 19!

BLUE EXORCIST

BLUE EXORCIST VOL. 19
SHONEN JUMP ADVANCED Manga Edition

STORY & ART BY KAZUE KATO

Translation & English Adaptation/John Werry
Touch-up Art & Lettering/John Hunt, Primary Graphix
Cover & Interior Design/Sam Elzway
Editor/Mike Montesa

Printed in the U.S.A.

Published by VIZ Media, LLC
P.O. Box 77010
San Francisco, CA 94107

10 9 8 7 6 5 4 3 2 1
First printing, June 2018

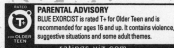

In the next volume...

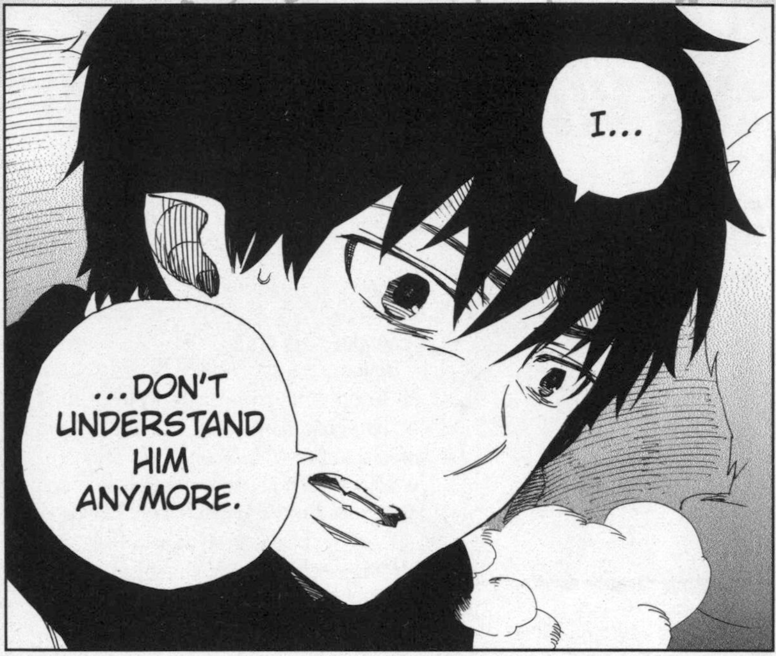
I...
...DON'T UNDERSTAND HIM ANYMORE.

Lewin Light, a.k.a "Lightning," has uncovered some disturbing truths in his investigation into the Illuminati. Some of those discoveries concern the origins of Father Fujimoto, the secrets of the Blue Night, and even Rin and Yukio's birth. As these facts start to point toward an even more unsettling conclusion, the Exwires head for Kyoto to celebrate a wedding. While everyone is enjoying the happy occasion, Rin must face the fact that he has lost touch with his brother, Yukio, whose struggles with the blue fire in his eyes are getting worse every day...

Coming October 2018!

...You're Reading in the Wrong Direction!!

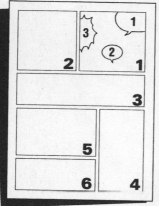

Whoops! Guess what? You're starting at the wrong end of the comic!

...It's true! In keeping with the original Japanese format, **Blue Exorcist** is meant to be read from right to left, starting in the upper-right corner.

Unlike English, which is read from left to right, Japanese is read from right to left, meaning that action, sound effects and word-balloon order are completely reversed... something which can make readers unfamiliar with Japanese feel pretty backwards themselves. For this reason, manga or Japanese comics published in the U.S. in English have sometimes been published "flopped"—that is, printed in exact reverse order, as though seen from the other side of a mirror.

By flopping pages, U.S. publishers can avoid confusing readers, but the compromise is not without its downside. For one thing, a character in a flopped manga series who once wore in the original Japanese version a T-shirt emblazoned with "M A Y" (as in "the merry month of") now wears one which reads "Y A M"! Additionally, many manga creators in Japan are themselves unhappy with the process, as some feel the mirror-imaging of their art skews their original intentions.

We are proud to bring you Kazue Kato's **Blue Exorcist** in the original unflopped format. For now, though, turn to the other side of the book and let the adventure begin...!

—Editor

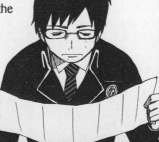

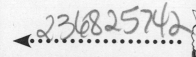